WINDOWS FOR
WORKGROUPS
MADE EASY

W. RONALD
- 1995 -

WINDOWS FOR WORKGROUPS MADE EASY

Tom Sheldon
with
Jim Sheldon

Osborne **McGraw-Hill**

Berkeley New York St. Louis San Francisco
Auckland Bogotá Hamburg London Madrid
Mexico City Milan Montreal New Delhi Panama City
Paris São Paulo Singapore Sydney
Tokyo Toronto

Osborne **McGraw-Hill**
2600 Tenth Street
Berkeley, California 94710
U.S.A.

For information on translations or book distributors outside of the
U.S.A., please write to Osborne **McGraw-Hill** at the above address.

Windows for Workgroups Made Easy

234567890 DOC 99876543

ISBN 0-07-881941-5

Publisher
Kenna S. Wood

Acquisition Editor
Frances Stack

Associate Editor
Jill Pisoni

Technical Editor
John Heilborn

Project Editor
Janet Walden

Copy Editor
Kimberly Torgerson

Proofreader
Carol Burbo

Indexer
Brown Editorial Service

Computer Designer
Stefany Otis

Illustrator
Marla J. Shelasky

Cover Designer
Compass Marketing

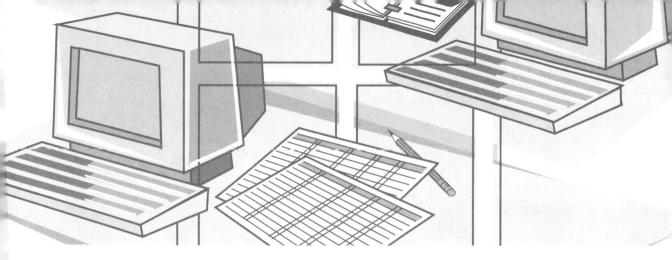

CONTENTS

Introduction xvii

1 ▪▪▪ **Windows Overview** 1
The Windows Desktop Metaphor 2
Mouse or Keyboard? 4
Mouse Usage and Terminology 4
Keyboard Usage and Terminology 5
Types of Windows 7
Windows as Icons 9
Window Elements 11
The Control Menu 11
The Menu Bar and Drop-Down Menus 11
Window Sizing Buttons 12
Scroll Bars 13
Borders 13
The Title Bar 14
Dialog Boxes 14
Multitasking with Windows 14
Cutting and Pasting with the ClipBook 15
Examining and Saving ClipBook Contents 17
Windows Accessories and Games 17

Control Panel Options for Customizing
   Windows 19

2 ▣ Starting Windows **23**
   Starting Windows 24
      Logging On 24
      What's Your Mode? 27
      Analyzing the About Program Manager
       Dialog Box 30
   Running Programs in Windows 30
      Starting Applications When Starting
       Windows 31
      Starting an Application from the StartUp
       Group 32
   Starting Windows Automatically 33
   Other Startup Considerations 34
      Minimizing RAM Usage 34
      Running Non-Windows Applications 35
   Logging Out and Exiting Windows 36
      Logging Out 37
      Exit Methods 37

3 ▣ Using the Windows Interface **41**
   Getting Around in Program Manager 42
      Mouse Techniques 42
      Keyboard Techniques and Speed Keys 48
   Moving Among Applications on the Desktop 52
      Switching Among Applications 53
      Using the Task List 54
   Resizing and Moving Windows and Icons 56
      Resizing Windows with the Mouse 56
      Using Scroll Bars 58
      Removing Scroll Bars 59
      Moving a Window 60
   Closing a Window 61
   Dialog Boxes 62
      Dialog Box Fields and Buttons 63

Using Dialog Boxes   68
Exiting Windows   69

4 ▉▉▉▉ Navigating the Windows Environment 71

Exploring the Program Manager   72
   Program Manager Groups   72
   Reorganizing the Program Manager   72
   Saving Program Manager Arrangements   79
Organizing the Desktop   80
   Window Switching Methods   81
   Organizing the Desktop with the Task List   81
Cut and Paste Operations   83
   Pasting to Another Application   85
   Saving the Clipboard Contents   86
   Closing Application Windows   88
Exploring the Control Panel   88
   Setting the Date and Time   89
   Changing the Color Scheme   90
Exploring the File Manager   91
   Using the File Manager   94
   Closing the File Manager   97

5 ▉▉▉▉ Using Windows Help 101

Accessing Help 102
   How to Get Help 103
Using the Help Menu 103
   Getting Context-Specific Help 104
Using Help Windows 104
   Scroll the Help Text and Choose a Topic 105
   Using Help Buttons 107
   Using the Help Menu Options 109
Other Help Formats 115

6 ▉▉▉▉ Customizing Windows: The Control Panel . . . 119

Color 120
   Creating Custom Color Schemes 121
   Creating Custom Colors 123

Fonts 125
   Windows, Your Printer, and Fonts 126
   Viewing, Installing, and Removing Fonts 128
Ports 131
Mouse 134
   Set Mouse Tracking Speed 134
   Setting the Double Click Speed 135
   Swapping the Mouse Buttons 135
   Mouse Trails 135
Desktop 135
   Desktop Pattern 136
   Fast "Alt+Tab" Switching 138
   Using a Screen Saver 139
   Putting Up Wallpaper 143
   Changing Icon Spacing 144
   Adjusting the Sizing Grid 145
   Setting the Cursor Blink Rate 146
Printers 146
International 146
Keyboard 148
Date/Time 148
Installing Drivers 149
   Adding a New Driver 150
Sound 151
Network 152
   Using the Network Utility 154
386 Enhanced Mode 157

7   Working with Files 161
DOS and Windows File Types 162
File-Naming Conventions 164
   File-Naming Strategies 165
   Using Wildcard Parameters to List Files 168
Directory Concepts 169
   Organizing with Directories 170
Using File Menu Options 171
   The File New Option 172

The File Open Option 172
Accessing Network Files 179
The File Save Option 181
The File Save As Option 182

8 ▬▬ Organizing Applications 185

Creating a New Group 186
   Creating a New Group Window 187
   Copying Program Items to a New Group 188
   Resizing and Arranging the New Window 189
   Saving Arrangements 190
Creating New Program Item Icons 190
   The New Option 191
   Creating a Document Icon 196
   Using the Setup Utility to Create Startup
      Icons 198
Other Program Manager Options 201
   Changing the Properties of a Group or Icon 201
   Deleting a Program Item or Group 205
The Startup Group 206
Chapter Wrap-Up 207

9 ▬▬ File Manager, Part I: Features and Options .. 209

The File Manager Window 210
   Restoring File Manager Default Settings 211
Customizing File Manager 212
   Suppressing Confirmation Messages 212
   Changing Fonts 214
   Displaying the Status Bar 215
   Displaying the Toolbar and Drive Icon Bar 215
   Minimizing File Manager on Use 215
   Save Settings on Exit 216
Working with Directory Windows 216
   Opening Another Directory Window 217
   The Split Bar 217
   Arranging Windows 219
   Windows Refreshment Time 220

Climbing the Directory Tree 220
   Expanding and Collapsing Branches 220
   Indicating Expandable Branches 222
Working with the File List 223
   Changing the File View 223
   Showing File Details 224
   Sorting the File List 225
   Listing Specific Files 226
Selecting Files 229
   Selecting Contiguous Files 229
   Selecting Noncontiguous Groups of Files 230
   Deselecting Files 231
   Using the Select Files Option 231
   The Toolbar 232
Creating Program Manager Startup Icons with
  File Manager 236
Starting Applications from File Manager 237
   Establishing Launch Windows 238
   The File Manager Run Command 241
   Drag-and-Drop Procedures 242

10 ▬▬ **File Manager, Part II: File, Directory, and**
  Network Commands **245**
Copying and Moving Files with the Mouse 246
Using the File Menu Commands 248
   Opening Selected Directories and Files 248
   Moving and Copying Files 249
   Deleting Files 251
   Renaming Files 252
   Viewing and Changing File Properties 254
   Printing from File Manager 256
   Program and Document Associations 257
   Searching for Files and Directories 259
Working with Directories 260
   Creating Directories 260
   Copying and Moving Directories 261
   Deleting Directories 263

Using Disk Commands 265
   Copying Disks 265
   Labeling a Disk 266
   Formatting Disks 267
   Make System Disk 268

11 ▬▬ Sharing and Accessing Network Files 271

Workgroups and Network Computers 273
What It Means to Share Your System 276
   File Security 277
   Disconnection Problems 281
   Monitoring Usage 282
Sharing Directories 282
   Sharing Directories on Your System 283
   Accessing Shared Directories on Other
      Systems 285
   How to Stop Sharing Directories 288
Chatting with Other Users 290
Monitoring Your System 291
   WinMeter 291
   NetWatcher 292
   Disconnecting Users 294
   Closing Files 294
Monitoring Server Usage with File Manager 296
Novell NetWare and Microsoft LAN Manager
   Support 296
   Accessing NetWare Servers and Resources 297
   Accessing LAN Manager Servers and
      Resources 300

12 ▬▬ Printing with Windows 303

The Printing Process 304
A Word About Fonts 305
Printing a Document 307
   The Print Setup Dialog Box 309
   Connecting to Network Printers 312
   The Print Dialog Box 316

The Control Panel Printer Settings 319
    Setting the Default Printer 319
    Bypassing Print Manager 320
The Print Manager 320
    Working with Print Jobs and Queues 323
    Print Manager Menu Options and Control
    Buttons 326
    The Options Menu 327
Sharing Printers on Your System 330
    How to Stop Sharing Printers on Your
    System 333
    Connecting and Disconnecting from Shared
    Printers 333
Using Printers on NetWare Servers 334

13   **The ClipBook Viewer** **337**
ClipBook Features 340
    The Clipboard 340
    Setting ClipBook Features 343
Working with Your Local ClipBook 345
Sharing a Local ClipBook Object 346
Connecting with Other ClipBooks 347
Using ClipBook Objects in Your Documents 348
    Object Linking and Embedding 349

14   **Creating Compound Documents** **353**
Understanding OLE Concepts 354
    Embedding 355
    Linking 357
    An Example of Linking and Embedding 357
OLE Components 359
    Servers and Clients 360
    Verbs 361
    Linking and Embedding 361
    Changing Embedded or Linked Objects 363
    Icons as Objects 363
Embedding Objects 366

Linking Objects 368
    Viewing and Updating Link Information 370
Embedding Icons 371
    Using Packager 372

15 ▬ **Microsoft Mail** **377**
Postoffice Components 379
Using Mail 381
    Connect to an Existing Postoffice 382
    Mail Startup Trick 383
    Changing Your Password 384
    Exiting Mail 385
Composing and Sending Messages 385
    Address the Message 385
    Type the Subject and Message 389
    Attaching Files to Messages 389
    Send the Message 391
Reading Messages You've Received 392
    Replying to Messages You've Received 392
    Forwarding Messages You've Received 393
Folders 393
    Creating a New Folder 394
    Moving Messages into Folders 396
Archiving and Deleting Messages 396
Message Templates 397
Message Finder 398
Working Offline 399
Administrative Tasks 399
    Creating the Postoffice 399
    Checking and Compressing Folders 403
    Postoffice Manager Duties 402
    Reinstating First-Time Startup 403
Enhancing Microsoft Mail 404

16 ▬ **Microsoft Schedule+** **407**
Appointment Book 408
    Viewing Your Appointments 409

Adding a One-Time Appointment 410
Recurring Appointments 415
Setting Access Privileges 421
Opening Other Users' Appointment Books 422
Exporting and Importing Appointments 423
Archiving Appointments 425
Task List 425
Adding A One-Time Task 425
Recurring Tasks 426
Viewing Tasks 426
Planner 428
Printing Appointments and Tasks 429
Setting Display Defaults 430
General Options 431
More About Schedule+ 432
Offline and Online Modes 432
Viewing Reminders at Windows Startup 433
Creating Resource Accounts 433
The Schedule+ Extensions 434

17 ▬▬ Network Games: Hearts 437
Hearts Basics 438
Begin Play 439
Passing Cards 441
Passing Strategy 441
Game Strategy 442

18 ▬▬ Network Administrator Information 445
Installing Windows for Workgroups 446
Network Hardware 447
Network Types 447
Installing Network Interface Cards 451
Windows for Workgroups Network
Communications 454
NetBEUI and NetBIOS 456
NetWare SPX/IPX Support 456
Windows for Workgroups Startup Files 457

Standard Mode 457
386 Enhanced Mode 458
Windows for Workgroups Initialization Files 459
The PROTOCOL.INI File 461
Network Settings in WIN.INI 463
Network Settings in SYSTEM.INI 464
Restricting Share Options 465
Completely Disabling Sharing 465
Disabling File Manager Share Options 465
Disabling Print Sharing 466
Server Priority Values 466
Setting Values for Each VM 468
Connecting with Novell NetWare Networks 471
Novell NetWare Drivers 472
Other NetWare Information 473
Connecting with LAN Manager Networks 474
Connecting to LAN Manager Servers 474
Using LAN Manager Security 475

A ▬▬ **Windows Modes and Memory** **479**
Types of Memory 480
Windows Operating Modes 482
Standard Mode and Memory 483
386 Enhanced Mode and Memory 484

B ▬▬ **Running Non-Windows Applications** **489**
Types of Applications 490
Non-Windows Applications 491
Non-Windows Applications Requiring
Expanded Memory 492
Memory-Resident Software 492
Working with Non-Windows Applications 493
Running Non-Windows Applications in a
Window 494
Copying and Pasting in Standard Mode 495
Copying and Pasting in 386 Enhanced
Mode 496

Setting Options for 386 Enhanced Mode 497
Using Program Information Files 500
Using the PIF Editor 502
Other Settings 503

C ▬ **Optimizing Windows' Performance** **507**
Choosing a Windows Mode 508
Improving the Performance of Non-Windows
Applications 509
Optimizing System Startup 510
Using Windows SYSEDIT 511
Changing the CONFIG.SYS File 512
The AUTOEXEC.BAT File 514
Improving Disk Performance 515
Hard Disk Cleanup 515
Disk Optimizing Techniques 517

D ▬ **Windows for Workgroups Resource Kit** **521**
The Resource Kit Utility Disk 522
NetMeter 523
Network Adapter Status (NetStat) Utility 523
Network DDE Share Manager 524
Phone Message Application 525
Mail 3.x Folder Conversion Program 525
Additional Files 525
Online Help Information 526

▬ **Index** **527**

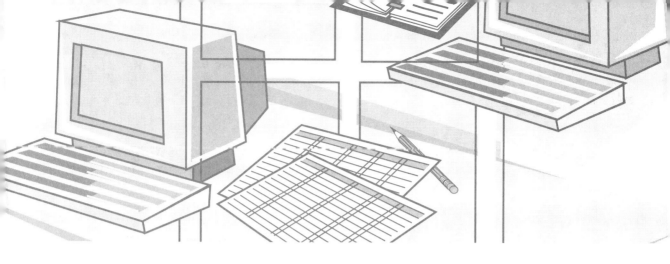

INTRODUCTION

Welcome to *Windows for Workgroups Made Easy*. This book explores Microsoft's network version of the popular Windows 3.1 operating system. Windows for Workgroups makes it easy for people to connect their computers, share information, and work together. You can send electronic mail (e-mail) to your associates, schedule group meetings, share files and printers, manage calendars, and work together on group projects. You can even play the card game Hearts over the network with up to three other players.

With Windows for Workgroups, any 80386 or later model system can act as a *server* and share its resources (files and printers) with other users on the network. Any other system connected to the network and running Windows for Workgroups can use those shared resources as a *client*. You can run the program on a system that is already attached to an existing network, or you can build a new network by adding network interface cards (NICs) and tying them together with network cable. A similar product called Workgroup Connection for MS-DOS contains all the software you need to connect an MS-DOS-based PC as a client to a Windows for Workgroups server.

At least 40 major computer manufacturers are preinstalling Windows for Workgroups on their systems in anticipation of the need for users to communicate in network environments. More than 100 independent software and hardware vendors have already developed products to support the new features in Windows for Workgroups. But, you can

begin working with other users right away. Windows for Workgroups includes an electronic mail program and scheduling program for workgroup use.

The purpose of this book is to help you learn how to use Windows and the new networking features of Windows for Workgroups. The importance of Windows and networking can't be overstated. Bill Gates, chairman and CEO of Microsoft, has said that "the integration of networking and workgroup features into Windows is an enormous and innovative step. Whether a company is small or large, people need to work together in groups, share information, quickly involve one another in decisions, and coordinate schedules and business activities. These everyday activities will be supported by the services built into Windows for Workgroups, and by existing and new applications that take advantage of the operating system's workgroup extensions. Windows for Workgroups makes group computing easier."

Windows for Workgroups provides developers with the features and tools they need to write Windows-based applications that take advantage of workgroup capabilities. This ensures that many network-compatible applications will be available. Applications can easily be extended to support the electronic mail functionality in Windows for Workgroups. For example, spreadsheets, word processing documents, or even voice-annotated messages can be sent to other users by attaching them to mail messages. Applications are being enhanced to take advantage of networking features. For example, Microsoft Excel and Microsoft Word for Windows upgrades automate common workgroup activities, such as document assembly and schedule tracking, forms routing and notification, information sharing, and application-specific workgroup tasks.

Companies with an existing network can use Windows for Workgroups as a client to bring new services and capabilities to their LAN users, such as workgroup-enabled applications, scheduling and network dynamic data exchange (DDE). The product is compatible with Microsoft LAN Manager and Novell NetWare and allows users to simultaneously access both network types at the same time. MIS managers and users can install and configure Windows for Workgroups in a single drag-and-drop action for both of these popular networks. This saves time and trouble and reduces desktop support issues. In

addition, Windows for Workgroups also works on other networks, such as Banyan VINES.

Windows for Workgroups Features

Windows for Workgroups provides several network applications and utilities so you can begin working with other users once your network is installed. Of course, Windows for Workgroups also includes all of the desktop accessories and utilities included with the Windows 3.1 product. Here are some basic advantages of connecting computers into a Windows for Workgroups network:

◆ Quick and easy file transfers among computers on the network

◆ Centralized file storage and backup

◆ Support for Object Linking and Embedding (OLE) over the network, which provides automatic updating of information in linked documents.

◆ Electronic mail and messaging

◆ Peripheral sharing of printers, hard drives, CD-ROM drives, and other devices

◆ Workgroup applications

You can transfer files without first copying them to a disk and then sending that disk to another user. You can also run applications stored on other computers and store the files you create with those applications on that same computer. When files are centralized in this way, backup and protection of data are easier to manage.

OLE, discussed in Chapter 14, makes group projects more practical. For example, you can insert a set of numbers or a graphic image from a document owned by another user in your document. An automatic link is established that ensures your document is updated whenever the original document is changed or updated.

Peripherals and printers attached to other users' systems are accessible so you can take advantage of laser printers, color printers, or CD-ROMs attached to those systems. This can help reduce the equipment requirements in your office. If you've been wanting your own laser printer, try justifying its purchase to management by reminding them that other users can share it over the Windows for Workgroup network.

Windows for Workgroups contains a handy Chat utility so you can type messages to other users and read their responses. It also includes several network utilities so you can monitor the way your system is being used by other network users and change your network configuration.

The following features and utilities are also part of the Windows for Workgroups package.

Microsoft Mail   Mail is an electronic mail service that lets users read, compose, forward, and reply to electronic mail messages, as well as manage messages they receive. You can attach an entire document to a mail message. The version of Microsoft Mail that ships with Windows for Workgroups is compatible with only one workgroup. If you need to connect with other workgroup postoffices on the network or to other e-mail systems, you'll need the additional support provided by the Microsoft Mail and Schedule+ Extensions for Windows for Workgroups.

Schedule+   Schedule+ is a full-featured graphical scheduling application that allows people to schedule group meetings and manage their daily calendars and task lists electronically. You can set up group meetings and view the schedules of other users. It is an excellent tool for people who are working together on group projects that must meet various deadlines.

Network DDE   Network DDE provides a way for users to create compound documents that share data across the network. You can insert information in your documents from documents owned by other users, even if those documents reside on other network computers. Network DDE ensures that changes made to the original documents are made in the documents where the information is pasted. For example, a group leader could create a compound document that contains information from the accounting department, graphics from the art department, and text from the marketing department. Each department can change its portion of the compound document as necessary. Every time the group leader opens the compound document to view or change its contents, any changes made by the departments are automatically made in the group leader's document.

Security   Windows for Workgroups offers security features that can lock out unauthorized users from using shared resources on the network. Users can share files and printers with other users on two levels. Other users on the system can either be given full access to a directory, or granted permission to read files but not modify them in any way. Access is granted by giving users specific passwords related to the level of security they should have. If more sophisticated security is required, Microsoft LAN Manager or Novell NetWare are recommended.

File Manager and Print Manager Improvements   Windows for Workgroups includes Windows File Manager improvements that simplify information sharing. A Toolbar provides a set of buttons for quickly executing commands that would normally be accessed by choosing options on a menu. New options provide commands for sharing directories and printers, or connecting with shared directories and printers on other users' computers.

Windows for Workgroups Packaging

Windows for Workgroups has everything that even nontechnical users need to install the product quickly and easily. Several software-only configurations provide an upgrade for Windows 3.0, Windows 3.1, and MS-DOS. Other configurations include software, network cards, and cables as listed here:

✦ Starter kits include all the software, network cards, and cables needed to connect two PCs in a complete Windows-based network. A starter kit is recommended for users with no existing network. The kit includes a 15-minute videotape that walks you through a step-by-step installation process. To expand the network, you purchase a user kit.

✦ User kits contain all hardware and software needed to connect an additional PC to the network.

✦ Software-only packages are available for users who are installing the operating system on PCs that are already networked, or for users who want to purchase their own network cards.

The starter kits and user kits are also available in the form of upgrade packages for current Windows 3.1 users. Software-only versions are

available in upgrade form for current users of Windows 3.0 and
Windows 3.1. Prices range from $99.95 to $849.95, U.S. suggested retail
price (SRP), depending upon the configuration. In addition, the
Workgroup Connection for MS-DOS product contains all the software
needed to connect an MS-DOS-based PC as a client to a Windows for
Workgroups network. Its SRP is $79.95.

NOTE: You can buy the software-only kits, then purchase network
cards and cables from alternate (and discounted) sources. You can
also install Windows for Workgroups on most existing networks.

System Requirements

Using the Windows for Workgroups operating system 3.1 for file
sharing and print sharing requires MS-DOS version 3.3 or later (version
5.0 is recommended); a PC using an Intel 386SX or later processor; and
3MB of RAM (4MB are recommended). Using Windows for Workgroups
without file and print sharing requires 2MB of RAM and a 286 or later
processor in standard mode and an Intel 386SX or later processor in
enhanced mode. A Microsoft mouse or other pointing device is strongly
recommended.

Additional requirements include a 5 1/4-inch or 3 1/2-inch
high-density disk drive and a hard disk with 9.5MB of available
memory (14.5MB are recommended); a VGA, super VGA, 8514/A, EGA,
or video graphics adapter and monitor compatible with Windows 3.1
(color VGA or better resolution is recommended); and a Microsoft
Windows-compatible network adapter card and cabling.

Setup and Administrative Information

Because Windows for Workgroups is a networking program that
involves many computers and many users, an administrator is usually
assigned to install the software and manage the network. An
administrator is not essential, but on large networks, it's important to
have someone on staff who is familiar with the network and how each
system has been installed. This administrator might also set policies for
sharing resouces and establish password access to those resources. Even

small networks will benefit from having at least one person who keeps track of the network and can assist other users in its use.

If Windows for Workgroups is not yet installed on your system, or if you need network administrator information, start by reading Chapter 18. It discussed networks and how to install the hardware, and it provides information for troubleshooting network problems. You will also learn some interesting administrative tricks and find out how to connect with other networks like Microsoft LAN Manager and Novell NetWare.

Windows Update Notes

We offer a set of update notes that keep you informed about the latest information and changes to Windows for Workgroups. The notes contain the following information:

✦ Update information from Microsoft Technical Support and the Microsoft Knowledge Base information service

✦ Known bugs, problems, and solutions

✦ Software and hardware compatibility information

✦ System and hardware notes

To order the notes, use the coupon in the back of this book. Send a check or money order for $12, made payable to Tom Sheldon. If you live in California, add 86 cents tax. If you live outside the United States, add $2 for shipping and handling. Please note that the price covers the cost of collecting and organizing the information, as well as printing, mailing, and handling.

CHAPTER

1

WINDOWS OVERVIEW

Welcome to the world of Microsoft Windows for Workgroups. Throughout, this book refers to Windows for Workgroups as simply Windows.

Windows gives you a brand-new way to work with computers that is not only more exciting, but also helps you be more productive. Applications (software) written to work with Windows have a similar look and feel. That means you can easily switch from one manufacturer's program to another's without having to relearn basic functions like opening, editing, printing, and saving documents. In addition, Windows provides a Clipboard feature, so you can "cut" text and graphics images from one application and "paste" them into another.

This chapter presents a guided tour of Windows. Its objective is to help you find your way around the screens and become familiar with Windows terminology.

The Windows Desktop Metaphor

The designers of Windows wanted to create an interface that everyone would find instantly familiar, so they employed a desktop metaphor. The entire computer screen is like a desktop, and windows are placed on this desktop in the same way you might arrange papers, calendars, notepads, calculators, and other workplace tools on your desk. The first window you see when you start Windows is shown in Figure 1-1.

Furthermore, when you do paperwork on your desktop, you might have several sheets of paper side by side or stacked on top of one another. In Windows, you can open several windows at once and place

The Program Manager is the first window you see when starting Windows for Workgroups
Figure 1-1.

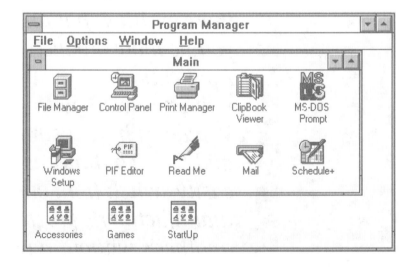

documents side by side for comparison, or stack them so you can shuffle through your work during the day. The advantage of having several projects open at once is that you can get at your work quickly when a client calls with a question or when the boss walks in. And you can copy information from one window to another. Figure 1-2 shows a spreadsheet open in one window, a notepad in another, and a word processing document in still another.

NOTE: All open windows rest on the desktop, which is basically the screen background area.

Although you can open several applications at once, only one window is *active* and responds to your immediate keyboard input. Clicking a window with the mouse makes it the active window and highlights its title bar; you can then start typing text or executing commands for that window. In Figure 1-2, the window titled "Notepad—NOTES.TXT" is the active window because its title bar is highlighted. Any text you type or

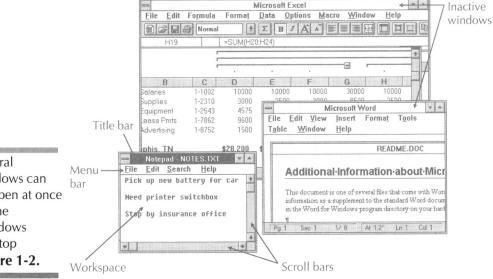

Several windows can be open at once on the Windows desktop
Figure 1-2.

commands you execute affect the active window; the other windows wait patiently in the background until you make them active.

The *workspace* is the area of the window where you type text, draw, or otherwise work with data. When the information in the workspace is saved to disk and given a filename, that name appears in the title bar. In Figure 1-2, you can see that the file NOTES.TXT is open in the Notepad window. The title bar helps you distinguish between open windows. Suppose you need to run two copies of the same application at once, to compare and edit documents—the title bars allow you to see which document is in each window.

NOTE: Some applications, like Microsoft Word for Windows, let you open multiple documents at once in the same application window, so you don't have to run more than one copy of the program. This saves memory.

Mouse or Keyboard?

Before continuing, you'll want to get familiar with your mouse and keyboard. The Windows interface works best with a mouse, and although you don't need one to take advantage of Windows' features, it's highly recommended that you use a mouse.

Mouse Usage and Terminology

If your system has a mouse, a pointer in the shape of an arrow appears on the screen. In the following illustration, the mouse pointer points to a button in the upper-right corner of the window:

To move the pointer, move the mouse along your desk or tabletop. (If you run out of room while moving the mouse, you can pick it up and reposition it.) Most mouse devices have two buttons, some have three. With Windows, you use only the left and right buttons.

This book employs the following terms to describe the actions of the mouse:

Term	Action
Point	Move the onscreen pointer by moving the mouse. Point the tip of the arrow to an object on the screen, such as a button, icon, or character.
Click	Press and immediately release a mouse button.
Click and hold	Press and hold down the mouse button until you complete an action.
Drag	Point at an object on the screen; then click and hold while moving the mouse. The object moves with the mouse.
Double-click	Click a mouse button twice quickly. This is the Windows/mouse equivalent of executing a command by pressing the Enter key.

Keyboard Usage and Terminology

You can use the keyboard instead of the mouse to access menu items on windows. (The *menu bar* that appears on many windows is explained in "The Menu Bar and Drop-Down Menus," later in this chapter.) This book assumes that most users have a mouse, but keyboard techniques are also covered for two reasons. First, they are sometimes faster to execute than mouse actions. Second, if your mouse is disabled, you'll need to use keyboard commands. This sometimes happens after changing your hardware configuration.

To access window menus with the keyboard, press the Alt key followed by another key related to the menu item you want to select. Most menu options are represented by an underlined letter or number that you press to activate the option.

For example, to open the File menu from the Program Manager menu bar,

you would press Alt-F, because *F* is the underlined letter in the File option. This File menu will open,

and you can then type the letter of the menu option you want to select. Note that you don't have to press the Alt key again once the menu is open; just press the underlined letter of the option you want.

As you work with Windows menus using the keyboard, keep the following in mind:

✦ Once you become familiar with menu options and the keys that activate them, you can use the keystroke method to execute a command without looking at the menu.

✦ Some menu options may not be available for your current activity. These options will appear "grayed out," as are the Move and Copy commands in the File menu shown previously. (When you select text or graphics to move or copy, these menu options will become available.)

✦ Some menu options have *speed keys*—special keys or combinations of keys that accomplish the same action as the menu option. In the previous illustration, the Move option, when available for use, can be executed by pressing F7. You'll want to get familiar with these speed keys, since they often are the fastest way to execute a command.

Types of Windows

1

It's important to understand the difference between the various types of windows that you'll see on the Windows desktop. Typically, the Program Manager appears after you start Windows, as shown in Figure 1-1. You double-click icons in the Program Manager to start programs, which appear in *application windows*. Programs such as Microsoft Word for Windows, Aldus Pagemaker, and Micrografx Designer run in application windows. Program Manager is itself an application window, but it is unique because you use it to start other programs. You can organize the way Program Manager looks to fit the way you work and the way you want to start your programs as you'll see in Chapter 8.

NOTE: Starting a program from the Program Manager is often called "launching" a program.

Application windows contain their own "subwindows" called *document windows*. The Program Manager window shown in Figure 1-3 has two document windows, Main and Accessories. Note that the Main and Accessories windows are positioned inside the Program Manager window. You cannot move the windows out of the Program Manager window and onto the desktop.

When you're working in a word processing application, a document window holds an actual document. But the term *document window* is a little misleading. In some applications, these windows might hold a list of files or artwork. In fact, the Program Manager has several document windows that are more appropriately referred to as *group windows*. Figure 1-3 shows the Accessories and the Main group windows. Other group windows appear as icons at the bottom of the Program Manager window. These group windows are temporarily closed, but you can open them by double-clicking the icons with the mouse.

Figure 1-4 shows two document windows open in the Microsoft Word for Windows application window. An application that uses document windows loads itself into memory only once. This saves memory because you open multiple documents from the single host program instead of loading multiple programs for each document. Each

The Main and Accessories group windows are part of the Program Manager window. They share Program Manager's menu commands, but cannot be moved outside of its window borders **Figure 1-3.**

Document windows

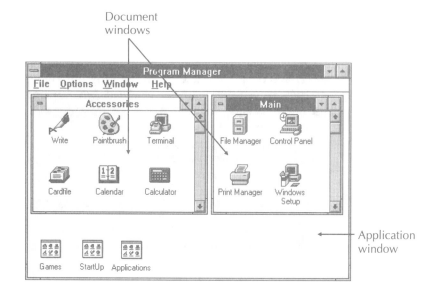

Application window

Document windows

In an application like Microsoft Word, one or more documents can be open at once, each in its own document window **Figure 1-4.**

document window shares the menus and other features of the host application. Document windows don't have menu options of their own because they share the menu options of the host application, as shown in Figure 1-4.

Windows as Icons

You can temporarily remove open windows from the screen when not in use by reducing them to icons on the desktop. This is called *minimizing* the window. Don't confuse the icon of a minimized program with the startup icons in the Program Manager Window. The name of the application and any files loaded in its workspace appear under the minimized program's icon on the desktop, as shown here:

Notepad -
README.TXT

Paintbrush -
BOXES.BMP

File Manager -
[d:\draw*.*]

When a *document window* is minimized, it appears within the host application window. For example, here is the Program Manager window with all its group windows minimized to icons:

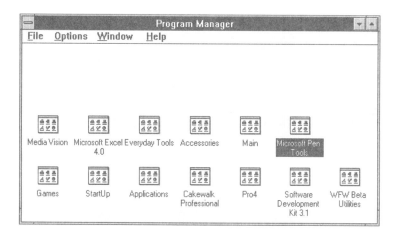

Double-clicking any of these icons opens the group so you can see the
icons within it. Use group windows in Program Manager to organize
your applications into meaningful groups. For example, you might
have a group called Newsletter that contains the programs and
documents used to create a monthly newsletter.

NOTE: An application remains in memory whether its window is
open or minimized. Reducing the window to an icon does not exit
the application—it's just a way to remove clutter from the screen so you
can work with other windows.

Keep in mind that applications with icons in the Program Manager
window are not running, as those on the desktop are. As shown in
Figure 1-5, the icons in Program Manager represent programs you can
start while icons on the desktop represent programs that are already

Double-click
icons in
Program
Manager to start
applications.
Icons on the
desktop
represent
applications
already loaded
in memory
Figure 1-5.

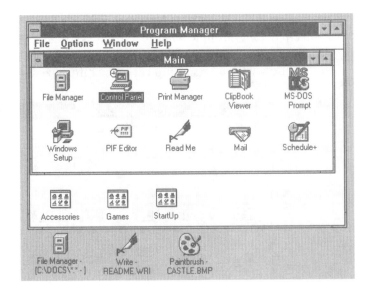

running in your computer's memory. Simply double-click the running program icon to open its window for use.

1

Window Elements

Now it's time to take a quick look at the individual elements of a window. The Program Manager window is used as an example, but most other windows have similar features.

The Control Menu

The button for opening the Control menu is located in the upper-left corner of every window. When you click the button, the Control menu shown here appears:

The Control menu has options for moving, sizing, minimizing, maximizing, and closing windows, but it's really designed for keyboard users who need to access functions that mouse users would perform by pointing, clicking, and dragging.

The Menu Bar and Drop-Down Menus

When a window has a menu bar at the top, and you select an option from the bar, a *drop-down menu* appears. Here is the File menu from the Program Manager:

You can select options from menus by pointing and clicking with the mouse, or by using keyboard techniques described in "Keyboard Techniques and Speed Keys" in Chapter 3.

Window Sizing Buttons

Click the buttons at the upper-right corner of a window to minimize it to an icon or maximize it to fill the whole screen. These Minimize and Maximize buttons are shown here:

When a window has been maximized, the Maximize button is replaced by the Restore button, as shown here:

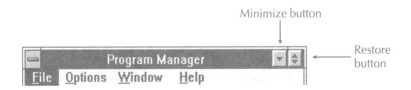

Click this button to restore the window to the size it was before being maximized.

Scroll Bars

1

Scroll bars appear on a window when all of its contents can't fit within the window. Most application windows have scroll bars, as shown in Figure 1-6. The scroll bars may appear on the right border for scrolling vertically, on the bottom border for scrolling horizontally, or both. You'll need a mouse to use scroll bars.

Borders

Borders define the limits of a window and you can adjust them to increase or decrease the window size. Mouse users can click and drag any window border or corner to *resize* the window. When you point to a border or corner, the mouse pointer changes to a double- headed arrow, as shown on the right-hand border of this window:

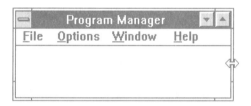

You then click and drag the pointer to resize the window.

Mouse users can use scroll bars to move vertically or horizontally through a document
Figure 1-6.

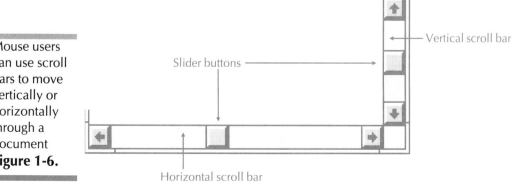

Slider buttons

Vertical scroll bar

Horizontal scroll bar

The Title Bar

You've already learned about the title bar that appears at the top of a window. One more thing to remember about the title bar is that, with a mouse, you can use the title bar to move a window to another location. Just point to the title bar, and then click and drag the window.

TIP: Here's an interesting trick you can use with the title bar. Double-click it to maximize the window, then double-click it again to restore the window to its original size.

Dialog Boxes

Menu options that include an ellipsis (...) display *dialog boxes* when selected. A dialog box contains a set of options that you set to affect how a menu command is executed. You use the mouse to select options or, in some cases, you type text in text fields. For example, you set options on the Print Setup dialog box shown in Figure 1-7 to specify how you want a document printed. You can choose different printers if more than one printer is connected to your system or network. You can also choose different paper sizes, orientation, and other options.

Multitasking with Windows

Windows lets you load and run several applications at the same time; this capability is called *multitasking*. Most of the time you'll probably

You use dialog boxes to choose options and specify settings for executing commands **Figure 1-7.**

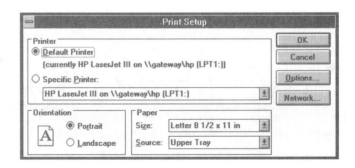

work with one application while others wait in background windows until you need them. However, Windows also lets you have a background application working on one task while you are doing something else in the active window. For example, a background application can sort a mailing list or print a document as you write a letter in another window.

Multitasking may slow your system down a bit, but in some cases the trade-off for multitasking is beneficial. Consider that your computer spends a lot of its time sitting idle while you type in your word processor. Thousands (or even millions) of potential processing cycles go to waste every time you pause to think or look at your notes. Multitasking lets your system use this idle time to handle other tasks in the background. Every time you pause, Windows jumps to the background application and continues processing.

To multitask several applications, start each application in its own window. Execute a task like sorting or printing for one application, and then go ahead and activate another window to work on something else. That's all you have to do.

NOTE: For multitasking to work properly, applications must be written to run under Windows. DOS applications can only be multitasked when running in 386 enhanced mode, as discussed in Appendixes A and B.

Cutting and Pasting with the ClipBook

The ClipBook accessory lets you move text or graphics from one application to another, or from one network computer to another network computer. Think of the ClipBook as an invisible bulletin board where you place text or graphics until you're ready to use them, either in the same document or in another application window. For example, you might create a company logo in Paintbrush and then paste it into a Write or WordPerfect document. Or, several users on a computer network might use ClipBook to share art or spreadsheet information they are assembling for a product brochure or a group project.

The ClipBook is really two utilities, the Clipboard and the Local ClipBook, as you can see in Figure 1-8. The Clipboard is a temporary

The ClipBook is two utilities: the Clipboard for temporary storage and the Local ClipBook for permanent storage.
Figure 1-8.

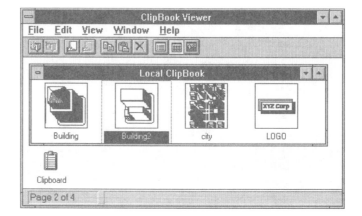

holding area for text or graphics (called "objects") that you've cut or copied from an application. The Local ClipBook is a permanent storage area for these objects. After you've captured an object from an application, you can reuse it immediately by pasting it elsewhere, or you can save it for future use by placing it in the Local ClipBook.

Almost all application windows have menu options for cutting and pasting information to and from the Clipboard, as shown here:

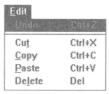

Cut, Copy, and Paste are Clipboard options, and are explained in the following table:

1

Clipboard Command	Function
Cut	Deletes the selected text or graphic and places it in the Clipboard, overwriting the current Clipboard contents.
Copy	Places a copy of the selected text or graphic in the Clipboard, overwriting the current Clipboard contents. The original is not removed, as with the Cut command.
Paste	Copies the contents of the Clipboard to the current insertion point position in a window. The contents of the Clipboard remain intact.

Examining and Saving ClipBook Contents

Look again at Figure 1-1, and you'll see a ClipBook icon in Program Manager's Main group. When you need to examine the graphics or text you've captured with the Cut or Copy command, you can double-click this icon.

Each time you copy or cut text or graphics, the existing contents of the Clipboard are overwritten. If you need to retain the contents of the Clipboard for future use, you can save it to the Local ClipBook (which saves the images to disk automatically). In Figure 1-8, notice how the Local ClipBook shows four images. These images are displayed as *thumbnails,* which are reduced versions of what the images really look like, You should save graphics and text objects to the Local ClipBook when you want to use again them during another session.

Windows Accessories and Games

The Program Manager contains two group windows called Accessories and Games. The Accessories window contains icons for starting various tools and utilities useful in your Windows work sessions. Here is the Accessories window and an explanation of the utilities it contains:

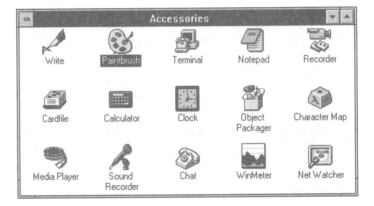

Utility	Function
Write	A word processor with character- and paragraph-formatting features
Paintbrush	A painting program for creating graphics images
Terminal	Lets you connect with other computers and data services over phone lines
Notepad	A small, easy-to-use note-writing utility
Recorder	Stores mouse movements and keystrokes so you can play them back later
Cardfile	A minidatabase that tracks names, addresses
Calendar	Keeps track of your appointments
Clock	Displays a digital or analog clock
Object Packager	Lets you create packages of data in one application and paste them into another
Character Map	Used to insert symbols and special characters into your text
Media Player	A utility for playing sound and multimedia devices
Sound Recorder	A utility for recording, editing, and playing back sounds

1

Utility	Function
Chat	A utility that lets you "chat" and share information between other users on your network
WinMeter	Graphically displays how your system is being used by other users on the network
Net Watcher	Displays a list of users accessing your system and lets you terminate those users' connections

The Games window lets you access games for entertainment when you're not so busy. The Games group contains the card games, Solitaire and Hearts, and the strategy game, Minesweeper. Hearts is a network card game, which means that four people on separate network computers can play the game together.

Control Panel Options for Customizing Windows

The Main group window in the Program Manager contains an icon called Control Panel. When you select the Control Panel icon, the following window appears:

Each icon in this window opens a utility for customizing various elements within Windows, as described in the following table:

Utility	Function
Color	Allow users to set the color schemes for Windows
Drivers	Installs and removes device drivers
Fonts	Adds and removes screen and printer fonts
Ports	Sets the speed and protocols of your system's serial ports
MIDI Mapper	Controls MIDI-attached devices
Mouse	Controls the way the mouse operates
Desktop	Changes the appearance of the desktop, including its colors and patterns, and the alignment of icons inside windows
Networks	Controls the connection of Windows to a network
Printers	Adds, removes, and configures printers
International	Sets country codes, language type, currency formats, and number formats
Keyboard	Sets the repeat rate and speed delay of the keyboard
Date/Time	Sets the date and time
Sound	Assigns sounds to system events
386 Enhanced	Controls the way applications run under 386 enhanced mode

CHAPTER

2

STARTING
WINDOWS

In this chapter you'll learn how to start Windows and begin using it, so it's assumed you've already installed the program on your hard drive. If not, refer to Chapter 18 for setup information.

During installation, Windows determines the type of computer, display monitor, mouse, and printers your system has, and whether you are connected to a network. Based on this information, Windows then starts up in a specific mode. In most cases, the startup method determined during installation will be the best for your day-to-day activities. However, every now and then you may want to start Windows in another mode, depending on the applications you intend to run or the tasks you need to do.

This chapter explains the operating modes for Windows, and examines some other startup and operations issues.

Starting Windows

To start Windows, turn your computer on and wait for the DOS prompt to appear. This will be the drive C prompt unless your system startup configuration has been altered, or your computer is attached to a network. You'll see the drive letter followed by a blinking cursor. Type **WIN** and press (Enter) to start Windows.

Logging On

When you start Windows, you see the Welcome to Windows for Workgroups dialog box shown here:

You use this box to specify who you are and your logon password. Windows then gives you access to resources and files on the network, based on your logon name. If this is the first time you are logging on, type a name in the Logon Name field and a password in the Password field. Use the mouse or press the (Tab) key to move between fields. Note that the logon name specified during Windows for Workgroups installation may already be in the Logon Name field.

NOTE: If others use this computer, each person should specify a different logon name and password in the Welcome to Windows for Workgroups dialog box.

2

Logging on to a network is important on networks that require security. The logon name and password you specify give you access to resources such as disks and printers on other network computers. Passwords are optional, but they provide file privacy and security on a network that many people use.

Users who share directories and printers on their computer can require that other users on the network enter a password before they can access the resources. For example, Figure 2-1 illustrates how Jane shares a directory on her system with other users. The directory might contain art files or spreadsheet files that other users need to access. Jane controls who can access the directory by specifying access passwords when she shares the directory. She then gives the password to Joe and

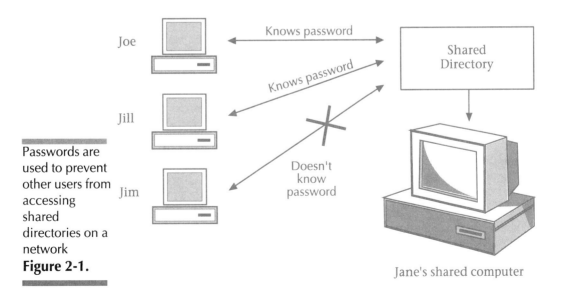

Passwords are used to prevent other users from accessing shared directories on a network

Figure 2-1.

Jill, but not Jim. Joe and Jill can access the directory and work with its files, but Jim is locked out until given the password.

Don't confuse your logon password with the passwords used to access shared directories on other network computers. When you start Windows for Workgroups, you type a *logon password,* then when you access shared directories or printers on other computers, you type a *resource access password.* However, there is an important link between your logon password and your resource access passwords. Windows for Workgroups creates a special password-list file based on your logon name and password, as shown in Figure 2-2. In this file, it records the passwords you type the first time you access a network resource on another computer. The next time you access that resource, Windows looks in the password-list file and uses the recorded password so you don't have to type it again. This one-time logon scheme gives you network-wide access through your logon password. However, it is extremely important that other users *not* know your password. They could log on using your name and password, then access resources that only you have authority to use. They could also cause damage to files using your logon name.

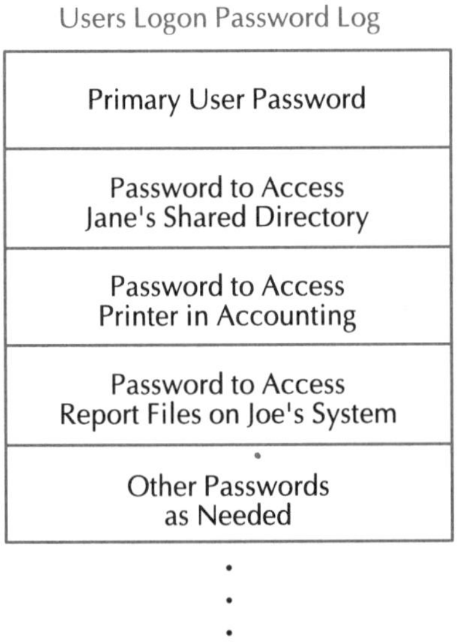

Users Logon Password Log

Primary User Password
Password to Access Jane's Shared Directory
Password to Access Printer in Accounting
Password to Access Report Files on Joe's System
Other Passwords as Needed

A password-list file keeps a record of the passwords you enter to access shared resources

Figure 2-2.

After filling out the Welcome to Windows for Workgroups dialog box, click the OK button. You'll then see the Program Manager window like the one pictured in Figure 1-1. You are now ready to work with Windows for Workgroups. Later, you'll learn how to change your password, which is a good idea to prevent security breaches. If your network has an administrator, he or she may require that you change your password on a regular basis.

CAUTION: Never leave your computer unattended if you are logged on to the network. A person could walk up to your system and gain unauthorized access to network resources using your logon name. Always log off or use a password-protected screen saver before leaving, as discussed at the end of this chapter.

What's Your Mode?

It's a good idea to begin by determining the *operating mode* in which Windows has started, and the way it uses computer memory. To view startup information about your Windows program, open the About Program Manager dialog box. To do so, first make sure that Program Manager is the active window, as shown in Figure 1-1. If not, click the Program Manager window to activate it (or press [Alt]-[Tab] until the Program Manager title bar is highlighted). If the Program Manager is reduced to an icon on the desktop, double-click the icon.

To open the About Program Manager dialog box, do one of the following:

Mouse users:	Click the Help menu option, and then click About Program Manager.
Keyboard users:	Press [Alt] to highlight the menu bar. Hold it down and press [H] to select the Help menu, then [A] to select the About option.

NOTE: In this book, key combinations like the preceding one will be expressed like this: [Alt]-[H][A].

You'll see the About Program Manager dialog box, similar to the one in Figure 2-3 appear on your screen. It displays the Windows version number and operating mode, available RAM (random access memory), and available system resources (explained later in this chapter in the section "Analyzing the About Program Manager Dialog Box"). Note that the About Program Manager box in Figure 2-3 is for a system running Windows in 386 enhanced mode; your Windows program may be running in standard mode.

Standard Mode   Standard mode is the normal operating mode for Windows running on systems with Intel 80286 processors and 2MB of memory. If you have an 80386 or 80486 system, you can also run this mode to get better performance, but you'll give up some of the features of 386 enhanced mode. You won't be able to share resources on your computer with other network users, but you will be able to access resources on other network computers. Before Windows can be started in this mode, you must type **NET LOGON** at the DOS prompt.

386 Enhanced Mode   386 enhanced mode is a multitasking mode that provides additional features for owners of Intel 80386 and 80486 systems—such as virtual memory, which treats disk storage as memory when you're running short on memory. Virtual memory is especially useful when you can't run a program because your computer doesn't

The About Program Manager dialog box shows the Windows version number, operating mode, and other Windows operating information.
Figure 2-3.

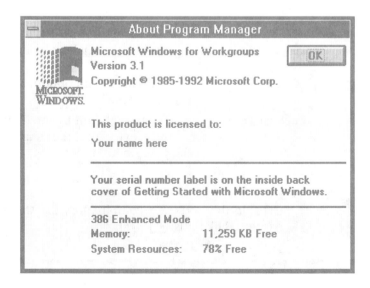

2

have enough memory. The 386 enhanced mode also gives you the ability to share your system's resources with other network users and a way to run DOS applications in separate windows (instead of full-screen). You can multitask DOS applications, which means they run simultaneously with other applications so you can do several things at once. Note that standard mode will multitask Windows applications, but not DOS applications.

Depending on the type of processor your system has, Windows starts in one of the two modes just described. Here are descriptions of system types and the modes they use:

✦ Intel 8088/8086-based systems will not run Windows for Workgroups. You can run Windows 3.0 on these systems.

✦ Intel 80286-based systems run Windows in standard mode only.

✦ Intel 80386/80486-based systems run Windows for Workgroups in 386 enhanced mode if 3MB or more of memory are available; otherwise, Windows runs in standard mode.

TIP: Although 386 enhanced mode provides additional features such as virtual memory, resource sharing, and the ability to multitask non-Windows (DOS) applications, using this mode may slow down your system. If you don't need these operating enhancements, use standard mode for better overall performance. However, if you have a high-performance system (80486 or better), you shouldn't see too much of a slowdown in 386 enhanced mode.

Windows normally starts in the mode it determines (during installation and setup) is best for your system. When you need to force Windows to start in another mode, use these startup command parameters:

Command	Mode
WIN /S	Type this command to start Windows in standard mode. Before doing so, type **NET LOGON** at the DOS prompt to start the network support software so you can access resources on other computers.
WIN /3	This command starts Windows in 386 enhanced mode.

Analyzing the About Program Manager Dialog Box

You don't have to type the startup commands just described to start Windows. They are used to "force" Windows to run in a specific mode. If you just type **WIN**, Windows starts in its default mode. If your system contains an 80286 processor and has 2MB of RAM, you'll see "standard mode" indicated in the About Program Manager dialog box. If your system has an 80386 or 80486 processor and has 3MB or more of memory, you'll see "386 enhanced mode" in the dialog box.

The amount of memory listed in the About Program Manager box indicates how much memory is available to your applications after DOS, Windows, and any startup applications are loaded. System Resources is not the same as available memory; rather, it indicates the amount of memory that Windows sets aside for its own use to track dialog boxes, buttons, messages, and menus. System resources may run low while available RAM remains high, usually because you're running too many applications at once. If this happens, you'll see "Out of memory" messages. Simply close applications you don't need and continue your work.

If you run out of memory when starting applications, you might try running Windows in 386 enhanced mode to take advantage of virtual memory. With this arrangement, your hard disk is used to make up for any lack of memory. As you work with Windows, check the About Program Manager dialog box periodically to determine if Windows is running efficiently and to see if you need to add additional memory.

T**IP:**   Appendix A provides a further discussion of modes and memory.

Running Programs in Windows

If you're anxious to run one of your Windows applications and you see its startup icon in the Program Manager, double-click it now to launch the program. If the group that holds the startup icon is minimized, double-click the group icon to open the group window, then double-click the application startup icon.

If an icon is not available for the program you want to run, or if you don't have a mouse, you can use the Program Manager Run command to get the application started. Do one of the following:

Mouse users:	Click the Program Manager File menu option to open the File drop-down menu; then click the Run option.
Keyboard users:	Press [Alt]-[F][R] to open the Run dialog box.

The following dialog box will appear:

In the Command Line text box, type the path and name of the program you want to run. For example, to run Microsoft Word for DOS located in the WORD directory on drive D, you would type **D:\WORD \WORD** in the Run dialog box.

Starting Applications When Starting Windows

In the preceding section "What's Your Mode?," you saw how to add the /S or /3 parameter to the Windows startup command to start Windows in one of its two operating modes. When you start Windows, you can also include the name of a program that you want to start immediately after Windows starts. For example, to start Windows and open Microsoft Word for Windows at the same time, enter the following startup command (assuming Word is in the C:\WINWORD directory):

```
WIN C:\WINWORD\WINWORD
```

Because the Program Manager is designed to make program startup easy, this command-line method is limited in its usefulness. It is normally easier to double-click the icon of a program you want to start.

However, if you use only one application in Windows, you can add this type of startup command to your computer's AUTOEXEC.BAT file to bypass the Program Manager altogether. It might be handy for teachers in a classroom environment, for example, to bypass Program Manager and get student users directly into the program you are teaching.

Perhaps you need to start a particular application and also specify one of the Windows run modes. To do this, type the mode parameter before the application name and path. The following command starts Windows in standard mode and immediately runs Word for Windows:

```
WIN /S C:WINWORD\WINWORD
```

If you have specified a program's directory in the PATH command of your AUTOEXEC.BAT file, you can omit the drive letter and path from the startup command. Assuming that the Word for Windows directory is on the path, you could type the following to start the program.

```
WIN /S WINWORD
```

TIP: You'll find an exercise for tailoring the AUTOEXEC.BAT file later in this chapter, in the section "Starting Windows Automatically."

Starting an Application from the StartUp Group

Another way to load an application when Windows starts is to include the startup icon of the program in the Program Manager StartUp group. The advantage of this method is that you can load more than one application at startup. These applications then rest on the desktop, ready for use.

In the following exercise, you copy the File Manager icon from the Main group to the StartUp group, using the Copy command on the Program Manager File menu. As you become more familiar with the programs and accessories you use most often, you can copy their program icons, as well, to the StartUp group. Note that this procedure *copies* the File Manager icon from the Main group, leaving the original File Manager icon in the group.

1. If Windows is not loaded, type **WIN** at the DOS command line and press Enter. Log on as described earlier.

2. At the Program Manager window, open the Main group window by double-clicking it with the mouse, or by pressing Alt-W and typing the number listed on the menu for the Main group.

3. Click the File Manager icon, or use the arrow keys to highlight it.

4. Press Alt-F C to select the Copy option from the File menu. The Copy Program Item dialog box appears, indicating the name and group of the currently selected icon (File Manager in the Main group).

5. To select the group you want to copy the icon to, click the down arrow in the To Group list box (or press ↓ on the keyboard) until StartUp appears, as shown here:

6. Click OK or press Enter to complete the operation.

The next time Windows starts, File Manager will automatically load into memory. You can add other icons to the StartUp group using the same procedure.

Starting Windows Automatically

You can include the Windows startup command in your computer's AUTOEXEC.BAT file if you want Windows to start automatically every time you turn your computer on. The AUTOEXEC.BAT file is located in the root directory of your C drive, and is explained fully in your DOS

manual. To edit the file, use the Windows Notepad editor to add the
WIN command as the last line in the file. Follow these steps:

1. Double-click the Accessories group, or press [Alt]-[W] to open the
   Window menu and then type the number of the Accessories group.
2. When the group opens, double-click the Notepad icon, or
   highlight it using the arrow keys and press [Enter].
3. When the Notepad window opens, press [Alt]-[F][O] to open a file.
4. The Open dialog box appears with the File Name field highlighted.
   Type **.BAT** and press [Enter].
5. When the file appears in the Notepad workspace, press [↓] until
   you reach the last line in the text. On a new line, type **WIN**.
   Follow this with any startup parameters, if desired—for example,
   to start in a specific mode or load an application.
6. Press [Alt]-[F][S] to save the file, and answer Yes to the inquiry about
   writing over the existing file.

Other Startup Considerations

Here are some things to keep in mind if some of your programs don't
run as expected, or if Windows runs short on memory. You'll find
additional information about memory, program startup, and
optimization of Windows in the appendixes.

Minimizing RAM Usage

You are less likely to have problems starting Windows or running its
applications if you reduce the amount of memory in use before you
start Windows. This is especially true if you need to run non-Windows
applications that require a set amount of memory.

The most likely cause of Windows startup problems is a conflict with
programs that are already loaded in memory before you start Windows.
Memory-resident programs (TSRs) such as pop-up utilities or special
drivers that are loaded at the DOS command prompt are such
programs. Check the contents of the AUTOEXEC.BAT and CONFIG.SYS
files in the root directory of your system, then use an editor or
Windows Notepad to remove any commands you think might be
causing conflicts. It's often best to load such programs after starting

Windows. In this way, Windows assigns memory to the utilities in a way that does not conflict with other applications. You can use the Notepad editor as described earlier in the section "Starting Windows Automatically." You'll find additional information on this subject in Appendix B.

TIP: To disable other programs' startup commands in the AUTOEXEC.BAT or CONFIG.SYS files, insert the REM statement before the startup command instead of removing the startup command completely. In this way, you can restore it later if necessary. Refer to your DOS manual for more details.

Running Non-Windows Applications

You can start non-Windows applications (one not designed to work with any version of Windows) after starting Windows. The benefit of running a non-Windows application under Windows is that you can easily switch from it to Windows and other applications, and even cut and paste information among windows.

When a non-Windows application runs in the Windows environment, it takes over the entire screen. However, if you are running in 386 enhanced mode instead of standard mode, you can run the non-Windows application in a separate, resizable window that does not have any of the typical Windows features such as drop-down menus and scroll bars. The application operates exactly the same as if it were started from the DOS command line. You can open such a window to access DOS, as shown in Figure 2-4, by double-clicking the MS-DOS Prompt icon in the Program Manager's Main group. At first, the whole screen is taken over by the DOS prompt. Simply press Alt-Enter to collapse it to a window similar to that in Figure 2-4.

TIP: When you're done with the MS-DOS Prompt window, type **EXIT** and press Enter to close the window.

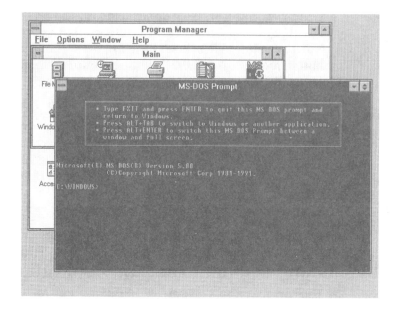

In 386 enhanced mode, you can access a DOS application, or the DOS command line prompt from a separate, resizable window.
Figure 2-4.

Since non-Windows applications were not written with Windows in mind, they are not capable of cooperatively sharing memory with other programs. Non-Windows applications tend to dominate memory. That's why you need to free up memory before starting Windows. For additional information on this subject, refer to Appendix B.

TIP: Upgrading to Microsoft's DOS 5.0 or Digital Research's DR DOS 6.0 will help you free up more memory to run non-Windows applications.

Logging Out and Exiting Windows

When you've finished using Windows, always remember to exit the program using the methods described in the following paragraphs. *Never* simply turn your system off while Windows is still running. Information in memory that has not been saved to disk would be lost.

2

Logging Out

As mentioned earlier, you should never leave your system unattended while you are still logged on. A person could gain unauthorized access to shared network resources through your logon account. You could simply exit Windows, but if you want to keep it running and still log out, follow the steps below.

1. Double-click the Control Panel icon in Program Manager's Main group. The Control Panel opens.
2. Double-click the Network icon in the Control Panel. The Network Settings dialog box appears.
3. Click the Logon button at the bottom of the dialog box. The following dialog box appears:

4. Click the Log Off button on the Logon Settings dialog box.

NOTE: It's usually easier to use a password-protected screen saver to prevent users from accessing your system while you are away. See Chapter 6 for more information.

Exit Methods

To exit Windows, first make sure the Program Manager is the active window by clicking its title bar, or press Alt -Tab until the title bar is highlighted. Then:

♦ To close Windows with the mouse, simply point to and double-click the Control menu button, as shown here:

♦ To close Windows with the keyboard, press [Alt]-[Spacebar] to open the Control menu, and then press [C] to select the Close option. Or,

♦ Use the speed key combination [Alt]-[F4]. (Notice that this and the other speed keys are listed on menus.)

When you quit Windows, this dialog box appears:

Normally, you would click OK or press [Enter] to execute your quit command, but, so you can continue with the exercises in the next chapter, click the Cancel button or press [Esc].

CHAPTER

3

USING THE WINDOWS INTERFACE

*This chapter presents a hands-on, step-by-step look at Windows. You see how to work with windows, menus, and control features, and how to get around in dialog boxes. If Windows is not already running on your computer, type **WIN** now to get it started.*

As mentioned in the previous chapter, Windows starts in the default mode for your computer, based on the processor type and memory. You'll need to log on to the Windows for Workgroups network before you see the Program Manager window.

Getting Around in Program Manager

You've already done some work in Program Manager—usually the first window you see when Windows starts. A picture of the default Program Manager screen is shown in Figure 3-1. The Program Manager window contains *groups* that are either open as windows or minimized as icons. In Figure 3-1, the Main group is open as a window, and its program startup icons are visible. The StartUp, Accessories, and Games groups are minimized as icons at the bottom of the Program Manager window.

The exercises in this section help you master the techniques for navigating in Program Manager with both the mouse and the keyboard.

Mouse Techniques

Windows is designed to take full advantage of a mouse, trackball, pen, or other pointing device. As you move the mouse device, a pointer moves on the Windows desktop. The pointer itself changes shape as you move it over different areas of the screen. It converts to an I beam (the *insertion point*) when you're editing text, and it changes to a cross-hair when pointing in the workspace of a painting or drawing program. A double-headed arrow appears when the pointer is over a window border, indicating the directions in which you can move the

The Program Manager as it appears the first time Windows is started, with the Main group open

Figure 3-1.

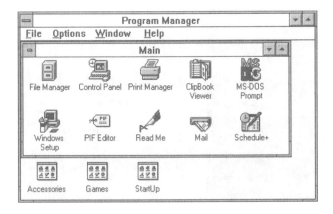

border. After choosing a command, you may see the hourglass, which tells you that Windows is working on a task and temporarily unavailable.

You can click just about anywhere on the desktop with the mouse. What happens when you click depends upon the location of the mouse pointer. In most cases, you click once to activate a Windows command or option, but in some locations you double-click the mouse, as you'll see in the following exercises.

3

Opening Menus and Choosing Options

The second line of a window, directly below the title bar, is the *menu bar.* It includes the names of one or more *drop-down menus.* To open a drop-down menu, click its name in the menu bar. The drop-down menu then opens to reveal a list of options that you can select by clicking the option with the mouse. You can also click a drop-down menu's title, then hold down the mouse button and drag through the menu options, releasing the mouse button when the option you want is highlighted.

In the following exercise, you click a *toggle option,* which is an option that can be set either on or off (enabled or disabled). When a toggle option is enabled, a check mark appears in front of the option. Clicking an unchecked option turns it on, and clicking it again turns it off.

1. Point to Options on the Program Manager menu bar, and click the mouse. The Options drop-down menu opens, and stays open when you release the mouse button.
2. On the Options menu, click the last option, Save Settings on Exit.

Clicking a menu option immediately executes it and closes the menu, so in this case, it's hard to see if the option was really turned on.

3. To confirm that the option was enabled, point again to Options on the menu bar, and click the mouse. The Options menu should now appear, with a check mark in front of the Save Settings on Exit option, as shown here:

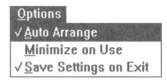

CAUTION: If the Save Settings option was already enabled, you may have just turned it off. Repeat Step 2 to turn it back on.

4. Now try a different technique to disable the Save Settings option. Point to Options on the menu bar; then click and hold down the mouse button. The menu opens.

5. While holding down the mouse button, drag through the menu until the Save Settings on Exit option is highlighted, and then release the mouse button. Releasing the button disables the option.

6. You can now open the menu again to make sure the check mark is gone. Click Options, note the absence of the check mark beside Save Settings, and click Options again to close the menu.

NOTE: For reasons discussed later in this chapter, we want the Save Settings on Exit option disabled.

Scanning Menus

You can use the mouse to scan menus when you're looking for a particular command or trying to remember which command is used to perform a task. Try this:

1. Click File on the Program Manager menu bar, and hold down the mouse button. The File menu opens.

2. While still pressing the button, drag the mouse to the right. As you drag, each drop-down menu opens.

3. Release the mouse when the menu you want is open.

NOTE: If you change your mind and don't want to select a menu option, press the (Esc) key.

3

Using the Minimize, Maximize, and Restore Buttons
Windows come in three sizes:

◆ A *minimized* window is an icon resting on the desktop.

◆ A *maximized* window takes up the entire screen. No other windows are visible until the maximized window is minimized or *restored*, which resizes it to its *customized* size (defined next).

◆ A *customized* window is one you have resized by clicking and dragging its borders and corners to make it any size you want.

Click the Maximize button, as shown here, to maximize a window:

When a window is maximized, its Maximize button converts to the Restore button, as shown here:

Click the Restore button to return the window to its regular or customized size. To minimize a window and reduce it to an icon, click the Minimize button positioned next to the Maximize or Restore button.

A typical procedure is to arrange windows in a *cascade* or *tile* formation on the desktop so you can see all your windows, as shown in Figure 3-2. You maximize the window you want to work with; then, when you're finished, you click the window's Restore button, and the cascade arrangement will reappear. You can choose Cascade or Tile from the Window menu to rearrange windows in this way.

A Word About Maximized Group Windows   Recall that group windows are subordinate to the Program Manager window. When you maximize a group window, its name displays in the title bar of the Main window, and its Restore button appears just below the buttons of the Program Manager window. For example, when the Main group window is maximized in the Program Manager, it looks like this:

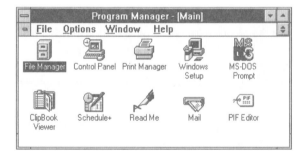

When a group window is maximized in Program Manager, you can't see other group windows or icons. Remember to click the Restore button to return the window to its original size.

Activating a Window

Athough you can have several windows open at once, only one of those windows can be active at a time. To activate a window, click the window once, or, if it is minimized to an icon, double-click its icon.

When a window is not visible because it is overlapped (hidden) by another window, you can move the overlapping window aside or

3

With the Task List, multiple windows can be placed in cascading (left) or tiled (right) arrangements **Figure 3-2.**

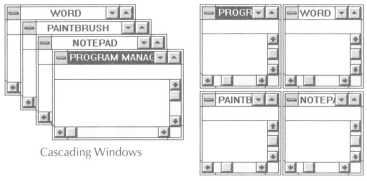

Cascading Windows

Tiled windows

minimize it to an icon. Another method is to pick the window you can't see from a list, as described here:

✦ To make a hidden group window active in Program Manager, choose its name from the Window drop-down menu.

✦ To make a hidden application window active on the desktop, double-click the desktop or press Ctrl-Esc to open the Task List, and pick the window from that list. (The Task List is covered in "Using the Task List," later in this chapter.)

TIP: You can also choose Cascade or Tile from the Window menu in Program Manager, to rearrange the windows so they are easier to see. (See Chapter 4.)

Starting Applications with the Mouse

With the mouse, starting an application is easy—just double-click the program icon of the application you want to start. In this exercise, you start the Clock application in the Accessories group. Before doing so, you need to open the Accessories group window. Follow these steps:

1. Locate the Accessories group icon at the bottom of the Program Manager window. If you can't find it, choose Accessories from the Window drop-down menu.

2. When the Accessories window opens, point to the Clock icon and double-click the mouse. The Clock appears on the desktop.

3. Minimize the clock by clicking its Minimize button. Note that the time is still discernible in the icon.

Keyboard Techniques and Speed Keys

Though Windows is designed primarily for use with a mouse, you can also use the keyboard. Keyboard techniques are presented here because some actions are actually easier to do with the keyboard, once you have learned the keystrokes. The most important key to remember when using keyboard techniques is the Alt key. You press it to access the menu bar and the Control menu of a window. You then press a letter key that represents the menu option.

As you work with Windows menus, you'll notice that speed keys are listed next to some menu options. If you don't feel like taking your hands off the keyboard to reach for the mouse, you can always press one of these speed keys to select the option.

Opening the Control Menu

The Control menu is important; it contains commands for resizing, moving, and closing the window. Every window—even the Program Manager—has a Control menu. To access the Control menu of a group window within Program Manager, press the Alt key followed by the − (hyphen) key. To access the Control menu of a program running in a separate window, press the Alt key followed by the Spacebar. Try the following exercise to see how this works:

1. In the Program Manager window, press Alt-Spacebar to open its Control menu. Notice that the options on the menu are commands that can also be invoked with the mouse, like Minimize and Maximize.

2. Press the Esc key to close the Control menu.

3. Press Alt–– (hyphen) to open the Control menu of the currently active group window. Notice the similarity in options, then press Esc to close the menu.

Remember that group windows in Program Manager are document windows with their own Control menus. Notice the subtle difference in the buttons shown here:

3

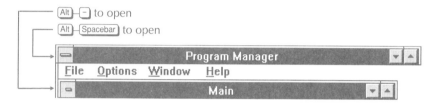

The symbol in the button for the Program Manager Control menu depicts a spacebar as a reminder; the Control menu button in the Main group window represents the hyphen key.

If you have a mouse, you may never need the Control menu, since most of its commands are easier to execute with the mouse. However, if you don't have the use of your mouse for any reason, you can always revert to keyboard methods for using Windows.

Accessing Menus and Menu Options

To access any menu bar, press the Alt key, then use the → or ← key to highlight the name of the menu you want to open. When the menu name is highlighted, press ↓ or Enter to open the menu. Once a menu is open, you can use the arrow keys to move through the list of options to highlight the one you want, and then press Enter to display its related dialog box or other screen. (There is an easier way to do all this, as you learn later, but for now, try this next exercise.)

1. Press Alt to access the menu bar. The first menu item, File, is highlighted. Press Enter to open the File menu, shown here:

2. Press the ⊡ key several times to open and examine each of the other menus.

   As you move from menu to menu, notice that the options in the menu bar, as well as the options on the drop-down menus, each have an underlined character in their name. Instead of using the arrow keys to highlight and select menus and menu options, you can press these underlined characters in combination with the Alt key to access the options much more quickly. For example, the combination of keystrokes to open the File menu and choose the Run option is Alt-F R. To some users, even the mouse method of accessing menus may seem awkward when compared to the Alt-key method.

Let's use this method to work with the Window menu. The names of windows or open documents are listed on the Window menu, preceded by a number. In the following steps you make the Accessories window active by choosing it from the Window menu:

3. Press Alt-W to open the Window drop-down menu.

4. Type the underlined number preceding the Accessories option on the menu. (The number representing each window may not always be the same. It changes, depending on the arrangement of windows and the addition of new windows.)

Selecting Other Group Windows

As you've just seen, you can open other group windows by choosing their names from the Window menu. Another method is to press Ctrl-Tab repeatedly until the title bar of the group you want is highlighted. If the group is minimized to an icon, press Ctrl-Tab until the icon name is highlighted, and then press the (Enter) key to open the group as a window.

In this next exercise, you practice opening, activating, and closing group windows.

1. Press (Ctrl)-(Tab) until the Games group icon is highlighted.
2. Press the (Enter) key. The Games group window opens and becomes the active window.
3. Press (Ctrl)-(Tab) until the Main group window is once again active.
4. Press (Ctrl)-(Tab) until the Games group is active.
5. Press (Alt)-(-) (hyphen) to open the Games group Control menu.
6. Press (C) to choose the Close option.

NOTE: In the Program Manager, the Close and Minimize commands both minimize a group window to an icon. However, when you are working with application windows, these two commands have different results. If you choose Close on the Control menu of an application window, the application is removed from memory, along with any documents in its workspace. You'll be asked to save the documents if you haven't already done so. So if you want to keep the application open and in memory for later use, choose Minimize from the Control menu instead.

Starting Applications with the Keyboard

The main objective of working in the Program Manager is to start applications. To do so, you must first open the group that holds the program icon for the application you want to start. Then highlight the application icon with the arrow keys and press (Enter).

The following exercise shows you how to open the Windows Control Panel:

1. Activate the Main group by choosing it from the Window menu, or by pressing (Ctrl)-(Tab) until the Main window's title bar or icon is highlighted.
2. Press (→) until Control Panel is highlighted.

3. Press the ⌨Enter⌨ key. The Control Panel window overlays the Program Manager window and becomes the active window.

Try pressing ⌨Ctrl⌨-⌨Tab⌨, and notice that it has no effect in the Control Panel. The ⌨Ctrl⌨-⌨Tab⌨ key combination is an exclusive feature of the Program Manager window. In the Control Panel, use the arrow keys to highlight the icons.

Returning to the Program Manager

When the Control Panel is open, it becomes part of the desktop, not the Program Manager window. Press ⌨Alt⌨-⌨Esc⌨ or ⌨Alt⌨-⌨Tab⌨ to switch between desktop windows. Try this:

1. From the Control Panel window, press ⌨Alt⌨-⌨Esc⌨ to switch to the Program Manager. The Control Panel window will probably be hidden behind the Program Manager window, depending on your window arrangment.

2. Press ⌨Alt⌨-⌨Esc⌨ again to return the Control Panel to the front.

Moving Among Applications on the Desktop

In the previous sections, you learned mouse and keyboard methods for accessing windows. In this section, you will learn techniques for working among open applications on the Windows desktop using the mouse and the keyboard.

When more than one window is open on the desktop, you can click the window you want to activate. You can also use keyboard methods to switch among windows, or open the Windows Task List to choose a window from a list. Since you can't always point to a window to make it active (windows may be overlapped by other windows, or the mouse may be inactive, as when you're working in some non-Windows applications), take a look at all of these other techniques:

✦ Use ⌨Alt⌨-⌨Tab⌨ to *preview* windows. Previewing is a quick way to scan through open applications. The title of each application is displayed. Minimized icons open when you release the mouse while the icon is highlighted.

♦ Use [Alt]–[Esc] to *switch* among application windows. The switching method lets you see the entire contents of each window as you switch. Minimized icons are only highlighted; you must press [Enter] to open an icon. Though this method is useful, in most cases you'll want to use the faster preview method.

♦ The *Task List* is opened from the keyboard by pressing [Ctrl]–[Esc], or by double-clicking the desktop. The Task List (fully described in "Using the Task List," later in this chapter) provides the same options for the desktop that the Window menu provides for Program Manager. You can use Task List to choose an application, or to arrange windows and icons on the desktop.

The keyboard methods available for moving among applications are summarized here:

Keystroke	Function
[Alt]–[Tab]	Previews windows and icons
[Alt]–[Esc]	Switches between full application windows and icons
[Ctrl]–[Esc]	Opens the Task List

TIP: You can reverse the window-switching order by holding down the [Shift] key while pressing [Alt]–[Esc] or [Alt]–[Tab].

Switching Among Applications

The following exercise demonstrates how to switch among applications using the mouse and keyboard.

1. In a previous exercise, you made the Clock available on the desktop as an icon. Open it as a window now by pressing [Alt]–[Tab] until the clock name appears and then release the keys.

2. Press [Alt]–[Tab] several times to switch among the windows that are currently open on the desktop. Try going in the other direction by pressing [Shift]–[Alt]–[Tab].

In the next steps, you start the DOS Prompt, which temporarily returns you to DOS so you can execute DOS commands. You then switch back to Windows using the Alt–Esc switching method.

3. Press Alt–Tab until Program Manager is listed; then release the keys.
4. Press Ctrl–Tab until the Main group is listed, and press Enter if it is an icon.
5. Double-click the DOS Prompt icon, or select it with the arrow keys and press Enter.
6. When the DOS prompt appears, press Alt–Esc to switch back to Windows.

When Windows reappears, the DOS Prompt icon rests on the desktop since you only switched away from it, rather than closing it. In this way, you can keep a program or task running in DOS while you switch back to Windows.

Using the Task List

The Task List is an integral part of Windows that is always available. You can use it to switch among applications and to reorganize the desktop. The Task List appears when you double-click the desktop or press Ctrl–Esc, and is useful when you can't see all the windows on your desktop:

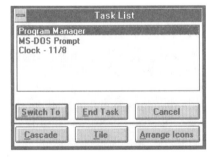

You can also select the Switch To option on the Control menu of any window to open the Task List.

The top portion of the Task List displays the names of currently running applications. To switch to an application, double-click its name with the mouse, or highlight the application name using the arrow keys and press `Enter`.

The buttons at the bottom of the Task List window are used to close a window (task) or rearrange the desktop, as described in the following table. Click the button, or press `Alt` along with the underlined letter on the button.

3

Task List Button	Function
Switch To	Switch to and activate the selected application
End Task	Close the selected application
Cancel	Exit the Task List
Cascade	Rearrange windows in a cascade layout
Tile	Rearrange windows in a tiled layout
Arrange Icons	Arrange the icons on the desktop

Practice using the Task List now by following these steps:

1. Double-click the desktop or press `Ctrl`-`Esc` to open the Task List.
2. Double-click Clock in the list box, or press `↓` to highlight Clock and then press `Enter`. Clock becomes the active window.
3. Use Task List to close an application. Repeat Step 1, and choose DOS Prompt from the list box.
4. Click the End Task button or press `Alt`-`E`. The following dialog box appears:

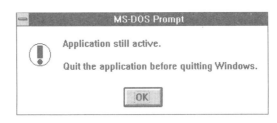

NOTE: This demonstrates that you can't end a DOS or non-Windows application from Windows without warning. Click the OK button in this case, but keep in mind that you'll normally need to close non-Windows applications using their regular exit routines.

5. Open Task List again by repeating Step 1. Then click the Cascade button to see how Windows rearranges the open windows in a cascade layout.

 ## Resizing and Moving Windows and Icons

You resize and move open windows for several reasons. Perhaps you want to see two windows side by side so you can view the contents of one window while working in another. In Program Manager, it's useful to resize group windows and arrange them to improve access to startup icons. In this section, you learn how to minimize, maximize, resize, and move windows on the desktop. Then in Chapter 4, you see how to reorganize the windows in the Program Manager using the techniques you learn here.

Resizing Windows with the Mouse

Every window has active borders and title bars. You can click and drag the borders with the mouse to resize the window.

NOTE: You may want to move a window before or after resizing it, by clicking and dragging its title bar. See "Moving a Window," later in this chapter.

The shape of the mouse pointer changes when it is pointed at a window's border or corner. The pointer becomes a double-headed arrow when it is over a window border, and a diagonal double-headed arrow when it is over a corner. The arrows indicate the directions in which you can move the borders or corners. When the mouse pointer converts to one of these symbols, you can click and drag the border or corner, and then release the mouse to resize the window.

In the following exercise, you resize the right border and then the lower-right corner of the Program Manager window. Keep in mind, however, that you can resize any border or corner using the methods described here.

3

1. Make the Program Manager window active by clicking it with the mouse, or by pressing [Alt]–[Tab] until its title bar is highlighted.

2. Point the mouse at the right border so you see the double-headed arrow pointer.

3. Click and drag the border to the right. As you drag, a shadow box appears to indicate the new size for the window, as shown next. Drag the border out about an inch, and then release the mouse to resize the window.

Now resize the window in two directions, by dragging its lower-right corner outward.

4. Point the mouse at the lower-right corner until you see the diagonal double-headed arrow pointer.

5. Click and drag down and to the right. As you drag, the shadow borders appear, as shown in the following illustration.

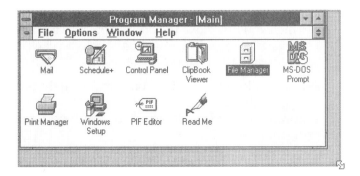

6. Release the mouse to resize the window.

TIP: You can click any border or corner to resize a window, but it's
most common to drag the lower-right corner because the right and
bottom portions of a window's contents are usually hidden.

Using Scroll Bars

Scroll bars appear at the right and bottom of a window when the entire
contents of the window's workspace can't be seen—usually after the
window has been resized. Scroll bars are only accessible with a mouse.
In this exercise, you reduce the Program Manager window until scroll
bars appear, and then scroll the window vertically and horizontally.

1. Resize the Program Manager window by clicking and dragging its
   lower-right corner inward. Do this until the horizontal and vertical
   scroll bars appear, as shown in Figure 3-3. You may need to click
   and drag inward several times, releasing the mouse each time.

2. Click the down-arrow scroll button on the vertical scroll bar
   several times. As you do this, the window contents scroll down,
   and the slider button moves down in the slider bar. Click until the
   slider button is at the bottom of the bar.

3. Now click the vertical slider button and drag it back up. When you
   get about halfway up the bar, release the mouse button. Notice
   how the contents of the window change.

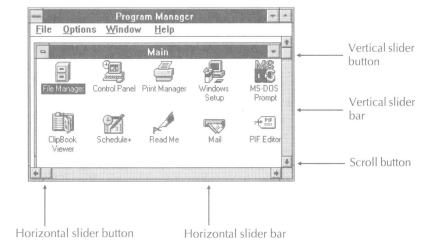

Vertical slider button

Vertical slider bar

Scroll button

3

Horizontal slider button   Horizontal slider bar

Resizing a window makes the horizontal and vertical scroll bars appear
Figure 3-3.

4. Click and drag up again, and watch how the contents of the window change depending upon where you release the slider button. Drag the slider button all the way to the top of the bar and release the mouse.

5. Position the mouse inside the vertical slider bar, and then click and release the mouse button.

NOTE: Clicking inside the slider bar moves the contents of the window one page at a time. A page is equal to the vertical height or horizontal width of the window itself.

If you want, try experimenting with the horizontal scroll bar, clicking the horizontal scroll buttons, slider button, and slider bar to see how the window contents move inside the window.

Removing Scroll Bars

When you want to see as much of a window as possible, expand it until its scroll bars disappear. In the previous exercise, you resized the

Program Manager until scroll bars appeared. Now reverse these steps to remove the scroll bars:

1. Drag the Program Manager vertical slider button all the way to the bottom, and the horizontal slider button all the way to the right. (Note that this is not a necessary step but will demonstrate an anomaly of the scroll bars that you will probably encounter.)

2. Click and drag the lower-right corner of the Program Manager window outward (right and down) several inches.

   Notice that the scroll bars don't go away immediately, because you scrolled the window contents to the bottom and to the right. You'll often see this effect when resizing a window to remove its scroll bars. Even though you've made the window large enough to make all its icons visible, they still need to be scrolled into view. Then the scroll bars will disappear.

3. To remove the scroll bars, drag the slider buttons back to the top and far left.

4. If the scroll bars still don't disappear, drag the lower-right corner out further.

5. Now drag the borders back in as far as possible to remove white space, but not so far that the scroll bars reappear.

Tightening the window borders in this way resizes the window to its optimum size. The entire window contents can be seen at once, yet the window doesn't take up too much space. Some windows, however, contain so much material that they dominate the desktop if opened in this way. You'll need to resize these windows, arrange them on the desktop in the best way possible, and use scroll bars to access any items that are out of view.

Moving a Window

Once you resize a window, you can reposition it next to other windows, or just move it out of the way. In this example, you drag the Program Manager window to the upper-left corner of the desktop; then you open the Clock window, resize it, and drag it out of the way to the lower-left corner of the desktop. In the last exercise, you resized the Program Manager window to its optimum size. It should now fit in the upper-right corner, leaving plenty of space on the desktop for other windows.

1. Point to the title bar of the Program Manager; then click and drag until the window is in the upper-left corner.

2. Double-click the Clock icon, which should still be resting on the desktop. (If it's not, open the Accessories group in the Program Manager and double-click the Clock icon.)

3. Resize the Clock window so it is approximately two inches square.

4. Point to the title bar of the Clock; then click and drag the window to the lower-right corner of the desktop.

   Try choosing Analog or Digital from the Clock Settings menu to change the way time is displayed.

Closing a Window

There are several different ways to close a window. Keep in mind that closing a window removes the program and its documents from memory. If you want to keep the window open but remove it from the desktop temporarily, minimize the window instead of closing it.

To close a window, double-click the Control button in the upper-left corner of the window. Alternatively, you can press (Alt)–(F4), or you can choose Close from the window's Control menu.

Closing the Program Manager window is the same as exiting Windows. To see how this works, follow these steps:

1. Double-click the Control button on the Program Manager window, and you'll see the following dialog box:

2. If you really wanted to close the Program Manager, you would click the OK button. For now, click the Cancel button to stay in Windows.

When you close applications, you'll see a warning message if that workspace contains an unsaved document. This warning message gives you a chance to save your work before the application closes.

Dialog Boxes

The *dialog boxes* that appear when you invoke Windows commands display information and additional parameters for commands or options. Dialog boxes usually appear after you select a menu option that is followed by an ellipsis (...), or as part of a command routine. In this section, you work with the Run command in the Program Manager, which presents the two dialog boxes shown in Figure 3-4. The Run dialog box at the top of the figure appears when you select Run on the Program Manager File menu. The Browse dialog box appears when you click the Browse button in the Run dialog box.

Many Windows commands use dialog boxes. As a result, you'll rarely need to look up a command's usage in a manual. The dialog boxes present you with all possible options in an easy-to-use format. Keep in mind that you do not need to change all options in dialog boxes. In most cases, the application supplies default settings that you can use to execute the command. Often it is only necessary to change one or two settings.

Dialog boxes consist of *fields*, and some fields are grouped together in boxes. You can turn field options on or off by clicking buttons or marking check boxes. You can also select options from scrollable list boxes or drop-down lists. When all options are set, click the OK button or press Enter to accept the changes. To cancel the dialog box, press Esc.

Although dialog box options and buttons are easily accessed with the mouse, you can also use the following keyboard techniques:

✦ Press Tab to jump from one field to the next. A dotted rectangle or highlight will appear in the currently selected area.

✦ Press Shift-Tab to move backwards through the fields.

✦ If you press Tab at the last field, you are returned to the first field.

✦ If a field has an underlined letter, you can press Alt and then press that letter to jump to that field.

✦ Press Spacebar to mark and unmark check boxes.

Dialog Box Fields and Buttons

3

Though every dialog box has a different set of options, the methods used to enter and edit options and settings are the same in any dialog box. Each type of field and button found in a dialog box is described in the following paragraphs.

Command Buttons

Command buttons let you execute or cancel the dialog box, or open another dialog box. For example, some windows contain a Help button that opens a window with help information about the current command. Notice that the Browse button in Figure 3-4 has an ellipsis (...), which means it will present another dialog box if selected.

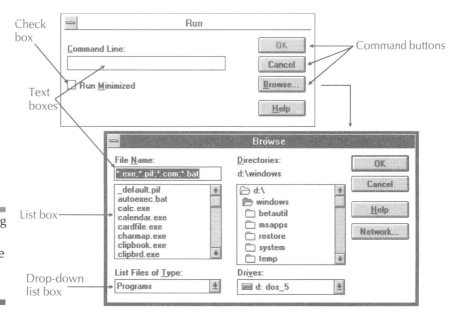

The Run dialog box and its related Browse dialog box

Figure 3-4.

Use the mouse to click the command buttons. With the keyboard, press
⟨Tab⟩ to move among them. As is shown in the following illustration, the
OK button on the Run box is highlighted:

NOTE: Pressing ⟨Enter⟩ is the same as clicking the OK button, so be
careful not to press ⟨Enter⟩ until you've set all necessary options and
are ready to execute the command.

Text Boxes

Text boxes are used to enter information for a command. For instance, in
the foregoing Run dialog box, you must type the filename of the program
you want to run in the Command Line text box. Sometimes text boxes
contain default information. Some text boxes will accept only numbers.

List Boxes

A list box holds the names of one or more items from which you can
select. You can scroll through the list by pressing the arrow keys on the
keyboard or by clicking arrow buttons in the list box's scroll bar. You
can also use the ⟨Pg Up⟩ and ⟨Pg Dn⟩ keys, or type the first letter of the item
you are looking for to quickly scroll through the list. As shown in the
Browse dialog box in Figure 3-5, selecting a file from the File Name list
box causes its name to appear in the File Name text box.

Drop-Down List Boxes

Drop-down list boxes initially display only one item. In Figure 3-5, the List Files of Type box and the Drives box are drop-down list boxes. Clicking the down-arrow button with the mouse opens the drop-down list, as shown in Figure 3-6. You can also press `Tab` to move to a drop-down list box, and then press the `↓` key on the keyboard to scan through the list. Press the `Tab` key when the item you want is highlighted.

Option Buttons

Option buttons (also called radio buttons) are toggles that let you turn an option on or off by clicking the button. When option buttons are grouped together in a box, only one button may be enabled. This illustration was captured from a Setup dialog box for a laser printer:

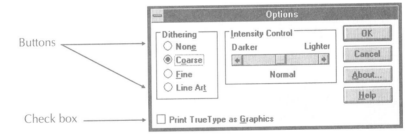

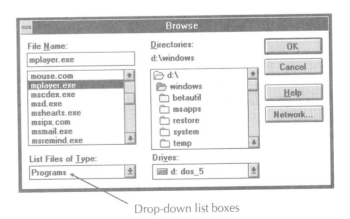

The File Name text box with a name selected from the list box

Figure 3-5.

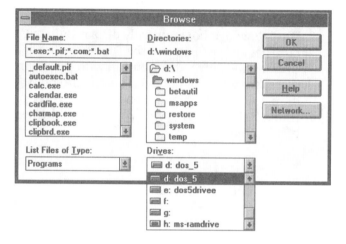

The Drives
drop-down list,
opened by
clicking the
down-arrow
button in the
list box
Figure 3-6.

Here only one of the four buttons in the box can be enabled, by
clicking the button with the mouse. If one button is already enabled
and you click another button in the box, the previously enabled button
is turned off. With the keyboard, you can turn on an option button by
pressing the (Alt) key and pressing the underlined letter of the button
you want to select. Repeat this action and you turn the button off.

Check Boxes

Check boxes work like option buttons; you mark them (enable them) to
turn the option on, and remove the mark (disable them) to turn the
option off. Unlike option buttons, however, you can mark as many
check boxes as are necessary to set the options and settings for a
command. In the following example, the box is from Microsoft Word
for Windows, and is used to set various preferences for a window and
the text displayed in it:

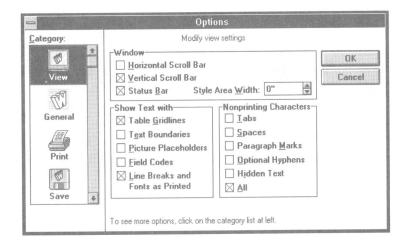

Warning and Message Boxes

Warning boxes are displayed when you attempt to execute a command improperly, or when Windows needs more information related to the command. The following box appears to confirm file deletions:

When a warning or message box appears, click (or select from the keyboard) one of its buttons, depending on the task at hand. If you choose the Cancel button, the entire command is cancelled.

Using Dialog Boxes

Now you'll put together all the information you've learned in this section about dialog boxes. In the following exercise, you open the Run dialog box and then start the File Manager.

1. Make sure the Program Manager window is active by clicking it with the mouse. Or press [Ctrl]-[Esc] and choose it from the Task List.

2. Choose Run on the File menu by clicking it with the mouse or pressing [Alt]-[F] [R]. The Run dialog box appears (see Figure 3-4).

Now you need to insert the name of the File Manager program in the Command Line text box. If you knew the name, you could type it in the box and click the OK button or press [Enter]. However, in the following steps, you use the Browse option to locate the filename and place it in the Command Line box.

NOTE: Keep in mind that this is an exercise in using dialog box features and contains more steps than you would typically need to access a file. Also, File Manager is normally accessed by double-clicking its icon. The Run command demonstrates an alternative method of starting it, or any application that doesn't have a startup icon.

3. Click the Browse button in the Run dialog box (or press [Alt]-[B]) to display the Browse dialog box (Figure 3-4).

4. Note the different fields of the dialog box. The Directories field on the right lists the disk drive and directory where your Windows files are located, and the scrollable list box contains the filenames.

5. Click the down-arrow scroll button in the Drives drop-down list box to see a list of alternative disk drives. (You can also press [Alt]-[V] to access the Drives field, and then press the [↓] key on the keyboard to open this drop-down list box.) Choose C or the drive where your Windows files are located.

6. Now press the [Tab] key several times until the File Name list box is highlighted. A dotted rectangle surrounds the first file in the list.

7. Press the [↓] key on the keyboard several times to scroll through the list of files.

8. Press W to jump to the files that start with *W*, and then press ↓ until WINFILE.EXE is highlighted. This filename now appears in the File Name text box.

9. Click the OK button or press Enter to select the WINFILE.EXE file. The complete path and filename now appears in the Command Line field of the Run dialog box.

10. Click in the Run Minimized check box (or press Alt-M). This will minimize File Manager when it starts. The Run Minimized option is useful when you want to load an application for later use.

3

11. Click the OK button on the Run dialog box, or press Enter, to start File Manager.

File Manager now appears as an icon at the bottom of the desktop. To open the File Manager as a window, double-click its icon; or hold down Alt-Tab until its name appears, and then release the keys.

Exiting Windows

That's it for this chapter. If you want to exit Windows and return to DOS, make the Program Manager window active and double-click its Control menu button, or press Alt-Spacebar and select Close from the Control menu.

CHAPTER

4

NAVIGATING THE WINDOWS ENVIRONMENT

In this chapter, you learn about Windows by exploring the Program Manager, the File Manager, and several of the Windows applications and utilities. In the Program Manager section, you see how to rearrange group windows and set options. You set the date and time within the Windows environment and change the color scheme of a window. In the File Manager section, you study the structure of the File Manager window and practice working with some files on your disks and hard drive.

Keep in mind that this chapter builds on the techniques you learned in Chapter 3, and introduces you to features you'll learn more about later.

Exploring the Program Manager

You've already seen how the Program Manager provides methods for organizing program icons into groups of applications based on the type of work you do. But the main purpose of the Program Manager is to "launch" applications, so this section shows you some interesting techniques for doing just that.

Program Manager Groups

When the Program Manager is initially installed, it contains at least four groups: Main, Accessories, StartUp, and Games. Two additional groups, called *Windows Applications* and *Non-Windows Applications*, may have been created to hold icons for applications already installed on your system.

Each group, except StartUp, contains application icons. If you have programs you want to start every time Windows starts you copy the icons for those programs into the StartUp group. This was covered in Chapter 2 when you copied the File Manager icon into the StartUp group. The File Manager, Notepad, and Calculator are useful startup utilities you can include in the group. (In addition, you can specify that the programs will run *minimized*, which means they appear as icons on the desktop after Windows finishes loading them.)

The Accessories group contains helpful programs you'll want to run daily. In the next section, you see how to rearrange the desktop so that the Accessories group is open and ready when Windows first starts.

Reorganizing the Program Manager

The initial arrangement of groups and icons in the Program Manager, described in the foregoing paragraphs, is useful when you're learning Windows, but as you become more familiar with the program, you may want to rearrange Program Manager to suit your own projects and working style.

Consider, for example, the contents of the Main group. Though its icons represent useful programs, you may find you don't really need to access these programs every day. The most practical Program Manager arrangement displays a group window of icons to start programs that you use most often, such as those in the Accessories group.

Figures 4-1, 4-2, and 4-3 show three possible arrangements of the groups within Program Manager. In Figure 4-1, the Main and Accessories groups are both open and arranged side by side. Not all icons are visible; rather, the most frequently used icons have been placed so you can select them without scrolling the window.

The Program Manager in Figure 4-2 places less emphasis on the Main group, which is minimized. Here the Accessories group is open as a window so its applications are easier to select. In this arrangement, the Main group is rarely needed because its most-used application, File Manager, has been added to the StartUp group and automatically loads when Windows starts.

4

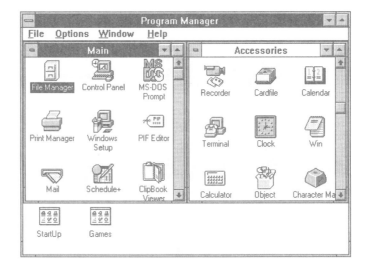

One method of arranging Program Manager is to place the Main and Accessories groups side by side
Figure 4-1.

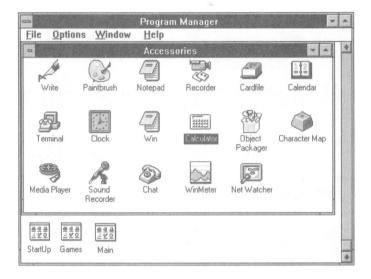

This Program
Manager
arrangement
places more
emphasis on
Accessories
than the utilities
in the Main
group
Figure 4-2.

Figure 4-3 depicts a custom arrangement in which part of the Main
group and most of the Accessories group are visible. The difference
between Figure 4-1 and Figure 4-3 may seem trivial, but the methods
used to arrange each configuration are quite different, as you'll see.

The following exercises show you how to create the arrangement in
Figure 4-1 using the Tile command, and then how to create the custom

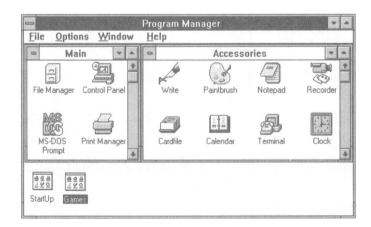

In a custom
window
arrangement,
you can
manually resize
the windows
Figure 4-3.

arrangement in Figure 4-3 by manually resizing windows. Throughout this book you'll be using programs in the Main group and Accessories group, so it's a good idea to keep the Main group window open for now. Later, you can create new groups and rearrange windows to accommodate the way you work.

Set Program Manager Options

Before continuing with the exercises, make the following changes using the Program Manager Options menu. First open the Options menu to view what options are already enabled. Recall that a check mark appears in front of items that are enabled. Do the following now:

4

1. Disable the Save Settings on Exit option.
2. Enable the Auto Arrange option.

The first step ensures that any changes you make to the size of windows and their arrangement are not saved for subsequent Windows sessions. The second step causes icons within Program Manager groups to automatically rearrange to fit within a resized group window.

Although the Save Settings on Exit option automatically saves changes you make to the Program Manager when you exit Windows, enabling it is not recommended. The reason is simple. During the course of a Windows session, you'll probably open groups and maybe even move windows out of the way to see other windows. If you exit without reorganizing and closing windows, you'll see that arrangement the next time you start Windows, which could be disorienting.

TIP: A better method for saving arrangements is to hold the Shift key and choose Exit Windows from the Program Manager File menu. You press this keystroke only when you're sure you want to save an arrangement. Doing so doesn't actually exit you from Windows, but it does save arrangements. Note that this method also works in the File Manager.

Move and Resize the Program Manager

Now you can begin creating the Program Manager arrangement in Figure 4-1. In this setup, the Program Manager window is moved to the upper-left corner of the desktop and resized so that it takes up about three-quarters of the space. This leaves room so you can see other application windows on the desktop, and yet provides enough room in the Program Manager for rearranging group windows.

1. Point to the title bar of the Program Manager; then click and drag the window to the upper-left corner of the desktop.

2. Point to the lower-right corner of the Program Manager window; then click and drag until the window covers about three-quarters of the desktop.

Tile the Group Windows

Now you can arrange the group windows within the Program Manager, using the Tile command from the Window menu. Follow these steps:

1. Make sure the Main group is open as a window. If it isn't, double-click its group icon to open it.

2. Open the Accessories group by double-clicking its group icon.

3. Choose Tile from the Window menu.

The two open group windows are now side by side, as in Figure 4-1.

The size of tiled windows and the number of visible icons in them depends on the original size of the Program Manager window. For example, when the Program Manager window is maximized and you select Tile, the group windows are tiled to fill all the available space. Try this on your newly arranged desktop by following these steps:

1. Click the Program Manager Maximize button to make the window fill the entire desktop.

2. Choose Tile from the Window menu. The two open windows are resized and fill the Program Manager window.

3. Now click the Restore button on the Program Manager. When the window is restored to its previous size, the tiling arrangement no longer fits the window. This demonstrates that you may need to

periodically retile your window arrangements if Program Manager is resized.

4. Choose Tile again, and resize the group windows to fit within the restored Program Manager.

Now that you understand how tiling works, you can adjust and retile the Program Manager window until it is arranged the way you like. You can enlarge the Program Manager window, and then retile to see more icons, or reduce the Program Manager window and retile so the window takes up less space on the desktop. Repeat the steps in the previous exercise until the Program Manager window fits optimally on your desktop.

4

Other Arrangements: Cascade and Custom

The Tile option resizes windows to fit within the boundaries of the Program Manager, making each the same size. You may, however, prefer an arrangement in which all icons within a group are visible. You can do this with the Cascade option on the Window menu, as follows:

1. Choose Cascade from the Window menu. The group windows are resized so you can see more icons, but only icons in one window are visible at the top of the arrangement.

2. Click the title bar of the back window to move it to the front.

3. If you can't see all icons in either of the windows you have observed, resize the Program Manager, and select Cascade again. Repeat this until the group windows are sized so that you can see all of the icons.

You can create the custom arrangement shown in Figure 4-3 by following these steps:

1. Enlarge the Program Manager window so you have some room in which to work. (Later, you can reduce the Program Manager window to surround the groups.)

2. Click the title bar of the Main group and drag it to the upper-left corner of the Program Manager window.

3. Click and drag the lower-right border of the Main window until it is approximately the size shown in Figure 4-3. You can make it

larger or smaller, depending on the number of icons you want displayed.

4. Release the mouse button to resize the window. The icons automatically rearrange to fit its new size (assuming the Auto Arrange option is enabled).

5. Repeat Steps 2 and 3 until the Main window is sized the way you want it to be.

6. Drag the Accessories window next to the Main group, and then resize its window. If there isn't room to make the Accessories window large enough to suit you, enlarge the Program Manager window.

7. Once the group windows are resized, adjust the Program Manager window border to remove excess white space.

NOTE: After resizing windows into a custom arrangement, excess space may exist between the icons and the bottom of the group windows. It's easy to move the group icons to reduce this effect; simply click the icons and drag them up. Then you can click and drag Program Manager's bottom border up to eliminate the white space.

Rearrange the Program Icons

If you've created your own custom Program Manager arrangement like that in Figure 4-3, you may want to refine it by arranging the icons so that most are visible without having to scroll the window. In this next exercise, you rearrange icons in the Main group.

1. Click the Maximize button on the Main window so that you can see all its icons.

The icons in the maximized window arrange themselves from left to right in one or more rows, depending on the size of the window. The left to right order is maintained in multiple rows if you shrink the window. The objective of this exercise is to reorder the icons so that the most important icons are still visible at the top of the window even when it is reduced in size.

4

2. To rearrange the Main group icons, click and drag them over one another. When you release the mouse button after moving an icon, notice how other icons move down through the list or trade places with the one you've moved. Work at rearranging the icons until they appear as shown here:

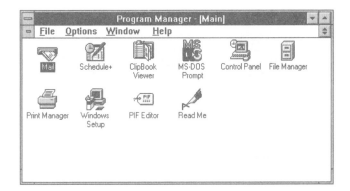

3. Now click the Restore button on the Main window. Notice that the icon order is maintained in the reduced window.

Saving Program Manager Arrangements

Once you've reorganized the Program Manager the way you like, you can save the changes so they appear the next time you start Windows. To save changes, follow these steps:

1. Press and hold the (Shift) key.
2. Choose Exit Windows from the Program Manager File menu.

This method of saving changes is superior to enabling the Save Changes on Exit option (on the Options menu) because it lets you save changes when you are sure you want them saved. As mentioned previously, enabling Save Changes on Exit would save any temporary rearrangements you made to Windows for the next session. This is not always what you'll want if you've been moving and resizing windows for the current session only.

Organizing the Desktop

As you work with Windows from day to day, you'll probably find that you usually want to open more than one application at a time. Typically, one application is left open while you work in another. You can then use the waiting application later without having to reload it. Having two applications open also allows you to cut and paste information between them, a powerful feature that is described in "Cut and Paste Operations" later in this chapter. But first let's examine some of the ways of organizing and navigating applications on the Windows desktop.

For this exercise, make sure your Program Manager window is arranged so that it looks similar to Figure 4-3. Activate the Program Manager, open the Accessories group window, and then follow these steps to open several applications:

1. Double-click the Notepad icon, so that the Notepad window appears on the desktop. (If you can't see the icon, scroll the window.)

2. Click the Program Manager window to make it active. If you can't see the window to click it, press [Alt]-[Tab] repeatedly until its menu bar is highlighted; then release the keys.

3. Double-click the Write icon in the Accessories group. The Write window is added to the desktop. By now, the desktop is getting cluttered, but you can still open other applications.

4. Double-click any blank part of the desktop to make the Task List appear, as illustrated next. (If you can't see the desktop, press [Ctrl]-[Esc] to bring up the Task List. You'll learn more about the Task List in a later section.)

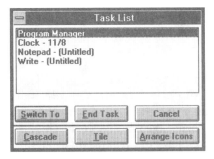

On the Task List you'll see all the currently open applications.

5. Open one more application: double-click the Paintbrush icon.

Window Switching Methods

A Windows session can have as many open applications as will fit in memory. There are three methods for switching among applications. You can try all three methods by following these steps:

1. Press [Alt]-[Esc] several times to switch among the open windows. This switching method displays the entire contents of each window, but it is slower than the scrolling method demonstrated in Step 3.
2. Press [Shift]-[Alt]-[Esc] several times to reverse the order of the switching.
3. Press [Alt]-[Tab] several times to scroll through a list of names of open windows.
4. Press [Shift]-[Alt]-[Tab] several times to reverse the scroll order.
5. Double-click the desktop (or press [Ctrl]-[Esc]) to open the Task List. In the List, double-click any application to activate it.

As you can see, there are several ways to activate an application window. You decide which is best based on the number of applications you have open. With many applications open, it's best to use the Task List, because you can double-click the application you want instead of cycling through all the open windows.

Organizing the Desktop with the Task List

The Task List isn't just for opening applications—it is also a helpful tool for reorganizing a cluttered desktop. You've already seen how to select an application from the Task List. Now here are some exercises using the Task List to make task switching easier.

1. Double-click a blank area of the desktop (or press Ctrl-Esc) to display the Task List.

2. Click the Tile button to resize and tile all open windows on the desktop.

TIP: When windows are tiled, you can see some of the contents of each window. This is useful if the same application is open in more than one window and you need to differentiate between the contents of each window. Simply click the Maximize button of the window you want to work in, and then restore the window when you're finished. Try this now.

3. Click the Maximize button on the Notepad window. Notepad opens to a full-screen display. Then click the Notepad Restore button to return it to the tile arrangement.

The tiled arrangement depends on the number of open windows. When four windows are open, for example, they are arranged in a checkerboard pattern on the desktop, as you see now. Try this next exercise to see another arrangement:

1. Click the Minimize button in the Program Manager window to reduce it to an icon on the desktop.

2. Open the Task List (double-click the desktop or press Ctrl-Esc).

3. Click the Tile option. The three open windows are arranged side by side.

4. To rearrange the windows in a cascade, reopen the Task List and click the Cascade button.

Now each window is larger and displays more of its contents horizontally than with the tile method. Click the Maximize button of any window you want to work in, and restore the window when you're finished.

4

Arranging Desktop Icons

When applications are not in use, there's no need to keep their windows open. It's better to minimize them to icons and thereby reduce desktop clutter; this also makes the applications easier to open if another application is running in a large window. Follow these steps to practice minimizing applications and arranging their icons.

1. Click the Minimize button of each open window.
2. Click and drag the icons to new positions anywhere on the desktop.
3. Double-click the desktop to open the Task List (or press Ctrl-Esc).
4. Click the Arrange Icons button to align the icons neatly at the bottom of the Desktop.

 T**IP:** The Arrange Icons button is useful when icons are moved out of place or you've closed some application icons and you want to adjust the position of those remaining on the desktop.

 Cut and Paste Operations

The *cut-and-paste* feature in Windows lets you copy or move text and graphics images from one place to another in a document, or from one application window to another. Commands for cutting and pasting are located on the Edit menu of nearly every Windows application.

Cutting and pasting is easy—first highlight the text or image you want to move. Then choose either Cut or Copy. A Cut removes the selected text or graphic from its current location and places it in the Clipboard; a Copy leaves the original text or graphic intact and places a copy of it in the Clipboard. With the text or graphic waiting in the Clipboard, click where you want it inserted, and select the Paste command to complete the operation.

 NOTE: Recall that the ClipBook contains the Clipboard viewer. The ClipBook doesn't need to be open for you to take advantage of the cut-and-paste feature. However, you can open ClipBook and double-click its Clipboard icon to see the text or graphics you cut or copied, and you can save the information for later use.

The following exercises demonstrate how the Clipboard works:

1. In an exercise in the foregoing section, you opened Notepad, Write, and Paintbrush in the Program Manager Accessories window. Make sure these applications are still open (double-click their icons if necessary) before you begin this exercise.

2. Activate the Notepad window. Then type the following text, and press the [Enter] key at the end of the line.

This is an example of copying and pasting text.

3. Notice that the arrow pointer has changed to an I-beam pointer. Place the I-beam pointer in front of the *T* in the word *This*, and click and drag to the end of the line. This highlights the line.

4. Choose Copy from the Edit menu, or press [Ctrl]-[C]. This puts the highlighted line in the Clipboard.

Remember, you don't need to have the Clipboard open to perform cut-and-paste operations, but you can view its contents at any time. In the section "Saving the Clipboard Contents," later in this chapter, you learn how to open the Clipboard and save its contents.

5. Press the [↓] key to remove the highlight from the text you selected in Step 3 and move the insertion point to the next line.

6. Click the Edit menu again. (Notice that Copy and Cut on the Edit menu are now unavailable because nothing is selected or highlighted in the Notepad workspace.) Select the Paste command from the Edit menu.

The text you copied to the Clipboard is pasted into the line where you have positioned the insertion point, just below the previous text.

Pasting to Another Application

Let's try pasting the same line into a different window (the text is still in the Clipboard). Follow these steps to paste it in the workspace of the Write application:

1. Click the Write window, or double-click its icon.
2. When the Write window opens, click Edit on its menu bar. Notice that it has the same Cut, Copy, and Paste options as the Notepad Edit menu.
3. Choose Paste from the menu, and the now-familiar line appears in the Write workspace.

Now try copying a graphic image from the Paintbrush window to the Write window. In this exercise, you open a file called LEAVES.BMP in Paintbrush, and use the Cutout tool in that application to outline part of the image and copy it to the Clipboard.

1. Click the Paintbrush window, or double-click its icon.
2. In the Paintbrush window, choose Open from its File menu, or press (Alt)-(F) (O).
3. Double-click the filename LEAVES.BMP in the file list; you'll need to scroll down the list until you see it.
4. When the LEAVES graphic appears, click the Scissors cutout tool, pictured here:

5. Once you've clicked the cutout tool, use it to surround some of the leaves. You don't need to be exact.

Move the mouse pointer to the Paintbrush workspace (it converts to a cross-hair pointer). Position this pointer in the upper left, and then click and drag to the lower right and release the mouse button. A dotted line surrounds the portion you outlined.

6. Choose Copy from the Edit menu. This puts the graphic in the Clipboard and overwrites the line of text you put there earlier.

7. Minimize the Paintbrush window.

8. Activate the Write window, and press Enter to start a new line. Select Paste from the Edit menu. The image is pasted in the Write document at the position of the cursor, as shown in Figure 4-4.

Saving the Clipboard Contents

You can open the Clipboard at any time to view or save its contents. The image from Paintbrush is still in the Clipboard after the last exercise; follow these steps to save that image to a file:

1. Activate the Program Manager window and double-click the ClipBook icon in the Main group. The ClipBook window opens, as shown in the illustration on the following page:

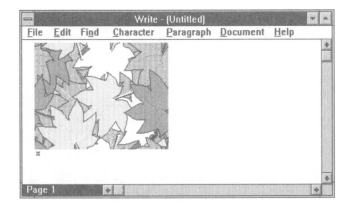

A Paintbrush image pasted to a Write document window
Figure 4-4.

4

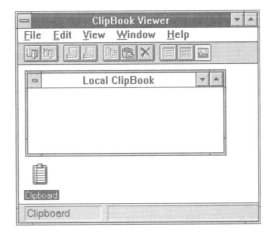

2. You can double-click the Clipboard icon to see the captured image.

3. Now place it on the Local ClipBook. Click the title bar of the Local ClipBook window, then choose Paste from the Edit menu.

4. The Paste dialog box appears as shown here:

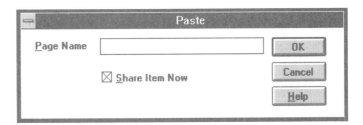

5. Type a name for this image (such as LEAVES).

6. Disable the Share Item Now option.

7. Click the OK button.

The image now appears in the Local ClipBook window. You can close the ClipBook. The image will be saved and available the next time you open ClipBook.

NOTE: Choosing the Copy or Cut command overwrites the current contents of the Clipboard. If you think you'll need something that's in the Clipboard for another use, you must save it to the Local ClipBook or choose Save As from the File menu.

Closing Application Windows

TIP: Before you go further in this chapter, follow the steps here to close the applications that are open on the desktop. This is especially important if your system is low on memory.

To close Notepad, Write, and Paintbrush, double-click the Control button in their respective windows. Or, if they are icons on the desktop, click the icon once, and then choose Close from the Control menu. Message boxes will appear and ask you if want to save the contents of Notepad and Write. Unless you want to save something that's there, just click the No button, and the applications will close.

Exploring the Control Panel

In this section you learn important techniques for *customizing* the look and operation of Windows by using utilities in the Control Panel. Double-click the Control Panel icon in the Program Manager Main window now, to display a window similar to this:

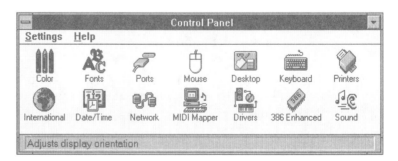

The utilities in the Control Panel are used to control your computer, printers, and various features of Windows. Here in Chapter 4 you examine the Date/Time utility and the Colors utility as an exercise in setting Window features.

Setting the Date and Time

Because files are tagged with the date and time when they are saved, and because this information can be used to sort and organize files, it is important that your system has the correct settings. To set a new date and time, double-click the Date/Time icon on the Control Panel. This is the Date & Time dialog box:

4

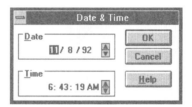

NOTE: Use the International icon on the Control Panel to change the format of the date and time display. This option is explained in Chapter 6.

To change the date or time, double-click the item you want to change, and then click the up- or down-arrow button repeatedly until the setting for each element is correct. You can also use the ⌨Tab key to move to any field and then type in a new setting.

The following exercise shows you how to set the date and time.

1. Double-click the month element in the Date field, or press the ⌨Tab key until it is highlighted.

2. Click the up- or down-arrow in the Date field to increase or decrease the value for the month element, or simply type in a new value.

3. Tab to the day element and repeat Step 2.

4. Tab to the year element and repeat Step 2.

5. If necessary, change the time field using the same procedure.

6. To save your changes, click the OK button or press ⌷Enter⌷. To quit without making the changes, click the Cancel button or press ⌷Esc⌷.

Changing the Color Scheme

You can change the color scheme of your Windows environment using the Color utility. Open it now by double-clicking the Color icon in the Control Panel. In the Color dialog box (Figure 4-5), the Color Schemes field at the top of the box lists the current color scheme. When you pick a color scheme, it appears in the sample window in the middle of the dialog box.

There are two ways to change color schemes: you can select one of the predefined color schemes in the Color Schemes field, or you can create

The Color dialog box lets you change the Windows color scheme

Figure 4-5.

your own custom color scheme by clicking the Color Palette button at the bottom of the dialog box. Complete details for creating custom color schemes are covered in Chapter 6.

Follow this exercise to choose one of the predefined color schemes:

1. In the Color dialog box, click the down-arrow button in the Color Schemes field, or better, just press on the keyboard.

2. Press the up- and down-arrow keys in the list box to scroll through and scan through the sample color schemes.

3. Highlight the color scheme you want, and click the OK button or press (Enter).

That's how easy it is to change the color scheme. Experiment with different schemes until you find one you like.

4

Exploring the File Manager

The File Manager helps you organize and manage programs and files on your hard disk filing system. A *file* is a collection of information, initially created in the memory of the computer and then saved to a disk storage device. All files have unique names. Hard drive filing systems that use DOS are organized into *directory* structures. Each directory is a separate area where you can store files; for instance, one directory might hold your business files, and another your personal files.

NOTE: Keep in mind that this section provides only a brief introduction to the File Manager. Chapter 9 contains a complete discussion. If you need more information about files, refer to Chapter 7.

The File Manager window is illustrated in Figure 4-6. Like the Program Manager, File Manager has its own document windows, but they are called *directory windows* because they list the files in a directory. The elements of the File Manager window are described in the next sections.

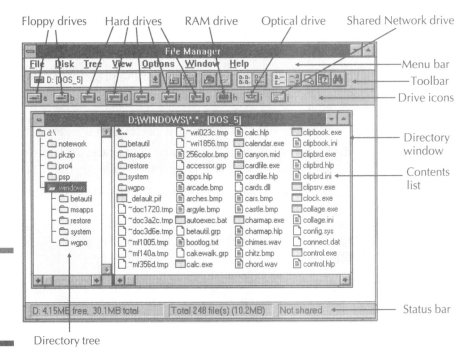

Floppy drives   Hard drives   RAM drive   Optical drive   Shared Network drive

Menu bar
Toolbar
Drive icons

Directory window
Contents list

Status bar

The File Manager directory window **Figure 4-6.**

Directory tree

Menu Bar   The File Manager menu bar contains commands for copying, moving, renaming, and deleting files or directories. It also contains options to change the way files are listed and the way the directory structure is presented.

Toolbar   The Toolbar provides quick access to some of the most used menu commands, as is shown in Figure 4-7. You simply click a button instead of choosing an option from the menu. You can customize the Toolbar to include options you use the most.

Drive Icons   The drive icons represent the disk drives available on your system. Clicking a drive icon displays the directory tree for that drive.

Directory Window   Directory windows provide a view of files in your directories. More than one directory window can be open at once, each

4

Toolbar buttons
in the File
Manager
Figure 4-7.

Connect		Connect to shared directory
Disconnect		Disconnect from shared directory
Share		Share a directory with other workgroup members
Stop Sharing		Stop sharing a directory
List Names		Display names only in directory windows
List All		Display all file information in directory windows
File Name Order		List by filename in alphabetical order
Extension Order		List by extension in alphabetical order
Size Order		List files in order of size
Date Order		List files in chronological order
New Window		Create a new directory window
Copy Files		Copy files or directories
Move Files		Move files or directories
Delete Files		Delete files or directories

presenting a list of files in a different directory. Each directory window includes drive icons, a directory tree, and a contents list (or files list).

Directory Tree   The directory tree represents the directory structure for the currently selected drive. Click a directory on the tree to display its files in the contents list.

Contents List   The contents list, also called the files list or file listing, displays the files of the directory that is currently selected in the directory tree. The following icons represent the various types of files:

File Icon	Description
	Executable files are program files and batch files. You can double-click these icons to start programs; thus the File Manager can be used to launch applications in the same way as Program Manager.
	Associated files are created by a Windows application, or have a filename extension recognized by an application. You can double-click the icons of associated documents to automatically load them into the workspace of the application that created them.

File Icon	Description
	Subdirectories that branch from other directories. Double-click a subdirectory icon to access the files stored in it.
	Parent directories have branching subdirectories. Double-click the parent icon to move back one level in the directory tree.
	The *other file* icon represents all other files that Windows does not recognize as program or associated files.

Using the File Manager

In these exercises, you get a chance to use File Manager and become familiar with what it can do. First, let's take a look at your Windows directory, which is normally on drive C, but may be on another drive in your system.

1. In the drive icon bar, click the drive icon where the Windows directory is located.
2. Click the Windows directory icon in the directory tree. The files list then displays the files in the Windows directory.

Change the Order of the Files List

The order of the files included in the files list can be changed using options on the View menu. In this next exercise, you sort the list by file type, which groups files by their filename extension.

1. Click View in the File Manager menu bar.
2. Click Sort By Type, press [Alt]-[V] [B] or click the Extension Order button on the Toolbar. Watch as the files are resorted in alphabetical order by their filename extension.

TIP: Listing files by type (filename extension) is a convenient order to use when you need to view or select a group of similar files. For example, scroll through the files list and notice that graphics files with the extension .BMP are grouped together.

Listing File Statistics

Use the View All File Details option to display additional information about files, such as their creation date and size:

4

1. Select View from the File Manager menu, and then All File Details. Alternatively, click the List All button on the Toolbar.

2. If you can't see all the file statistics, enlarge the File Manager window, and then enlarge the directory window.

Now you see more than just the filenames and icons. Files are listed in rows with the size, date, and other information.

Listing Only Executable Files

You can specify which files you want to include or exclude from the File Manager files list, thus restricting this display to only the files you want to work with. In this exercise, you reduce the file listing to only executable program (.EXE) files. Note that .EXE files are programs you can start by double-clicking their icons.

1. Select the View command and choose the By File Type option. The following dialog box appears:

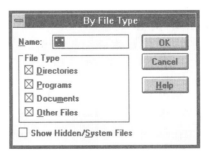

Initially, the Name field includes the file specification *.*, which lists all files. The File Type box offers you another way to specify which files to list: Just mark or unmark the check box for the file types you want included or excluded from the list.

2. Unmark the check boxes for Documents and Other Files. Leave only the Directories and Programs check boxes marked.

3. Click the OK button or press [Enter].

The contents list in File Manager now displays a list of directories and executable program files in the Windows directory. Other files are excluded from the list.

Starting Programs from File Manager

Now that you have the .EXE files listed in File Manager, you can double-click any of them to start those programs. Most of the .EXE files you see in the files list are the same programs that are started when you double-click an icon in the Program Manager. Note CLOCK.EXE (the Clock), CALC.EXE (the Calculator), and CONTROL.EXE (the Control Panel). As mentioned, File Manager just gives you another way to start these programs. Try it now by following these steps:

1. Point to CALC.EXE and double-click. The Calculator opens on the desktop.

2. Click the Calculator Minimize button.

3. Locate NOTEPAD.EXE and double-click its icon. If you already have Notepad loaded, another copy will open in another window. Minimize this window for use in the next exercise.

Loading Associated Files

Associated files are linked, by means of their filename extensions, to the applications that created them. For example, the Notepad editor creates files with the extension .TXT, and the Calendar utility creates files with the extension .CAL. You can double-click an associated file to open it in the workspace of the application used to create it.

Follow these steps to change the files list and open an associated file.

1. Select the View command and choose the By File Type option.

2. When the By File Type dialog box opens, mark only the Documents check box. (After the last exercise, you need to unmark Directories and Programs.)

3. Click the OK button or press Enter.

4. When the files list reappears, double-click WINLOGO, which is associated with the Paintbrush application. The file is loaded in the Paintbrush workspace.

Thus File Manager provides a quick way to view and open your various document, graphics, and other files. To do the same in Program Manager, you would need to create a startup icon for the document in a group, or start the application and then open the document.

4

Opening a Second Directory Window

You can open a second directory window and view two sets of files side by side for comparison. Try this now:

1. Select the Window command from the File Manager menu bar and choose New Window, or press Alt-W N.

2. The new window duplicates and overlaps the first window. To see both windows, choose Cascade from the Window menu.

3. In the directory tree of the new window, click an icon for a directory different from the one selected in the first window. The files for that directory are then listed in the new window, and the title of the window changes.

TIP: To open a new window for another disk drive, double-click the icon of the disk in the current window.

Closing the File Manager

When you're ready to close the File Manager, first take a look at the status of the Save Settings on Exit option on the Options menu. If this feature is enabled, any changes you made to directory windows and menu options will be retained for your next File Manager sessions.

However, because the changes made in these exercises are not necessary to normal operation of the Windows environment, it's important that you make sure this feature is not enabled.

Save Settings on Exit is a toggle, so if the check box is marked, just select it again to turn it off. You can now double-click the Control button or choose Exit from the File menu to quit File Manager.

CHAPTER

5

USING WINDOWS HELP

In this chapter, you learn how to use the Windows help system. Nearly every window contains the Help option on its menu bar. Use Help to obtain information, assistance, and even tutorials on Windows applications.

Help opens as a separate window that you can keep handy on the desktop as you work with applications. You can search for help text, or simply scroll through it to view the help text in order.

You can also place "bookmarkers" in the help text at locations you want
to refer to later, or even add your own help text or comments.

Accessing Help

You can access help information in two ways: You can select the Help
option on the menu bar of a window to access help for any topic
related to the application running in the window. Or, you can
highlight a particular command or menu option and press the F1 key
to get help related to that item. For example, if you highlight the Run
command on the Program Manager File menu and press F1,
instructions for using Run are displayed, as shown in Figure 5-1. *Help
windows* are resizable and movable, and have a menu bar, buttons, and
other typical Windows features. They can even be minimized and kept
on the desktop for periodic reference.

Think of the help system as a reference book with a table of contents,
index, and glossary. Most applications have their own "book" of help.
The F1 key lets you immediately display a specific part of the book
that is related to the task you are working on. To view help information
for an entire application from the beginning, click the Help option on

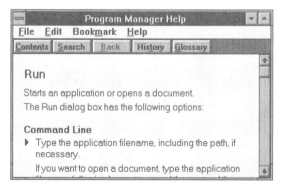

A typical Help
dialog box
Figure 5-1.

the application menu bar or press ⟨Alt⟩-⟨H⟩. You'll see drop-down menus similar to these:

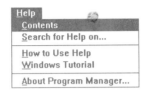 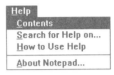

The Help menu on the left is from the Program Manager, and the one on the right is from Notepad. Both menus have options in common, such as Contents and Search for Help on. Search for Help on helps you locate any topic in Help. Some applications have their own tutorials, like the Windows Tutorial option on the Program Manager menu.

How to Get Help

To get help, either open the Help drop-down menu or press the ⟨F1⟩ key to display specific help information related to the task you are working on. A third method is also available in some applications; you can press ⟨Shift⟩-⟨F1⟩ to change the mouse pointer to a question mark, and then click the area of the screen for which you want help. The exercises in the rest of this chapter illustrate these techniques. Before starting the exercises, make sure the Program Manager is active.

 ## Using the Help Menu

In the Program Manager, choose Help from the menu bar to open the Help menu. Choose the Contents option to open the Help window. The Help window contains a list of topics displayed in green or as underlined letters. Now minimize the Help window by clicking its Minimize button. You will see the following Help icon at the bottom of the desktop:

The Help window is now out of the way, but easily accessible when you need it.

Getting Context-Specific Help

You can get help information related to the command you're using by pressing [F1]. In the following exercise, you display help for the Run command on the Program Manager File menu:

1. Activate the Program Manager window, and open the File menu.
2. Press the [↓] key to highlight the Run option (*don't* click the option).
3. Press [F1] to display help for the Run command.
4. Reduce the size of the Help window, and notice that the help text rearranges itself to fit the new window shape.
5. You don't need to read this help now, so close the Help window by double-clicking its Control button.

Some dialog boxes have buttons for accessing help. In this way, you can execute a command and then get help about the command's options. Try this:

1. Choose Run on the File menu.
2. Click the Help button in the dialog box. When the help for the Run command is displayed, notice that the size you gave the Help window in the previous exercise is retained.
3. Close the Help window.
4. Press [Esc] to close the Run dialog box.

Using Help Windows

Help windows look much the same as other windows, except they also have a set of buttons used to navigate the special contents of the window. In the following exercises, you learn how to work with Help windows. Before you start the exercises, you need to open the Program Manager Help window by choosing Contents from the Help menu.

TIP: Keep in mind that you can resize Help windows and position them beside their related application windows. This makes it easy to reference help information when you need it. Alternatively, you can keep Help windows minimized, and maximize them when you need their information.

Scroll the Help Text and Choose a Topic

5

To scroll through help text, click the down-arrow button on the scroll bar, or press the [Pg Dn] key. You can click any topic that is highlighted in green or underlined. Follow these steps to practice getting help on various topics:

1. Choose Contents from the Program Manager Help menu if the Help window is not already open.

2. Click the topic called "Organizing Applications and Documents" under the How To heading in the contents list. The following Help window appears:

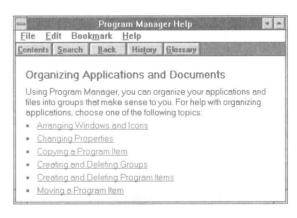

Notice that this topic has branching topics of its own. As you click each topic, you move further into the help text. You use the Back button under the Help window menu bar to move back to your starting place.

3. Click the topic "Creating and Deleting Groups."

Now you see help text that describes how to create and delete groups. Notice the green or underlined words within the text itself. These are *glossary items*. You can click a glossary item to get a quick description of the term.

4. Click the glossary item "title bar" to display the glossary text shown in Figure 5-2.
5. Click the glossary reference to remove it from the screen.

This section has shown you how to move into different levels of help text. The next section shows you how to move back through the help text.

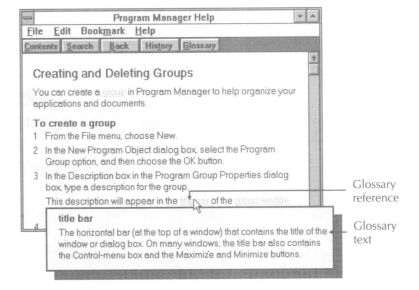

Glossary reference window opened for the selected "title bar" topic
Figure 5-2.

Using Help Buttons

Every Help window has a set of Help buttons, as illustrated here:

These buttons are used to navigate through the help text, or to quickly relocate to other topics. Some Help windows include the << and >> buttons; they are used to browse back and forth through help topics. Here is a list of the buttons and their functions; they are discussed in detail in the paragraphs that follow:

Help Button	Function
Contents	View Help window contents
Search	Search for specific help topics
Back	Move back one help topic
History	View history
Glossary	Display a list of glossary items
<<	Browse backward
>>	Browse forward

5

Viewing the History

Every topic you access while using a Help window is recorded automatically in a history file. You can then display the history file and use it to jump back to any previous topic. In the last exercise, you advanced into the Program Manager help text twice by clicking two topics. To view these steps and return to any one of them, click the History button or press Alt-T. You'll see a listing of steps similar to this:

To return to any topic in this history list, double-click the topic with the mouse. The help text for the topic is displayed in the Help window.

The History button provides a convenient way to browse through help text. It lets you advance several steps into a help topic, and then quickly return to the top level and continue with another topic.

The Back Button and Browse Buttons

The Back button is used to go back one step in the help text. You can click this button several times to retrace your steps to any point, and then branch off to another topic.

The forward browse button (>>) and the backward browse button (<<) that appear on some Help windows let you step forward or backward through each major topic in the help text. The << button moves backward through the help topics, and the >> moves forward through the help topics. Click the button with the mouse, or press [Alt]-[<] or [Alt]-[>].

Displaying the Table of Contents

To return to the beginning of the help text and display its list of topics, click the Contents button. Try this now to return to the beginning of the Program Manager help text.

Searching for Topics

You can quickly locate any help topic using the Search button or by choosing Search for Help on from the Help menu. Try the following exercise to locate help for the options on the Program Manager File menu:

1. In the Program Manager Help window, click the Search button. You'll see the Search dialog box (Figure 5-3).

2. In the top text box, where the blinking cursor appears, type **S**. Keywords that start with *S* are displayed in the list box in the top half of the Search dialog box.

3. Double-click "Starting Applications" to view a list of topics that have this keyword in their text. The lower list box then displays these topics (see Figure 5-3).

4. Double-click any topic in the lower list box to see that help text.

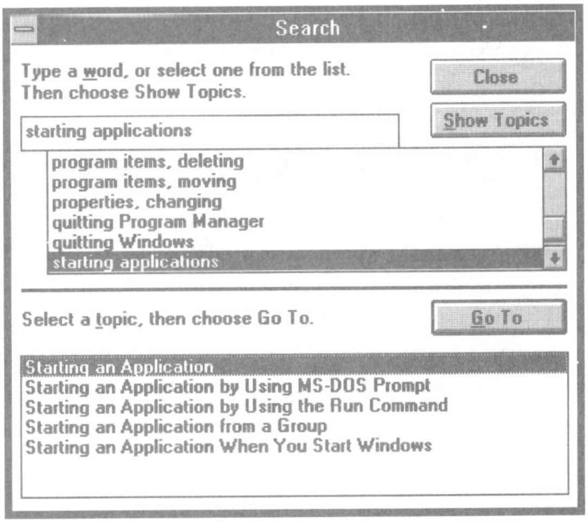

The Search
dialog box for
finding help
topics
Figure 5-3.

5

The Show Topics button and the Go To button can be used instead of
the mouse instructions in the foregoing exercise. To use the Show
Topics button, first highlight a keyword in the upper list box, and then
choose the Show Topics (Alt-S) button. When the topics appear in the
lower list box, you can highlight a topic and choose the Go To (Alt-G)
button to display the help text for that topic.

Using the Help Menu Options

Now let's take a look at the options on the Help window menu bar. In
the Program Manager Help window, select each option as you read the
following text:

♦ The *File* menu gives you options for opening the help text of
another application, or printing the currently displayed help topic.

♦ The *Edit* menu has options for copying a block of help text to
another application, and annotating (adding to) help text.

♦ The *Bookmark* menu is used to insert a placeholder in help text so
you can quickly refer back to a point in that text at any time.

♦ The *Help* menu provides help about the help system itself.

This section steps you through the menu options. Before beginning, make sure the Program Manager Help window is still open. If it isn't, open it now.

The File Open Option

Most Windows applications have their own help text, which is in a file (with a .HLP extension) stored in the Windows directory of your hard drive. You can look at the help information for any application, even if it's not running, by choosing Open on the File menu of any currently open Help window. This is most useful for teachers or managers who need to create a set of instructions for other users. You can open the help text file of any application, and then use the Copy option on the Help Edit menu to copy specific topics to another document. Do the following exercise to practice opening another help topic:

1. Make sure the Program Manager Help window is still open. If not, choose Contents from the Program Manager Help menu.

2. Choose the Open option on the File menu. You'll see this dialog box:

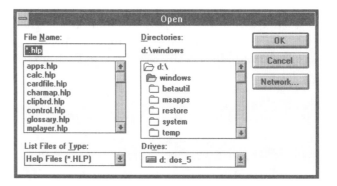

3. Double-click CALC.HLP at the top of the File Name list.

The Help window title bar now displays "Calculator Help," even though the calculator is not running.

Printing a Help Topic

Printing the text of a help topic is one of the most useful things you can do with the Help system. In this next example, you print a list of the standard keystrokes used by the Calculator.

1. Click the topic "Use Standard Calculator Functions" under the Keyboard heading, to display the keyboard methods for accessing the Calculator.
2. Choose Print Topic from the File menu to print the topic.

To print other topics, first display the topic, and then choose the Print Topic option on the Help File menu.

5

TIP: Print the contents of any help topic to create an instant quick-reference that you can post next to your computer or place in a help binder.

Copying a Help Topic

Teachers, instructors, and managers can open a help file and copy its text to a file in a word processor. Printed or on-line collections of these help topics can be expanded or abbreviated, or otherwise customized, to train students and employees.

Use the Copy option on the Help Edit menu to place the text of any help topic in the Clipboard. You can then paste the help text into another application. In the following exercise, you copy the Standard Calculator Functions help information to the Notepad editor and save it for later use.

1. Make sure the Using Standard Calculator Functions topic is still displayed. If not, use the Help window History button and choose it again from the list of Calculator help topics.
2. Select Edit in the menu bar, and choose the Copy option. You'll see the following dialog box:

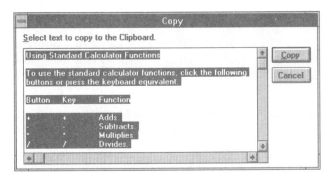

3. Click the Copy button to copy the entire text into the Clipboard.

4. Start Notepad by double-clicking its icon in the Accessories group of the Program Manager.

5. When the Notepad window opens, choose Paste from the Edit menu to place the help text in the workspace.

6. Save the text by choosing Save As from the File menu. When the Save As dialog box appears, type **CALCKEYS** in the File Name text box, and click OK or press ⌷Enter⌷.

7. Close the Notepad window, and make the Calculator Help text window active again. If you can't see the Help window to click it, press ⌷Ctrl⌷⌷Esc⌷ and choose its name from the Task List.

You'll get a chance to use this CALCKEYS file later for other exercises.

NOTE: You can highlight any part of the text by clicking and dragging through it with the mouse.

The Annotate Option

The Annotate option in the Help Edit menu lets you add *annotations* (notes and comments of your own) to any help topic. When you add an annotation, a paper clip appears at the beginning of the topic's help text. Try adding a comment to the current (Calculator) Help window by following these steps:

1. Choose Annotate from the Edit menu. You'll see this dialog box:

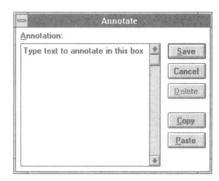

2. In the large text box where the blinking cursor appears, type the following:

   This topic has already been printed.

3. Click the Save button (Alt-S).

4. Scroll to the top of the Calculator help text until you see the paper clip symbol.

5. Click the paper clip to display the Annotate dialog box, and you'll see your annotation. Press Esc to return to the Help window.

You can remove an annotation at any time by clicking the Delete button (Alt-D) on the Annotation dialog box. The Copy and Paste buttons in that box let you copy existing annotations from one annotation box to another.

Defining Bookmarks

Bookmarks mark a place in a help file to which you want to return later. Bookmark titles are then added to the Bookmark menu. Here's an exercise to define a bookmark:

5

1. The Standard Calculator Functions help text should still be visible in the Help window. Select Bookmark from the menu bar, and choose the Define option from the menu. You'll see this dialog box:

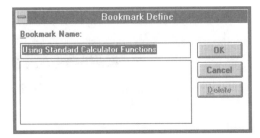

2. In the bookmark name field where the cursor is flashing, type **I was here!** in the top field. Click OK or press Enter.

NOTE: The lower field is used to select and delete an existing bookmark.

3. Open the Bookmark menu. You'll see your new bookmark on the drop-down menu, as shown here:

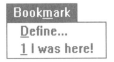

You can use bookmarks in topics you need to access quickly. Bookmarks are saved from one session to the next. When you don't need a bookmark any longer, open the Bookmark Define dialog box,

click the bookmark to delete in the list at the bottom, and click the
Delete button (Alt-D).

Other Help Formats

Some Windows applications, such as Microsoft Mail and Microsoft
Schedule+, use a collapsible help system. All the major topics are listed
with buttons that you click to expand the topic, or a list of subtopics.
Figure 5-4 illustrates the Microsoft Mail help window. If you click any
of the plus (+) buttons, a list of subtopics appear. You can then choose
one of these subtopics to read help information. Note in Figure 5-4 that
when the button labeled Using the Address Book is clicked, the
temporary window appears showing subtopics.

5

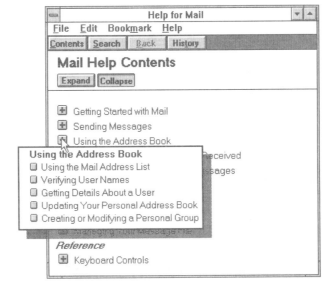

In a collapsed
help system,
you click
buttons to
display more
topics or help
text
Figure 5-4.

In Figure 5-4, note the Expand and Collapse buttons under the help heading. Initially, all help text topics are collapsed. If you click Expand, you'll see a list similar to that shown in Figure 5-5. The subheadings now appear under each main topic heading. You can choose either expanded or collapsed listing methods, depending on your preference.

When a collapsed list is expanded, you see all the subtopics under each main heading **Figure 5-5.**

CHAPTER

CUSTOMIZING WINDOWS: THE CONTROL PANEL

To customize your Windows environment, you use the Control Panel utilities, illustrated on the following page. For example, you use the Printers icon to add and configure printers to work with Windows. You can also personalize your Windows screen by changing the color scheme or displaying pictures on the Windows desktop.

To begin working with the Control Panel, double-click its

icon in the Program Manager (or select it with the keyboard), and you'll
see a Control Panel window similar to this:

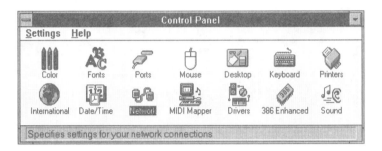

There are three categories of options on the Control Panel:

✦ **Window and desktop options**   Choose the color of window
borders, menu bars, text, and other features with the Color utility.
To alter the desktop pattern, cursor blink rate, and window spacing,
use the Desktop utility.

✦ **Hardware settings**   Set the operations of the keyboard, mouse,
serial ports, and printers with the Keyboard, Mouse, Ports, and
Printers utilities, respectively.

✦ **Software settings**   Control the internal settings of your
system—date and time, language and currency formats, keyboard
operation, and screen fonts—with the Date/Time, International,
Keyboard, and Fonts utilities, respectively. The Network utility is
used to log on to networks and modify various network settings.

The sections in this chapter describe each of the Control Panel utilities in
detail, except for MIDI Mapper, which is beyond the scope of this book.

Color

The Color utility lets you change the color of window borders, title
bars, menu text, and so on. Choose one of the Windows predefined
color schemes, or design your own.

Double-click the Color icon in the Control Panel to display the Color
dialog box pictured in Figure 6-1. The highlight should be in the Color

The Color
dialog box
Figure 6-1.

Schemes drop-down list box. To scroll through the options in this box, click the down-arrow button with the mouse, or press the ⬇ key on the keyboard. As you scroll through the list, the sample window (in the center of the Color dialog box) takes on the currently selected color scheme so you can see what it looks like. Click OK or press Enter to select a new color scheme.

Creating Custom Color Schemes

Windows 3.1 comes with a number of predefined, named color schemes. These are all listed in the Color Schemes box. If you don't like these schemes, you can create your own. To create a custom color scheme, you pick a window element you want to change (border, title bar, window text, and so on), and then choose a new color for it from the Basic Colors palette. Once you've created a scheme you like, you can save it and make it the current color scheme.

Mouse users can click any part of the Color dialog box to change settings. If you're using the keyboard, press the Tab key to move among the fields. Don't press Enter until you're completely finished, because that closes the dialog box.

6

The following exercise shows you how to create your own custom color scheme:

1. Click the Color Palette >> button in the lower part of the Color dialog box. The Color dialog box expands, as shown in Figure 6-2.
2. Click the down-arrow button on the Screen Element list box until Desktop is highlighted.
3. In the color boxes of the Basic Colors area, notice that the current color is surrounded by a black border. Click White in the lower-right corner to select white for the desktop color.
4. Choose Menu Bar from the Screen Element list.
5. Click a new color in the Basic Colors area to change the color of the menu bar.

Repeat Steps 4 and 5 to change any screen element you want, watching the sample window on the left as you select each new color. Once you've designed a color scheme, save it by following these steps:

1. Click the Save Scheme command button ((Alt)-(A)) to display the following dialog box:

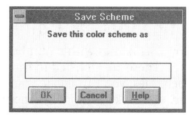

2. Type a name for your scheme in the text box.
3. Click OK or press (Enter) to save the scheme.

To edit your color scheme, highlight its name in the Color Schemes box and make changes as outlined in the previous procedure. Or click the Remove Scheme button ((Alt)-(M)) to delete it altogether. To make your new scheme active, display its name in the Color Schemes list box, and click the OK button or press (Enter).

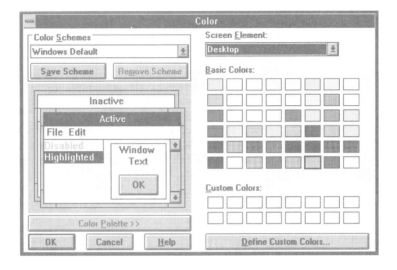

The Color
dialog box,
fully expanded
Figure 6-2.

Creating Custom Colors

You can also create your own colors for use in the color schemes. Open
the Color dialog box from the Control Panel; then click the Color
Palette >> button to display the expanded Color dialog box (Figure 6-2).
Next, click the Define Custom Colors button to open the Custom Color
Selector box, shown in Figure 6-3.

The slider bar and text boxes on the Custom Color Selector box are
used to adjust the mix of red, green, and blue (RGB Color Model), or
the hue, luminosity, and saturation (HLS Color Model) that make up
colors. All of these concepts are described in the following paragraphs.

✦ The large color refiner box, or grid, is for selecting a color by using
the mouse.

✦ The luminosity slider bar to the right of the color refiner box is used
to change the luminosity of the current color.

✦ Click the Color|Solid box to pick a dithered or solid version of the
current color.

✦ In the value boxes, select or enter numeric values for colors, rather
than using the mouse methods.

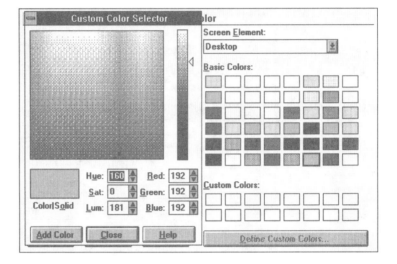

The Custom
Color Selector
box
Figure 6-3.

Once you've created a color, you click the Add Color button to add the new color to one of the 16 Custom Color boxes.

When you use the Custom Color Selector, you need to understand the following terminology about the custom colors you are creating. *Hue* is the intensity of red, blue, and green that combine to make the color, and corresponds to a *horizontal* movement across the color refiner box. *Saturation* is the purity of a color (or its lack of gray content), and corresponds to a *vertical* movement in the color refiner box. *Luminosity* is the brightness of a color on a scale from black to white.

You can also mix colors by specifying the darkness or brightness of their red, green, and blue elements. When the Red, Green, and Blue fields are set to 0, the color is black. When all three fields are set to 255, the color is white. Any combination in between is a custom color.

Because some monitors are incapable of displaying the full range of colors supported by Windows, a dot pattern is used to approximate the color as closely as possible. This is known as *dithering*. As you work with a color, the Color|Solid box displays the dithered color on the left. The box on the right is the closest solid, or nondithered, color that can be displayed. Once a custom color is created, you can choose between the dithered or solid version of that color by clicking in either side of the Color|Solid box.

This next exercise shows you how to create and add a custom color:

1. Start by dragging the luminosity slider bar pointer about midway on the scale.

2. In the color refiner box, point to the approximate color you want. (You'll see a cross-hair color refiner cursor.)

3. To make adjustments to the color, drag the mouse around in the refiner box or slide the luminosity pointer. Watch the colors in the Color|Solid box until you see a dithered or solid color that you like.

4. Try making some finer adjustments by clicking the up- or down-arrow buttons of the value boxes below the refiner box. Click and hold these buttons to get an idea of how hue, saturation, and luminosity determine the position of the pointers in the refiner box or luminosity bar.

5. Add the new color to a box in the Custom Color field by clicking either the dithered or solid color in the Color|Solid box, and then clicking the Add Color button.

6

The new custom color will fill the first available color box in the Custom Colors field. To change a custom color, click its color box and follow the above procedure again. Use your custom colors to design custom color schemes.

Fonts

Fonts are sets of characters with a specific typeface that can be altered by changing their size and using different type styles, like italic and boldface. Using varied fonts can change the look and readability of your documents. In most applications, fonts are changed by opening a fonts dialog box. To understand fonts and how they are translated on your screen and printer, follow these steps to open Windows Write and choose Fonts from the Character menu:

1. Double-click the Accessories group in Program Manager.

2. Double-click the Write icon.

3. Choose the Fonts option from the Character menu, and you'll see the dialog box shown in Figure 6-4.

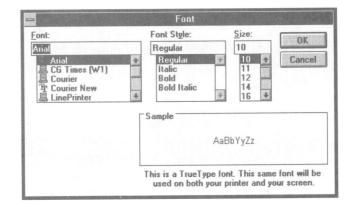

The Font dialog box in Windows Write is used to change the formatting of selected characters
Figure 6-4.

The Font dialog box includes list boxes for selecting a font, font style, and font size. Scroll through the Font list now by clicking the down-arrow button or pressing ⬇ on the keyboard. Watch the Sample box as you do this, and notice that fonts are either printer fonts or TrueType fonts (explained next).

Windows, Your Printer, and Fonts

The fonts available in the character formatting menus of any Windows application depend partly on the currently installed printer. For example, the fonts named AvantGarde, Bookman, and Zapf Dingbats will appear when a PostScript laser printer is installed. If you install a dot-matrix printer, a different set of fonts is available. Special printer definitions are added when you install printers during Windows Setup or with the Printer utility on the Control Panel. These printer definitions tell Windows what it needs to know about your printer and its fonts.

Windows 3.1 includes a new kind of *scalable font* called TrueType. You can reduce or enlarge these fonts to many different sizes. In addition, their appearance on the screen is very close to the printed version. TrueType fonts will print on any graphics-capable printer, so you are not limited to the fonts built into your printer.

It is important to make a distinction between the fonts displayed on the screen and those printed by the printer. Windows uses *screen fonts* to display characters as near as possible to how they will look when printed. Sometimes the match isn't perfect, but it's close enough for you to get a good idea of what you'll get on paper. Character size and spacing is sometimes off, but the location of line breaks and the spacing of lines will be accurate enough to give you an idea of the page layout. The advantage of TrueType fonts is that they look good on the screen and in your printed documents.

To better understand fonts, consider the following methods your printer uses to print text.

Built-in Printer Fonts   A font that your printer already knows how to print is called a *built-in* font. To work with this font, the printer does not need additional information from the computer, except a direction for which style and size to print. When using built-in printer fonts, you are limited to the range of fonts, styles, and sizes available in the printer. In some printers, the available fonts can be expanded by adding font *cartridges*, or by sending font descriptions stored in the computer to the printer's memory.

6

Computer Fonts   Instead of using a predefined font built into the printer, you can generate fonts in the computer and send them to the printer as graphic information. Windows puts the printer in *graphics mode* and makes it print any font, style, or size you request. The TrueType fonts supplied with Windows 3.1 are scalable in the range of 4 points to 127 points and can be printed on any graphics-capable printer supported by Windows.

N**OTE:** Printer fonts have corresponding screen fonts. The screen fonts mimic the way the font appears when printed. In some cases, you can acquire a screen font that provides an even better match to your printer's fonts, by contacting the manufacturer of the printer or by buying third-party font packages.

Viewing, Installing, and Removing Fonts

The Fonts utility on the Control Panel is used to install new fonts, or to install screen fonts for the fonts built into your printer. You can also use the Fonts utility to optimize system memory by removing fonts you don't use. In this section you'll see how to remove a font from memory and then reinstall it, using the Fonts utility.

NOTE: Keep in mind that most third-party fonts come with their own installation programs. Before using the Fonts utility, refer to the installation manual for any third-party fonts you have purchased.

Start the Fonts utility by double-clicking its icon in the Control Panel. You'll see the Fonts dialog box pictured in Figure 6-5.

To view currently installed fonts, scroll through the Installed Fonts list box. This displays a sample of each font in the lower box, as you scroll in the Installed Fonts box. As you scroll through the list, you'll see

The Fonts utility lets you view, add, and remove screen and printer fonts

Figure 6-5.

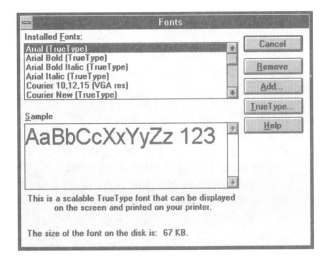

TrueType fonts and other fonts. For example, the Courier 10,12,15 font in the Installed Fonts list in Figure 6-5 is a screen font for VGA monitors. It may be used to display a built-in printer font on screen.

Adding Fonts

Fonts are available from a wide variety of sources. You can buy them off the shelf, or you can download them from bulletin board systems (BBSs) such as the Windows forums on CompuServe. To make new fonts available to Windows applications, you need to install them using the Fonts utility. In the following example, fonts downloaded from a CompuServe Windows forum are stored in the directory TRUETYPE on drive C.

1. Choose the Fonts icon from the Control Panel. The Fonts dialog box appears, as shown in Figure 6-5.

6

2. Click the Add button on the Fonts dialog box.

3. Choose the drive and directory where the fonts are located in the Drives and Directories list boxes. The available fonts will be listed, as shown here:

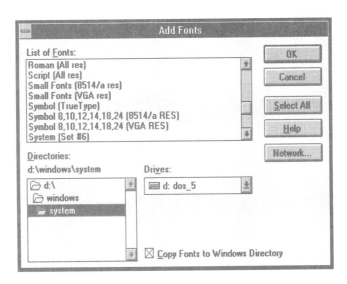

4. Click the fonts you want to add, or click the Select All button to add them all.

5. Click the option Use Fonts from Selected Directory if the fonts are already stored on your hard drive, otherwise Windows will make a duplicate copy of the font files in the directory. Leave this option blank if you are copying the files from a floppy disk or from another source such as a network server. Windows will then copy the files for you.

6. Click OK to install the new fonts.

Using TrueType Fonts

By default, Windows displays TrueType fonts in the Fonts dialog boxes of your applications. In some cases, you may prefer to use only your printer's fonts. In other cases, you may prefer to use TrueType fonts exclusively. To change the type of fonts that Windows displays, click the TrueType button on the Fonts dialog box to display the TrueType dialog box, as shown here:

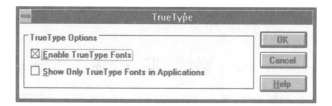

Mark the Enable TrueType Fonts check box to use TrueType fonts, or clear the box to use your printer's fonts only. Mark the Show Only TrueType Fonts in Applications check box to use TrueType fonts exclusively, or clear it to see all installed fonts. Note that checking this option frees memory for other applications.

Removing Fonts

There are two options available for removing fonts. You can remove a font to free memory for other applications, but keep the font available on disk if you need it in the future. Or you can permanently remove a font from your system by removing the disk file of the font. This not only frees memory, but makes disk space available as well.

To remove a font, follow these steps:

1. Choose the Fonts option in the Control Panel.
2. Highlight the font you want to remove in the Installed Fonts list box.
3. Click the Remove button. The dialog box shown here appears:

4. To remove the font from disk as well as from memory, mark the Delete Font File From Disk option.
5. Click Yes to remove the font.

6

Freeing Memory by Removing Fonts

As mentioned earlier in this chapter, there are two methods of freeing system memory by removing fonts.

To free the greatest amount of memory, click TrueType on the Fonts dialog box to display the TrueType dialog box. Then mark the Show Only TrueType fonts in Applications option on the TrueType dialog box. Alternatively, clear the Enable TrueType Fonts option to remove all TrueType fonts from memory. Note that doing so does not remove the fonts from disk. You can reenable them at any time.

The second method of freeing memory is to remove individual fonts using the Remove button on the Fonts dialog box. In this way, you can selectively remove only the fonts you don't use, rather than all the TrueType fonts or all the non-TrueType fonts as described in the previous paragraph.

Ports

The Ports utility in the Control Panel is used to configure the serial ports on the back of your computer. Most computers have only one or two serial ports, but the Ports utility has options for configuring up to four. Each serial port is referred to as COM1, COM2, and so on. Serial ports are used to connect modems and serial printers to your computer.

However, the Ports utility is primarily used to configure a port for a serial printer.

NOTE: If a modem is attached to one of your serial ports, use the modem's communications software to configure the port, rather than the Windows Ports utility.

Double-click the Control Panel Ports icon to display the following dialog box:

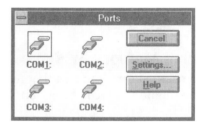

Here you can view and change the configuration for any port, by highlighting the icon for the port and then clicking the Settings button (Alt-S). If you're not actually setting up a COM port, but just learning about Windows, you can still follow along with this discussion to learn more about communications settings.

For this example, highlight the icon for COM1. Click the Settings button or press Alt-S to open the Settings dialog box for the COM1 port, as shown here:

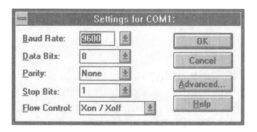

Following are descriptions of the settings in this box. To change a setting, click the down-arrow button to display a list of options and then click a new option.

NOTE: In each case, the setting should match the requirement for the device that is connected to that port.

Baud Rate   The *baud rate* is the speed at which information is transmitted through the port. Click the down-arrow button in the Baud Rate field to see the choices in the list box.

6

Data Bits   The *data bits* setting is the length, in bits, of each character sent. The bit size is either seven or eight. Match this to the setting of the device you are connecting.

Parity   *Parity* is an error-checking parameter used by some devices. If the printer or remote device connected to the port uses parity, you must determine the type, and then select the appropriate setting in the Parity list box.

Stop Bits   *Stop bits* are used to indicate the beginning and ending of each transmitted character.

Flow Control   *Flow control* provides a way for the receiving device to tell the sending device to temporarily stop sending data because it has more than it can handle at the moment. After the current data is printed or processed, more can be sent. The Xon/Xoff setting is software-level handshaking and is most commonly used. The Hardware setting designates hardware-level handshaking, which takes place between pinouts on the serial connectors. Handshaking is usually not required when the baud rate is lower than the printer speed, in which case you can designate None.

TIP: To duplicate the settings of one port to another, use the mouse to drag the port icon with the existing settings to another port icon.

Mouse

To change the operating characteristics of your mouse or other tracking device, select the Mouse icon on the Control Panel. You'll see the following dialog box:

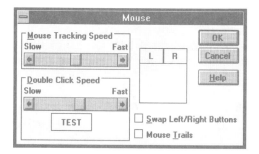

Set Mouse Tracking Speed

When the dialog box first opens, the slider button in the Mouse Tracking Speed box is flashing. Changing the position of this button allows you to change the speed at which the mouse pointer moves across the screen in relation to the movement of the mouse.

Try sliding the Mouse Tracking Speed button all the way to the left, and then drag the mouse pointer on the desktop to try the new speed. Then slide the button all the way to the right, and drag the mouse pointer again to try the new tracking speed. Then set the slider button in the position you prefer, and go on to the next section.

TIP: Beginning users, or those of you who are creating precise drawings may want to set the mouse for slower tracking. As you become more familiar with your mouse, you can increase the tracking speed as desired.

Setting the Double Click Speed

The Double Click Speed setting tells Windows when to interpret two mouse clicks as a double-click, by defining the length of time between the two clicks. Here's an exercise to practice using the slider bar for this setting:

1. Click the slider button in the Double Click Speed box, and slide it to the left.
2. Try double-clicking with the mouse in the TEST box below the slider bar. When your double-click speed matches the new setting, the TEST box changes colors.
3. Slide the button to the right, and test the double-click speed again in the TEST box.
4. Set the slider button to the position you prefer.

6

Swapping the Mouse Buttons

If you are left-handed, you can swap the functions performed by the left and right mouse buttons. Just click in the Swap Left/Right Buttons check box (this is a toggle setting). When the box is checked, the right button becomes the button used for the majority of tasks, such as selecting items and executing commands.

Mouse Trails

Click the Mouse Trails option to leave a trail of mouse pointers as you drag the mouse. This option takes effect immediately. It is most beneficial for liquid crystal displays (LCDs) like those on notebook computers, where screen response is slow.

After making changes to the Mouse dialog box, click the OK button or press (Enter) to return to the Control Panel.

Desktop

The Desktop utility lets you change certain features of the desktop: the desktop color and pattern, the cursor blink rate, and the grid that windows "snap" to when they are resized. Double-click the Control

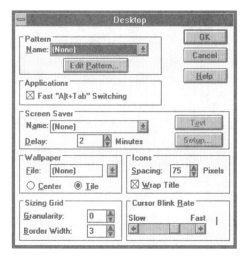

The Desktop
dialog box and
its many features
Figure 6-6.

Panel Desktop icon now to display the dialog box shown in Figure 6-6.
The options in this dialog box are described in the following paragraphs.

Desktop Pattern

The first time you start Windows, there is no desktop pattern—only the
color of the desktop you selected in the Color dialog box (discussed
earlier in this chapter). Using the Pattern features in the Desktop dialog
box, you can change the appearance of the desktop to a pattern,
providing a background that helps differentiate windows and icons on
the desktop, or just because you want to see something new. You can
install a predefined pattern, like Critters, Quilt, Waffle, or Weave, or
create patterns of your own.

Installing a Pattern

Follow these steps to install a pattern on the desktop:

1. Click the Edit Pattern command button ((Alt)-(P)). You'll see the
   following Desktop-Edit Pattern dialog box:

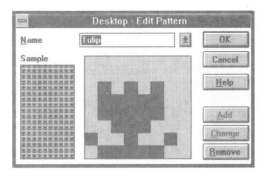

2. Press ⊕ on the keyboard to open the Name drop-down list box. Continue to press the ⊕ key repeatedly to display each name and pattern.

3. Highlight the Tulip pattern; then click the OK button or press Enter.

4. Although the Pattern Name list box now displays the name of the Tulip pattern, to make it appear on the desktop you have to click the OK button in the Desktop dialog box (or press Enter). Do this now to see how the pattern appears on the desktop.

6

Changing the Pattern Colors

You can change the color of the desktop pattern, as well as its background, to make items on the desktop easier to see and read. These changes are done in the Color utility, as discussed earlier in this chapter. Let's change the colors of the pattern you have added to your desktop.

1. Return to the Control Panel, and double-click the Color icon.

2. Click the Color Palette >> button to open the dialog box.

3. In the sample window, click Window Text, or select it in the Screen Element list box.

4. Select any color box from the Basic Colors area. This will be the color for the tulips in the desktop pattern.

5. Click the desktop in the sample window, or choose Desktop in the Screen Element list box.

6. Choose a color that you want as the underlying background color for the tulips.

7. Click the OK button or press [Enter], and look at the results on your screen.

Repeat these steps to try other colors in your patterns.

Editing a Pattern

You can also create your own Desktop patterns, as described in this next exercise.

1. Open the Desktop dialog box.
2. Click Edit Pattern ([Alt]-[P]). The Desktop-Edit Pattern dialog box appears, with the current pattern and its color visible in the Sample box.
3. Click the elements or *bits* in the editing area to turn them on or off. Experiment by clicking at various locations and watch as the pattern changes in the Sample box.
4. When you've created a pattern you like, save it by typing a new name in the Name field and clicking the Add button ([Alt]-[A]).
5. Click the OK button or press [Enter].

The new pattern name now appears in the Pattern Name list box. To place this new pattern on the desktop, click OK or press [Enter].

In the Desktop-Edit Pattern dialog box, the Add, Change, and Remove buttons are used to edit, save, or delete existing patterns. After editing a pattern, you can click Change and save it under that pattern name. However, it's best to save patterns under new names so you won't lose the original ones. To do so, begin typing a new name in the Name box; the Add button can then be used to save the pattern under a new name. To remove a pattern you have created, highlight its name in the Name box and press the Remove button.

Fast "Alt+Tab" Switching

When you press [Alt]-[Tab] on the keyboard repeatedly to switch among windows, the name of each window appears. Releasing the keys causes the selected window to appear. You can change this switching method by disabling the Fast "Alt+Tab" Switching option. When you do so, the title bar of each window appears while pressing the key combination. You should try both options to see which you prefer.

Using a Screen Saver

The Screen Saver feature blanks the computer monitor screen or displays a moving object until a key is pressed or the mouse is moved. On some screens, this prevents an image from burning itself onto the screen when left on too long. Although most screens these days are not susceptible to screen burn, screen savers still have an important role. You can use them to temporarily lock out others from tampering with your computer while you are away. Use the Screen Saver options in the Desktop dialog box to designate the type of screen saver you want and the interval of inactivity that must pass before the saver takes over the screen.

Here is an exercise to install a screen saver:

6

1. Open the Desktop dialog box, and click the Screen Saver Name field. A list of available screen savers appears, as shown here:

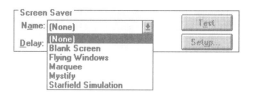

2. Click Starfield Simulation.
3. In the Delay text box, type the number of minutes of inactivity you want to pass before the screen saver comes on. For this example, type **1**.
4. Click the Test button to see a sample of the screen saver.
5. Move the mouse or press any key on the keyboard to return to normal screen mode.

If you want, select any of the other screen savers and click the Test button to see how they look. The Marquee screen saver is described in "Creating a Marquee" later in this chapter.

Customizing a Screen Saver

You can change the features of a screen saver by selecting it and then clicking the Setup button. Follow these steps to change the look of the Starfield Simulation screen saver:

1. Make sure the Starfield Simulation screen saver is selected in the Name list box; then click the Setup button. You'll see the following dialog box:

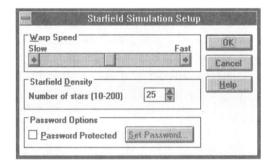

2. To change the speed of the moving starfield, click the slider button in the Warp Speed field and drag it left or right toward Slow or Fast.

3. To change the starfield density (number of stars), click the up- or down-arrow buttons in the Starfield Density text box.

4. Click the OK button or press Enter to execute the changes, and click the Test button to see the changes.

You can also change the settings of the Mystify and Marquee screen savers. When you open their Setup dialog box, click the Help button to view instructions for setting options.

Setting a Password

Setting a password for a screen saver prevents others from accessing your system when you're not around; this is especially useful when you have an application running, or if the desktop is set up in a way you don't want disturbed. It is also important when you are connected to network resources that others should not access while you are away. You can use a screen saver to lock your network connection instead of logging off the network.

CAUTION: Before you decide to use a password, keep in mind that typing a password to recover your screen every time it blanks may be a hassle. Only use a password when necessary, like when you're leaving your desk for a while. If you do set a password, *don't forget it.*

To change the password for the Mystify screen saver, follow these steps:

1. Choose Mystify in the Screen Saver Name field, and click the Setup button.
2. Click the Password Protected check box to make the Set Password button available.
3. Click the Set Password button. The Change Password dialog box appears, as shown here:

6

4. Type a password in the New Password box, and type it again in the Retype New Password box. *Memorize the password,* and then click OK or press [Enter].
5. When the Mystify Setup dialog box returns, click OK or press [Enter] to return to the Desktop dialog box.
6. Change the Delay value to one minute (if it isn't already set), and click OK or press [Enter].
7. Don't touch the keyboard or mouse for one minute. When the screen saver takes over, press any key. The password dialog box appears.
8. Type the password you entered in Step 4 to return to Windows.

NOTE: If you forget the password for a screen saver, you'll need to restart your system to get back into Windows. You should then turn the screen saver off.

Creating a Marquee

The Marquee screen saver is unique—it lets you define your own message to display on your screen during periods of inactivity. For example, if your system is busy sorting a large list of addresses and you don't want this process interrupted, a marquee message of "Don't Touch!" is appropriate. You might also create a marquee to inform co-workers that you've gone to lunch, or create a marquee that gives an instructional message like "Press any key to see a demo."

To create a marquee message, follow these steps:

1. Select Marquee from the Screen Saver Name list box; then click the Setup button. You'll see the Marquee Setup dialog box, as shown here, with text scrolling in the Text example field:

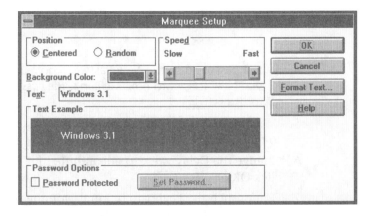

2. Type the marquee text in the Text field.

3. Click the Format Text button; then pick a font, style, size, and color for the text. Click OK.

4. In the Position box, choose where you want the text to scroll—across the center, or randomly on the screen.

5. In the Speed box, select a scrolling speed for the marquee.

6. Choose a color in the Background Color box.

7. If you want a password, fill out the Password Options box as described in the last exercise.

8. Click OK or press Enter to return to the Desktop dialog box.

9. In the Screen Saver Delay box, enter a delay value if desired.

10. Click the Test button to test the marquee, and then press any key to return to the Desktop dialog box.

11. If you are happy with the marquee, click OK or press Enter to close the Desktop dialog box and execute the changes.

6

Putting Up Wallpaper

The Wallpaper option lets you display a Paintbrush bitmap file on the desktop, as a single display or in a tiled pattern. Thus you can display a picture or a list of birthdays and important phone numbers as the desktop background. You can draw bitmapped images in Windows Paintbrush, or you can use images provided in the Windows directory. Try placing one of them on the desktop using this exercise:

1. From the Control Panel, open the Desktop dialog box.

2. In the Wallpaper area, click the down-arrow button beside the File list box.

3. Select WINLOGO.BMP in the file list. (The .BMP signifies a bitmap image file.)

4. Click the Center button; this tells Windows to center the picture on the desktop.

5. Click the OK button or press Enter.

The Desktop dialog box closes, and the Windows logo covers the desktop, overlaying any desktop patterns you may have selected previously.

Try other images, following the same steps. Note that most images are much smaller and are designed for tiling. Select LEAVES.BMP, and click the Tile button in the Wallpaper box. When you click OK or press (Enter), the image is tiled (repeated) in a consistent pattern. Your desktop looks like your front yard in Fall.

TIP: Feel free to experiment with the other image files in the Wallpaper list box, but keep one thing in mind if your system is short on memory: wallpaper images may require as much as 164K of RAM, so you may want to remove wallpaper from your desktop when you are running large applications.

Creating Your Own Wallpaper   You can create your own wallpaper images, using Windows Paintbrush. One practical example is to create a wallpaper image using scanned pictures of your kids or your friends; then type in their birthdays and other information under each picture. You might also create a list of phone numbers or other important information.

Changing Icon Spacing

The options for Icons in the Desktop dialog box let you change the default spacing between icons, and set the Wrap Title feature on or off. Figure 6-7 shows how the settings in the Icons box affect the icons on the desktop of a VGA display. In the first line of icons, the Spacing value is 75 pixels, and the Wrap Title option is off. Notice that icon titles overlap. In the middle row, spacing has been increased to 100 pixels, and the titles no longer overlap. In the last row, spacing is again at 75 pixels, but Wrap Title is on—this is the best layout when you have a lot of icons on the desktop.

In this exercise, you'll increase the spacing between icons.

1. In the Control Panel, click the Desktop icon.
2. In the Icons area of the Desktop dialog box, click the up-arrow button in the Spacing text box until the spacing value is 100.
3. Mark the Wrap Title check box, if it is not already marked.
4. Click the OK button or press (Enter).

Change the
spacing
between icons
and the setting
of the Wrap
Title feature to
make icons
easier to see on
the desktop
Figure 6-7.

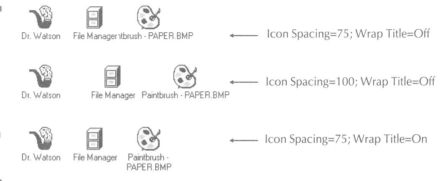

5. The changes in icon spacing will not take effect until you rearrange the icons. To do this, open the Task List by double-clicking the desktop or pressing Ctrl-Esc.

6. When the Task List appears, click the Arrange Icons button. Then you can observe the changes you've made.

Adjusting the Sizing Grid

The Sizing Grid box in the Desktop dialog box controls the *granularity* of the desktop. Granularity is like an invisible grid pattern on the desktop that windows "snap" to when being moved or resized. The purpose of the grid is to help you align windows and give your Desktop a neat appearance. The granularity value is initially set to zero, but you can set it from 1 to 49, with each increment representing 8 pixels. (To get an idea of pixel size, note that the default border width is 3 pixels.) Just setting the grid to 1 makes it easier to align windows when moving or sizing them.

There is also an option in this box to change the border width of desktop windows. If you are having trouble differentiating windows on the desktop, you can increase their border width to make them easier to see or grab when resizing.

To set the Granularity and Border Width values, follow these steps:

1. From the Control Panel, open the Desktop dialog box.

2. In the Sizing Grid box, click the up-arrow button in the Granularity text box until the value is 5. This sets a grid that is 40 pixels wide.

3. Click the up-arrow button in the Border Width text box until the value is 5 pixels.

4. Click the OK button or press Enter.

At the desktop, notice that the window border is now wider. Now try sizing the Program Manager window with the mouse or keyboard. Notice that the window border snaps to the new grid pattern. In most cases, a grid pattern of this large size is only useful if you have a large monitor and are working in a higher resolution, such as 1024 × 768 pixels.

Setting the Cursor Blink Rate

Use the Cursor Blink Rate option to change the rate at which the cursor blinks. You can set the blink rate so that you can more easily find the cursor when editing documents in Windows Write, Notepad, or other Windows applications. Here's how to change the blink rate:

1. Open the Desktop dialog box in the Control Panel.

2. Click and drag the button in the Cursor Blink Rate slider bar. As you do, watch the blinking cursor on the right until it is blinking at the rate you want.

3. Click the OK button or press Enter to set the new blink rate.

Printers

The Printers icon is used to install and configure printers. You can also use it to select a different port for a printer, or to install new fonts. For a complete discussion of the Printers utility, refer to Chapter 12.

International

Use the International icon to set country-specific formats for elements such as date, time, currency, numbers, and keyboard settings used in Windows. The default settings are for the United States, so you won't need to make any changes to these settings unless you are using

Windows in another country or under other special conditions. The International dialog box is shown in Figure 6-8.

If you need to use different international settings, select your country from the Country list box. This updates all the other settings in the International dialog box. However, if you need to specifically customize the date, time, and currency formats, click the appropriate field in the dialog box and enter changes as necessary. To see how selecting a different country affects the other settings in the dialog box, try the following exercise:

1. Open the International utility by double-clicking its icon in the Control Panel.

2. The highlight is in the Country drop-down list box. Press the [Alt] key, and then the [↓] key on the keyboard. As you scroll through the list, notice the changes in the other fields and in the formats at the bottom of the dialog box.

3. To select a new country, highlight its name in the Country list box, and click OK or press [Enter]. To cancel the dialog box without changing the country, click the Cancel button or press the [Esc] key.

If your country is not listed in the Country list box, you can pick a country that has the most appropriate settings, and then make additional changes in the other fields of the dialog box to match the formats used in your country.

6

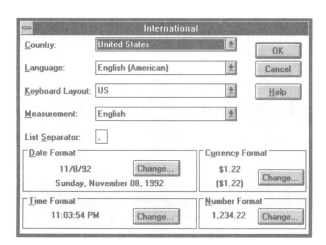

The International dialog box

Figure 6-8.

Keyboard

To adjust the operations of your keyboard, use the Keyboard icon on the Control Panel. You can adjust the delay, which is how long a key must be held down before it starts repeating, and the repeat rate, which is how fast the key repeats as you hold it down. To change the delay and repeat rate, follow these steps:

1. Select the Keyboard icon on the Control Panel, and you'll see this dialog box:

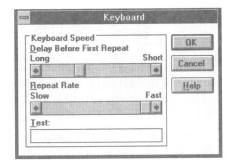

2. To adjust the delay interval, click the button in the Delay slider bar and slide it left or right.
3. To adjust the repeat rate, click the button in the Repeat Rate slider bar and slide it left or right.
4. Test the new settings by placing the cursor in the Test box and holding down a key.
5. Adjust the slider buttons until the settings are as you want them; then click OK or press [Enter] to save the changes.

Date/Time

To set a new date and time, select the Date/Time icon on the Control Panel. (If you worked through Chapter 4, you've already had the opportunity to change the date and time.) If you have a mouse, double-click the portion of the date or time that you want to change; then type a new value or click the up- or down-arrow keys on the dialog box. Click the OK button or press [Enter] to save the changes.

Installing Drivers

The Drivers utility is used to install new drivers as they become available. Many of the drivers are associated with Windows' multimedia capabilities. Double-click the Drivers utility to display the following dialog box:

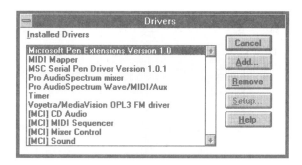

6

Note the following regarding the Drivers utility:

✦ Use Drivers to install preexisting drivers for sound cards, such as those listed in the previous illustration.

✦ Use Drivers to install the driver file supplied with a new hardware device you've attached to your system.

✦ Device drivers for a mouse, keyboard, display, and network, as well as international key code support, are installed with the Setup utility in the Program Manager Main group.

✦ Device drivers for printers are installed with the Printer utility.

✦ You must remove an existing driver before installing a new version over it.

TIP: If you have a CD-ROM drive, install the [MCI] CD Audio driver so you can play CD audio disks in the drive.

Adding a New Driver

Microsoft supplies some drivers for sound and MIDI (Musical
Instrument Digital Interface) devices on the Windows disks. Other
devices must be copied from disks supplied by manufacturers, or from
the Microsoft Driver Library (MDL). The MDL is available via modem
on the Microsoft electronic downloading service at (206) 637-9007, or
you can call Microsoft Customer Support at (800) 426-9400.

To install a new driver, follow these steps:

1. Open the Drivers dialog box.
2. If you are installing an updated version of a driver, highlight the
   existing driver and click the Remove button.
3. Click the Add button to display the following dialog box:

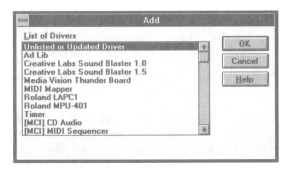

4. A list of available drivers on the Windows disk set is listed. Choose
   the driver to install and click the OK button.

To install a driver from a floppy disk, use the Unlisted or Updated
Driver option. In the remaining part of this example, the SPEAKER.DRV
file (available from Microsoft) is added to allow .WAV sound files to be
played on the computer's speaker.

5. Click the Unlisted or Updated Driver option in the Add dialog box,
   then click the OK button. The Install Driver dialog box appears,
   asking for the letter of the drive containing the driver disk.

6. Place the floppy disk in the appropriate drive and click OK. In a moment, the following dialog box appears, which lists the speaker driver (or any other driver you may be installing):

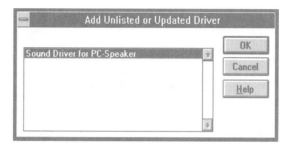

7. Choose the driver if it is not highlighted and click OK to install it.

6

Driver Settings

When a driver is installed, you may need to adjust some of its settings, such as the interrupts or I/O ports. Refer to the device's manual for details on how the settings should be made for your device. When installing the speaker driver, adjustments are made to its pitch and volume in a dialog box that appears after the driver copies to your system. You can change the setup for most drivers by highlighting the driver entry on the Drivers dialog box and clicking the Setup button.

NOTE: Once a driver is installed, you must restart Windows to enable it.

Sound

Use the Sound utility in the Control Panel to assign various .WAV file sounds to system events. Sounds play through an optional sound board such as the Creative Labs Soundblaster, or through your system's speaker if you have the SPEAKER.DRV file installed, as discussed in "Installing Drivers," earlier in this chapter. The following dialog box appears when you double-click the Sound icon:

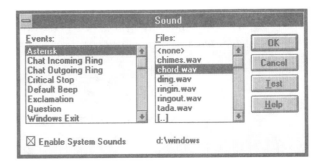

A list of events appears on the left and a list of sounds appears on the right. Do the following to assign a sound:

1. Click any event.
2. Click a sound to assign to it.
3. Click the Test button to hear the sound.
4. If you don't like the sound, try another. When all the sounds are the way you want, click the OK button.

Network

Use the Network icon to control your network connection settings in the Windows for Workgroup environment. You can change your logon name and the name that identifies your computer. You can also add yourself to a different workgroup or create new workgroups. Let's review these concepts before discussing the options on the Network dialog box.

Logon Name   When you start Windows for Workgroups, the logon dialog box appears as shown here:

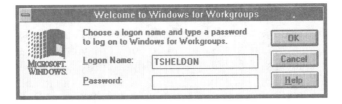

If you are the default user for a computer, your logon name appears in the Logon Name field of the dialog box. If you are not the default user, you must type your logon name in this field. The Network icon in the Control Panel is used to add new users for a computer or change the name of existing users. Your logon name is used to keep a log of passwords you use to access resources like directories and printers on other users' computers.

Computer Name   Every computer in the network has a specific computer name. You see these names when you attempt to connect with and share the resources of other computers, as shown in Figure 6-9. Note that computer names should be somewhat descriptive so users can easily determine exactly which computer to connect to. A name like "MY_COMPUTER" doesn't give other users a clue as to which system it is or what resources it has (CD-ROM, laser printer, and so on.). Instead, use descriptive names up to 15 characters long that define the office location or user of the system and possibly the resources attached to it. You can use the Network icon in the Control Panel to change a computer's name, as shown in Figure 6-10.

6

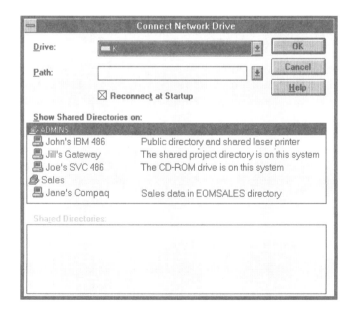

A list of computer names appears when you attempt to connect with other computers on the network.
Figure 6-9.

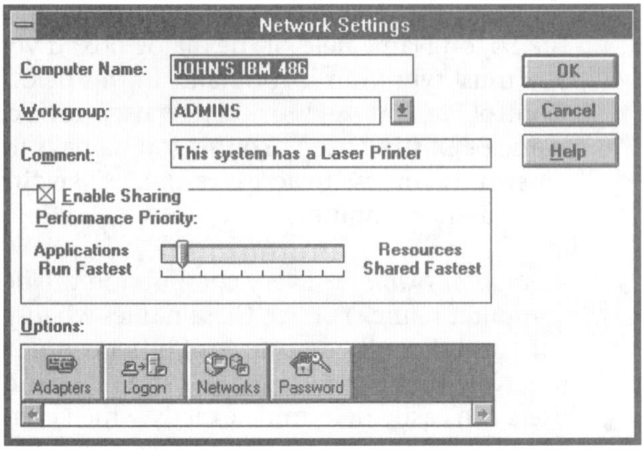

The Network
Settings dialog
box
Figure 6-10.

Workgroup   All computers on a network belong to a workgroup. On a small network, every computer may belong to the same workgroup, but on large networks, workgroups provide a way of organizing users and computers. For example, in a small workgroup, you would probably know exactly where a computer named "John's IBM" is located and what resources it has available. In a large organization, there are usually many Johns and many IBM systems, so it's necessary to organize computers into workgroups such as ACCOUNTING, SALES, DIVISION-A, SECOND-FLOOR, and so on. Then, if you want to access John's computer, you first specify the John in the ACCOUNTING group, not the John in the SALES group or another group. In Figure 6-9, note the two workgroups ADMINS and Sales. Each workgroup has a sublist of computers that you can access. If necessary, you can change the workgroup a computer belongs to by opening the Network utility in the Control Panel. So for example, if Jane moved from the Sales department to ADMINS, she or the network administrator would use the Network utility in the Control Panel to change her workgroup name.

Using the Network Utility

When you choose the Network icon in the Control Panel, a dialog box similar to Figure 6-10 appears. You can make the following changes on the dialog box:

Computer Name Field   Type in a new name for the computer. This name appears to other users when they attempt to access shared resources on the network. You should use a name that describes the computer and differentiates it from other computers on the network. It should help other users recognize the location of the computer or the resources it has to share. You can type up to 15 characters in the Computer Name field.

Workgroup Field   As mentioned previously, workgroups categorize the computers on a network to make network resources easier to find and select. For example, group all the computers in the accounting department in a workgroup called ACCOUNTING and group all the computers in the sales department in a workgroup called SALES. A user who needs to access accounting information, would scan the list of computers in the ACCOUNTING group. You can change the group a computer belongs to by selecting a new group from the drop-down list. You can also create a new group by simply typing its name in the Workgroup field.

6

Comment   You can type comments in this field to further expand the description of a computer and the resources it has. As shown in Figure 6-9, these comments appear when other users attempt to access the resources of other computers. They appear on the right in the Show Shared Directories On field.

Enable Sharing   This box is normally enabled, but you can unmark it to disable sharing on your system. Typically, you would disable sharing if you need to run an application that requires the full attention of your system's processor. When this box is disabled, other users can't access your system. Their access would slow your system down. When you're done running the special application, be sure to mark the Enable Sharing option so other users can access your system once again.

Performance Priority Slider   You can adjust the slider in the Network Settings dialog box to adjust how much of your system's processing time is given to your applications and how much is given to other users on the network when network sharing is enabled. If your applications seem to run too slow, adjust the slider to the left. If your system is primarily a server for other users, adjust the slider to the right to give those users more processing time. See Chapter 18 for more information.

Changing Logon Settings

You can change the logon settings of Windows for Workgroups by clicking the Log On button at the bottom of the Network Settings dialog box. The dialog box pictured here appears:

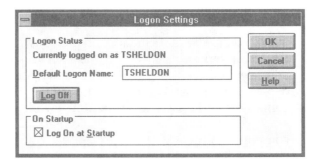

You can do the following activities in the dialog box.

The Log On Button   This button appears if you are currently logged off the network. You click it to log on.

The Log Off Button   This button appears if you are currently logged onto the network. To log off the network, click the Log Off button. You log off if you need to leave your computer for awhile and you don't want other users to access network resources under your logon name. Remember that your logon name has special access rights on other network computers that only you are authorized to have. If you don't log off, other users may access those resources using your logon name. Alternatively, you can exit Windows to log off the network, or install a password-protected screen saver.

Default Logon Name Field   The name specified in the Default Logon Name field appears on the logon dialog box when Windows starts. On computers that several people use, this name should typically be the name of the primary computer user, for convenience. If two or more people use the computer, specify the name of the user who logs on most frequently.

On Startup Field   The On Startup field lets you specify whether users log on when they start Windows, or later when they want to access the network. If this box is enabled, users log on when Windows starts. If this box is disabled, users must open the Network icon in the Control Panel, choose Logon, and click the Log On button that appears on the Logon Settings dialog box.

Changing Password Settings

You can change your password by clicking the Password button at the bottom of the Network Settings dialog box. The dialog box shown here appears:

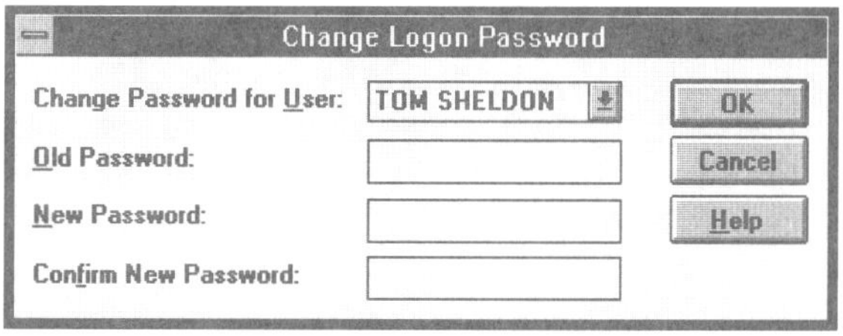

6

You type your old password in the Old Password field, then type a new password in the New Password field. Type the new password again in the Confirm New Password field.

System administrators who know a user's password can use this dialog box to change the password for the user.

386 Enhanced Mode

Windows can run in 386 enhanced mode on 80386 or 80486 systems. When Windows starts in this mode, a 386 Enhanced icon appears in the Control Panel. Clicking the icon displays this dialog box:

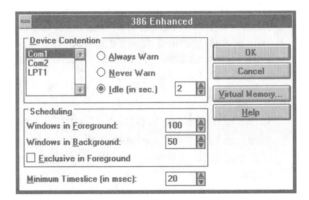

The Virtual Memory button is used to install or change the settings of
the swap file used to swap memory from RAM to disk. The dialog box is
used to set the following options for multitasking non-Windows
applications:

✦ *Device Contention*   These options set alarms that warn you when
   applications simultaneously access devices such as printers and
   modems. The warnings are designed to keep you aware of how
   applications are working in the background, so you can adjust other
   settings.

✦ *Scheduling Options*   These options specify the percentage of
   processor time used by applications in the foreground and
   background.

These settings are explained in Appendix B. If you need to multitask
non-Windows applications, refer to this Appendix for more
information.

CHAPTER

7 WORKING WITH FILES

Windows works together with the DOS operating system to manage, among other things, the files on your computer's hard drives. As you work with files in Windows, you must still follow the rules and regulations for DOS-level files, but Windows makes it easier to organize and use your files. This chapter discusses how the Windows and DOS file systems work together, and provides exercises to familiarize you with methods for listing, saving, and retrieving files in Windows. You'll also see how files are accessed on shared network computers.

DOS and Windows File Types

Files are collections of information, initially created in the memory of the computer, and then saved to a disk storage device. On DOS-based systems, directories are used to organize the hundreds of files that are typically stored on the hard drives and floppy disks. Directories give you a way to separate and organize your files into distinct groups, in the same way a filing cabinet uses drawers, hanging folders, and file folders to separate groups of files.

Keep the following guidelines in mind as you work with files in Windows:

✦ Files on the same disk or in the same directory must have unique names.

✦ Filenames consist of an eight-character name and a three-character extension, separated by a period. Similar types of files often have the same extension.

✦ Files are portable. They can be copied to other disks or directories.

✦ Files vary in size during their lives. When no longer needed, they can be deleted to make room for other files.

✦ The location of a file is important. You may need to specify its drive letter and directory name when accessing the file. This information is called the *search path* (or just *path*) to the file.

Files can contain many different types of information. The name of a file usually indicates what type of file it is, as discussed in the following section.

Program Files   *Program files* contain computer-readable code written by programmers. When you open and look at the contents of a program file, all you see is a string of code that looks like scrambled text. The names assigned to program files have *filename extensions* such as .COM and .EXE. These files are often called *executable* files, meaning that you can execute the program by typing its filename at the DOS prompt. Double-clicking a program icon in Program Manager executes a .COM or .EXE file.

Support Files   Some programs use auxiliary *support files* that also contain program code, but are not executable independently. Support files have filename extensions such as .OVL (overlay), .SYS (system), .DRV (driver), and .DLL (dynamic link library). You'll often see these files in the same directory as your program files.

Text Files   *Text files* contain readable, alphanumeric characters that follow the American Standard Code for Information Interchange (ASCII) format. These files are often called ASCII files and can be opened by a wide range of programs on many types of computers, not just those with DOS systems. Text files are easily transferred to other systems over a telephone line, using a modem.

Formatted Text Files   *Formatted text files* contain text and special codes that define how the text is formatted. They must be converted before you can open them in an application besides the one used to create them.

Graphics Files   *Graphics files* contain graphics information in several possible formats. The most common is the *bitmap* image format, which saves the actual dot-by-dot representation of the screen image. Other types of graphics files contain the actual series of commands used to create the image; when this type of file is opened, the commands are replayed to create the image.

Data Files   *Data files* contain information such as that created by a database or spreadsheet program. These files are readable only by the creating application, or by an application that can translate the information in the files to its own format. Data file information is separated in various ways to form the *fields* of a database or the *cells* of a spreadsheet. Common formats are comma-delimited files for databases, and SYLK (Symbolic Link) or DIF (Data Interchange Format) for spreadsheet data. Note that some data files may not contain special formats and are really simple text files.

NOTE: This book divides files into two broad categories: program files and document files. Applications like Windows Write and Notepad are stored on disk as program files. The files you create with these applications are document files, and may contain text, graphics, and other types of data. Document files are loaded into the workspace or document windows of Windows applications.

File-Naming Conventions

It is important to understand the conventions used to name and open files. Files within the same directory cannot have the same name, but you can use names that have characters in common as part of a strategy to keep your files organized. Windows gives you a warning message if you try to create a file with a name that's already in use.

The basic filename consists of an eight-character *name,* followed by a period and then an optional three-character *extension.* The filename may be fewer than eight characters, but any characters beyond the maximum eight are truncated. Here is a typical filename:

YOURFILE.TXT

Another important aspect of a filename is its location, or path. When referring to files not in the current directory, you need to include the drive and directory along with the actual filename. For example, if the YOURFILE file referenced previously were in the WINWORD directory on drive D, its complete path would be

D:\WINWORD\YOURFILE.TXT

Notice that backslashes are used to separate the directory and filename information, and a colon always follows the drive letter.

NOTE: In Windows, you don't need to type the drive and path. Instead, you typically choose them from drop-down lists.

When you connect your computer to a network, file-naming conventions change slightly. Every computer on the network has a *server name,* and each shared directory on the computer has a *share name.* When you need to refer to files on other computers, you specify the server name and share name, in addition to the filename. The format used to refer to a file on another network computer is as follows:

*servername**sharename**filename*

For example, to access a file called JANBUDG.WRK in the shared directory called DATA on the network computer called ACCTDEPT, you would specify the following filename:

```
\\ACCTDEPT\DATA\JANBUDG.WRK
```

As you'll learn later, it is possible to use these types of filenames in the File Open and File Save As dialog boxes of Windows applications that are compatible with Windows for Workgroups.

NOTE: For more information about file-naming conventions, refer to your DOS manual.

File-Naming Strategies

To keep your files organized and to help you remember the contents of files, it is useful to develop a strategy for naming your files. You can use the filename and its extension to describe a file's contents, the program that created it, and possibly the type of data in the file (text, graphics, or numbers).

7

Filename Extensions

Many programs automatically add a filename extension when you save a file. Table 7-1 lists the extensions attached to filenames by the Windows accessory programs. These extensions are used whenever you save a file, unless you specifically type a different extension after the filename. Notice that Paintbrush is capable of creating three different types of files, each with its own extension. You use filename extensions to list and work with specific files. For example, you could list all files with the extension .WRI to see the documents you've created in Windows Write.

Table 7-2 lists other extensions you can use when creating files with the Windows accessories or any other program. (These extensions are commonly used in the computer industry.) As with the accessories listed in Table 7-1, other Windows applications frequently add their own filename extensions to files you save. For example, Microsoft Excel spreadsheet files usually have the extension .XLS; Lotus 1-2-3 worksheet files may have the extension .WKS or .WK1.

Program	Extension	Meaning
Paintbrush	.BMP	New Paintbrush bitmap image
Paintbrush	.MSP	Old Paintbrush bitmap image
Paintbrush	.PCX	PC Paintbrush bitmap image
Calendar	.CAL	Calendar file
Clipboard	.CLP	Saved Clipboard image
Cardfile	.CRD	Index card file
Program Manager	.GRP	Group information file
PIF Editor	.PIF	Program Information File
Recorder	.REC	Set of Recorder macros
Notepad	.TXT	Notepad text file
Write	.WRI	Windows Write text file
Terminal	.TRM	Terminal phone list
Initialization	.INI	Windows initialization files
Sound Recorder	.WAV	Wave Sound files
Media Player	.MID	Midi Sound files

File Extensions Used by the Windows Accessories
Table 7-1.

Extension	Usage
.BAK	The backup version of an edited file (some programs create these automatically)
.BAT	Reserved for DOS batch files
.DAT	Commonly used for data files
.DTA	Another extension commonly used for data files
.DOC	Commonly used for document files
.HLP	Commonly reserved for help files
.MNU	Commonly used for menu files
.MSG	A message file
.TMP	Commonly used for temporary files

Common Filename Extensions
Table 7-2.

Associating Files and Programs   Filename extensions can help you locate the files created by a particular program. In fact, the extension is used to *associate* a document with the program that created it. You can double-click associated files to simultaneously start up an application and load the document into its workspace. If you save files with extensions other than those associated with the program, you'll need to create a new association. You learn more about associations in Chapter 9.

Filenames

The filename itself can be used to describe and categorize the contents of files. Try to create filenames that make sense to you and others. Names like NOTE.TXT and FILE.DOC are meaningless if you create dozens of notes and files because you'll soon lose track of their contents. A name like JANREPRT.TXT is a little better at describing the contents of a report file for January, but if you have several report files for January, you'll need to be even more specific.

A strategy for naming monthly report files created with Excel is listed here. The filename includes the report type and date of creation:

7

    RA92130.XLS (REPORT A, 1992, JAN 30)
    RB92130.XLS (REPORT B, 1992, JAN 30)
    RC92130.XLS (REPORT C, 1992, JAN 30)
    RA92228.XLS (REPORT A, 1992, FEB 28)
    RB92228.XLS (REPORT B, 1992, FEB 28)
    RC92228.XLS (REPORT C, 1992, FEB 28)

At first these filenames may seem cryptic, but consider the strategy: The R designates the files as reports (filenames containing budgets would start with B). The second letter indicates the type of report; here three separate reports are created at the end of each month (A, B, and C). Next comes the report date, followed by the .XLS extension added by Excel.

NOTE: In the foregoing strategy for naming files, putting the year first, then the month, then the day, for the report date makes it easier to list the files later.

Using Wildcard Parameters to List Files

Wildcard characters can be used as substitutes for any letter or group of letters when specifying filenames. The question mark (?) is used to represent a single character, and the asterisk (*) to represent two or more characters. Wildcards are typically used to list files at the DOS level, but you can also use wildcard characters when working with Windows dialog boxes and the File Manager.

Let's use the previous list of monthly report files as an example to see how wildcard parameters are used to specify files. If you specify RA*.*, all files that start with "RA" are listed:

    RA92130.XLS
    RA92228.XLS

The specification R???1*.* lists all files that start with "R" and that have a "1" (January) in the fifth position:

    RA92130.XLS
    RB92130.XLS
    RC92130.XLS

And the specification RA??1*.* lists only the "RA" file for January:

    RA92130.XLS

Notice how the ? serves as a placemarker; that is, any character may occupy its position. The *, on the other hand, is used to represent any group of characters in the filename, and the extension.

This next exercise will help you learn how to use wildcards. Start File Manager now by double-clicking its icon in the Main group of the Program Manager. When the File Manager window appears, follow these steps to view the files in the WINDOWS directory:

1. Click the C drive icon (or the drive where your Windows directory is located) to list the directories on that drive. You can also press the [Ctrl] and the drive letter keys on the keyboard to accomplish the same thing.

2. Point to the Windows directory icon in the tree listing on the left and click. The window on the right now lists the files in the Windows directory.

3. Now let's use wildcard characters to list files that have the .TXT extension. Choose By File Type from the View menu.

4. The By File Type dialog box appears. Notice that the Name field includes the ***.*** wildcard specification , which displays all files. If you execute the command with this specification in the Name field, you'll list all files. To list only files with the extension .TXT, type ***.TXT** in the Name field.

5. Click the OK button or press Enter.

A list of the files that have the extension .TXT is displayed. Notice that the title bar of the window includes the file specification *.TXT as a reminder of the file types listed in the directory window.

Use the foregoing procedure again, to list other groups of files. For example, type ***.EXE** in the Name box (Step 4) to list the Windows executable program files. Next, try entering **PROG*.*** to see files related to the Program Manager. Finally, put the ***.*** designation back in the Name box to display the complete list of files in the directory window.

7

Directory Concepts

Directories provide a way to separate files on hard drives in much the same way you would organize files in a filing cabinet. The following illustration shows a *directory tree* from the File Manager:

The top folder icon is the *root* directory. All disks and drives have a root directory, and all other directories on that disk or drive branch from that root. In the illustration you can see that the DOS and WINDOWS directories branch from the root directory; they are *subdirectories* of the root. The WINDOWS directory has two subdirectories of its own, SYSTEM and DESIGNER, and DESIGNER has a subdirectory called SAMPLES.

NOTE: The terms directory and subdirectory are often used interchangeably. You could say that the SYSTEM *directory* is a *subdirectory* of the WINDOWS directory.

As mentioned earlier in this chapter, in "File-Naming Conventions," you may need to specify the full path of a file when referring to a file outside of your current directory. For example, if a file named HOUSE.DRW is in the SAMPLES subdirectory of the previously illustrated directory tree, it has the path shown here (assuming it is stored on drive C):

C:\WINDOWS\DESIGNER\SAMPLES\HOUSE.DRW

In most cases, you won't need to type out such long path names when working with files. The Windows File Manager allows you to open two windows side by side to make copies of files between directories or do other work within directories. In other Windows applications, a dialog box helps you pick the drives and directories where files are located, as described later in this chapter.

Organizing with Directories

You can use directories to organize your files on disk. For instance, all related programs should be stored in their own directories, separate from other programs. This directory is usually set up by an application when you run its installation utility. In addition, it's a good idea to store the data files for an application in another separate subdirectory.

This prevents the data files from mixing with the program files, making it easier to find and list the data files for a particular program.

Backing Up Data Files   To make backup of critical data files easier, store those files in a separate directory. Then, when you need to back up the files, you simply back up the one directory. Consider the following illustration, which shows several data file subdirectories branching from the DATA directory:

This arrangement makes it easy to back up all the subdirectories that branch from DATA with a single command. Unlike program files, data files change constantly, so it makes sense to group and back them up together. It doesn't mean you should not back up program files, but you can typically do so less often. The directories that hold program files should be backed up after you've made important changes to their configuration or setup parameters. You'll then have a backup of your new setup, as well as the original program diskettes. But data files typically change daily, so it's a good idea to back them up as often as necessary. A subdirectory tree similar to that described above makes backup easy.

7

Using File Menu Options

In this section you explore the Windows commands and dialog boxes for opening, saving, browsing, and searching for files. What you've learned about files and directories so far in this chapter will help you access the common features of these commands. Their features are the same throughout a wide range of Windows applications, so you only need to learn them once.

For the exercises in this section, open Notepad by double-clicking its icon in the Accessories group of the Program Manager. When the

Notepad window appears, click the File menu option. The first four options on the File menu are used to open and save files in many Windows applications. What you learn about them in Notepad applies to other applications, as well.

The File New Option

Use the File New option to clear the screen of any existing work and begin a new file. If the existing work has not yet been saved, Windows will ask if you want to save it before clearing the screen.

Some applications, such as Word for Windows, let you open several documents at once. In this case, the workspace is not cleared when you select New. Instead, another document window opens for the new file. You can thus edit two documents at once, compare their contents, cut and paste text or graphics between them, and so forth. Keep in mind that each new document window requires additional memory, so the number of new document windows you can open is limited.

The File Open Option

The File Open option lets you open an existing file. Select Open on the Notepad File menu now, to display the Open dialog box shown in Figure 7-1.

The File Open
dialog box
Figure 7-1.

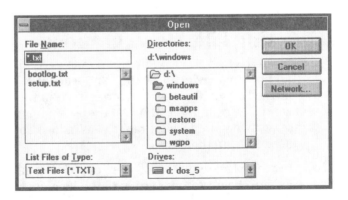

This dialog box has four areas where you can make selections or type text. If the file you want to open is in the current drive and directory, just type its name in the File Name text box and press Enter. To open a file on a different drive or in a different directory, first select a drive in the Drives list box and/or select a directory in the Directories list box. Later, you'll see how to open a file on a shared network drive by clicking the Network button. Changing the drive or directory causes a new list of files to appear under the File Name text field. You can then double-click one of the files to open it.

 NOTE: To narrow down the list of files, if you know part of the filename of the file you want to open, type a wildcard file specification in the File Name text field. This is discussed in greater detail in "Change the File Listing," later in this chapter.

The following steps outline a typical procedure for opening a file:

1. Choose Open from the Applications File menu.
2. Choose a drive in the Drives drop-down list box.
3. Choose a directory in the Directories list box.
4. Double-click the file you wish to open in the File Name list box.

The following exercises help you become familiar with the File Open dialog box and techniques you can use to search for and list files.

Pick a Drive

When you first see the Open dialog box, the highlight is in the File Name text box. Look at the Directories and Drives fields. They display the location of the files listed in the File Name field. If you need to look at files on other drives and directories, you'll need to change these fields. If the drive and directory are correct, type the name of the file you want, or select it from the File Name list box and click the OK button. In this exercise, you pick the drive where your WINDOWS files are located. Even if WINDOWS is already your current directory, work through this exercise for practice.

7

1. Click the down-arrow button in the Drives list box. You'll see a list similar to this one:

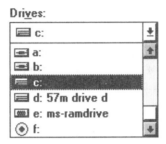

Drives:

- c:
- a:
- b:
- c:
- d: 57m drive d
- e: ms-ramdrive
- f:

2. Your current drive is highlighted. Scan through the list by clicking the arrow buttons on the scroll bar, then click the drive that contains your WINDOWS directory and files. If you're not sure, select drive C, then drive D and so on until you see the WINDOWS directory appear in the directory list.

Notice that the contents of the other fields in the dialog box change to reflect the contents of the new drive. You can follow this same procedure to list the files on a floppy disk or any other drive in your system.

NOTE: Of the icons in the previous illustration, drive E is a RAM drive, and drive F is a CD-ROM optical disk.

Pick a Directory

Before opening or saving a file, you always need to make sure you are in the correct directory on a drive. Though files in the same directory have unique names, two files in different directories may have the same name—they are distinct only because they are in different directories. Be sure the directory is correct before opening a file.

Just above the Directories list box you'll see the name of the current directory. To select a new directory with the mouse, double-click the directory's icon or name in the list box. If you can't see the directory you want, click the down-arrow button until the directory moves into view, and then double-click its icon or name. Try this:

1. Select the Directories list box by pressing [Alt]-[D].

2. Press the [↑] key on the keyboard until the root directory is highlighted, as shown here:

Note that the current drive is C in this illustration; your drive may be different if you chose another drive in the last exercise.

7

3. Press [Enter]. This changes the listing so it shows the subdirectories that branch from the root directory. You can also simply double-click the root directory icon. The Directories list box will now look similar to this:

Notice that the current directory is listed at the top as c:\ and its icon is an open folder.

4. Select the WINDOWS directory. (If you can't find the WINDOWS directory, you need to switch to the drive where that directory is located.)

Once you select the WINDOWS directory, a list of its subdirectories appears under its folder icon, and a list of files in the directory appears in the File Name list box.

Change the File Listing

Now you're ready to work with the File Name text box and list box. The previous exercises showed you how to use the Drives and Directories list boxes to make the WINDOWS directory the current directory. These next exercises assume you are still in the WINDOWS directory.

When you first bring up the Open dialog box, the highlight is in the File Name text box. Often you can type a filename and press [Enter] to load the file, assuming the drive and directory are set correctly. But if you're not sure of the filename and the list is long, you can type a wildcard file specification in the File Name text box to shorten the list and display files that closely match it.

NOTE: To open a file, you can also type in the full path and filename regardless of what directory or drive is showing.

Note that *.txt currently appears in the File Name text box because you're using Notepad, which creates files with the .TXT extension. This file specification automatically appears whenever you start Notepad. Other applications use different file specifications. For example, Windows Write creates files with the .WRI extension. When you first open Write's Open dialog box, the File Name text box contains *.wri, and files with this extension are listed in the File Name list box.

To change the File Name listing:

1. Make sure the highlight is still in the File Name text box. If it isn't, double-click the box.
2. Type *.**INI** in the text box and press [Enter]. A listing of .INI files appears, similar to the following:

File **N**ame:

*.ini
clock.ini
control.ini
excel.ini
fish!.ini
msd.ini
progman.ini
system.ini
win.ini

3. Press [Tab] to access the file listing. Note that the first file is surrounded by a dotted line.

4. Press the [↓] key on the keyboard until the file WIN.INI is highlighted or press W to quickly jump to that part of the listing. As you scroll, notice that each filename appears in the File Name text box.

5. Click OK or press [Enter] to open the WIN.INI file.

7

NOTE: The WIN.INI file, and other .INI files, contain Windows startup parameters that advanced users often edit using Notepad.

6. You don't need to have this file open now, so choose New from the Notepad File menu. This clears the workspace.

There are several other techniques for listing files. For instance, you can change the parameter in the List Files of Type text box, or you can specify other wildcard parameters in the File Name field. Try the following:

1. Choose Open from the File menu. In the Open dialog box, notice that the previous file specification is in the File Name text box.

2. Type **PROG*.*** and press [Enter]. You'll see the following listing:

File Name:

3. Try another wildcard specification, using the ? parameter, too. Type **???INI.***and press Enter. You'll see a list like this:

File Name:

4. Choose a file specification from the List Files of Type box. Click the down-arrow button in the field, and the following appears:

List Files of Type:

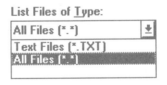

5. Highlight the All Files [*.*] option in the list. Press Enter, and you'll see the complete list of files in the WINDOWS directory.

In some applications, there may be more options in the List Files of Type box. For example, in the List Files of Type box for Paintbrush, shown next, you can choose from three different types of graphics files that Paintbrush can open:

List Files of Type:

BITMAP file (*.BMP; ±

BITMAP file (*.BMP; ↑
MSP file (*.MSP)
PCX file (*.PCX)   ↓

On the other hand, in Notepad, you won't be able to load all the files
you see listed with the *.* file specification. Because Notepad is a simple
text editor, you can only open text files, such as those with the
extensions .TXT, .INI, and in some cases .DOC and .DAT.

Accessing Network Files

Click the Network button in the Open dialog box to access files in
shared directories on other computers attached to the network. When
you click the Network button, the dialog box in Figure 7-2 appears.
Note that this same dialog box appears when you click the Network
button in Save As dialog boxes.

When you first open the dialog box, you'll want to focus on the list of
workgroups and computers in the Show Shared Directories On box. In
Figure 7-2, ADMINS is a workgroup and the computers listed under its
members. When you first open the Connect Network Drive dialog box,
you may only see a list of one or more workgroups. Double-click the
workgroup that contains the computer you want to connect to, then
choose the computer from that list.

7

NOTE: If you previously connected with a network drive, click the
down-arrow button in the Path field to see if it is listed there. Then
you can select it.

Follow the instructions below to connect with a directory on another
computer and access a file in that directory. Remember that these
procedures are similar if you are saving a file to a network drive.

1. Choose Open from the File menu of your application.

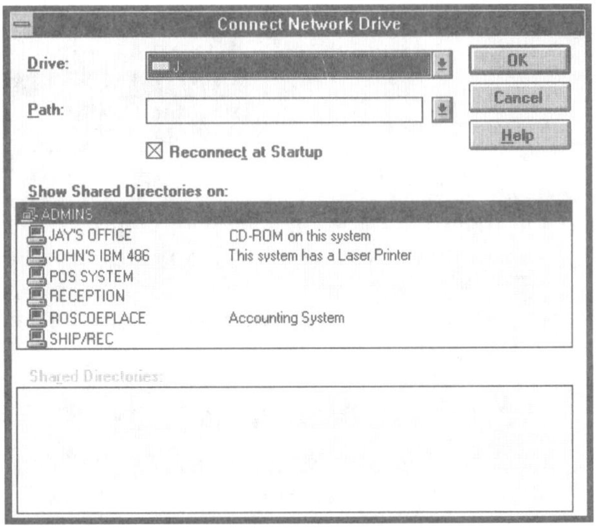

The Connect
Network Drive
dialog box
appears when
you click the
Network button
on Open and
Save As dialog
boxes.
Figure 7-2.

2. Click the Network button in the Open dialog box to display the Connect Network Drive dialog box similar to Figure 7-2.

3. If you can't see the list of computers for a workgroup, double-click the icon for the workgroup to display that list.

4. Double-click the icon of the computer you want to connect to. A list of shared directories on that computer appears in the Shared Directories box at the bottom of the Connect Network Drive dialog box.

5. Click once on the directory you want to access.

The servername and sharename of the directory now appear in the Path field of the Connect Network Drive dialog box. Clicking OK at this point will give you access to the files in the directory. However, you can make two further changes before doing so, but these are optional:

✦ *Choose a different drive* Click the down-arrow button in the Drive field to choose a different drive letter for the connected directory. Usually, Windows recommends the next available drive. For example, if you have two local hard drives (drive C and D), Windows will recommend drive letter E as the letter for the drive. This letter will appear in the Drives drop-down list box on the

Open menu the next time you need to access or save a file. In most cases, however, there is little need to change this drive letter.

✦ *Reconnect at Startup*   Make sure this option is enabled if you want the network drive connection available the next time you start the application(s). Even if you exit Windows, the drive connection is reestablished the next time you start the application.

After you have set all the options on the Connect Network Drive dialog box, click the OK button. The Open dialog box reappears with the new drive letter and name listed in the Drives and Directories fields. You can now choose a file on the shared directory from the list in the File Name field that contains the computer you want to connect to.

Double-click a workgroup icon to see a list of computers in that workgroup. In Figure 7-2, the computers under the ADMINS workgroup are displayed.

7

The File Save Option

The File Save option is used to save a file using the name that appears in the title bar. This assumes you previously saved the file and assigned a name to it using the Save As option. If you choose Save, and the file has not yet been named, the File Save As dialog box appears.

NOTE: Keep in mind that the Save option saves changes without asking for verification. In most cases, this will be fine, but there may be times when you want to load a file, edit it, and then save it under a different name. You should then use the Save As option to rename the file before saving it.

Some applications have a Read Only check box that you can mark to force a file to be saved under a different name, thus preserving the original. Alternatively, you can mark files as read-only using the Properties command in the File Manager to prevent them from being altered. Files that are used in this way are often referred to as *template* files.

The File Save As Option

The Save As option on the File menu is used to save a file for the first time and specify its filename. It also lets you save an existing file under a new name. The File Save As dialog box has the same features as the File Open dialog box, including the network button which lets you save files on network computers with shared directories. You type the new name for the file in the File Name text box, and specify the drive or directory in which you want to store the file in the Drives and Directories boxes.

The following exercise will familiarize you with the Save As box:

1. Open Notepad if it is not already open.
2. Type your name at the flashing cursor in Notepad's workspace.
3. Choose the Save As option in the File menu, or press [Alt]-[F][A]
4. When the Save As dialog box opens, notice its similarities to the File Open dialog box. This is the common Windows dialog box format that you'll see in many other applications.
5. Type **NAME.TXT** in the File Name text box, and click OK or press [Enter].
6. Choose New from the File menu to remove the NAME.TXT file from the screen.
7. Type some other text, such as the make of your car, and select the Save As option again.
8. Type **NAME.TXT**, and click OK or press [Enter]. In a moment, the following dialog box appears:

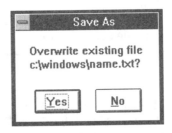

Because NAME.TXT already exists, Windows warns you that you're about to overwrite an existing file.

9. Click the No button, or press [Alt]-[N]

When you select No in answer to the "Overwrite...?" prompt, the Save As dialog box remains active, so you can try a different filename. Notice that the File Name list box contains grayed-out filenames. You can scan this list to see what filenames are already in use, and avoid any conflicts. In addition, this list is helpful when you're saving files that follow a naming strategy. You can display the file list to remind you of the naming scheme, or to see what names are already in use. Or you might need to choose an option in the Save File As Type field to see a different list of files.

You're now at the end of this tutorial. You can click the Cancel button or press the [Esc] key to close the Save As dialog box, and then close Notepad or reduce it to an icon for future use.

7

CHAPTER

8 ORGANIZING APPLICATIONS

In this chapter, you learn how to organize the applications, utilities, accessories, and other program items in the Program Manager. You'll see how to create new startup icons and group windows, and rearrange startup icons into new groups that best fit the way you work. You'll use some of the techniques you learned in previous chapters to resize windows and move them to other locations. In this way, you create an arrangement that shows only the icons that you want to see and hides those you don't often use.

Creating a New Group

To have easy access to the applications and documents in your system, it's a good idea to arrange them according to your work habits. Windows lets you move a program icon into another existing group, or create new groups as you need them. For example, you can organize all of the applications and tools that you use for writing into a window called "Writing Tools," and all the applications and tools that you use to create pictures and art into a window called "Drawing Tools."

Figure 8-1 illustrates two groups that contain *document startup icons*. When you set up document icons (described in "Creating a Document Icon," later in this chapter), double-clicking an icon starts the program represented by the icon itself, and loads a document represented by the name under the icon. Creating group windows such as these improves your access to the files you work with regularly. Note that the DAILY group has startup icons for business and personal appointment calendars, a Notepad TIMELOG, and a Notepad DAILY file. The COMPANY NEWSLETTER group includes startup icons for many different files and programs that you might use when creating a newsletter.

The initial organization of the icons in the Program Manager window may very well be helpful as you're learning to use Windows, but eventually you'll find it beneficial to reorganize these icons to fit your personal taste and the way you work. The following exercise demonstrates how to create a new group window and add program items to it.

Groups help
organize the
way you work
Figure 8-1.

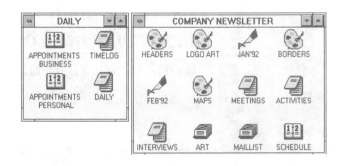

Creating a New Group Window

This exercise shows you how to create a new group window using the New command on the Program Manager File menu. The group will be named Everyday Tools.

1. Choose New from the Program Manager File menu. This opens the New Program Object dialog box, shown here:

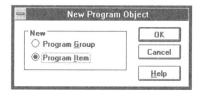

2. Click Program Group (if it is not already selected) to indicate that you want to create a group, not an icon for a group.

3. Click the OK button or press [Enter] to display the Program Group Properties dialog box:

8

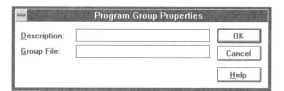

4. Start with the blinking cursor in the Description text box, and type **Everyday Tools**

NOTE: Leave the Group File box blank; Windows supplies this using the first eight characters from the Description box. The group file will hold information about the group, such as its name and the icons it contains.

5. Click the OK button or press [Enter].

When the dialog box closes, the Everyday Tools group appears in the Program Manager as an empty group window. Now you're ready to add program startup icons to the new group.

Copying Program Items to a New Group

Now that the group window exists, you can add application and document icons to it. In this next exercise, you copy existing application icons from the Main and Accessories windows to the Everyday Tools window.

Start by considering which Windows applications and accessories you'll want to include in the Everyday Tools window. For this example, let's copy the File Manager, Control Panel, Print Manager, Write, Paint, Calendar, and DOS Prompt icons to the new window. Later you can add other icons to the group to fit your needs.

The easiest way to copy icons from one window to another is by dragging them with the mouse. However, if you prefer to type the destination group name, you can use the Copy command on the Program Manager File menu. To copy an icon from the Main group to the new Everyday Tools group, follow these steps:

1. Open the Main group window. Make sure you can still see at least a part of the Everyday Tools window, so you can click it later to select it. (You could resize both windows and place them side by side, but it is not necessary for this operation.)

2. Press the Ctrl key, and then point to the File Manager icon in the Main group. Click and drag the icon to the Everyday Tools group while holding down the Ctrl key. A copy of the icon now appears in the new group.

CAUTION: If you fail to hold down the Ctrl key while dragging, the icon will be moved, not copied. Moving an icon removes it from the source group and places it in the destination group.

3. Repeat Step 2 and copy the Control Panel icon to the Everyday Tools group.

Now try the keyboard method. Copy the Print Manager from the Main group to the Everyday Tools group, as follows:

1. Make the Main group active by pressing ⒜lt–Ⓦ and choosing it from the Window menu.
2. Use the arrow keys to highlight the Print Manager icon.
3. Press ⒜lt–Ⓕ Ⓒ to choose Copy from the Program Manager File menu. Note that the resulting dialog box describes the operation you are performing, as shown here:

4. Press the ⏷ key until the Everyday Tools group name appears in the To Group box, and then press Ⓔnter.

8

On your own, copy the DOS Prompt, ClipBook Viewer, Mail, and Schedule+ icons in the Main group window to the Everyday Tools group, using either the mouse or the keyboard method described previously. Next, copy the Chat, WinMeter, and Net Watcher icons from the Accessories group to the Everyday Tools group. First open the Accessories group, and then use the mouse or keyboard method to copy the icons.

Resizing and Arranging the New Window

Once you've finished copying the icons as described in the previous paragraphs, close the Main and Accessories windows; then follow these steps to resize and move the Everyday Tools window:

1. Click the Program Manager Options menu; if the Auto Arrange feature is not checked in the drop-down menu, enable it now.

2. Resize the Everyday Tools group window to fit around its icons. Point to a border or corner of the window, then click and drag. The icons will rearrange as you change the window's size.

3. Move the resized window to the upper-left corner of the Program Manager.

The Everyday Tools window should now look like Figure 8-2.

Saving Arrangements

Once you've arranged Program Manager, you need to make sure the new arrangement is available the next time you start Windows. To immediately update the changes, hold down the (Shift) key and choose Exit from the File menu. You won't exit Windows, but your changes are saved for your next session.

Creating New Program Item Icons

In this section, you'll create icons for program items, using the New command on the Program Manager File menu. In addition, you'll learn about using the Setup utility to automatically search your hard drives for applications and create startup icons for them.

The resized, rearranged Everyday Tools group
Figure 8-2.

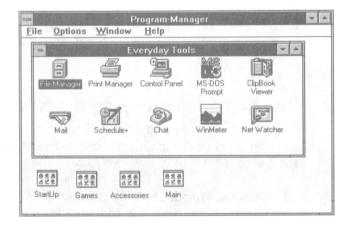

The New Option

The New option on the Program Manager File menu is used to create new program item icons, as well as new groups. In this example, you create a new program startup icon in the Main group window for a program called SYSEDIT. This program resides in the directory named \WINDOWS\SYSTEM and is used to edit your system startup files and the Windows startup files.

Follow these steps to add the new startup icon:

1. The Main group window was minimized in the last exercise, so activate it now by double-clicking its icon.

NOTE: To add a program item to a group, you must first make the group active.

2. Choose New from the File menu to open the New Program Object dialog box.

3. This time you are creating a new program item icon, so click the Program Item button; then click OK (or press Enter). You'll next see the following Program Item Properties box (which is described in the next section):

8

Working with the Program Item Properties Box

The text boxes of the Program Item Properties box allow you to describe to Windows all it needs to know about a new program item. In most cases, you don't need to fill out all the fields, but you'll find examples of all of them as you work through this section. Below are descriptions of each box and button in the dialog box.

Description   In the Description box, type the name you want to appear under the icon or in the title bar of the window that runs the program.

Command Line   In the Command Line box, type the name of the executable (.EXE or .COM) file used to start the program, with a drive letter and path if necessary. Optionally, you can include the name of an associated file to load with the application when it starts, thus creating a document icon. Recall that a document icon starts an application and loads an associated document file into its workspace. If you don't know the name of the file, you can click the Browse button in this dialog box (explained shortly) to activate a search.

Working Directory   In the Working Directory box, type the name of the directory where you want the application to open and save files. The program itself doesn't have to be in this directory, but it will access files in this directory while it runs. Use this field to specify a data directory that separates the files created by the application from other data files.

Shortcut Key   In the Shortcut Key box, specify a keystroke used to start the application. For example, you could assign the keystroke Ctrl-Alt-W to an icon for a word processing program. Note that keystrokes must include either Ctrl-Alt or Ctrl-Shift-Alt. In the Shortcut Key text box, if you type a single character such as W, Ctrl-Alt will automatically be added, making the shortcut key Ctrl-Alt-W. Press Shift and a letter to create a Ctrl-Shift-Alt keystroke.

Run Minimized   Check the Run Minimized box if you want the application to reduce to an icon on the desktop whenever the program starts. This is useful if you have set up the application to start when you turn your system on, but you don't always use it right away.

Browse   If you don't know the name of the executable file to enter in the Command Line field, press the Browse button to open a dialog box so you can search for the file.

Change Icon   Use the Change Icon button to select an icon to use for the program.

To complete the creation of the SYSEDIT startup icon, indicate the Description and Command Line properties of the program item, as described in the following:

1. The blinking cursor should be in the Description field. If it isn't, click the text box or press [Alt]–[D].

2. For Description, type **SYSEDIT**. This is the name that will appear under the icon.

3. Press [Tab] to jump to the Command Line text box. Here you need to specify the command that starts the SYSEDIT program. If you know the drive, directory, and filename where the program is stored, you can type them in the Command Line field. Or you can browse the files on your hard disk to locate the .EXE or .COM file, as discussed next.

Browsing for the Filename

8

NOTE: As you work through this exercise and some of the others that follow, you'll notice that Windows programs and accessories open and save files in the Windows directory—this happens unless you indicate otherwise. As you know, this book assumes your Windows directory is C:\WINDOWS. However, if you've installed Windows on another drive, or are accessing it from a network drive, you'll always need to specify the appropriate drive and directory. As you work through the remaining exercises in this chapter, you'll be reminded when it's important to include the correct path.

The Browse button in the Program Item Properties box is a handy tool—it lets you locate the .EXE and .COM files in your system. The Browse dialog box has the same features as the Open dialog box you learned about in Chapter 7. This exercise will step you through its use; if you need more information, refer to Chapter 7.

NOTE: Although .EXE and .COM files are generally selected in the
Browse dialog box to start programs, .PIF files (discussed in
Appendix B) and .BAT files (discussed in your DOS manual), can also be
selected. In addition, you can list and select an associated document file
using the Browse dialog box.

1. From the Program Item Properties dialog box, click the Browse
   button, or press ⁅Alt⁆–⁅B⁆. You'll see the dialog box shown in Figure 8-3.

2. In Figure 8-3, the files in the Windows directory are listed when
   you first open the dialog box. If you're not sure where your own
   Windows files are located, here's your chance to find out. The path
   to these files will be displayed above the Directories list box in
   your Browse dialog box, and you should write this down for future
   reference, especially if it is a path other than C:\WINDOWS.

3. In the Directories list box, note the subdirectories that branch
   from the Windows directory. In this example, you need to access
   the SYSTEM subdirectory, so look for the SYSTEM subdirectory
   icon, and double-click it with the mouse. This displays a listing of
   executable files for that subdirectory.

4. Drag the slider button in the File Name scroll bar until you see the
   filename SYSEDIT.EXE, and click that filename.

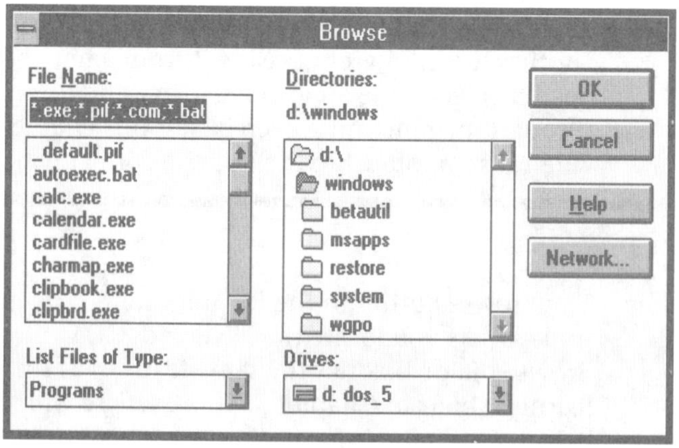

The Browse
dialog box is
used to locate
.EXE and .COM
files to assign to
program item
icons

Figure 8-3.

Browse		
File Name:	**Directories:**	OK
.exe;.pif;*.com;*.bat	d:\windows	Cancel
_default.pif	📁 d:\	Help
autoexec.bat	📂 windows	Network...
calc.exe	📁 betautil	
calendar.exe	📁 msapps	
cardfile.exe	📁 restore	
charmap.exe	📁 system	
clipbook.exe	📁 wgpo	
clipbrd.exe		
List Files of Type:	**Drives:**	
Programs	💾 d: dos_5	

5. Click the OK button or press ⏎ Enter. This inserts the path and filename of the SYSEDIT.EXE file into the Command Line field of the Program Item Properties dialog box.

NOTE: The Browse dialog box also has a Network button, as discussed in Chapter 7. You can click this button to create startup icons for programs or documents on the shared directories of network computers.

Selecting the Icon

Now choose an icon for the SYSEDIT program.

1. In the Program Item Properties dialog box, click the Change Icon button, or press Alt – I. Here is the Change Icon dialog box:

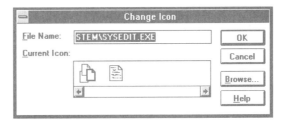

2. Two icons are shown in the display area for SYSEDIT. Double-click the icon on the left.

NOTE: Later you'll learn how to choose from a larger list of icons.

Completing the Task

There are several other items in the Program Item Properties dialog box that you might need to designate for some programs, but not for

8

SYSEDIT. For example, there is no need to mark the Run Minimized box because SYSEDIT is a utility that you'll normally use as soon as you start it. Also, a working directory is not required because SYSEDIT uses files in the root and Windows directories only.

NOTE: You can add a shortcut key by clicking in the Shortcut Key box and typing **S** or some other letter.

To complete the creation of the SYSEDIT icon, click the OK button or press Enter, and the icon appears in the Main group window. To test your new icon, double-click it with the mouse or press the shortcut key you assigned. Once you've made sure your icon works, you can close SYSEDIT again—you won't need it until a later chapter, when you modify the startup procedure of your computer and Windows.

Creating a Document Icon

A *document icon* is a program item icon that starts an application and loads a document in that application's workspace, in one step. This section shows you how to set up a document icon in the Everyday Tools group; but first, you create a document to associate with the icon, as discussed next.

Creating the Time Log Document

The Notepad accessory has a unique time logging feature that inserts the date and time in a file every time you open it. You can use this feature to create a date/time-stamped log of notes or events. Follow the steps here to create the time log file:

1. Activate the Accessories group in Program Manager by double-clicking its icon, or choose its name from the Window menu.

2. Start Notepad by double-clicking its icon.

3. When the Notepad window appears, type **.LOG** on the first line. Do not include spaces or tabs before this entry, be sure to include the period, and use all capital letters for LOG.

4. Save this file by choosing the Save As option from the File menu.

5. When the Save As dialog box appears, type **TIMELOG** in the File Name text box, and make sure the Windows drive and directory are selected in the Directories field. Click OK or press ⌷Enter⌷ to save the file.

Every time you open the TIMELOG file, the time and date will be inserted after the last line. You can then type a note or record of some activity under the time stamp. Now add some notes to this "diary" file.

6. Select the Notepad File command and choose Open on the menu.

7. Type **TIMELOG** in the File Name field, and click OK or press ⌷Enter⌷.

8. Under the date and time entry, type the following text:

   This is an exercise for Windows 3.1 Made Easy.

9. Press ⌷Alt⌷–⌷F⌷ ⌷S⌷ to save the file.

10. Repeat these steps to add a few more lines to the TIMELOG file, and get an idea of how the file will look after you've opened it several times.

8

TIP: The Notepad time log is an excellent tool for those who need to track their time for billing or record-keeping purposes, or for keeping track of telephone calls. The icon you're about to create will make the file easy to access.

Creating the Document Icon

Now you're ready to create a document icon for the TIMELOG file in the Everyday Tools group window. Follow these steps:

1. Move the Notepad window out of the way for now by clicking its Minimize button.

2. Activate the Everyday Tools group in the Program Manager by clicking it or choosing it from the Window menu.

3. Select the File command and choose New from the File menu.

4. When the New Program Object dialog box appears, select Program Item and click OK. You'll then see the Program Item Properties dialog box (shown previously in Figure 8-3).

5. The blinking cursor will be in the Description text box; type **TIMELOG** as the name to appear under the icon.

6. Click in the Command Line box, and type the following command (assuming the file is stored in the Windows directory):

   NOTEPAD.EXE TIMELOG.TXT

NOTE: Because TIMELOG.TXT is associated with Notepad, you could type just TIMELOG.TXT. This example shows how you would type a startup command for a non-associated document. In addition, it is important to enter the command as shown here because you will work with this entry again later in this chapter, in "Changing the Properties of a Group or Icon."

7. Click OK to execute your entries, and the new TIMELOG icon will appear in the Everyday Tools group window.

The command you typed in the Command Line field first loads Notepad, and then opens the TIMELOG.TXT file. Note that the name of the file is specified as a parameter after the program name. Now try opening the time log again, by double-clicking the new TIMELOG icon. You'll see your time log file, with the latest time and date inserted in the bottom line.

Using the Setup Utility to Create Startup Icons

The Windows Setup utility offers yet another way to create startup icons for applications. You are probably already familiar with Setup from the installation routine. Another task Setup can do for you is search your hard drive for executable files and create startup icons for those it finds. You usually do this for DOS-based programs since most Windows-based programs install their own icons during setup.

Start the Setup utility now by double-clicking the Setup icon in the Main group window of the Program Manager. You'll see a window similar to this one:

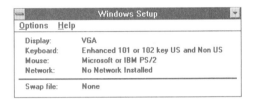

Follow these steps to create a new application startup icon using Setup:

1. Select Options, and choose Set up Applications to display the following dialog box:

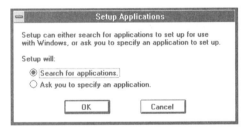

2. Select the button marked "Search for applications," and then click the OK button.

TIP: If you just need to set up one application, select the button marked "Ask you to specify an application," then specify the path and name for the application startup file.

Setup now will do all the work of searching for the applications on your hard drive. (The other button in the Setup Applications dialog box works similarly to the Browse button in the Program Item Properties box.) Next, you'll see the following dialog box:

8

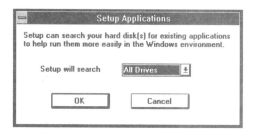

3. Click the drives to search and/or click Path to search the directories specified on the DOS path. More than one option can be selected.

NOTE: Searching the path is often the most efficient way to have Setup do a search, but the programs must be on the path.

4. You'll see the Setup Applications dialog box; it will look like Figure 8-4 with a different listing of files.

On the left of the Setup Applications dialog box is a list box containing filenames of applications that are not currently set up as program item icons. (Every system is different, of course, and your list will represent what's available on your computer.) In the list box, choose the programs you want to add to Program Manager. For example, if your system runs with DOS 5, you'll probably see QuickBASIC in the list box, and you can select it. Continue with the program setup process:

A Setup
Applications
dialog box
Figure 8-4.

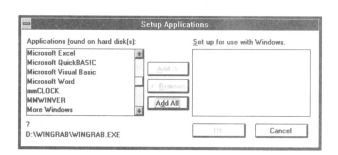

5. Click to select the filenames of the applications you want to add to Program Manager, and click the Add button. The applications then appear in the list box on the right. To add all the applications, click the Add All button.

If you've selected an item on the left and you decide you don't want to add it, simply click it again to deselect it. If you've already moved an item to the right list, and you don't want to install it, select the item, then click the remove button.

6. When you are done selecting applications, click OK or press ⟨Enter⟩.

Windows Setup will create icons for the applications you selected, in a group called Applications or a group called Non-Windows Applications. You can open these groups now to see where your new application icons appear.

Other Program Manager Options

In this section, you learn how to change the properties of existing groups and program items, how to delete program items, and how to make applications start every time you start Windows.

Changing the Properties of a Group or Icon

The Properties option on the Program Manager File menu is used to change the properties of the selected group or program item icon. You work with the same Program Item Properties box that you use for adding a new group or icon (Figure 8-3). Remember these guidelines:

✦ To change the properties of a group, it must first be reduced to an icon; otherwise, Program Manager assumes you want to change a program item icon in the group window.

✦ Group properties that you can change include the group's name and the name of the group file.

✦ Program item properties that you can change include all those that were available when you created the item, including the item name, command line, working directory, icon, and shortcut key.

In this exercise, you change the properties of the TIMELOG icon you created previously.

1. Click the TIMELOG icon in the Everyday Tools group window.
2. Select the Program Manager File command, and choose Properties from the File menu.

The Program Item Properties dialog box is displayed, and includes the information you entered when creating the TIMELOG program item. One property you can change is the command line. Previously, you typed NOTEPAD TIMELOG.TXT in the command line field, but since files with the .TXT extension are associated with Notepad, they automatically load into its workspace. For future reference, you can leave out Notepad from the command line. Try this now by making the following changes:

3. Double-click the Command Line text box with the mouse.
4. Type **TIMELOG.TXT**. (Make sure you include the .TXT extension; without it, the file will not load.) Press ⏎Enter to accept the new field text, but don't click OK yet. Leave the Properties box open for the next exercise.

Creating a Shortcut Key

A *shortcut key* makes it possible to start an icon from the keyboard. This is convenient if the icon's group is not open or visible. Try adding a shortcut key to the TIMELOG icon.

1. In TIMELOG's Properties box, click the Shortcut Key field.
2. Press ⓣ to make Ctrl-Alt ⓣ the shortcut for opening the TIMELOG file.
3. Do not click OK yet; leave the Program Item Properties dialog box open.

Notice that when you press ⓣ, Windows inserts CTRL + ALT + T in the Shortcut Key text box. Shortcut keys use the Ctrl-Alt and Ctrl-Shift-Alt key combinations to avoid conflicts with other Alt-key assignments used by Windows. Write the shortcut key on a list for future use.

Changing Icons

The startup icon suggested for the TIMELOG file is the same icon used for Notepad. However, because in this case you are configuring a document icon to load a specific document (the time log) into Notepad's workspace, you'll want to change the icon to look more like a document. Here's how to change the icon:

1. Click the Change Icon button; this displays the Change Icon dialog box.

In the Change Icon dialog box, the File Name field contains the name of the Notepad executable file. Notice that only one icon is displayed in the Current Icon display area. Most programs written for Windows contain at least one icon, but some provide several. In this case, there isn't much of a selection, but you can "borrow" an icon from another application by typing the application's filename in the File Name field. In the remainder of this exercise, you use the Browse button to find the PROGMAN.EXE file in the Windows directory and borrow an icon from that program's extensive list.

2. In the Change Icon dialog box, click the Browse button to open the Browse dialog box. You'll see a list of files in the Windows directory.

3. For future reference, let's look at the icons available in the MORICONS.DLL file. Select MORICONS.DLL, and then click OK. The Change Icon window returns, with a large list of icons as shown next. Use the scroll bar to scan the list.

8

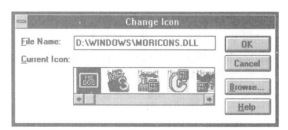

4. Scroll through the list by dragging the slider button right, then left.

5. To see a more generic assortment of icons, click the Browse button again, then click to select PROGMAN.EXE (Program Manager), and click OK. The assortment of icons in the Current Icon display area now displays the following:

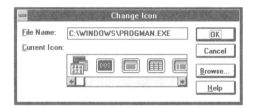

6. Scroll left and right through the display. One excellent use for TIMELOG is to track telephone calls, so select the telephone icon by double-clicking it. The new icon now appears in the lower-left corner of the Program Item Properties box.

7. Click OK or press Enter to save all the changes you have made to the TIMELOG icon in the last few exercises.

Defining a Working Directory

Most of the applications and accessories that come with Windows automatically open and save files in the Windows directory. However, you've learned how saving document files in separate directories is a practical way to organize your hard disk—for example, you might create a directory called DOCS for Write document files, and another called ART for Paintbrush files. The Working Directory field in the Program Item Properties dialog box lets you specify the directory where an application will open and save its files.

To see how this works, let's start the DOS Prompt to see what its default working directory is, and then return to Windows and change that directory.

1. Double-click the DOS Prompt icon in the Main group of the Program Manager. (You may have moved this icon into your Everyday Tools group; if so, double-click it there.)

2. You'll now see the name of the Windows directory. (If you don't, type **PROMPT pg** at the DOS prompt and press Enter.)

When you work at the DOS level, it's likely that you'll want to work in a directory other than Windows. To redefine the DOS Prompt icon so it opens to another directory, do the following:

3. Type **EXIT** at the DOS prompt to return to Windows.
4. Make sure the DOS Prompt icon is highlighted, then select the Program Manager File command and choose Properties from the File menu.
5. Click the Working Directory text box and type **C:\DOS** (or type the path of a directory you want to use when you start the DOS Prompt).
6. Click OK or press Enter to save the changes.
7. Double-click the DOS Prompt icon again. When the DOS prompt appears, the DOS directory will be the active directory.

You can make similar changes to your other program items to ensure that files created with those programs are stored in specific directories. For example, create a directory called \DOCS, then change the Working Directory property of the Write icon to \DOCS. Then, the files you create with Write are automatically stored in that directory.

8

Deleting a Program Item or Group

The Delete option on the Program Manager File menu is used to delete the currently selected group or program item.

NOTE: A group must be reduced to an icon before it can be deleted.

CAUTION: Deleting a group also deletes any program item icons within the group. If you want to save any of the items, move them to another group before deleting the group.

To delete a program item or group, first reduce it to an icon, and highlight the icon. Press the Del key or choose Delete from the File menu. Windows displays a message box asking if you really want to delete the icon. Answer Yes to go ahead with the deletion, or No if you change your mind.

The Startup Group

The Startup Group has special significance in the Program Manager: any program item copied to this group will automatically start when Windows starts. Open the Startup Group now to see if it contains any program item icons. If you worked through the exercises in Chapter 2, the File Manager icon should be in the group. You can use this next exercise to add some other icons to the Startup Group:

1. If the File Manager icon is not included in the Startup Group, copy it there now by dragging its icon from the Main group. *Make sure to hold down the* Ctrl *key while dragging the icon.* This makes a copy of the icon in the Startup Group and leaves the original icon in the Main group.

TIP: It's better to copy icons to the Startup Group rather than move them there. If you ever need to close an application that started automatically with Windows, restarting the application will be easier when its icon is in a familiar group like Main or Everyday Tools. Typically, you leave the Startup Group reduced as an icon during your Windows sessions, so it isn't as readily available.

2. Copy the Clock icon from the Accessories group to the Startup Group, pressing Ctrl as you drag.

3. Copy any other icons for applications you want to start whenever Windows starts.

Now you need to make sure the applications in the Startup Group reduce to icons on the desktop when they start, because it's unlikely you'll need to use all of them immediately after your system starts.

4. Click and highlight the File Manager icon in the Startup Group.

5. Click the File menu option in Program Manager and choose Properties in the File menu.

6. When the Program Item Properties dialog box appears, mark the Run Minimized box.

7. Repeat these steps for the Clock and any other icons you may have copied into the Startup Group.

Chapter Wrap-Up

Now that you've made changes to the Startup Group and to other Windows settings, you can try exiting Windows and then restarting it. Before doing so, however, make sure to save any changes you've made. Hold down the [Shift] key, then choose exit from the File menu. The next time you start Windows you'll see all the changes you made, including icons on the desktop for programs you added to the Startup Group.

Notice that the Clock displays the correct time, even when minimized to an icon. You can leave it minimized all the time if you don't mind looking at the time in such a small format. If you can't make out the time, try changing the display by choosing Analog or Digital on the Clock's Options menu. If you still can't read the display, just open the Clock window and resize it to any size you like.

8

CHAPTER

FILE MANAGER, PART I: FEATURES AND OPTIONS

File Manager is a Windows program that lets you display and work with the drives, directories, and files on your local hard disk or on the hard disks of shared network computers. If you are familiar with DOS, you'll find most of the commands you normally use to copy, rename, delete, and manipulate files, but presented now in a graphical interface which is much more intuitive than the DOS command line. In addition, File Manager has added many features that make it easier to list files and select the ones you want to work with. You can manage these files in a number of ways, the most important of which are listed here:

✦ Copy and move single files or groups of files by clicking and dragging their icons to other drives or directories.

✦ Delete or rename files or groups of files.

✦ Start executable program files by double-clicking their icons.

✦ Open documents by double-clicking their icons.

Of course, File Manager has many more features that you'll learn about as you read through this chapter and Chapter 10. You read about some of these features in Chapter 4, but here in Chapter 9 are more thorough explanations. It is assumed you have an understanding of the file and directory concepts discussed in Chapter 7.

The File Manager Window

The first time you start File Manager, it looks similar to the window pictured in Figure 9-1. (If your File Manager screen looks different, don't worry—in a moment you'll get a chance to restore the File Manager default settings.) Like the Program Manager, File Manager holds document windows within its borders, but in File Manager these windows are called *directory windows* because each displays the contents of a single directory. Directory windows have the following features:

✦ The *menu bar* has menu options for working with files and changing the features of File Manager.

✦ The *drive icon bar* depicts each of the floppy drives, hard drives, RAM memory drives, and network drives available to File Manager.

✦ The *Toolbar* gives you push-button access to the most popular menu options, and you can customize it to fit your own needs.

✦ The *directory tree* depicts the directories on the drive that is currently selected in the drive icon bar.

✦ The *contents list* shows the files for the directory selected in the directory tree.

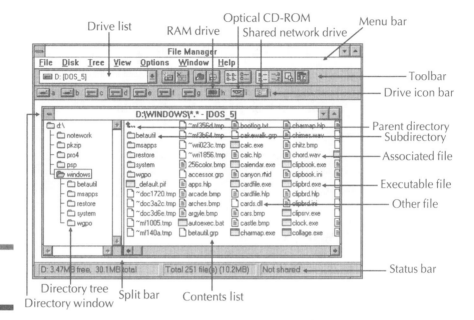

The File
Manager
Figure 9-1.

+ A *split bar* separates the directory tree and contents list. You can
  click and drag the split bar left or right to enlarge either side of the
  directory window, or you can remove the split altogether and
  display only directories or only files.

+ The *status bar* displays important information about the selected
  drive, such as the number of files and their total disk space.

Restoring File Manager Default Settings

The following steps restore the File Manager default settings so you can
work through the exercises in this chapter. You'll rename the
WINFILE.INI file in the Windows directory, which holds the
configuration information File Manager reads every time it starts. This
information includes the size of the window, the settings on the
Options menu, and the contents of directory windows. When the file is
renamed, File Manager won't find it and will thus create a new file
using default settings.

1. First make sure the Save Settings on Exit option is not enabled. Open the File Manager Options menu; if the Save Settings on Exit box is checked, click it to turn it off.

2. Select File, and choose Rename from the File menu.

3. When the Rename dialog box appears, type the following in the From text box. (If your Windows directory is on a drive other than C, replace C in the entry with the correct drive letter.)

   C:\WINDOWS\WINFILE.INI

4. In the To text box, type the following, again substituting the appropriate drive letter if necessary.

   C:\WINDOWS\WINFILE.TMP

5. Exit File Manager, and then restart it by double-clicking its icon in the Program Manager.

File Manager now creates a new WINFILE.INI file with the default settings.

You're now ready to continue with the exercises in this chapter. After you finish the chapter, if you want to restore the previous settings, first delete WINFILE.INI, and then rename WINFILE.TMP to WINFILE.INI using the Rename command on the File menu. However, this chapter shows you how to create your own arrangements, so you might not want to restore your old settings.

Customizing File Manager

You can customize File Manager in a number of ways. For example, you can change the fonts that display filenames, turn the status bar on or off, or change the way File Manager asks you to confirm your commands. The options discussed in this section are on the File Manager Options menu.

Suppressing Confirmation Messages

When you delete or copy files in File Manager, warning messages appear asking you to confirm your actions. If you feel these confirmation messages are unnecessary, you can use the Confirmation option on the Options menu to turn some or all of them off. Choose Confirmation now to display the following dialog box:

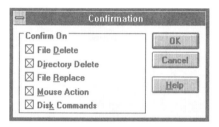

Marking these check boxes controls confirmation messages for the following operations:

Option	Operation
File Delete	Deleting files
Subtree Delete	Deleting directories and subdirectories
File Replace	Overwriting a file that already exists
Mouse Action	Copying and moving files using mouse click-and-drag techniques
Disk Commands	Disk-management commands such as FORMAT

If you are a new user, leave all these options checked until you become more familiar with File Manager operations.

Controlling File Deletions

In some cases, it's advantageous to temporarily turn off a confirmation request. For example, you can disable the File Delete confirmation when you're deleting large groups of files and you're sure it's safe to delete all the files. *Be sure to turn the option back on,* so you'll be cautioned as usual when deleting files in the future.

Another way to control file deletion confirmations is in the Confirm File Delete dialog box. For example, when the File Manager File Delete confirmation option is turned on, you see a dialog box similar to the following when you try to delete a group of files:

9

You can click the Yes to All button if you're sure the remaining files should be deleted. Or you can selectively delete individual files by clicking the Yes or No buttons as this confirmation box appears for each file. Click Cancel to keep the remaining files and stop the delete command.

Changing Fonts

To change the font used to display filenames in directory windows, choose the Font option on the Options menu. You'll see the Font dialog box shown in Figure 9-2.

Here's how to change the font:

1. In the Font list box, use the scroll bars or arrow keys to scroll through, and click the font you want to use.

2. In the Font Style list box, choose a style for the font you want to use.

The Font dialog box is used to change the file listing text in a directory window to another font, style, and size **Figure 9-2.**

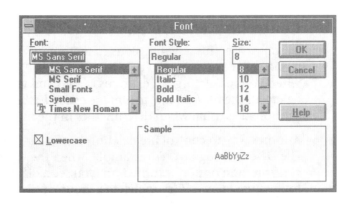

3. Choose a font size in the Size box. Keep in mind that large fonts reduce the total amount of information you can see in the window.

4. If you prefer uppercase letters, click the Lowercase check box to turn this option off.

5. A sample of your selected font appears in the Sample box at the bottom of the dialog box. To see what the font looks like in the File Manager listing, click the OK button or press Enter to accept your selection.

Displaying the Status Bar

The status bar at the bottom of the File Manager window displays the following useful information about disk space and file sizes for the currently selected disk:

✦ When a directory is selected, you'll see information about the drive at the left of the status bar, and about the directory at the right of the status bar.

✦ When a file is selected, the status bar tells you the size of the file.

✦ When multiple files are selected, the status bar indicates the number of files and their total number of bytes.

You can turn the status bar off and on by choosing Status Bar from the Options menu. Turning the status bar off is not usually necessary unless the desktop is so crowded that you need to make the File Manager window as small as possible.

9

Displaying the Toolbar and Drive Icon Bar

If you need more room to work in the File Manager, you can turn off both the Toolbar and drive icon bar by disabling the Toolbar or drive icon bar options in the Options menu. However, disabling these options is not recommended.

Minimizing File Manager on Use

When the Minimize on Use option is enabled, File Manager reduces to an icon whenever you double-click an application startup file. To see how this works, try the following exercise:

1. Select Options, and click the Minimize on Use option to turn it on.
2. In the File Manager directory tree, click the Windows directory (if it is not already selected).
3. Locate CARDFILE.EXE in the file listing for the Windows directory, and double-click the icon. This starts the Cardfile application and minimizes Program Manager to an icon.
4. Close Cardfile now to save memory.

If you want the Program Manager to minimize in this way whenever you start applications, keep the Minimize on Use option marked; otherwise, click it again to disable it.

Save Settings on Exit

When the Save Settings on Exit option on the Options menu is enabled, any settings you make during a File Manager session are saved for the next session. Settings that are saved include the marked options on the Options menu, changes to directory windows and their contents, and the rearrangement of directory windows within the File Manager. You can click this option now if you want to save the settings you make while working through this chapter.

When the Save Settings on Exit option is on, any windows that are open when you exit File Manager will be reopened in the next File Manager session. Usually, this isn't a problem; however, to avoid screen clutter in the next session, you may want to close any unnecessary windows, or any windows you don't want reopened, before you leave File Manager or disable the Save Setting on Exit option. You can save any new arrangements you make by holding the Shift key and choosing Exit from the File menu. This saves the new arrangement but doesn't actually exit Windows.

Working with Directory Windows

The first time you start File Manager using its default settings only one directory window is open, and it fills the entire File Manager window as shown in Figure 9-1. You can open additional directory windows to display files on other drives and directories.

Opening Another Directory Window

Multiple directory windows are opened to display the contents of several drives and directories. To set up a new directory window, do the following:

1. Choose New Window from the Window menu.

2. Choose Tile from the Window menu to arrange the two windows. Notice the title bar in each window indicates the current directory, but the original window is labeled 1 and the new window is labeled 2.

3. In the upper window, click the DOS directory, or any other visible directory.

TIP: A quick way to open a new directory window is to double-click the drive icon for another directory window. A new window for that drive appears.

The Split Bar

9

Within the directory window, the split bar divides the directory tree and the contents list. Drag the bar to the left to provide more space for file listings in the contents list, or to the right to get a wider view of the directory tree when necessary. You can also remove the split altogether, and display only the directory tree or only the file listing.

To drag the split bar and change the allocated space for either side of the window, click and hold the bottom of the bar and drag it with the mouse. Note that when the mouse pointer is over the split bar, it changes to a double-headed arrow, as shown here:

In one of the windows you now have open, try moving the split bar to the left so you can see more files in the contents list.

NOTE: You can also move the split bar by choosing the Split option on the View menu, and then using the ⊣ or ⊢ key to move the split bar.

To remove the window split entirely, select the View menu, and choose Tree Only to display only the directory tree, or Directory Only to display only files for a selected directory. Here's an example of a window that displays only the tree; the window has been resized, and all branches of the tree have been opened.

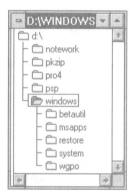

Here's an example of a directory window that shows the file list only:

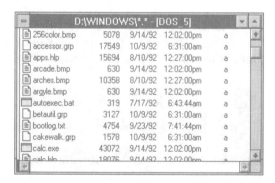

Note that files are listed vertically, along with size and creation date information. Later in this chapter you'll learn how to customize the file listings.

Arranging Windows

When more than one directory window is open, you can rearrange them by using the Cascade and Tile options on the Window menu, or by dragging them with the mouse. You can also minimize them, as shown in Figure 9-3.

Directory window icons take on the name of the directory they list, as well as the type of files listed. The icon itself indicates the listing method. In Figure 9-3, the left icon lists the root directory tree only, the middle icon lists files only from the Windows directory, and the right icon lists both the directory tree and files from the HPFAX directory. Note the difference in the icons and the names under the icons.

9

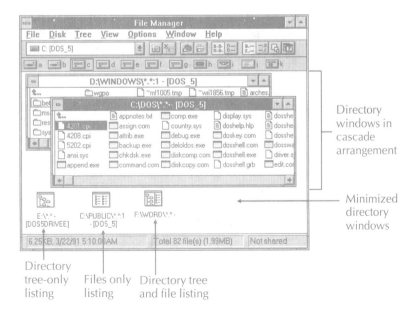

Directory windows in cascade arrangement

Minimized directory windows

Minimized directory windows
Figure 9-3.

Directory tree-only listing   Files only listing   Directory tree and file listing

Windows Refreshment Time

No, it's not time to take a break. The Refresh option on the Window menu is used to update the list of files in a directory window in the following situations:

✦ To update the list of files for a floppy disk drive after changing the floppy disk in the drive

✦ When you've performed a file operation outside the File Manager that affects the file list, and the list has not yet been updated in the directory window

✦ When you restore a minimized directory window and you want to make sure its file list is current

✦ To update network drive file lists

Climbing the Directory Tree

The directory tree displays the directories and subdirectories of the currently selected drive. To select a different drive, click one of the drive icons at the top of a directory window. On a network, some drive icons will represent shared directories on the network or directories on the file server of a NetWare network.

To display the list of files in another directory, click that directory icon in the directory tree. Alternatively, if the highlight is in the directory tree, press the arrow keys on the keyboard to scroll through the tree. As each directory is highlighted, its files are listed in the contents list. When a directory has branching subdirectories, use one of the methods described next to access files in the subdirectory.

Expanding and Collapsing Branches

The following exercise demonstrates how you can expand and collapse the directory tree. Before you begin, make sure the Windows directory is displayed in a directory window. If it isn't, click the directory window you want to use, or choose New Window from the Window menu. Next, click the icon of the drive that holds the Windows directory, and then click the Windows directory icon.

When a drive contains many directories and directory levels, the entire tree may not fit in the window. By collapsing the directory tree, you display only certain levels of files. You can shrink the tree by collapsing the entire tree or by collapsing specific branches.

1. Collapse the entire directory tree by double-clicking the root directory icon.

2. Double-click the root directory icon again to expand the branch. Now the first level directories branch from the root, similar to the directory tree shown here:

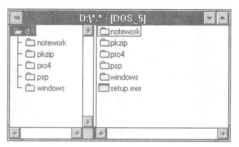

Note that the directory list will display few if any files for the root directory in most cases. The root directory usually only holds the startup files and all other directories branch from it.

3. Click the root directory icon. To see another way to collapse a directory, press ⊟; then press ⊞ to expand it.

4. To display the branching subdirectories of the Windows directory, double-click its directory icon, or highlight it and press ⟨Enter⟩. The System directory and possibly others will appear, depending on your setup.

5. Click the System directory icon, or press the ⬇ key to select it. The files of this directory are displayed in the contents list on the right.

6. Now close the directory tree under the Windows directory. You can do this any of three ways:

   ✦ Double-click the Windows directory icon.

   ✦ Highlight the Windows directory and press the minus (⊟) key.

   ✦ Highlight the Windows directory, select Tree from the menu bar, and choose Collapse Branch.

9

7. Now expand the entire directory tree. Select Tree and choose Expand All, or press Ctrl-*. When a directory tree is completely expanded, as many branches as will fit in the window are displayed.

8. Try collapsing a few branches by double-clicking the directory at the top of each branch.

Indicating Expandable Branches

Expanding the entire directory tree is a convenient way to see all directories and branching subdirectories for the selected drive. However, if the list is long, you can't see the entire tree, and you'll need to scroll through it using the arrow keys or the scroll bar.

The Indicate Expandable Branches option on the Tree menu provides another way to view the directory structure. Selecting this option causes a plus sign to appear in the icons of directories that have branching subdirectories, or a minus sign when the directory is already fully expanded. In this way, you don't need to expand every branching subdirectory to know that subdirectories exist. The following exercise demonstrates this feature.

1. Double-click the root directory to collapse it, or highlight it and press the minus (-) key.

2. Select Tree, and choose Indicate Expandable Branches from the Tree menu.

Plus signs appear in the icons of directories that have branching subdirectories that you can expand. Minus signs appear in the icons of directories that are already expanded.

TIP: The Indicate Expandable Branches feature is a remnant of Windows 3.0, and causes File Manager to run more slowly. If you don't need this feature, turn it off.

Working with the File List

The File Manager lets you select files from a list and then execute commands that affect the selected files. The following sections help you learn how to manipulate the file lists in directory windows. First let's examine the options on the View menu that let you change how files are listed.

Changing the File View

The File Manager View menu lets you change the way files are listed in the contents list. Here is the View menu:

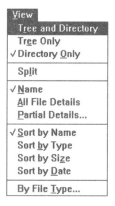

The first four options were discussed previously. This section is concerned with the remaining options on the View menu.

The options are also available by clicking the buttons on the Toolbar shown here:

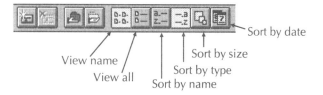

9

Showing File Details

The Name, All File Details, and Partial Details options on the View menu or Toolbar let you change the amount of information displayed about each file. You can display just the filename in a directory window, or you can also display the following information:

✦ The size of the file in bytes

✦ The date the file was created or last modified

✦ The time the file was created or last modified

✦ The *attributes,* or "status flags" of a file, which indicate if it can be changed and erased, or if it has been backed up

Let's display some additional information for the files in the Windows directory.

1. Click the Windows directory icon in a directory window.

2. To display detailed information about each file, click the View All File Details button on the Toolbar. The file information is listed in rows, like the listing in Figure 9-4.

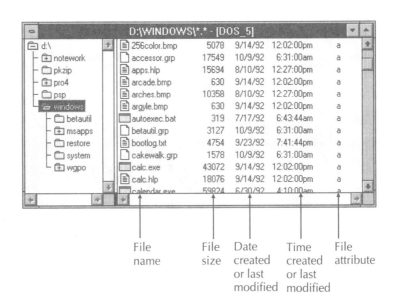

The All File Details display for files

Figure 9-4.

The first column lists the filename and shows its icon. The second column shows the size of the file in bytes. The third and fourth columns list the date and time the file was created or last modified. In the last column are the current attributes of the file, which are flags that designate the read and write status of a file (see "Viewing and Changing File Properties" later in this chapter), and whether it has been backed up.

Customizing the File Details Listing

Typically, the All File Details option is preferred for listing information about files. Sometimes, however, you'll need to make a directory window as small as possible. If so, select the Partial Details option on the View menu to select which file details you want. Choose this option now, and you'll see the following dialog box:

If you previously selected All File Details, all of the options in the Partial Details box will be marked. To turn any option off, click its check box, and then press the OK button. This removes the items from the file list, and you can reduce the size of the window accordingly.

Sorting the File List

The four Sort By options on the View menu or Toolbar change the order in which files are listed. This makes it easier to see and select groups of related files. Here are the Sort By options:

◆ *Sort By Name* is the default option. Files are sorted by the first eight characters of the filename.

♦ *Sort By Type* arranges files by their filename extension. For example, all executable (.EXE) files are listed together, all Write (.WRI) files are listed together, and so on.

♦ *Sort By Size* puts files in size order, with the largest file first. This option is useful when you need to find and delete large files to make room on a disk.

♦ *Sort By Date* lists files together by date; this may be the date they were first created or the date they were last modified. Files with the most recent creation or modification date are listed first, and the oldest files are last. You can scroll to the bottom of the list to see if there are any old files that need to be deleted.

Listing Specific Files

You can use the By File Type option to specify exactly which files you want to list, using wildcard characters or special check-box options. Choose the By File Type option on the View menu to display the following dialog box:

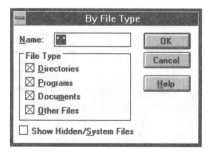

The Name field is highlighted when this dialog box first opens. To see how wildcard characters are used to display specific file groups, try this next exercise. Before you begin, make sure the Windows directory is still the current directory.

1. In the Name text box, type ***.TXT**, and press Enter to list all files with the extension .TXT.

2. Choose the By File Type option again. This time type ***.BMP** in the Name field, and press Enter to list Paintbrush bitmap files.

3. Choose the By File Type option once again. Type ***.EXE** in the Name field, and press (Enter) to list the program files with the extension .EXE.

4. Click the DOS directory icon in the directory tree. Notice that for this directory, too, .EXE files are grouped and listed in the contents list. You can use this trick when you're looking for specific files in various directories: click the directory icons one after the other (or use the Search command).

5. Choose the By File Type option one more time, type the wildcard characters ***.*** in the Name field, and press (Enter). This specifies that all files with all extensions should be displayed.

Now try selecting some of the options in the File Type box of the By File Type dialog box. You use these options to specify exactly the type of files you want in a listing. Each option is defined here:

✦ *Directories* Check this box to include the names of any subdirectories that branch from the current directory in the file listing.

✦ *Programs* Check this box to include executable files with the extensions .EXE, .COM, .BAT, or .PIF in the file listing.

NOTE: If you want to start applications from the File Manager by double-clicking their icons, you'll need to mark the Programs option so that executable files for the programs are listed.

9

✦ *Documents* Check this box to include associated document files in file listings. (Recall that associated files are those created by Windows accessories or associated with a Windows application. You can double-click associated files to open the application and the associated file in one step.)

✦ *Other Files* Check this option to list all files not included in the previous options.

◆ *Show Hidden/System Files* Turn on this option when you want to display files with the Hidden or System attribute. DOS creates these files and typically hides them in directory listings at the DOS level to prevent them from being accidentally deleted by users. Though you can display these files in a directory window, there is little reason to do so since they are rarely changed, moved, or deleted.

Try choosing each of these options, and various combinations of them, in the By File Type dialog box to see how the file list is affected. For example, consider this combination:

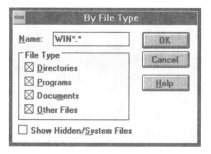

This displays all files with the first three characters WIN. Now choose the By File Type option again, and set it as shown here:

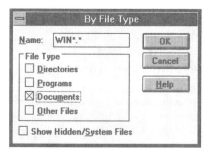

This setting reduces the file list further, displaying the WIN files only if they are also associated document files.

Selecting Files

Before you can execute a File command, you need to highlight files for the command to act upon. You'll use the selection techniques when working with file commands in Chapter 10. In the exercises that follow, you select files in the Windows directory, so begin by specifying the file listing you want, as follows:

1. Open the View menu, and choose the By File Type option.
2. Type ***.*** in the Name field.
3. Mark all the File Type boxes.
4. Click the OK button or press ⏎Enter⏎.

NOTE: Keyboard methods for selecting files are not covered in this section. For a list of keyboard selection techniques, refer to the File Manager Help window.

Selecting Contiguous Files

Contiguous (adjacent) files are easy to select. Simply click the first file you want to select, hold down the ⏎Shift⏎ key, and click the last file. If the last file you want to select is not visible in the window, you can scroll the list. The following exercise demonstrates this selection technique:

9

1. Rearrange the contents list by clicking the Sort by Type button. Notice that files with the extension .BMP are listed near the top.
2. Click the first .BMP file in the list.
3. Press and hold the ⏎Shift⏎ key, and then click the last .BMP file in the list. If you have a long list of bitmap files, it may be necessary to scroll down the list using the scroll bar. Don't worry if the first file you selected scrolls out of sight; all files in between it and the next file you click will be highlighted and selected, as long as you keep the ⏎Shift⏎ key depressed when you click.

TIP: To quickly jump to a file in a list, type the first letter of the file's name.

Selecting Noncontiguous Groups of Files

When the files you want to select as a group are not listed together, but scattered throughout the file list, they are referred to as *noncontiguous* files. Sometimes you can't group these noncontiguous files using the Sort By options or wildcard characters, but you can still select them as a group. To do this, hold down the Ctrl key as you click the icon of each file you want to select. Try these next two exercises to see how this works:

1. The .BMP files should still be selected from the last exercise. Select View and choose Sort By Name to list files in filename order. Notice that the .BMP files remain selected, even though they are no longer listed contiguously.
2. Select some other files. Hold down the Ctrl key and click several scattered .EXE files in the list, such as CARDFILE.EXE and PBRUSH.EXE.

Selected files remain selected until you click another file without holding down the Shift or Ctrl key. Files also remain selected as you scroll through the file list looking for other files to select. Try the following exercise to select scattered executable files.

1. Scroll to the beginning of the list. Click the first .EXE file you see, which should be CALC.EXE. Notice that the files you selected previously are no longer selected when you click this new selection.
2. Hold down the Ctrl key and continue selecting other .EXE files, scrolling through the list as needed. Files remain selected as you scroll through the list.
3. Add a contiguous group to the noncontiguous selections you just made. With the .EXE files still selected, hold down both the Ctrl *and* Shift keys, and click another file in the list. All files in between are added to the current selection list.

Deselecting Files

If you change your mind about selecting a file, you can easily remove it from the selected group (deselect it), by pressing the Ctrl key and then clicking the file's icon. Similarly, you can deselect a whole group of selected files by holding down the Shift key and clicking the files' icons. These techniques are handy because it is often easier to select a large group of files and then deselect one or two that you don't want than it is to select all the files you want individually. Try this method in the following example:

1. Scroll to the beginning of the contents list, and click the first file.

2. Hold down the Shift key and click the last file you can see in the window. This selects all the visible files in the window.

3. Hold down the Ctrl key and click some files at random within the selected group. This deselects the files.

4. Hold down both the Shift and Ctrl keys, and click a selected file. All files between this and the last file selected are thus deselected.

Using the Select Files Option

The Select Files option on the File menu provides a versatile alternative to selecting files by clicking them with the mouse. Choose Select Files to display the following Select Files dialog box:

9

To select files using the Select Files dialog box, type a file specification in the File(s) text box, using wildcard characters. Initially, the specification *.* is suggested in this field, but you can type over it. These next steps help you practice with this dialog box:

1. If files are currently selected in the contents list, deselect them by clicking the Deselect button in the Select Files dialog box.

2. Double-click in the File(s) field, type *.**EXE**, and press the Select button. All executable files in the directory window will be highlighted.

3. You can continue to add more selections. For example, double-click in the File(s) field and type *.**BMP**, then click the Select button.

NOTE: The Set Selection dialog box can be closed and reopened without losing your current selection of files in the contents list.

4. Click the Close button to close the Set Selection box; the files you selected remain selected.

5. Scroll to the beginning of the list.

6. Now deselect all files that start with C. Choose Select Files from the File menu, type **C*.*** in the dialog box, and press the Deselect button. Filenames starting with C are deselected.

TIP: Use the Select Files option whenever you know the filenames or extensions of the files you want to select. Use the mouse selection methods (described in the previous section) when you don't know the filenames or you prefer to scroll through the file list and search for files. You can also combine both selection methods.

The Toolbar

The Toolbar contains a set of push buttons that you can click to quickly execute various menu commands. File Manager has a set of default buttons (as shown in Figure 9-1) that you can use to share and connect with network drives or to change the way files are displayed in directory windows. You can, however, change these buttons to suit your own needs as discussed in this section.

To change the Toolbar, choose Customize Toolbar from the Options menu or double-click the Toolbar background. The dialog box in Figure 9-5 appears. On the left in the Available Buttons box is a set of buttons you can add to the Toolbar. On the right in the Toolbar Buttons box are the current Toolbar buttons. You simply click the button you want to add in the Available Buttons box, then click the Add button to move it to the Toolbar Buttons box. When you click the OK button, the new button is added to the Toolbar.

Scroll through the Toolbar Buttons box to see that it is in the same order from top to bottom as the buttons in the Toolbar are listed from left to right. Also notice the Separator option, which places a space between the buttons on the Toolbar.

Adding a New Toolbar Button

Let's walk through the process of adding a new button to the Toolbar. In the following exercise, you'll add a button that opens the Search dialog box so you can search for files on your local hard drive or on the network.

1. Double-click the Toolbar background to open the Customize Toolbar dialog box.

2. Select the position in the Toolbar Buttons list where you want to place the new button. Remember that this list is displayed left to right on the Toolbar itself. If you want the new button all the way to the right on the Toolbar, scroll to the bottom of the list and click the last item, which should be a separator.

9

The Customize Toolbar dialog box is used to change the buttons on the Toolbar
Figure 9-5.

3. If you want a separator space between the existing Toolbar buttons and the new Search button, double-click Separator at the top of the Available buttons list.

 NOTE: You can also single-click an item in the Available Buttons list, then click the Add button to add it to the list on the right.

4. Scroll through the Available Buttons list box until you see the File—Search button, which has a "binoculars" icon.
5. Double-click the File—Search button to add it to the Toolbar Buttons box on the right.
6. Click the Close button to add the File—Search button to the Toolbar.

The Search button now appears on the File Manager Toolbar. To add more buttons, follow a procedure similar to the one above. If you run out of space on the Toolbar, you'll need to remove some of the buttons, as described next.

Removing Toolbar Buttons

If you run out of room on the Toolbar, or simply never use some of its buttons, you can remove them by following the procedure below. The first method can be executed without opening the Customize Toolbar dialog box.

1. Hold down the (Shift) key.
2. Click the button you want to remove and drag it off the Toolbar. When you release the mouse, the button is removed.

The next method is performed from the Customize Toolbar dialog box. This method is best if you are adding and rearranging other buttons on the Toolbar in the same session.

1. Double-click the Toolbar background to open the Customize Toolbar dialog box.

2. Scroll through the Toolbar Buttons list until you find the button you want to remove.

3. Double-click the button, or click it once and click the Remove button.

4. Click the Close button. The button is removed from the Toolbar.

Rearranging the Toolbar Order

You can rearrange the order of the buttons on the Toolbar by following the steps below. There are two methods. The first is the best and you can do it without opening the Customize Toolbar dialog box.

1. Hold down the Shift key.

2. Click the button you want to move with the mouse and drag it to another position. When you release the mouse, the button moves to the new position.

To rearrange the Toolbar from the Customize Toolbar dialog box, follow the steps below. You use this method if you are also adding or removing buttons to or from the Toolbar.

1. Double-click the Toolbar background to open the Customize Toolbar dialog box.

2. In the Toolbar Buttons box, click the button you want to move.

3. Click the Move Up or Move Down button until the button is in a new position that you like.

4. Click the Close button to save the new arrangement.

Resetting the Toolbar

If you want to revert to the original Toolbar, simply open the Customize Toolbar dialog box by double-clicking the Toolbar background, then click the Reset button. When you click the Close button, the list reverts to its default setting as you see it in Figure 9-1.

Creating Program Manager Startup Icons with File Manager

File Manager provides an interesting way to create startup icons in Program Manager groups. When you add a new application and want to create a startup icon for it, simply locate its .EXE file in the File Manager and drag and drop the file icon on a group in the Program Manager. The file icon supplies Program Manager with all the file property information it needs to create the startup icon, including the path and name of the executable file that starts the program.

Document startup icons can be created in the same way. In the following exercise, you create a document icon for a Calendar file in the Program Manager Everyday Tools group. (If you didn't create this group in Chapter 8, substitute the Accessories group in the following steps.) First you need to create the Calendar file. Here's how:

1. In File Manager, locate CALENDAR.EXE in the Windows directory window and double-click its icon. Sort the list alphabetically if you have trouble finding the file.

2. When the Calendar window opens, select File and choose the Save As option. Type **DAILY** in the File Name text box. Make sure the Windows directory is selected in the Directories list box.

3. Click the OK button. Calendar saves the file with the extension .CAL.

4. You don't need to add appointments now, so close the Calendar window.

Next you need to locate the new DAILY.CAL file in the Windows directory.

5. Click anywhere in the file list of the Windows directory, and type **D**. This places the highlight on or near the DAILY.CAL daily file.

Now you need to arrange the File Manager and Program Manager windows so they are both visible. In particular, the Everyday Tools group icon or window needs to show in the Program Manager.

6. Move the File Manager window to the right, but make sure you can see the icon for the DAILY.CAL file. You may need to resize the window.

7. Move the Program Manager window to the left, and arrange its group windows so you can see all or part of the Everyday Tools group.

8. In the File Manager, click the DAILY.CAL file icon and drag it to the Program Manager. As you drag the icon, notice that it turns into a No symbol (a slashed circle) when it's over areas where the icon can't be dropped.

9. When the icon is over the Everyday Tools group (or the Accessories group), release the mouse button.

A Calendar icon appears in the group window. To check its properties, you can click it and choose the Properties option on the Program Manager File menu. You can also double-click the icon to open Calendar and use the daily calendar file.

The Setup utility, as discussed in Chapter 8, is probably the best way to install new program icons, but the drag-and-drop method described in the foregoing exercises is the best one to use when you need to create startup icons for document files. In contrast, the next section describes how you can use File Manager (instead of Program Manager) as the place to open all applications and documents in Windows.

9

Starting Applications from File Manager

The icon-oriented Program Manager provides an excellent means of starting your applications and organizing them into meaningful groups. However, with this method, only the programs and documents for which you have created icons are easily accessible. The File Manager, on the other hand, offers an alternative "launching platform" that provides wider access to the files on your system. For example, to start the Notepad editor from File Manager, you can double-click its file icon in the same way you double-click the Notepad icon in the Accessories group of the Program Manager. In addition, the document files are easily opened by double-clicking their icons in the File Manager file lists. To take advantage of this feature, you can list all your document files in a directory window, as described in the next section, "Establishing Launch Windows."

File Manager also provides ways to organize your programs and files for easy launching. First, files are already organized into directory groups, making them relatively easy to find. If you can't find a startup file or a document, you can use the Search command as described in the next chapter. Second, files you want to look at can be extracted from directory lists and sorted for easier viewing. For example, you might list all the executable (.EXE) files in a directory and hide all the rest.

Establishing Launch Windows

In this section you'll see how to set up File Manager for use as a program launcher to replace Program Manager. The arrangement described here and pictured in Figure 9-6 is only a suggestion, based on the files in the Windows directory. Consider organizing your own system so associated document files are in one or more special data

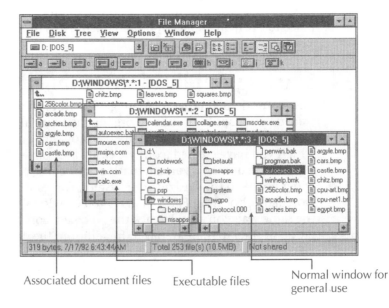

File Manager directory windows organized for program launching
Figure 9-6.

Associated document files   Executable files   Normal window for general use

directories. Here are some suggestions for organizing File Manager to access the files on your system.

✦ Create a "normal" directory window, containing a directory tree and contents list, that shows all files (*.*) in the selected directory. This will be your "working window"—you can use it to list the contents of other drives and directories when necessary.

✦ Create directory windows that list executable (.EXE) files so you can easily start programs.

✦ Use a directory window that lists documents sorted by their filename extensions to help you easily find files associated with programs.

The last two windows suggested in the previous list need not be split, since you won't be changing the directory within the windows. When you want to view another directory, you can always use the first "working window." Let's take a closer look at these three window arrangements.

The Working Window

You use this window for general use to display the contents of any directory. If you're still in File Manager, you should already have a directory window open. Make sure it displays the directory tree and file list; if necessary, choose Tree and Directory from the View menu. Resize the window so that other windows are available on the desktop. Alternatively, you can use the Cascade or Tile option on the Window menu to reorganize all the windows into the desktop arrangement that works best for you.

9

Creating an Executable Files Window

Here are the steps to create a new directory window exclusively for executable program files:

1. Choose New Window from the Window menu. (You can skip this step if you already have a second directory window open.)

2. Make the second window active (if necessary), and make sure the drive that holds the directory you want is selected. Then click the Windows directory in the directory tree.

3. Remove the split bar and display only the file list (select View and choose Directory Only).

4. Now list only .EXE files in the window. Select View, choose By File Type, and type ***.*** in the Name text box. In the File Type box, unmark and turn off all options except Programs. Click OK or press [Enter].

5. Click the Name button on the Toolbar to display only the names and icons of the files listed in the window.

6. Click the Sort by Name button on the Toolbar to sort the list in filename order.

You now have an organized list of executable program files. You can resize the window now, if necessary, but later you'll put all three of your new directory windows in the cascade arrangement.

Creating the Documents Window

Now create a window that lists only documents:

1. Make sure the window you just created is active, then open the Window menu and choose New Window. A new window appears that looks like the window you just created.

2. To list documents only, choose By File Type from the View menu. Type ***.*** in the Name field. In the File Type box, mark the Documents option and unmark all the other options. Click OK or press [Enter].

3. Click the Sort By Type button on the Toolbar to organize the listed files by their filename extensions.

Organizing and Saving the Arrangement

Now you can organize the three windows in a cascade arrangement on the desktop. Since the working window has a directory tree and is used to view other directories, place it on top. Click it now to make it active, and then choose Cascade from the Window menu. You'll get an arrangement similar to Figure 9-6.

Now you can launch applications by double-clicking their icons in the executable files window, or you can open documents by double-clicking their icons in the document window.

NOTE: To save this arrangement for the next File Manager session, hold down the (Shift) key and choose Exit from the File menu.

The File Manager Run Command

The Run command on the File menu opens a dialog box in which you can type the name of an executable program file you want to start. You use this option to start programs that don't have startup icons, or that aren't visible in a directory window. When the dialog box first opens, the name of the file currently selected in the contents list is displayed in the Command Line text box. If that entry is an executable program file, you can type the name of a document after it to load that document into the program's workspace when it opens.

In this exercise, you add parameters to a command in the Run dialog box:

1. Highlight the file NOTEPAD.EXE in the contents list of the Windows directory.
2. Select File and choose Run. NOTEPAD.EXE appears in the Command Line text box.
3. Type a space after the filename, and then type **TEST.TXT** after the space, as shown here:

9

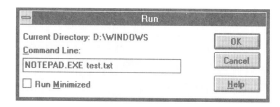

4. Click OK.

5. If the file exists, Notepad will load it into its workspace. If the file doesn't exist, you will see the following message box:

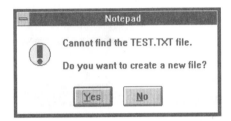

Click Yes to open a new file with the name TEST.TXT.

6. Close Notepad by double-clicking its Control button.

TIP: Some DOS commands use special parameters. You can use the Run dialog box to enter these parameters when executing the commands.

Drag-and-Drop Procedures

You can use the drag-and-drop method to quickly open documents in File Manager. First start an application, and then open a directory window in File Manager that lists document files for the program. Click one of the document files and drag it to the running program's window or icon. The document then appears in that program's workspace. The following exercise demonstrates how Notepad files can be opened using drag-and-drop.

1. In the File Manager, open a window on the Windows directory.

2. Double-click NOTEPAD.EXE to start the Notepad editor.

3. Minimize the Notepad window so it appears as an icon on the desktop, and make sure you can see the icon.

4. Locate the README.TXT file in the Windows directory. Click the file icon, and drag its icon over the Notepad icon on the desktop. The README.TXT document immediately opens in Notepad's workspace.

5. Now click another document and drag it to the Notepad window. The new document immediately opens in the workspace.

The advantage of this drag-and-drop method, compared to double-clicking the document icon, is speed. With Notepad already in memory, you can quickly load and view a document. Drag-and-drop is also useful when you are trying to identify files by viewing their contents. You can drag and drop any document that is associated with an application.

9

CHAPTER

10

FILE MANAGER, PART II: FILE, DIRECTORY, AND NETWORK COMMANDS

In Chapter 9, you learned about File Manager features and how to customize File Manager for your own use. In this chapter, you learn about the file, directory, and network commands available on File Manager menus.

Many of the commands you'll find on File Manager's File and Disk menu are similar to the commands you may be accustomed to using at the

DOS command prompt. In this chapter, you'll learn how File Manager commands can replace or substitute for DOS commands. We start out with a description of mouse techniques for copying and moving files, then explore file and disk-related commands.

Copying and Moving Files with the Mouse

You can move and copy files in File Manager using mouse techniques or menu commands. Mouse techniques are easiest to use, assuming both the source file icons and the icon for the destination directory are visible on the screen. If the icons are not visible, you'll need to open and arrange windows to make them visible, or use the Copy or Move menu commands.

NOTE: Copying a file makes a duplicate of that file in the destination. Moving a file removes the file from its original location and places it in the destination.

The following techniques help you copy and move files. If you are copying or moving more than one file, it is assumed you have already selected those files as described in Chapter 9.

✦ *Copying files from one directory to another* Hold down the Ctrl key, then click and drag the file or selected files from the source to the destination. The files are duplicated in the destination directory.

✦ *Copying files from one drive to another* Do not hold down the Ctrl key. Simply click and drag the file or selected files to the drive icon in the icon bar, or to a directory window for the destination drive. The source or destination drive can be a shared directory on a network computer.

✦ *Moving files from one directory to another* Windows assumes you want to move files when clicking and dragging, so you don't need to hold down a key. Simply click and drag the file or selected files to the destination.

✦ *Moving files from one drive to another*   Hold down the [Alt] key and click and drag the files to the destination. The source or destination can be a shared directory on a network computer.

In the following exercises, you get a chance to copy and move files. Before starting, create a new directory on your system that you can use for the exercises.

1. Make sure that the Windows directory is the current directory.

2. Select File and choose Create Directory to display the following dialog box:

```
┌─────────────────────────────────────────────────┐
│ ▬                Create Directory                 │
├─────────────────────────────────────────────────┤
│  Current Directory: D:\WINDOWS      ┌───────────┐ │
│                                     │    OK     │ │
│  Name: ┌──────────────────────────┐ └───────────┘ │
│        │                          │ ┌───────────┐ │
│        └──────────────────────────┘ │  Cancel   │ │
│                                     └───────────┘ │
│                                     ┌───────────┐ │
│                                     │   Help    │ │
│                                     └───────────┘ │
└─────────────────────────────────────────────────┘
```

Since the current directory is Windows, the new directory will branch from it.

3. Type **TEMP** in the Name field, and click the OK button or press the [Enter] key.

The new TEMP directory icon appears as a branching directory of the Windows directory. Now you can copy files to it using mouse click-and-drag methods.

4. The Windows directory should still be selected. Select View and choose Sort By Type.

5. Select all the .WRI files: Scroll the directory window file list until the .WRI file is in view, then click the first file, hold down the [Shift] key, scroll down if necessary, and click the last file.

6. Hold down the [Ctrl] key, click anywhere in the selection of contiguous files, and drag left. The mouse pointer changes and appears as an icon with three overlapping files.

10

7. Drag the files' icon to the TEMP directory icon in the directory tree.

8. When a rectangle surrounds the TEMP directory icon, release the mouse. You'll then see the following dialog box:

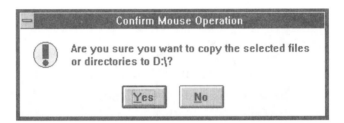

9. Here you must confirm the mouse operation; click the Yes button to confirm the copy.

You have now copied the .WRI files to the new directory.

Using the File Menu Commands

The File menu holds a set of commands that you use to manipulate the files and directories you've selected in directory windows. You examine each command as you work through the following sections.

CAUTION: Keep in mind that some commands on the File menu act on the currently selected directory in the directory tree. For example, if you click the Windows directory in the directory tree, and then choose the Delete option on the File menu, the dialog box will suggest deleting the Windows directory! So be sure to read all warning boxes as you work.

Opening Selected Directories and Files

File Open does basically the same thing as the [Enter] key. If you select a directory icon in the directory tree and choose File Open, the directory's branching subdirectories are displayed. If you select an .EXE file in the contents list and choose File Open, the program starts. If you select an associated document and choose File Open, the associated application is started and the document is loaded into its workspace.

Moving and Copying Files

File Move and File Copy are used to move or copy files and directories. Use these commands when you can't click and drag files because the source files or directories are not visible in a directory window, or when the destination directory is not visible in a directory window. The Move and Copy commands have the following advantages over mouse methods:

◆ If you know the filenames and locations of the files you want to copy or move, you can use Copy and Move to copy or move files without first opening directory windows and selecting the files.

◆ If the source files are visible in a directory window but the destination directory icon or window is not visible, you can click the files to copy or move, choose the Copy or Move command, and specify the destination.

◆ When using Copy or Move, you can use wildcard characters to specify the exact files to copy or move. This method may be easier than clicking each file or using the Set Selection dialog box.

◆ Copy and Move are available even if your mouse is disabled.

◆ You can specify a shared network directory as the source or destination, even if you are not connected to the directory. You specify the source or destination in the following format, as discussed in Chapter 7.

　　*servername**sharename**filename*

10

First let's look at the Move dialog box:

Move

Current Directory: D:\WINDOWS

From: D:\WINDOWS

To:

OK | Cancel | Help

In this dialog box the Windows directory name appears in the From text box, because its icon was highlighted when the Move command was selected. If any files are selected in the directory window when you select Move, their names will also appear in the From field of the dialog box. You can double-click in the From field to specify new parameters or to insert more parameters after the existing path information. In the To text box, type the drive and directory where you want to move the files.

Here is an example of the Copy dialog box:

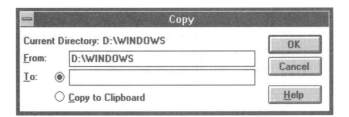

Once again, the current path and any selected files in the directory window appear in the From text box. You can type over the From box contents with your own file specification, by first double-clicking in the field. The following exercise demonstrates how to copy the Paintbrush .BMP files from the Windows directory to the TEMP directory you created earlier in this chapter. Since Copy lets you specify the path where files are located, you don't need to change directories before executing the Copy command.

1. Select File and choose Copy.
2. Type **C:\WINDOWS*.BMP** in the From text box. As usual, you'll want to replace drive C with the letter of your own Windows drive, if it is different (as shown above).
3. Type **C:\WINDOWS\TEMP** in the To text box.
4. Click OK to copy the files.

When Windows copies the files, notice that it does not display any warning or confirmation messages. This is because the files do not exist yet in the TEMP directory, and they are not being overwritten or deleted.

NOTE: The Copy to Clipboard button in the Copy dialog box is used when linking and embedding objects such as Paintbrush graphic files into a document.

Deleting Files

One of the easiest ways to delete a file or directory is to click its icon with the mouse and then press the ⌈Del⌋ key. A warning message appears asking you to confirm your deletion request—unless you have turned confirmations off as described in "Suppressing Confirmation Messages" in Chapter 9.

The File Delete command is used to specify the path and filename of the files or directories you want to delete. In the following exercise, you delete the Paintbrush .BMP files you copied to the TEMP directory.

1. Select File and choose Delete to display the following dialog box:

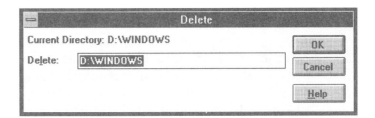

If any files are selected, their names appear in the Delete field.

2. Type **C:\WINDOWS\TEMP*.BMP** in the Delete field. This will delete all files with the extension .BMP in the TEMP directory.

3. Click the OK button to execute the deletion request.

If file deletion confirmations are still enabled, the following dialog box will appear for each file to be deleted:

10

To go ahead with the deletion, click the Yes button; click No to keep
the file. To delete all remaining files that match the specification, click
the Yes to All button. Another simpler way to delete files is to highlight
them with the mouse, then press the [Del] key.

TIP: The Confirm File Delete box can be used as a way to selectively
delete files. First select a group of files using any method you find
convenient. Next, choose Delete. You are then asked, one file at a time,
if you want to delete the selection. At this point simply click Yes or No.

Renaming Files

File Rename lets you change the names of your directories and files. If
you choose Rename with a directory or file highlighted in the contents
list, that path and filename appear in the From text box of the Rename
dialog box. In the following illustration, the file TEST.TXT in the From
field can be renamed by typing a new name in the To field.

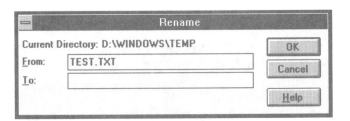

CAUTION: Don't rename files that belong to programs. If you do, the program won't be able to locate them.

Renaming groups of files using wildcard characters is a little tricky. There must be a common element in the names of all the files. For example, the following illustrates how you would rename the two .TXT files listed in the From text box to files with the extension .DOC:

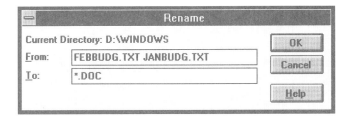

This next example illustrates how you would rename the files NEWDATA1.DBF, NEWDATA2.DBF, and NEWDATA3.DBF to OLDDATA1.DBF, OLDDATA2.DBF, and OLDDATA3.DBF:

10

This next example illustrates how you would rename the files
NEWDATA1.DBF, NEWDATA2.DBF, and NEWDATA3.DBF to

In this Rename dialog box, the From text box calls for all filenames starting with NEWDATA and having the extension .DBF to be renamed. The question mark holds the place of the eighth character of the filename, which differs for each file in the group. The To text box specifies that OLD will be the first three characters of the new filenames.

Viewing and Changing File Properties

You can display the attributes, or *properties,* of files and directories with the File Properties option. These properties are assigned to files to protect them from unauthorized changes or accidental deletion, or to designate whether the files should be backed up. The properties are discussed in the following sections.

NOTE: When working with shared network drives, the Properties dialog box looks slightly different and has additional features. These features are discussed in Chapter 11.

Read Only   Files marked R, Read Only, cannot be changed or deleted unless the Read Only attribute is removed. This option is useful on shared network drives as a way to prevent users from changing or accidentally deleting files. However, it is not fully secure. If, for example, another user has full security rights in the directory, he or she could simply remove the protecting attribute. Chapter 11 covers protecting files on networks.

Archive   When a file is first created, or when it is altered, its Archive flag (A) is set on. DOS commands such as BACKUP and XCOPY look at the Archive flag to determine if a file should be included in an incremental backup (the periodic backup of files that have changed since the last backup). During the incremental backup, the Archive flag is set off so the file is not included in the next backup. If the file changes in the meantime, its Archive flag is once again set on and it will be included in the next backup.

In most cases, you won't need to worry about the Archive bit (flag). However, there may be times when you want to manually set it to include or exclude a file from a backup. For example, to create a second set of backup disks, it may be necessary to set the archive bit on for files in directories you want to back up.

Hidden   Files marked Hidden (H) will not appear in a DOS file listing, and will only appear in directory windows if the Show Hidden/System Files check box is marked in the By File Type dialog box (discussed in "Listing Specific Files" earlier in this chapter).

System   Files marked System (S) are DOS files that are hidden in DOS file listings, and only appear in directory windows if the Show Hidden/System Files check box is marked in the By File Type dialog box (discussed in "Listing Specific Files" earlier in this chapter).

To get an idea of how attribute flags work, try the following exercise:

1. Click the Windows directory in the directory tree.
2. Scroll through the list and click the file README.WRI.
3. Select File and choose Properties to display the dialog box shown in Figure 10-1.

   The dialog box displays the file's size, date and time of creation or last modification, and path name. Any attributes set for the file are marked in the Attributes area. For this example, apply the Read Only attribute to the file, then note what happens when you try to make changes to it.

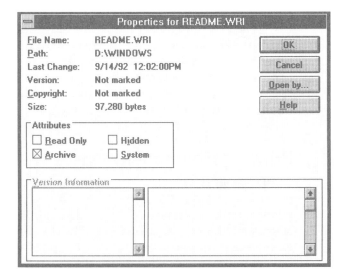

10

The Properties dialog box
Figure 10-1.

4. Click the Read Only check box in the Attributes area, and then click the OK button or press Enter.

5. Back at the File Manager, double-click the README.WRI file icon to start Write and load the file.

6. When the file opens, type your name or any text at the blinking cursor; then select File and choose the Save option. The following dialog box appears:

Because you have set the Read Only attribute on for this file, it cannot be saved with the changes you've made. You'll need to save the changes with a different name to keep the original intact. To do so, you would choose the Save As option from the File menu. For now, click OK to close the message box and close the window without saving.

Using the Read Only attribute is how template files are protected from accidental erasure or change. A *template* is a document used to create other documents. For example, a template might contain your company logo and address. The Read Only template file is opened, saved under a different filename, and used to create a letter, while the original template is preserved for future use.

Printing from File Manager

In File Manager, you can print a document by *dragging and dropping* its icon on the Print Manager, but the Print Manager must be running as a window or icon on the desktop for this to work. In addition, only associated files can be printed with the drag and drop method. The exercise that follows shows you how to print a Notepad file without having to start Notepad and load the file in its workspace.

1. The Print Manager must be running before you can drag and drop files on it. To start the Print Manager from the File Manager, double-click the file PRINTMAN.EXE in the Windows directory.

2. Make the File Manager window active; then click the Windows directory icon to make its files appear in the contents list.

3. Locate the file BOOTLOG.TXT, and click and drag the file to the Print Manager icon.

4. When the icon for the file is over the Print Manager icon, release the mouse; this causes the file to be printed.

Another way to print in File Manager is with the Print option on the File menu. Click the file you want to print, select File, and choose Print. When the Print dialog box appears, the file you selected is listed in the Text field. Click the OK button to print the file. Alternatively, you can just type the name of the file you want to print in the field.

Program and Document Associations

As you have learned, associated document files are linked to their creating program by means of the filename extension. For example, when you double-click a .TXT file, its associated application, Notepad, starts and the file is loaded into its workspace. Other Windows associations include Write and its .WRI files, as well as Paintbrush and its .BMP and .PCX files.

The File Associate command lets you create your own file associations. For example, if you add a new program that creates files with the extension .ZAP, you can use the Associate command to link the .ZAP files with the program. Then you can easily double-click the .ZAP files to quickly open them together with the program. Alternatively, you might want to associate .ZAP files with Notepad.

10

 CAUTION: Be careful not to associate a particular filename extension with more than one application. If you do, the last program you associated with the document is started when you double-click the document.

Documents created by Windows applications are already associated. The File Associate command is your tool for linking non-Windows applications with the documents they create, or to change associations. For example, you could remove the .TXT association from the Notepad and assign it to another text editor of your choice.

Assume for this exercise that you want the TIMELOG files that you create with Notepad to have the extension .LOG, rather than the usual .TXT extension associated with Notepad. The following exercise associates the .LOG extension with Notepad. Keep in mind that the .TXT extension also remains associated with Notepad (unless you remove it).

1. Select File and choose Associate from the File Menu to display the following dialog box:

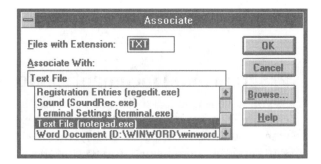

TIP: If a file is highlighted in the contents list, its extension is displayed in the Files with Extension text box of the Associate dialog box. You can save a step when associating files by first clicking a filename that has the extension you want to associate.

2. The cursor will be in the Files with Extension text box; type **LOG** (the period is not necessary) as the extension you want to associate.

3. In the Associate With list box, find Text File (notepad.exe) and click it. (You can also type in the name of the program if you know it, or click the Browse button to search for a program filename.)

4. Click the OK button (or press ⟨Enter⟩) to establish the association between the .LOG extension and Notepad.

To remove an association, open the Associate dialog box, type the extension in the text field, and choose None in the Associate With list box (or type it in yourself).

Searching for Files and Directories

The File Search option is used to locate files and directories within your disk filing system or within shared directories. You can search for a file by specifying its full filename, or by specifying a partial name and using wildcard characters. In the following exercise, you look for files with the filename extension .SYS on the current drive.

1. Select File and choose Search; you'll see this dialog box:

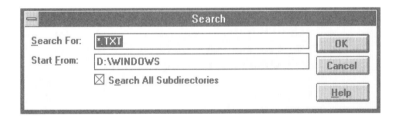

2. Type ***.SYS** in the Search For text box.
3. Type **C:** in the Start From field. (If your Windows directory is on another drive, replace C with the appropriate drive letter.)
4. Mark the Search All Subdirectories box, and click the OK button.

10

In a moment, you'll see a Search Results dialog box similar to this one:

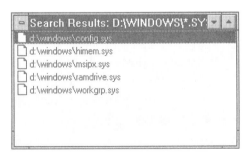

Scan through the list box and note that .SYS files are listed in several different directories, including the DOS and Windows directories. The Search Results window displays files like any other directory window. You can click any file in the list and execute the commands on the File menu or click and drag the files to other drives or directories. In addition, if executable files are listed, you can double-click them to start their programs.

Working with Directories

You can create, copy, and move directories in the File Manager. When copying or moving directories, File Manager can copy an entire directory tree or branches of it to a new directory or disk. It's easy to delete directories as well, but you'll want to use caution when you do, because File Manager will also delete a directory's branching subdirectories unless you specify otherwise.

Creating Directories

The Create Directory option on the File menu is used to create new directories. Before selecting the option, click the directory from which you want the new directory to branch. Alternatively, you can type the full path for the new directory in the Create Directory dialog box.

In a previous exercise, you created the TEMP subdirectory under the Windows directory. In this exercise, you create a new subdirectory that branches from TEMP.

1. Make sure a directory window is open to the drive that holds the Windows directory. Select the directory window that displays files in your Windows directory (or create a new directory window).

2. Double-click the Windows directory icon to display its subdirectories, if they are not visible.

3. Click the TEMP subdirectory.

4. Now you're ready to create the new subdirectory. Select File and choose Create Directory, and you'll see this dialog box:

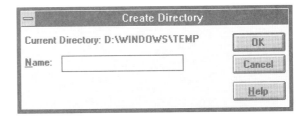

5. In the Name text box, type **LEVEL3** as the name of the new directory. (This name is used as an example only. It has no significance except to indicate that this is a "level 3" subdirectory.)

6. Click OK or press ⌈Enter⌋. This creates the new directory as a branching subdirectory of the TEMP directory.

Another way to create this level 3 subdirectory is to type its full path name in the Name field of the Create Directory dialog box. For example, in the foregoing exercise, you could skip Steps 1 through 3 altogether, and begin at the Create Directory dialog box; in the Name field, you would enter C:\WINDOWS\TEMP\LEVEL3.

Copying and Moving Directories

When you copy a directory, Windows makes a duplicate at the new location. When you move a directory, Windows deletes the original directory after it is moved to the new location. Copying and moving directories are useful ways to create a new directory structure on another drive, or to reorganize a drive. Remember that any branching subdirectories of a directory are copied or moved along with it, unless you specify otherwise.

NOTE: You can copy an entire directory and its subdirectories from one network computer to another. This is useful for making backups, or for duplicating the file structure of one computer on another system.

In this exercise, you practice moving the TEMP directory and its branching subdirectory, LEVEL3, to the root directory. In this way, TEMP will branch from the root, not from the Windows directory.

1. Click the drive icon for the Windows directory, if it is not currently active.
2. If you can't see the Windows directory's branching subdirectories, including TEMP, double-click the Windows directory icon.
3. Click and drag the TEMP directory's icon over the root directory icon. When the rectangle appears over the root directory icon, release the mouse button.
4. A confirmation message asks if you are sure you want to move the directory; choose Yes.

In a moment, you'll see the new structure of the directory tree. If you can't see the LEVEL3 directory, scan down through the list to find it, or double-click the TEMP directory to open its subdirectory tree.

Typically, you'll move rather than copy directories from one location to another. Copying creates duplicates of every file, which wastes disk space. In the instances when you really want to copy an entire directory, hold down the ⌃Ctrl key and drag the directory icon to the new location. To copy directories between different drives, simply click and drag. To move directories between drives, hold down the ⌥Alt key while clicking and dragging.

NOTE: Directories are copied, not moved, to another disk by default, because Windows assumes you want to keep the original directory in place. To actually move a directory to another disk, hold down the ⌥Alt key while you drag the directory icon.

TIP: You can also use the File Copy and File Move commands to copy directories. The advantage of using this method is that you can type the exact path where the directory should be copied.

Deleting Directories

In this section, you delete the TEMP directory. You have learned in previous exercises how to copy and move files to it, and how to move the directory to another location. Now it's time to delete this practice directory so it doesn't take up space on your hard drive. To delete a directory, highlight its icon in the directory tree and press the ⌑Del⌑ key. Alternatively, select File and choose the Delete option; then type the path and directory name.

When deleting directories, you'll want to be aware of the current confirmation settings in your Windows environment. Choose Confirmation from the Options menu now to display the Confirmation dialog box, and note the following settings:

✦ *File Delete*   If the File Delete confirmation is enabled, File Manager will ask you to confirm your commands to delete files in a directory and its subdirectories. Make sure this option is turned on, because you'll always want to make careful choices about deleting all files.

✦ *Subtree Delete*   If the Subtree Delete confirmation is enabled, File Manager will ask you to confirm your commands to delete a directory and each of its subdirectories. It is recommended that you always leave this option on so you'll be warned before you complete a deletion that might include a subdirectory you may have forgotten about.

Make sure all the confirmation options are set, and then follow the steps here to delete the TEMP directory:

10

1. Click the TEMP directory and press the ⌑Del⌑ key. The following dialog box appears displaying the name of the TEMP directory:

2. Click the OK button or press Enter. You then see the following confirmation box:

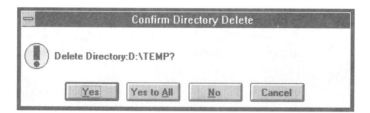

If you click the Yes button in the Confirm Directory Delete dialog box, File Manager starts deleting files in the TEMP directory, asking you to confirm the deletion of each branching subdirectory. If you click the Yes to All button, File Manager automatically deletes each subdirectory without asking for confirmation. It is recommended that you always choose the Yes button technique.

3. Click the Yes button in the Confirm Directory Delete dialog box. You'll see a confirmation box similar to this:

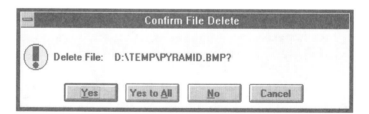

If you click Yes in the Confirm File Delete dialog box, a similar confirmation request will appear for each file to be deleted in the directory. Don't choose the Yes to All button unless you're sure you want to delete every file.

4. In this case, click the Yes to All button in the Confirm File Delete dialog box.

5. The Confirm Directory Delete dialog box appears for the LEVEL3 subdirectory. Click the Yes button to delete the directory.

All of the remaining files are deleted, and the TEMP directory is removed. You are not asked to confirm the deletion of the files in the LEVEL3 directory because you clicked the Yes to All button in Step 4.

TIP: If you want to delete the files in a directory but not its branching subdirectory, click the No button when the Confirm Directory Delete dialog appears for the directory you want to keep. This leaves the directory structure intact.

Using Disk Commands

The first four options on the Disk menu are used to work with floppy disks and hard disks. You can copy files between floppy disks, change a disk's electronic label, and format disks. The Disk menu also contains network options that are discussed in the next chapter. Floppy disk options are covered in the following sections.

Copying Disks

Choose the Copy Disk option on the File Manager Disk menu to copy the contents of one disk to another. The operation is similar to the DOS DISKCOPY command. You cannot copy to different disk types (for example, from 5 1/4-inch disks to 3 1/2-inch disks). The disk you want to copy is called the *source* and the disk you want to copy to is called the *destination*. If you only have one floppy drive, you must swap disks in the drive to make a copy. If you have two floppy disks, the Copy Disk dialog box shown below appears:

10

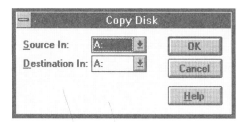

Choose the location of the source disk in the Source In field and the location of the destination in the Destination In field. If the second drive is a different format, you can't use it. Instead, specify the same drive letter in both the Source In and Destination In fields. Windows asks you to change disks. If the first and the second disk drive are the same type, you can specify the letter of each drive in each of the fields.

Click the OK button to begin the copy operation. Windows first asks for the source disks, then displays a dialog box that shows its progress as it reads the source. It then asks for the destination disk and copies the files it has read from the source to that disk. When the operation is complete, you can remove the disk and label it properly.

Labeling a Disk

The Label Disk option on the Disk menu is used to change the electronic label on disks. You see this label at the top of directory windows, or when you list a directory of a disk with the DOS DIR command. The electronic label is used by programs to identify which disk is in a drive. In some cases you may need to change this label if you are using an old disk for a new purpose. Or you can change it for esthetic reasons if you prefer to display a different name in directory windows. A disk label cannot exceed 11 characters.

◆ *Changing Hard Drive Labels*   Click the drive icon of the disk you want to change, then choose the Label Disk option on the Disk menu. Type the new disk label and click the OK button.

◆ *Changing Floppy Disk Labels*   Place the disk in a floppy drive, then click the icon for that drive. Choose the Label Disk option from the Disk menu, type the new label, and click the OK button.

NOTE: You cannot change the label of a shared disk that you are attached to.

Formatting Disks

The Format Disk command on the Disk menu is used to format floppy disks. When you choose the command, the following dialog box appears:

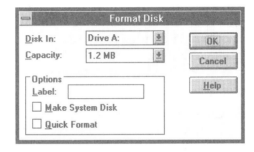

Follow these steps to format a floppy disk:

1. Place a disk to format in the floppy drive you want to use for formatting.

2. Choose the Format Disk command.

3. Choose the disk drive where you place the floppy disk in the Disk In field.

4. Choose the Capacity for the disk in the Capacity field.

NOTE: Normally, you'll use the default or highest capacity for a disk, but keep in mind that some older personal computers can only read disks formatted to a lower capacity.

5. Type an electronic name for the disk up to 11 characters long in the Label field.

6. Enable the Make System Disk field to make the disk bootable. Enabling this option adds the DOS system files to the disk. If the disk will only be used for data storage, don't enable this option, since the system files take up room on the disk.

7. Enable the Quick Format field to erase a disk that was previously formatted.

NOTE: When a disk is quick formatted, its file allocation table (FAT) and root directory are deleted. It is not scanned for bad sectors, but all space on the disk is made available for new files. Because this option removes all directories and subdirectories, it is a quick way to prepare old disks for new uses. However, if you suspect a disk has bad sectors, do not enable this option.

8. Click the OK button to begin disk formatting. A dialog box displays the progress, and you can continue with other tasks while the disk is being formatted.

When the format is complete, you are asked if you want to format another disk. If you choose Yes, the Format Disk dialog box stays open with some of the parameters you previously set so you can format another disk. If you choose No, the dialog box closes.

Make System Disk

The Make System Disk option adds the DOS system files to a previously formatted disk. The system files make the disk bootable, so you can start a computer with it. Note that this option accomplishes the same thing as enabling the Make System Disk field on the Format Disk dialog box covered previously.

NOTE: You cannot copy the system files to a formatted disk if you have copied other files to the disk.

To make a system disk, place a blank formatted disk in a floppy drive, then choose the Make System Disk menu option. When the dialog box opens, choose the drive where the floppy disk is located and click the OK button.

CHAPTER

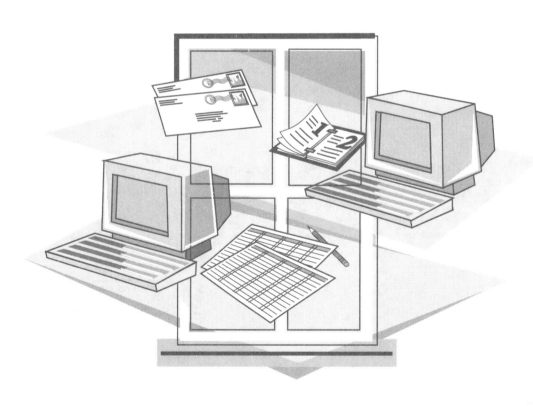

11

SHARING AND ACCESSING NETWORK FILES

This chapter covers methods for sharing directories on your system with other users and to access shared directories on other systems. If you share resources such as directories, files, and printers on your system with other network users, your computer is a server system. Other computers which access resources on server computers are known as clients. The type of computer you have and

271

the Windows mode you use determine whether your system can be a client, a server, or both, as described here:

✦ If you have an 80386-based (or later model) computer and start Windows in 386 enhanced mode by typing **WIN /3** at the DOS prompt, your computer can be both a client and a server. Note that your system may automatically start in 386 enhanced mode, so you can simply type **WIN**.

✦ If your system starts in standard mode, you can only be a client. You cannot share resources with other users.

Starting methods were discussed in Chapter 2. If your computer boots up as a client system only, refer to the sections in this chapter that discuss accessing shared directories and skip over the sections that discuss sharing directories.

Windows for Workgroups allows connections to Microsoft Windows NT servers, LAN Manager for OS/2 servers, LAN Manager for UNIX servers, Microsoft Network (MS-NET) servers, and Novell NetWare servers. A Windows for Workgroups computer can also act as a server for all of these networks except Novell NetWare. When you connect with these servers, their directories appear as drive icons on the File Manager drive icon bar, or in directory listings when opening or saving files in network-compatible applications.

Connecting computers together in a Windows for Workgroups environment has many advantages. You are no longer isolated as a single user, but become part of a group of users who share files and resources. In theory at least, your computing power and productivity increase. Here are some of the advantages of connecting systems with Windows for Workgroups:

✦ Sharing of peripherals such as printers, hard drives, CD-ROM drives, and other devices.

✦ Quick and easy file transfers among computers on the network.

✦ Centralized file storage and backup, which makes it easier to manage and protect a company's valuable data.

✦ Support for object linking and embedding (OLE) over the network, as discussed in Chapter 14. OLE simplifies group projects that utilize information, graphics, and other components from many different users.

✦ Electronic mail and messaging among users on the network.

✦ Use of workgroup applications such as Schedule+ that let you coordinate your work with other users.

Workgroups and Network Computers

This book assumes that your computer network has already been installed by a network administrator. When you start your system and Windows, one or more directories may already be shared on your computer and you may already have access to shared directories on other systems. You can access the files on other computers using File Manager. You can also access files on network computers from many network-compatible applications by choosing the Open option or Save As on the File menu of those applications. This section explains the network environment to help you better understand where and how network files are accessed, and the methods you use to refer to computers on the network. Note the following:

✦ Every computer on the network is assigned a *computer name* and a workgroup. Computer names must be unique and should be descriptive. For example, a computer name can describe the user of the computer, the type of system, what the system is used for, or the type of files stored on the system. The computer names appear in dialog box listings that you can browse through as discussed in Chapter 7 and later in this chapter.

✦ Windows for Workgroups uses the concepts of *workgroups* to organize computers into groups. When computers are grouped together under meaningful names, you can quickly locate a shared computer you need to access. For example, if you needed a file on a computer in the accounting department, you might scan the list of computers under a workgroup called ACCOUNTING.

✦ In small companies, everybody can belong to the same workgroup, but for large companies, it is often necessary to create two or more workgroups to categorize users and reduce problems associated with similar names. Typically, a network administrator decides which workgroup a computer (and its users) belongs to when a network is installed.

Let's look at an example that clarifies the benefits of workgroups. Figure 11-1 illustrates a typical office environment. There are four departments and three users in each department. One user in each department is a manager. There are several ways to organize the users in this company. Figure 11-2 illustrates how workgroups and shared computers would appear in browse dialog boxes for two different arrangements. The workgroup arrangement on the left groups managers and regular users together. The workgroup arrangement on the right groups users into their departments. Descriptions of both arrangements follow.

By Job Description   This arrangement, shown on the left in Figure 11-2, logically groups network computers by the type of user, not by the department location. For example, all the managers are made a part of a workgroup called MANAGERS. Typically, a manager's computer might have special files that the rest of the users in the department or other departments need to access. They can quickly locate any manager's computer by browsing the list of computers under the MANAGERS workgroup.

By Department   This arrangement, shown on the right in Figure 11-2, is based on the physical location of a computer, which is easy to

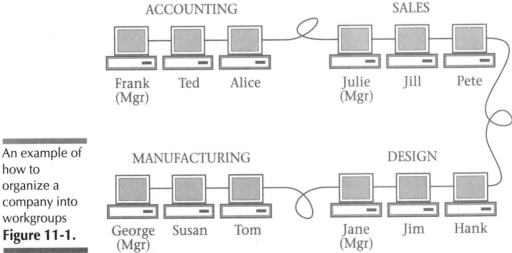

An example of how to organize a company into workgroups

Figure 11-1.

ACCOUNTING

Frank (Mgr)   Ted   Alice

SALES

Julie (Mgr)   Jill   Pete

MANUFACTURING

George (Mgr)   Susan   Tom

DESIGN

Jane (Mgr)   Jim   Hank

MANAGERS
Frank
Julie
George
Jane
USERS
Ted
Alice
Jill
Pete
Susan
Tom
Jim
Hank
ACCOUNTING
Frank
Ted
Alice
SALES
Julie
Jill
Pete
MANUFACTURING
George
Susan
Tom
DESIGN
Jane
Jim
Hank

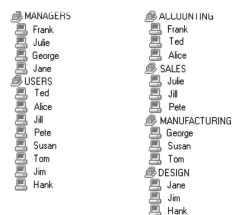

Two possible ways that the company might appear in browse dialog boxs
Figure 11-2.

remember. A user can quickly connect with another computer by browsing the list under the department name.

Another type of arrangement assumes that one computer in each department is primarily used as a server. No users actually sit at the keyboard of the system and use it, because its resources are *dedicated* to sharing files with other network users. In Figure 11-1, assume that an additional computer is added to each department to operate as a dedicated server. For this installation, a network administrator might create a workgroup arrangement like the one shown in Figure 11-3.

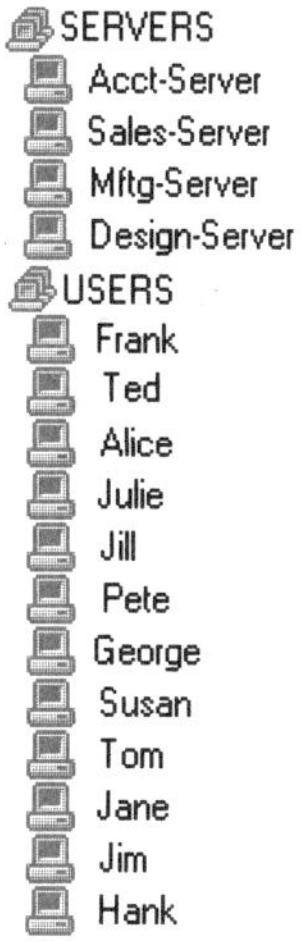

SERVERS
Acct-Server
Sales-Server
Mftg-Server
Design-Server
USERS
Frank
Ted
Alice
Julie
Jill
Pete
George
Susan
Tom
Jane
Jim
Hank

A workgroups list organized into dedicated file servers and users
Figure 11-3.

Notice that all users are included in a workgroup called USERS, and the dedicated servers in each department are included in a workgroup called SERVERS. This makes it easy for users to quickly locate servers or other users.

What It Means to Share Your System

Windows for Workgroups is a peer-to-peer file-sharing system. That means other users can access files and peripherals on your system, and you can access files and peripherals on other systems. There is mutual sharing. Compare this to dedicated file-server networks like Novell NetWare, in which all users access files on a centralized file server rather than on other users' systems. Centralized networks such as NetWare have benefits. Performance increases and file storage is centralized, which makes backups and file protection easier.

On a peer-to-peer network such as Windows for Workgroups, the performance of a shared computer is affected because its processing time is divided between the local user and network users who access the system's shared resources. The WinMeter utility lets you monitor exactly how much of your system's processing time is allocated to network tasks and how much is allocated to the programs you are running. If performance drops to much, it may be necessary to stop sharing your computer with other users. You temporarily stop sharing your system by opening the Networks utility in the Control Panel and disabling the Sharing option as shown in Figure 11-4.

Keep in mind that it may be impractical or impossible to stop sharing your system if other users need access to its files or peripherals. If performance drops too much, you'll need to move file and peripheral-sharing functions off your computer to another computer, such as a centralized and dedicated file server. Of course, you can remain connected to the Windows for Workgroups network for mail and message sharing, and to access the new dedicated server. On large networks, it makes sense to dedicate machines as file servers. On smaller networks with limited resources, a system that is used the least by a local user makes a good server, assuming it has the processing power and storage requirements to act as a server.

Disable the Enable Sharing option on the Network Settings dialog box to temporarily disable network sharing
Figure 11-4.

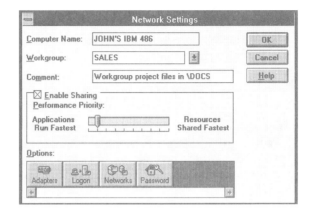

Also remember that you have a responsibility to other network users who access shared resources on your system. Make sure shared directories are available when they need them and make sure the files they store or access in the directories are safe and protected from unauthorized users. This requires that you set various password security features and that you back up your system on a regular basis.

File Security

Security and privacy of files is a concern in a network environment in which users access files on other users' systems. For example, you wouldn't want another user to access confidential data such as personnel files.

Windows for Workgroups provides security features that let you share only those directories you want to share. In addition, you can restrict users' access to shared directories on two levels.

Read-Only Directory Rights   Users who have read-only access rights can view files in a shared directory, but they can't change or delete the files.

Full-Access Directory Rights   Users who have full-access rights to shared directories can change existing files, add new files, and delete files. Grant this right with caution.

11

NOTE: When you share a directory, users have access to all its subdirectories.

You grant rights to directories by creating a password for the read-only access right and another password for the full-access right in the Share Directories dialog box as shown in Figure 11-5. This dialog box appears when you choose Share As from the Disk menu in File Manager. You first click one of the buttons in the Access Type field, depending on the type of access you want to give users. The Depends on Password option lets you specify both types of user access. You then fill in the Password fields. In this example, users with the password RAISIN have read-only access and users with the password INDIANA have full access.

How to Administer Access Rights

When do you grant read-only access rights and when do you grant full-access rights? If users need to change the files in a shared directory, they will need full-access rights. Read-only access rights are assigned in the following situations.

Program Directories   If the files in a directory are program files only, users should be granted read-only access rights to prevent them from accidentally changing or deleting files in the directory. They can still

The Access Type and Password field in the Share Directory dialog box are used to establish user access rights to a shared directory
Figure 11-5.

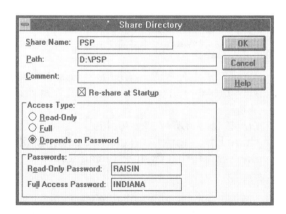

run programs in the directory as usual. This feature is especially important with Windows applications that save changes users make to the interface in .INI (initialization) files. For example, when you change and save the arrangement of Program Manager or File Manager windows, those changes are stored in .INI files. If you're sharing programs on your system with other users and you don't want them to make such changes, give them read-only access to the directories. Then their changes won't be written to your .INI files.

NOTE: Make sure that all users are licensed for programs that are shared on the network.

Database Files   A database is a file that contains customer lists, accounting information, and other sequential data divided into records and fields. Some users should only view information in the database, while others can both view and change information. Grant read-only access in database directories to users who should only view the information and full access to users who can both view and change it.

Template Files   A template is a file that users read and change. However, users should not save changes they have made back to the template file. When a user tries to save a file, a Save As dialog box appears so the changed version can be saved with a different name and in a different location. This preserves the original template file for future use. For example, a directory might contain a file with standard text such as a letter of recommendation or response to a product query. A user who needs the text reads the file, makes necessary changes, prints it, then saves it to another location (or discards the changes). Users who are authorized to make changes to the template are given the full-access right to the directory.

If you grant users full access to a shared directory, you can still protect individual files from change applying a read-only attribute. As covered in Chapter 10, first select the file, then choose the Properties command on the File Manager File menu and enable the Read-Only option. Keep in mind that this is not a completely secure approach. A user who really wants to change the file can open the Properties dialog box and remove

11

the read-only attribute. However, it does protect files from being inadvertently changed.

File and Record Locking

On a network, only one user should have access to a file at the same time to ensure that one user doesn't overwrite changes made to a file by another user. For example, assume Joe opens the file TEST.DOC. In the mean time, Sally opens the same file, makes some changes, and saves the file. Then Joe saves his changes. In doing so Joe overwrites any changes made by Sally. Windows for Workgroups locks files so only one user can access them at the same time, thus preventing overwrites.

The exception to this rule is a multiuser record-locking database, such as a mailing list or reservation system. A record in the database holds a block of information, such as the accounting records of a single customer. Databases are typically made available company-wide and stored in one location. In fact, networks are often installed for the sole purpose of providing database access to a large group of people. Each user accessing the database typically gets one record at a time and that record is locked to prevent others from accessing it while it is in use.

Accessing Password-Protected Shared Directories

The first time you access a password-protected shared directory, you type the password in a dialog box similar to this one:

Note the Save this Password in Your Password List field. If this field is enabled, the password is stored in the password list so you don't need to type it the next time you access the directory. The password list is

tied to the logon namc and password. Whcn you log on, thc passwords needed to access shared directories are made available. However, this can pose security problems. If another user discovers your logon password, they can logon and gain access to the shared directories on other systems that only you are authorized to access. To prevent this security problem, you can disable the Save this Password in Your Password List field, but you'll then need to remember the passwords and type them every time you access the shared directory. Your network administrator may have established a policy for this procedure, depending on the security requirements at your company.

Disconnection Problems

Once you share a directory and give other users access to it, you must ensure that the directory is always available when they need it. You might also be responsible for ensuring that the files in the directory are properly backed up.

When Windows starts, it attempts to reconnect with shared directory connections that were established in previous sessions. If those directories are no longer shared or Windows is not running on the other system, a message dialog box similar to the following appears.

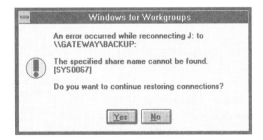

When you connect with a shared network drive, you can specify a one-time connection, or a reconnection every time you start Windows. Referring ahead to the Connect Network Drive dialog box in Figure 11-7, you would disable the Reconnect at Startup option so Windows doesn't reconnect the next time you start Windows. Note also that you can disconnect from a shared drive at any time by choosing the Disconnect Network Drive option on File Manager's Disk menu.

11

Monitoring Usage

You can share your system with other users if you have an 80386 or later model system. However, performance may drop, or users may access files in a shared directory you don't want them to have or that you want to use yourself. The following utilities help you monitor how other users are accessing your system:

WinMeter   This utility graphically displays how much of your processor's time is allocated to sharing functions and how much is allocated to the programs you are running.

NetWatcher   This utility displays the names of users who are accessing your system and the files they are using. You can disconnect a user or close a file they have open.

Chat   This accessory lets you connect with another user and "chat." A split window displays messages you type and messages received from the other user. You can use this utility to send messages to other users. For example, you might need to tell another user that a file is currently available in a shared directory, or that you need to shut your system down and the shared directory will be temporarily unavailable.

You'll learn more about these utilities later in this chapter.

Sharing Directories

You use the File Manager to share directories on your system, or gain access to directories shared by other users. Figure 11-6 shows the File Manager Toolbar buttons you can click to share and stop sharing directories on your system, or connect with and disconnect from shared drives on other systems. The list of drives on the Toolbar displays a list of the most recent shared directories you've been connected to. If you are not currently connected to one of the drives, you can select it from the list to connect to it.

When you share a directory on your system, you can set how you want other users to access your system. In other words, you can let users read files but prevent them from changing or deleting the files. Likewise, other users can give you full or limited access to their directories.

If you've connected with a shared directory on another system, it appears as a directory window in File Manager and you can access it as if it were a local directory. You can also connect with shared directories from within many Windows applications by choosing the Open or Save As options on the File menu and clicking the Network button on the dialog boxes. However, note that connections from within applications are only maintained during the time the application is open. You will not see directory windows for the connections in File Manager unless you specifically connect to the directory in File Manager.

NOTE: CD-ROM drives can be shared like any other drive. The Microsoft CD-ROM Extensions (MSCDEX.EXE) version 2.21 (or later) must be loaded on the workstation that the CD-ROM drive is physically connected to. Refer to your CD-ROM drive manual for installation instructions. Note that you will need to include the /s switch when loading the command.

Sharing Directories on Your System

To share a directory on your system, you open the Share Directory dialog box in the File Manager as pictured previously in Figure 11-5. Before opening the dialog box, you can first click the directory you want to share. If you don't, you'll need to type the name of the directory in the dialog box.

To open the Share Directory dialog box, click the button on the Toolbar as pictured in Figure 11-6, or choose Share Directory from the Disk menu. A dialog box similar to Figure 11-5 appears with the name of the currently selected directory in the Path field. The following sections discuss the fields and how you might fill them out.

11

File Manager Toolbar buttons for working with network drives
Figure 11-6.

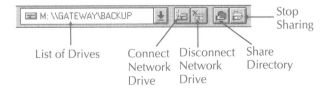

List of Drives

Connect Network Drive

Disconnect Network Drive

Share Directory

Stop Sharing

Share Name   Windows automatically inserts the directory name in the Share Name field, but you can change this name if you prefer to use a more descriptive name. The Share Name can be up to 12 characters in length.

TIP: You can hide a shared directory by including a dollar sign ($) at the end of its file name. This prevents unauthorized users from seeing it in their browse list. Refer to "Hiding Shared Directories" in this chapter for more information.

Path   The Path field lists the currently highlighted directory icon. To change the path, double-click the field and type over the existing entry.

Comment   Any text you type in the Comment field is seen by other users when they open the Connect Network Drive dialog box and browse through a list of shared directories. You could include comments like "Administrative use only" or "Project X files are on this system" to help users locate the directories they need to connect with.

Re-Share at Startup   If you want the directory shared every time you start Windows, make sure this option is enabled. If you only want to share a directory during your current session, disable this box.

Access Type field   Click one of the following options, based on the type of access you want users to have:

✦ *Read-Only*   Click this option to let users read files in the directory, but not change them. If you check this field, you can also type a password in the Read-Only Password field to restrict users' access to the directory. You give this password to only those users who can access the directory with the read-only privileges.

✦ *Full*   Click this option to let users both read and change the files in the directory. Users will be able to add, change, and delete files. To restrict who has access to the directory, type a password in the Full Access Password field. If you don't type a password in the field, all users on the network will have full access.

◆ *Depends on Password* This option lets you specify two levels of password access, one for read-only access and one for full access. Type a password for each in the fields at the bottom of the dialog box, then give the passwords to users based on the type of access they should have.

Be aware that other users may establish permanent connections to your shared directories. If you stop sharing the directory or don't turn your system on, they won't be able to access the shared directory. Of course, you are the one who controls how and when users access the directory, so you can stop sharing it at any time. However, if you do stop sharing the directory, send a mail message as a courtesy to other users and tell them the directory is no longer available. This also prevents unneeded service calls when other users "think" the system is misbehaving. You can use the NetWatcher utility to see who is sharing your directories and you can use the Chat or Mail programs to warn those other users that you won't be sharing the directory.

Hiding Shared Directories

You can prevent the name of a shared directory from appearing when other users browse your system for available directories. Simply include a dollar sign ($) at the end of the Share Name. You can use this feature to thwart unauthorized users from connecting with your directories. For example, you might share a directory with the name PRIVATE$. You then pass this directory name on to the users who are authorized to access the directory. Other users won't see it in their browse list. Of course, if they discover the name, they can connect with the directory, so it is not a fool-proof security measure. You should also use password security to prevent unauthorized users from accessing the directory.

Note that the name used appears in the drop-down file list box, along with the hidden string used to access the directory. Another user could conceivably walk up to the machine and look at this list to view the name of the hidden directory.

Accessing Shared Directories on Other Systems

To access a shared directory on another system, first click the down-arrow button in the list of drives box as shown on Figure 11-6. If you were recently connected to the directory, its name appears on the

11

list. Click the name to connect with the directory. If the name is not on the list, click the Connect to Shared Directory button on the Toolbar in File Manager, or choose Connect Network Drive from the Disk menu. A dialog box similar to Figure 11-7 appears. You can also check on this dialog box for previously connected directories. Click the down-arrow button in the Path field to see a list of the most recent connections and click the one you want if it is available.

To connect with a directory that is not on the drop-down list box in the Path field, start by selecting a computer in the Show Shared Directories on field. The list in this box is either collapsed or expanded, just like the directory tree list in a File Manager directory window. Follow the steps below to pick a computer and shared directory:

1. Double-click a workgroup icon to expand it and see the list of shared computers in the workgroup. Note that the workgroup list may already be expanded, so you can skip this step.

2. Click the shared computer in the expanded list you want to connect with. A list of shared directories appears at the bottom of the dialog box.

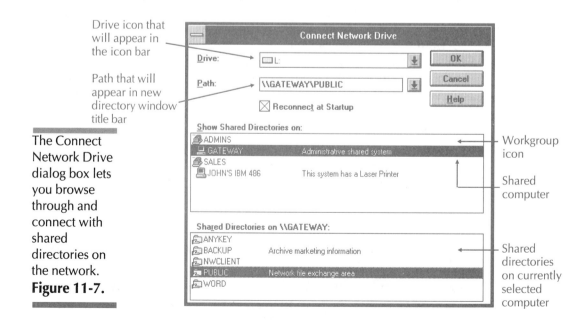

Drive icon that will appear in the icon bar

Path that will appear in new directory window title bar

The Connect Network Drive dialog box lets you browse through and connect with shared directories on the network.
Figure 11-7.

Workgroup icon

Shared computer

Shared directories on currently selected computer

3. Click the directory you want to connect with at the bottom of the dialog box. Its name is appended to the Path field. In Figure 11-7, the Path field indicates that the PUBLIC directory is selected.

As discussed under Hiding Shared Directories in the previous section, some directories are hidden. You will not see them listed in the Shared Directories field of the Connect Network Drive dialog box. However, if you know the name of the directory, type it in the Path field. Be sure to type "$" at the end of the name.

4. Now you can change the drive letter in the Drive field, but it is usually not necessary.

You can use the drive letter when referring to the shared directory, rather than typing its complete path. If necessary, you can use the letter of a drive that is already assigned to a shared directory. Doing so disconnects the current shared directory assignment and assigns the drive letter to the new shared directory. The drive letter you select will appear on the File Manager drive icon bar.

5. If you want to reconnect to this shared directory every time you start Windows for Workgroups, make sure the Reconnect at Startup box is enabled.

Keep in mind that the directory may not be shared every time you start your system. For example, a user might temporarily share a directory so you can transfer files. In this case, disable the Reconnect at Startup box so Windows doesn't attempt to reconnect with the directory in the future. If you don't disable the option, Windows displays error messages when it starts to inform you that it attempted to connect with an unavailable shared directory.

6. When everything is set the way you want, click the OK button to create the new shared directory connection.

If the directory is password protected, the following dialog box appears:

11

```
┌─────────────────────────────────────────────────────────┐
│ ▬              Enter Network Password                     │
├─────────────────────────────────────────────────────────┤
│ You must supply a password to make this connection:  ┌────────┐ │
│                                                      │   OK   │ │
│                                                      └────────┘ │
│                                                      ┌────────┐ │
│ Drive Letter:    L:                                  │ Cancel │ │
│                                                      └────────┘ │
│ Resource:        \\GATEWAY\PUBLIC                    ┌────────┐ │
│                                                      │  Help  │ │
│ Password:        │                              │    └────────┘ │
│ ⊠ Save this Password in Your Password List              │
└─────────────────────────────────────────────────────────┘
```

Type your password in the dialog box to gain access to the directory. If you don't want to save the password to access this directory with your logon password, disable the Save this Password in Your Password List option. For security reasons, your network administrator may require that this option be disabled to prevent users who have obtained your logon password from also gaining access to your directory connections.

If the Open New Window on Connect option on the Options menu is enabled, Windows creates a directory window for the new directory connection. If you disable this option, you can still access the directory by double-clicking its drive icon in the icon bar.

How to Stop Sharing Directories

Once you're done sharing directories, or using a shared directory on another computer, be sure to disable the sharing. If you don't stop sharing a directory on your system, users will see it in their lists of available drives, and may connect with the directory when you don't want them to. If you've established a connection to a shared directory on another system and no longer need it, be sure to disable the connection. It takes longer for your system to boot up for each drive it needs to connect to, and as mentioned previously, error messages appear when Windows tries to connect to directories that are no longer shared.

Stop Sharing a Directory on Your System

To stop sharing a directory on your system, click the Stop Sharing icon on the Toolbar, or choose Stop Sharing on the Disk menu. You'll see a dialog box similar to the following. Click the directory you want to stop sharing, then click the OK button.

If other users are still connected to the directory, you see a warning box similar to the following. You might need to contact other users (using Chat or Mail) to inform them that a shared directory on your system will no longer be available. Use the NetWatcher utility described later to find out who's accessing your system so you can send them a message. Click the Yes button to stop sharing the directory.

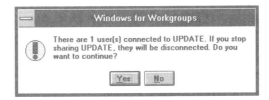

Disable a Connection to a Shared Directory

To disconnect from a directory on another system, click the Disconnect Directory button on the Toolbar, or choose Disconnect Network Drive on the Disk menu. You'll see a dialog box similar to the following. Click the drive you want to disconnect from, then click the OK button.

11

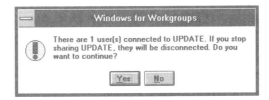

Chatting with Other Users

The Chat accessory provides a convenient way to converse with another user over the network. While a phone call might be more convenient, all messages typed with Chat can be copied and saved. In addition, you can insert blocks of text from documents and send them to other users. The standard Cut, Copy, and Paste commands are available on the Chat Edit menu for doing this. When you start Chat, a screen similar to the one shown in Figure 11-8 appears.

The three icons at the top left are used to dial another user, answer when another user calls you, or hang up a connection. You can also choose the same options from the Conversation menu. When you click the dialer icon, the standard network dialog box features for connecting with other computers appears. Simply click the workgroup icon and computer icon of the computer you want to chat with. You'll see a message that your computer is dialing the other system. The other system beeps, and the Chat icon appears on its desktop with the handset "rattling" in the holder. The person you are calling then double-clicks the icon to answer the call. To end the conversation, click the Hang-up icon, or choose Hang Up from the Conversation menu.

Messages you type appear in the upper window and messages received from the other users appear in the lower window. You can change this window arrangement by choosing Preferences from the Options menu. The following dialog box appears:

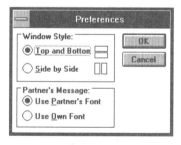

In the Window Style box, choose one of the window arrangements. You can also choose which font to use by clicking an option in the Partner's Message field. If your partner is sending formatted messages, be sure Use Partner's Font is selected. If you want to change the default font used by Chat, choose the Font option on the Options menu. If you want to change the background color, choose the Background Color option on the Options menu.

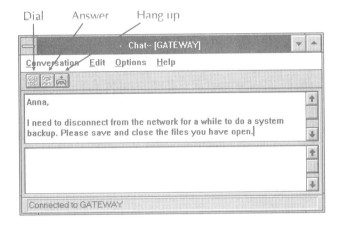

The Chat utility
Figure 11-8.

Monitoring Your System

WinMeter and NetWatcher are utilities that you can use to monitor other users' activities on your shared system. Both utilities are discussed in the following sections.

WinMeter

WinMeter graphically displays the amounts of computer processing time allocated to your programs and to network users. Double-click the WinMeter icon in the accessories group now and you'll see a display similar to this:

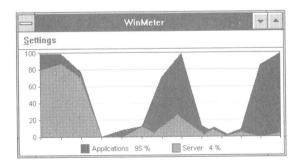

The display changes constantly depending on your activities and the activities of other users accessing your system.

11

You can change the colors and the sampling rate for WinMeter by opening the Settings menu.

◆ To change the colors, choose Application Color or Server Color from the Settings menu.

◆ To change the sampling rate, choose either 1 Second, 15 Seconds, 1 Minute, 5 Minutes, or 10 Minutes from the Settings menu.

◆ To see more of the graph, choose the Hide Title bar option from the Settings menu.

TIP: To restore the title bar from this mode, click the WinMeter window, then press the (Esc) key.

NetWatcher

You can use NetWatcher to monitor the directories and files accessed by other users and disconnect those users if necessary. Figure 11-9 shows a typical NetWatcher display. A list of users accessing your system appears on the left of the screen under the menu bar and Toolbar. Click one of these users to display a list on the right of the resources they are using.

The NetWatcher menu bar has three buttons: Properties, Disconnect, and Close File. Note that you can choose similar options on the Connection menu.

Properties   You can view the properties of a user by clicking the user's name, then clicking the Properties button, or by choosing Properties from the Connection menu. You'll see a window that describes the user and the user's logon time.

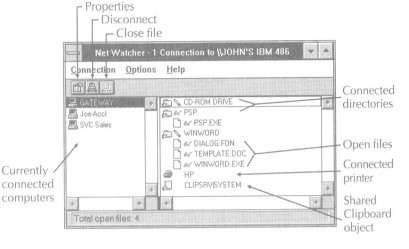

NetWatcher displays a list of users accessing your system and the resources they are using
Figure 11-9.

Disconnect   You can disconnect a user by first clicking the user's name, then clicking the Disconnect button (or by choosing Disconnect from the Connection menu).

Close File   You can close a file that another user is accessing by first selecting the file, then clicking the Close File button (or choose Close File from the Connection menu). The main reason for closing a file is because a user has inadvertently left it open and another user needs to access the file.

The Options menu contains options for changing the features of the NetWatcher window. These options are Toolbar, Status Bar, Refresh, and Split Window.

Toolbar   Choose this option to turn the Toolbar on or off.

Status Bar   Choose this option to turn the Status bar on or off.

Refresh   Choose this option to refresh the display of users if you feel it is not up to date. The display is refreshed automatically every 20 seconds.

Split Window   Choose this option to move the split in the window either left or right.

11

Disconnecting Users

You can disconnect a user with NetWatcher by first clicking the icon of the computer you want to disconnect, then clicking the Disconnect button. You'll see a screen similar to the following:

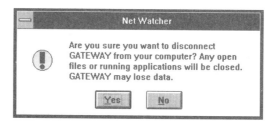

Be careful when disconnecting users. The user may have open files with important data that might be lost when you disconnect the user's system. Before you disconnect the user, send a message to the user so work can be saved. Remind them that they can save existing work to their own system, if necessary.

Closing Files

You can close a file another user is accessing with the NetWatcher Close File command. Windows for Workgroups locks other users out of files that are open to prevent file overwrites and data corruption. If you are sure a user is done with a file and has saved the changes, you can close the file to give other users access to it.

You might close a file because the user went off to lunch and inadvertently left it open on the system.

You might also close a file because a user has illegally opened one of your files. Keep in mind that once the file is in the memory of the user's system, you can't do anything to stop the person from reading it or saving it on his or her system. However, you can prevent the user from saving any changes (or destruction) of the file back on your system. You must act quickly, however, as discussed in the next section.

To close a file from NetWatcher, first click the computer that is using the file from the list on the left, then click the file you want to close, and finally click the Close File button. The dialog box shown here appears. Click Yes if you are sure you want to close the file.

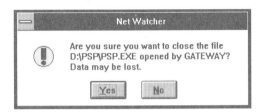

File Overwrite Precaution

Be aware that closing a file does not remove the file from the memory of a user's system. The file remains open, and the user can save it to his or her system. The user can also save a closed file back to your system and overwrite your originals! This is a problem if the reason you closed the file in the first place was to prevent a user from changing or corrupting the file.

To prevent a user from saving a closed file back to your system, immediately follow these steps to change the access right of the shared directory where the file resides:

1. In File Manager, click the icon of the shared directory the user has access to.
2. Click the Share As button.
3. Click the Read-Only option, then click the OK button.

Windows displays a message that the user currently connected may not be able to save their files. That's exactly what you want to accomplish.

You should follow this procedure with care. Changing a shared directory to read-only status may prevent unauthorized users from saving changed files, but it locks other users out as well. They can, however, save the file on their own system or another shared directory until you've re-shared the directory.

11

TIP: Your best defense against unauthorized access is to use password protection when sharing directories.

Monitoring Server Usage with File Manager

The NetWatcher utility has options for disconnecting users and closing files they have open. You can also close files from within File Manager. To view how an entire shared directory is being accessed by network users, follow these steps:

1. In the File Manager, click the icon of the directory you want to check.

2. Choose Properties from the File menu.

3. When the Properties dialog box opens, click the Open By button. You'll see a dialog box similar to Figure 11-10.

4. If you want to close a file, choose the file in the list box and click the Close File button.

Another way to close a file that another user is accessing is to first click the file in the directory window, then choose Properties from the File menu. When the Properties dialog box opens, click the Open By button, then click the Close Files button on the resulting dialog box.

NOTE: The Windows for Workgroups Resource Kit has additional utilities that network managers can use to monitor and manage the network. Refer to Appendix D for more information.

Novell NetWare and Microsoft LAN Manager Support

Windows for Workgroups lets you connect with and share the resources on Novell NetWare and Microsoft LAN Manager servers. Support for

The Open Files dialog box lets you view file users from File Manager and close files open by users
Figure 11-10.

these operating systems is loaded when you install Windows for Workgroups, or you can install the support later by accessing the Network icon in the Control Panel. Click the Network button on the dialog box and choose the network support you want to install.

Accessing NetWare Servers and Resources

When Novell NetWare support is installed, several changes are made to the AUTOEXEC.BAT and CONFIG.SYS files that you'll need to be aware of. The LASTDRIVE command in CONFIG.SYS determines the number of local and shared Windows for Workgroups drives you can have. In other words, it determines the number of drive icons you see in the File Manager, based on the local physical drives installed in your system (including CD-ROM and RAM drives), and the number of shared directories that appear as drives. Typically, Windows for Workgroup changes this to LASTDRIVE=P, which allows you to have up to 16 local drive assignments, including the shared directories you connect with using Windows for Workgroups. The first NetWare drive takes on the letter following the LASTDRIVE setting, typically Q. If you need to create other local drive assignments, increase the LASTDRIVE setting. If you need more NetWare drives and have unused drive letters for your local system, reduce the LASTDRIVE setting.

11

NOTE: Log onto your NetWare server before starting Windows for Workgroups. First switch to the Logon drive (typically Q), then type Logon. You can also include the logon commands in your AUTOEXEC.BAT file.

The commands MSIPX and NETX are added to the AUTOEXEC.BAT file. MSIPX loads the internetwork packet exchange software that lets your network card communicate on the network to the NetWare server and is dicussed further in Chapter 18. If you already had NetWare support installed before setting up Windows for Workgroups, the original IPX.COM file used for NetWare support is removed. NETX.COM provides DOS operating system support for accessing the NetWare operating system.

To connect with NetWare drives, follow these steps:

1. In File Manager, choose the Connect Network Drive option.

2. Click the NetWare button. The Network - Drive Connections dialog box appears, as shown in Figure 11-11.

3. Choose a drive letter in the Data drives list that you want to assign to the new mapped directory.

4. Click the Browse button to search for a directory on the NetWare server. The dialog box shown here appears:

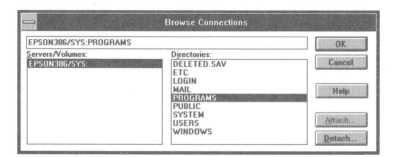

The text field at the top will display the directory name as you select it from the lower list boxes. You can also directly type the name in the top field.

The Network -
Drive
Connections
dialog box is
used to map a
drive letter to a
directory on a
NetWare server
Figure 11-11.

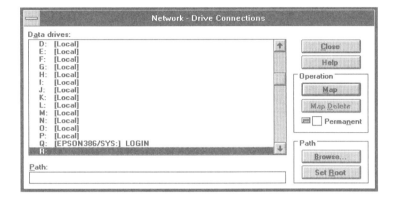

5. Double-click a server or volume name in the Servers/Volumes list box. The name appears in the top field.

6. Click a directory name in the Directories field on the right, or double-click a directory name to see its branching subdirectories. The directory (and subdirectory) names appear in the top field.

7. Once you've created the path to the directory you want to map, click the OK button. The Network-Drive Connections dialog box reappears with the directory path name in the Path field at the bottom.

8. Click the Map button to map this directory path to the drive letter you selected in the Data drives field.

9. If you want this path mapped to a drive letter every time you start Windows, enable the Permanent check box.

10. Click the Set Root button to make the drive appear as the root directory. This is necessary when running some applications.

You can continue to map other drives by following the same procedures. When you're done, click the Close button to return to File Manager. Icons for the new mapped drives appear on the drive icon bar and a directory window opens for the drive if the Open New Windows on Connect option is enabled on the File Manager Options menu.

11

In the Browse Connections dialog box, note that you can select a previously mapped data drive and click the Map Delete button to remove the drive mapping.

Accessing LAN Manager Servers and Resources

In order to connect with a LAN Manager network, at least one user on the Windows for Workgroup network must have a name that matches the name of the primary domain on the LAN Manager server. Once connected to the network, Windows for Workgroup users can access shared resources on the LAN Manager server, and users of other workstations connected to the LAN Manager server can access shared resources on systems in the Windows for Workgroup network.

To set options for LAN Manager, double-click the Network icon in the Control Panel. Click the Network button. If LAN Manager support was not installed when Windows for Workgroups was installed, you can install the support from this dialog box. Click LAN Manager on the left, then click the Add button. You will be asked to insert the appropriate disks.

If LAN Manager is installed, click its name on the right, then click the Settings button to make changes to the settings. Enable the Log On To LAN Manager Domain check box if you want to log on to LAN Manager whenever you start Windows for Workgroups. Type the domain you want to log on to in the Domain Name box. You can also change passwords by clicking the Set Password button. After you've made these changes, you must quit out of the dialog boxes, then restart Windows. Access to all LAN Manager resources is obtained in the same way you access Windows for Workgroup resources. Chapter 18 provides more information on LAN Manager for network administrators.

CHAPTER

12

PRINTING WITH WINDOWS

Printing a document in any Windows application is a relatively simple task; typically you choose the Print option from the application's File menu. There may be some slight variation in the way the Print command is listed or used, but its basic operation is essentially the same from one application to the next. There are, however, some behind-the-scenes details about printing that you should know, and they are covered in this chapter.

Before you can use a printer with Windows, you must install a *printer driver* to provide Windows with information about your printer, such as its graphics printing capabilities, how it handles paper, and which fonts it uses. Driver installation is normally done during Windows Setup, but you can use the Printers utility on the Control Panel at any time to change the way a printer is set up, to add a new printer, or to remove a printer. Windows for Workgroups lets you use printers attached to other network users' computers. You must install a printer driver on your own system for any "remote" printer you intend to use.

This chapter assumes that printer drivers are already installed for your printers. If this is not the case, choose the Printers icon in the Control Panel and click the Add button to install your printer drivers. Return here when your printer installation is complete.

The Printing Process

When you need to switch between two or more printers, specify different paper sizes, specify different printing orientations, and so forth, choose Print Setup on the File menu of the application you are working in. For example, open Windows Write and choose the Print Setup option on the File menu. The Print Setup dialog box is pictured in Figure 12-1. Methods for changing the print options are described in the illustration.

Print Manager

To print a document, use the Print command on the File menu of your application. The Print Manager then appears as an icon on the desktop, as shown here, for the duration of the print job. You can open the Print Manager and view or change the order of jobs in the Print Queue. You can also share your printer or connect with other network printers, as discussed later.

Another way to print is to drag document icons from the File Manager and drop them onto the Print Manager while Print Manager is running as a window or icon on the desktop.

Print Manager sends your document to the printer in the background as you continue working on other tasks. Documents are held in the Print Manager queue until they can be printed. You can view documents in the queue, change their order, or remove them, as long as they haven't yet started to print.

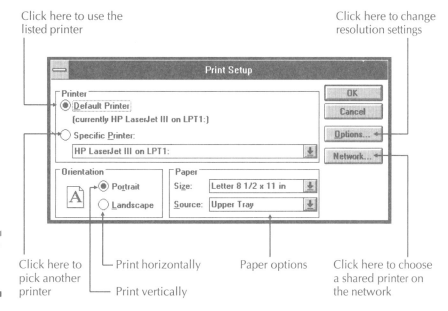

Click here to use the
listed printer

Click here to change
resolution settings

The Print Setup
dialog box
Figure 12-1.

Click here to
pick another
printer

Print horizontally

Print vertically

Paper options

Click here to choose
a shared printer on
the network

A typical Print dialog box is pictured in Figure 12-2. It has options for
specifying the range of pages to print and the number of copies to
print. In some cases, you can specify the quality of the printout from
low resolution for drafts to high resolution for final copies.

You learn about the Print command, Print Setup, and the Print
Manager in the following sections. The exercises guide you through the
steps of printing a document using Windows Write.

A Word About Fonts

12

The fonts that appear on character formatting menus of Windows
applications are either TrueType fonts, fonts specific to your printer,
third-party fonts, or screen fonts. In most cases, you'll want to print
with the TrueType fonts, which include Arial, Courier, Symbol, and
Times New Roman. TrueType fonts are scalable fonts; that is, you can
change their size over a large range. They are also designed to print just
as (or better than) they appear on the screen. The character size,

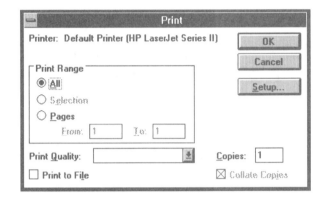

A typical Print
dialog box
Figure 12-2.

character spacing, and line spacing you see on the screen closely match
the appearance of the printed document.

Documents with TrueType fonts will have a consistent appearance
when printed on any Windows-supported printer, except for
differences introduced by the printing capabilities of the printer itself.
That means you can send documents to other users to print on their
printers, knowing the printout will look similar to your own.

The non-TrueType fonts listed on character formatting menus are
usually fonts built into the printer you've installed. For example, in the
Font dialog box shown here,

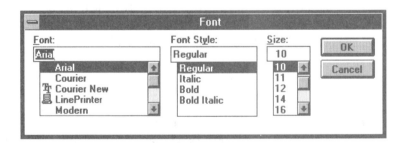

Arial and the Courier New font are TrueType fonts, as designated by the
TT icons next to their font names. The other Courier font is a printer
font as indicated by the printer icon.

When you install and select a PostScript printer, the Font dialog box displays font listings similar to these:

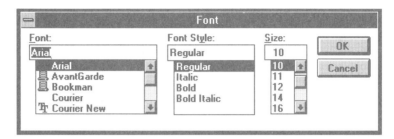

Notice that, in addition to TrueType fonts, PostScript fonts like AvantGarde and Bookman are available.

Since all Windows-supported printers can print TrueType fonts, this chapter assumes you've activated TrueType fonts. If you haven't, follow these steps before you do the exercises in the chapter:

1. Double-click the Control Panel icon in the Program Manager Main group.

2. Double-click the Fonts icon.

3. When the Fonts dialog box opens, make sure the Use TrueType option is marked. If it isn't, click it and then click the Close button.

Printing a Document

In the next few exercises, you work through the steps of printing a document, but first you need a document to print. Follow these next steps to create a document called FONTTEST that contains a sampling of several different fonts. When you're done, you will print the font test sheet to use in the future as a guide when assigning fonts to text.

1. Start Write by double-clicking its icon in the Program Manager Accessories window.

2. When the Write window opens, choose Fonts from the Character menu.

3. When the Font dialog box opens, click Arial in the Font list box. You may need to scroll to the top of the list to see it.

12

4. Click 12 in the Size box.

5. Click the OK button or press (Enter).

6. Type the following text in the Write workspace, and press (Enter) at the end of the line:

This is Arial 12 point regular

Repeat Steps 2 through 6 twice, first for TrueType Courier New and then again for TrueType New Times Roman. In Step 6, be sure to type the correct name for the font you've selected.

Now add one of the fonts that's specific to your printer by following these steps:

1. From the Write menu bar, open the Font dialog box.

2. Choose a non-TrueType font, such as Roman. (Remember, non-TrueType fonts are not preceded by the TT icon.)

3. Choose a font size of 12, and click the OK button.

4. Type the following text on a new line:

This is Roman 12 point regular, a non-TrueType font

5. Choose Save As from the File menu.

6. Type **FONTTEST** in the File Name field.

7. Click OK or press (Enter).

When you are done, the Write window will look similar to the following:

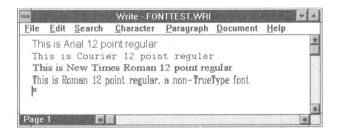

You can continue to add more font samples on your own. The printout will serve as a handy guide that you can post near your computer.

The Print Setup Dialog Box

Before printing a document, you may need to change the settings of a printer or switch to another printer. To do this, choose Print Setup on the File menu to open the Print Setup dialog box (Figure 12-1). Before you try printing the FONTTEST document, work through the following sections to learn the features of the Print Setup dialog box.

Choosing a Printer

When you have more than one printer, follow these steps to choose the printer you want to use:

1. In the Printer area of the Print Setup dialog box, click the down-arrow button in the Specific Printer list box until you see the printer you want to use; then click the printer name.
2. You'll make other selections in this dialog box later, but for now click OK to accept the new printer and close the dialog box.

Figure 12-3 shows what the Print Setup dialog box looks like when several printers are available. In Figure 12-3, the HP LaserJet III printer is attached to LPT1, and the IBM Color Printer is attached to LPT2. In addition, the HP LaserJet III attached to FILE is used to print PostScript documents to a disk file, as described in the next section. If you need to connect to a network printer, refer to "Connecting to Network Printers" later in this chapter.

Several printers available in the Specific Printer list box
Figure 12-3.

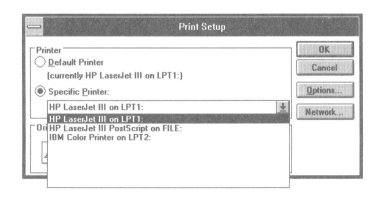

12

NOTE: It is not uncommon to install multiple drivers for a single printer, as is the case in Figure 12-3. The HP LaserJet III PostScript and HP LaserJet III are the same printer; the first is used when the removable PostScript font cartridge is installed, and the second is used when the cartridge is removed. Printing speed improves with the cartridge removed, but PostScript fonts become unavailable.

Using Print Files   A *print file* contains all the information required to print a document at a later time, even when the application that created the document is not running. You can create a print file with a Windows application by sending print output to a file instead of a printer. You can then send the file to a friend or co-worker to print on their printer. To print the file, the user need not start the application that created the file.

To create print files, start the Printers utility in the Control Panel and install the driver for the printer on which the document will be printed. Click the Connect button and specify FILE as its connection port.

When you print a document to a printer attached to a file connection port, Windows asks for the name of the file where it will store the print information. Once the file is created, you can copy it to disk and give the file to other users. You can even send it to a user over the network. There are three ways to print the print file:

✦ In the File Manager, drag and drop the icon for the print file to the running Print Manager.

✦ Select the Print command in the File Manager and specify the name of the print file in the text field.

✦ Use the COPY or PRINT command at the DOS prompt, as described in your DOS manual. For example, the following DOS COPY command prints a file called JANBUDG.DAT to the printer connected to the first parallel port (LPT1):

COPY JANBUDG.DAT LPT1

Setting Print Orientation

The choices shown in the Orientation area of the Print Setup dialog box (Figure 12-1) are for Portrait (vertical) or Landscape (horizontal) printing mode. Clicking one of these buttons changes the paper icon on the left representing the print orientation. Choose Landscape when you are printing wide spreadsheets and tables, or graphics that are wider than they are tall.

Choosing Paper Size and Source

In the Paper area of Print Setup, select the size and source of the paper to print on. Click the down-arrow button on the Size list box to view a list of paper sizes. Make sure you select the correct paper size so that pages will properly eject from the printer.

For Source, choose the paper tray where your printer will get paper, or the method it will use to advance paper as it prints. For a printer that has multiple trays, the list box will present different paper sizes or forms. For example, one tray might hold company stationary and another might contain regular or legal-size paper. When manual feed is selected from the list box, the printer waits for you to insert a sheet of paper or envelope in the manual feed slot.

Setting Other Options

Click the Options button on the Print Setup dialog box to display the Options dialog box. Not all options boxes will be the same. You can click the Help button for details. The following dialog box appears for most printers:

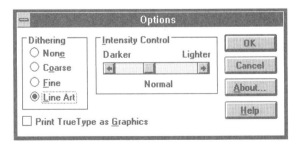

This dialog box is used to adjust the screen resolution when printing graphic images. The options are described in the paragraphs that follow.

After setting the options you want, click the OK button or press Enter to return to the Print Setup dialog box, and click OK there also.

Dithering   The dithering options let you specify the fineness of detail in graphic images when color images are printed on black-and-white printers. The option you select in the dithering box works in conjunction with the Intensity Control slide bar to control the conversion of colors to gray scale.

You can achieve the maximum number of dots per inch by selecting Fine or Line Art. The Fine and Line Art options work best on high-resolution printers like laser printers. The Line Art option converts some colors to patterns for special effects, so you'll need to experiment with the colors available in your applications when using this option.

Select Coarse to use larger dots, and None to print images with no gray shading at all.

Intensity Control   The Intensity Control slider bar allows you to darken or lighten the dot pattern when Coarse, Fine, or Line Art is selected in the Dithering box. You'll need to experiment to get the intensity that's right for your art. For example, in Paintbrush, yellow is the lightest color, but sliding the Intensity Control slider bar all the way to the Darker end causes yellow to print black. Sliding the bar toward Lighter makes colors that normally print black on black-and-white printers appear in various shades of gray. When Line Art is set, the nondithered colors on the left of the color bar in Paintbrush change intensity.

TrueType Fonts as Graphics   Mark the TrueType Fonts as Graphics option when you want to overlap graphic images onto text. When this option is enabled, it prints TrueType fonts as bitmap graphics. You may need to set this option on some printers that have problems printing TrueType fonts.

Connecting to Network Printers

One of the advantages of Windows for Workgroups is that you can use shared printers on other computers. You connect with these printers using the Print Setup dialog box, or the Print Manager as discussed later in this chapter.

Install a Printer Driver

Before you can use a shared printer on another system, you must have a printer driver for that printer installed in your system.

NOTE: If your printer driver is already installed, but not connected with a network printer, proceed to the next section, "Connecting the Driver to a Network Printer."

To load the driver, follow these steps:

1. Double-click the Printers icon in the Control Panel.
2. Click the Add button to install a new printer driver.
3. In the List of Printers field, choose the name of the shared network printer and click the Install button. You'll be asked to insert one or more of the Windows for Workgroups diskettes or a special drivers diskette supplied by the printer manufacturer.
4. When the newly installed printer name appears in the Installed Printers field, make sure it is highlighted, then click the Connect button and choose a port on the Connect dialog box. If you have a printer attached to your physical port LPT1, choose LPT2 or LPT3.
5. Click OK to complete the operation, then continue with the next section to connect the new printer driver to a physical printer on a network computer.

NOTE: If you don't have enough ports for both your local printers and the network printers you want to attach to, refer to "Adding Additional Ports" later in this section.

12

Connecting the Driver to a Network Printer

This section explains how to connect a printer driver on your system with a network printer. If you are continuing from the previous section, click the Network button on the Connect dialog box. If you are connecting an existing driver to a network printer, you can click the

Network button on the Print Setup dialog box of any application. The Connect Network Printer dialog box appears as shown in Figure 12-4.

The first step is to click the down-arrow button in the Path field to see if a previously connected printer is listed. If the printer is listed, click the printer, then click the OK button. If the printer is not listed, work through the following sequence, which is similar to the procedure covered in the last chapter for connecting to a shared network directory.

1. In the Show Shared Printers On field, double-click the workgroup that the computer with the attached printer belongs to.

2. When the workgroup expands, pick the computer that the shared printer is connected to. If you are not sure which computer it is connected to, click each computer icon to see a list of names and descriptions for the printers in the Shared Printers On field at the bottom of the dialog box.

3. When the printer you want to access appears in the Shared Printers On field, click it. The full path to the printer then appears in the Path field.

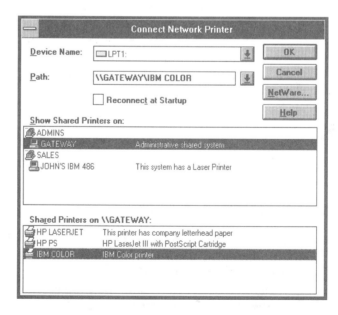

The Connect Network Printer dialog box is used to connect with a shared network printer

Figure 12-4.

4. In the Device Name field, choose a port to attach the printer to. Do not choose a physical port that is already in use by another printer attached locally to your system.

   Note that the port you choose for the network printer does not need to be physically installed on your system. Instead, Windows uses a fictitious port name so that you can print from your applications. If you send a print job to the port, Windows redirects it over the network to the computer that the shared printer is attached to. If you don't have enough port names, refer to the next section, "Adding Additional Ports."

5. Enable the Reconnect at Startup option if you want this printer connection every time you start Windows.

When everything is set the way you want, click the OK button. The name of the shared printer then appears in the Specific Printer drop-down list box of the Print Setup dialog box.

Adding Additional Ports

If you have printers attached to your local system and you connect with shared printers on other systems, you may use up the three default port names LPT1, LPT2, and LPT3. To add additional port names, follow these steps:

1. In File Manager, double-click the WIN.INI file icon. Notepad opens with the file in its workspace.
2. Scroll through the file until you see the section header called [ports]. You can also choose the Find command on the Search menu to locate this line.
3. In the [ports] section, locate the line that reads LPT3:=. Insert new lines underneath it as shown in the following. You don't need to add all the entries, only those for the additional ports you need, up to LPT9.

   LPT4:=
   LPT5:=
   LPT6:=
   LPT7:=
   LPT8:=
   LPT9:=

12

4. Save the file and restart Windows.

When you restart Windows, you'll have additional ports on which to assign shared network printers. Keep in mind that these are not physical ports, so you can't assign them to actual physical printers attached to your own system. You can only use them to refer to network printers.

The Print Dialog Box

This section describes how to print your FONTTEST document now that the printer is set up. The steps listed here help you print the file, and the options on the Print dialog box are discussed in the paragraphs that follow.

1. On the Write File menu, choose Print to display the Print dialog box, shown in Figure 12-2.

NOTE: The Print dialog box pictured in Figure 12-2 is specific to the Write application. Examples of other Print dialog boxes are presented later in this section.

2. Make sure All is selected in the Print Range box, to print the entire document.
3. Click the down-arrow button in the Print Quality list box, and then click the highest resolution listed.
4. Make sure the Print to File option is not marked, and that 1 is indicated in the Copies text box.
5. Click OK or press Enter to print the document.

If you are printing to a local printer and you haven't shared any of your printers, the Print Manager icon appears briefly on the desktop. The document is temporarily placed in a Print Manager queue and then

sent to the printer. When the document is printed, examine the text to see how the fonts look when printed.

Now let's explore the options of the Print dialog box.

Specifying the Print Range

The Print Range box contains options for specifying how much of your document to print.

✦ *All*   Choose this to print the entire document.

✦ *Selection*   Choose this to print the currently selected text in the document. This option is not available unless you have selected some text.

✦ *Pages*   This lets you print a range of pages. When you choose this option, you can specify the range to print in the From and To boxes.

Choosing Print Quality and Resolution

You set the print quality based on the type of image being printed and how you want it printed. In most cases, you will want to print with the highest quality available; however, if you need draft copies, want faster printing, or just want to save some ink or toner, pick a lower resolution.

In some cases, an image may shrink when you specify a high resolution, and it may be necessary to pick a lower print quality to print the image at a reasonable size. For example, if you create a graphic image at 75 dots per inch (dpi) and print it on a 300 dpi printer, the image may shrink to about a quarter of its original size. This is because the dot size on your screen is larger than the dot size on your printer. So while 75 dots may produce a 1-inch line on your screen, they produce only a 1/4-inch line when printed.

Many applications print at the size you intended by scaling images up on high-resolution printers or down on low-resolution printers. However, in some painting and drawing applications (such as Paintbrush), you can set an option called Use Printer Resolution to print an image at the printer's resolution. Thus you can work with an "exploded" view of an image on the screen, and then print it in a smaller, higher-resolution format.

12

Setting Other Print Options

Here are descriptions of the other options in the Print dialog box:

✦ *Print to File*   As discussed previously, you can send a document, including its formats and printer codes, to a file for later printing or printing on other systems. This print file can be copied to disk and sent to another user for printing on his or her system.

✦ *Copies*   Here, you specify the number of copies to print.

✦ *Collate Copies*   Mark this option to print your document in reverse order on sheet printers that normally stack pages with the printed side up.

NOTE: The Setup button in the Print dialog box opens the Print Setup dialog box so you can change the printer settings. Clicking this is the same as choosing Print Setup from the File menu.

Print Dialog Boxes in Other Applications

Print dialog boxes for other Windows applications have features related to those applications, or may have common features arranged in a different format. For example, here is the Paintbrush Print dialog box:

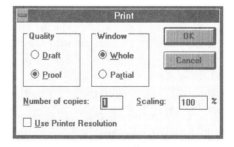

In this dialog box, choose Draft in the Quality box for faster printing, or choose Proof to print the highest quality. To print only part of a picture, choose Partial in the Window box, and then outline the part of the picture to print. The Scaling percentage text box lets you reduce or

enlarge the image, and you can mark Use Printer Resolution to match
the dot resolution of the image with the printer resolution, as discussed
in "Choosing Print Quality and Resolution" earlier in this chapter.

The Control Panel Printer Settings

There are two options available on the Control Panel Printers dialog
box of interest here. The first is used to turn Print Manager on or off.
The second is used to establish a default printer.

NOTE: You can also establish connections to network printers from
the Printers dialog box. Click a printer, then click Connect and
click the network button. A dialog box similar to Figure 12-4 then
appears, and you can follow procedures under "Connecting to Network
Printers" earlier in this chapter.

Setting the Default Printer

If more than one printer is connected to your system, one printer can
be designated the default printer. When applications are started, they
will use the default printer unless another printer is selected in the
application's Print Setup dialog box. Here's how to select a default
printer:

1. Select the Printers icon on the Control Panel. The Printers dialog
   box appears, similar to that shown in Figure 12-5.

The dialog box
for the Control
Panel Printers
icon
Figure 12-5.

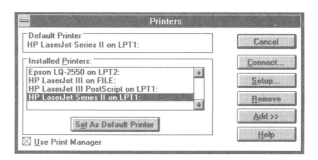

12

2. In the Installed Printers list box, click the printer you want to operate as the default printer.

3. Click the Set As Default Printer button.

4. Click OK to close the dialog box and accept the setting.

Bypassing Print Manager

The main purpose of Print Manager is to send printing information to your printers while you work on other tasks. However, when you are printing complex graphic images, it may be better to disable Print Manager to improve the printing speed. Print Manager also reduces system performance when in use, but the trade-off is that you don't need to wait for your document to finish printing before starting other work. To disable Print Manager, follow these steps:

1. In the Control Panel, click the Printers icon to display the Printers dialog box (Figure 12-5).

2. In the lower-left corner of the dialog box, unmark the Use Print Manager check box to turn the feature off.

3. Click OK to close the dialog box and accept the setting.

NOTE: Be sure to enable Print Manager after printing the graphics.

The Print Manager

Print Manager works as an intermediary between your Windows applications and your printer. It accepts print jobs from the applications, places them in a queue, and sends them to the printer in the proper order. You can start working on other tasks almost immediately after sending a document to the Print Manager. Non-Windows applications are not handled by the Print Manager, and instead are printed directly by the application, so there may be some delay before you can resume working.

Print Manager is also the control area for network printing. You can
share printers on your system from Print Manager, connect with shared
printers, or stop sharing and disconnect from network printers.

With Print Manager, it's not necessary to schedule your long and
complex print jobs after hours just so you can keep your computer
available for important tasks during the work day. For example, if one
of your clients calls and needs information, you can quickly access that
information on your system even though Print Manager is printing
your document. There's no need to stop the print job and finish it or
reprint it later. Print Manager can be assigned various priority levels
based on how much or little of your processor time you want allocated
to printing.

Print Manager holds print jobs in a queue until they can be printed. If
the printer is offline or out of service, Print Manager displays an
appropriate message and holds the jobs until the printer is again
available. If you attempt to exit Windows while print jobs are in a Print
Manager queue, a warning message appears and asks if you want to
discard the print jobs.

Most Print Manager features are shown in Figure 12-6. Descriptions of
Toolbar buttons are listed in Table 12-1.

The Print
Manager with
three available
printers and a
print job
waiting in the
queue of the
first printer
Figure 12-6.

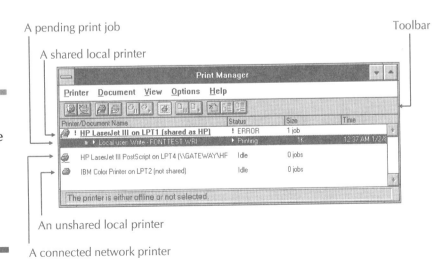

A pending print job

A shared local printer

Toolbar

An unshared local printer

A connected network printer

12

Click		To
	Connect network printer	Connect to a network printer.
	Disconnect network printer	Disconnect from a network printer
	Share printer as	Share your printer with others. This button appears only if Windows for Workgroups is running in 386 enchanced mode.
	Stop sharing printer	Stop sharing your printer with others. This button appears only if you are running Windows for Workgroups in 386 enhanced mode.
	Pause printer	Temporarily stop a printer from printing.
	Resume printer	Enable a printer to resume printing.
	Set default printer	Specify the selected printer as the default printer for Windows-based applications.
	Pause printing document	Temporarily keep the selected document from printing.
	Resume printing document	Enable a document to resume printing.
	Delete document	Delete the selected document.
	Move document up	Move the selected document closer to the top of the queue, making it print earlier.
	Move document down	Move the selected document closer to the bottom of the queue, making it print later.

The Toolbar
Buttons
Table 12-1.

Working with Print Jobs and Queues

You can view the files in the Print Manager queue and change the order in which they will be printed. You can also remove files from the queue. The following exercise gives you a chance to see how Print Manager works:

1. Activate the Write window and make sure the FONTTEST document is open.
2. Take your printer offline or turn it off.
3. Choose Print from the File menu and click OK to accept the default settings in the dialog box.

The Print Manager icon appears on the desktop, along with a message that the file is being printed. Because your printer is offline, the following message box appears:

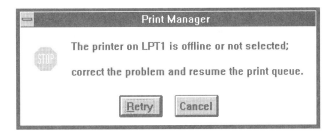

If this message were to appear during a normal printing operation, you would either turn the printer on, set it online, load paper, or fix any other problem the printer might be having. Then you would choose the Retry button. For the purpose of this exercise, however, let's take a look at how files stack up in the print queue:

4. Open the Print Manager by double-clicking its icon in the Program Manager, and leave your printer offline. The Print Manager window looks similar to Figure 12-6.

12

Notice in Figure 12-6 that the message bar says the printer on LPT1 is either offline or not selected. Three printers are listed in the work area, and the file waiting to be printed is listed in the queue under the first printer. Your Print Manager dialog box will look different, depending on the number of printers installed. Now send another print job to the Print Manager:

5. Click the Write window, select File, and choose Print.

6. Click OK to print the document. Once again, the Print Manager error message appears.

7. Click the Cancel button in the message box.

8. Repeat Steps 5 through 7 one more time to send yet another print job to the queue. The Print Manager window now looks like the one shown in Figure 12-7.

9. Open the Print Manager again, and notice that the three print jobs are waiting in the queue to be printed. In the next section you rearrange these print jobs.

Rearranging Queued Print Jobs

You can rearrange print jobs in the queue. Suppose you want to print the third job before the second job. In this exercise, the queued files have the same name and contents, but you can tell the difference between them by looking at the date and time of each job. The printer icon in front of a print job name indicates that it is ready to print, and

The Print Manager window with three print jobs waiting in the queue of the first printer
Figure 12-7.

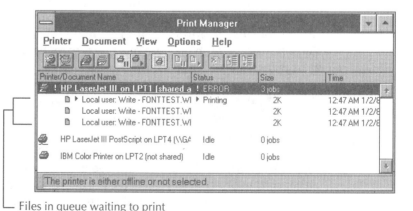

Files in queue waiting to print

theretore can't be rearranged. Let's switch the order of the second and third jobs in the queue:

1. Point to the third print job in the queue, and click and hold the mouse button. The mouse pointer changes to an up-arrow icon.
2. Drag it up to the second job. The mouse pointer changes to an .
3. Release the mouse button to switch the jobs.

Since the filenames are the same, look at the time on the right of the print jobs to confirm that they have switched positions in the queue.

NOTE: You can also click the Move Document Up or Move Document Down buttons on the Toolbar, or choose similar options on the Document menu to rearrange print jobs.

Pausing and Resuming Print Jobs

If you share the printer on your own system with other users, you can pause a print job and resume it at a later time. Note that you can't pause the printing of your own documents on your own system unless you take the printer offline, but you can pause them if they are sent to a shared network printer. To pause a print job, do the following:

1. Click the document you want to pause.
2. Click the Pause Printing Document button on the Toolbar, or choose the similar option from the Document menu.

To resume printing of a document, do the following:

1. Click the document you want to print.
2. Click the Resume Printing Document button on the Toolbar, or choose the similar option from the Document menu.

12

Pausing and Resuming Printers

Occasionally, a printer may stop printing or stall because it is out of paper or needs servicing. The top printer (HP LaserJet III) in Figure 12-7 is stalled and reports an error in its Status column. Additionally, you might pause a printer yourself to change paper or service the printer in other ways. To pause a printer for servicing, do the following:

1. Click the icon of the printer you want to pause.
2. Click the Pause Printer button, or choose the similar option from the Printer menu.

After fixing the problem, you can resume printing by working through the following steps. If you have been working the examples in this section, your printer is still stalled. You can place your printer back online and follow these steps to resume printing. Before doing so, you might want to refer to the next section to remove two of the example print jobs and avoid wasting paper.

1. Click the icon of the stopped printer.
2. Click the Resume Printer button, or choose the similar option from the Printer menu.

Deleting Print Jobs

To remove a document from the print queue, follow these steps:

1. Click the print job.
2. Click the Delete Document button on the Toolbar or choose the related option from the Document menu.
3. When the confirmation box appears, answer Yes if you really want to delete the print job.

Print Manager Menu Options and Control Buttons

The Print Manager has two important menus. The first is the Options menu, which lets you change the priority and features of the Print

Manager. The second is the View menu, which lets you turn the display of file information on or off, and lets you work with network queues.

The Printer Menu

The Printer menu has options for pausing and resuming a printer; connecting to and disconnecting from shared network printers; and sharing or not sharing your local printers. These options can also be selected from the Toolbar, the network printer options are covered later under "Using Printers on NetWare Servers."

View Menu Options

Some of the following View menu options may not be available if you are not connected to a network.

◆ *Time/Date Sent*   When this option is on, the Print Manager window display includes the time and date that the file was sent to the Print Manager queue.

◆ *Print File Size*   When this option is on, the Print Manager window display includes the file size.

◆ *Status Text*   This displays the status of printers when enabled.

◆ *Refresh*   When you are connected with a network printer, the Refresh option is used to get the latest list of files waiting in the queue of network printers.

◆ *Other Network Printer*   Displays a list of documents sent to a printer that you are not connected to. Use this box to check the status of other printers. For example, you might be trying to locate an available printer. Type the network path for the printer in the Network Printer box.

The Options Menu

12

The options menu has a number of choices for customizing the Print Manager. Each is described here:

◆ *Toolbar*   This option is normally enabled to display the Toolbar. If you want to remove the Toolbar, disable this option.

✦ *Status Bar*   The status bar displays messages about the activities of the Print Manager. You can disable this option to reduce the size requirements of the window.

✦ *Font*   Choose this option to change the font used to display text in the Print Manager window.

✦ *Set Column Width*   Choose this option to change the width of the columns in which status information is displayed. Follow these steps to adjust the columns:

1. Choose Set Column Width from the Options menu.

2. Move the mouse to the status area. A two-headed arrow appears.

3. Move the arrow left or right to adjust the first column.

4. Click the right mouse button to move to the next column.

5. Move the mouse to adjust the columns, then click the right mouse button to adjust the last column.

6. Click the left mouse button to complete the operation.

The Background Printing Option

The Background Printing option on the Options menu is used to set the priority (the amount of your system processors time that is allocated to printing) and the amount that is allocated to running programs. Choose this option to display the dialog box in Figure 12-8.

Set the options on the Background Printing dialog box as described in the following sections.

Use the Background Printing dialog box to change the allocation of processor time given to printing on your system
Figure 12-8.

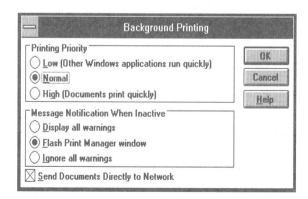

Low, Normal, and High Priority   The Low, Normal, and High priority settings let you control how much time Print Manager gives to print jobs in the background as you work with other applications. In any multitasking environment, every running application is given a portion of processor time. The portion you give Print Manager is determined by selecting Low, Normal, or High priority.

With *Low priority,* print jobs are given less processor time as applications are given more processor time. Use Low priority when you want to print while you continue to work in a foreground application. This option ensures that your application is given the full complement of processor time when it is working on a task; the print jobs continue printing when the application is not busy.

With *Normal priority,* print jobs and applications are allocated processing time somewhat equally. Your application may slow down some when more information is sent to the printer. You might want to start printing with this option enabled, and then switch to Low priority if your application is running too slowly or High priority if you need to quickly finish the print job.

In *High priority,* print jobs are given a larger processor share than applications. Choose this priority level for your print jobs when you are working in applications that don't require a lot of processor time—for instance, when typing unformatted text in an application such as Notepad.

The print priority setting depends on the type of application you're using. A database application that is sorting a mailing list requires almost 100 percent of your processor time, so printing may pause until the sorting task is complete, depending on the job priority and the application. On the other hand, when working with a word processor, your system idles every time you stop typing. This idle time can be put to use for printing. If Low priority is selected, the idle time is given to the Print Manager, and you won't see much of a slowdown when you resume typing. With High priority selected, you'll see interruptions as Print Manager occasionally sends more text to the printer.

Display All Warnings   When the Display all warnings option is enabled, Print Manager messages are displayed immediately.

12

Flash Print Manager Window   Select the Flash Print Manager window option if you want the Print Manager title bar or its icon on the desktop to flash when Print Manager needs to display a message. You then open or activate the Print Manager to view the message.

Ignore All Warnings   Turning the Ignore all warnings option on prevents messages from being displayed if the Print Manager window is inactive or reduced to an icon.

Send Documents Directly to Network   Enable this option to print directly to a network printer. It improves performance by bypassing the Print Manager. If disabled, documents sent to network printers are tracked as if they were sent to your own printer.

NOTE: See your network administrator for more information about using the printers on your network.

Sharing Printers on Your System

Windows for Workgroups lets you share a printer attached to your system with other users, or use a shared printer on another system. To share printers, your system must be an 80386 or later, running in 386 enhanced mode. Table 12-1 defines the buttons on the Toolbar you use to work with network printers.

To share printers attached to your system with other users, click the Share Printers icon on the Print Manager Toolbar, or choose Share Printer As on the Print menu. A dialog box similar to the following appears:

The first step is to choose one of the printers attached to your system to share in the Printer field. If you have only one printer, it appears in the field. Fill out the rest of the field in the dialog box based on the following information.

Printer   Your default printer appears in the Printer field. If other printers are attached to your system, you can choose one of them in the drop-down list box.

Share as   In the Share as field, type a name that will identify the printer for other users. For example, you can specify its type or its location in your building.

Comment   Use the Comment field to provide users with additional information, such as the type of paper loaded, or the hours that nonadministrative employees can use the printer.

Password   If you want to limit access to the printer, type a password in the Password field, then give that password to only those users who can access the printer.

Re-share at Startup   Enable this option if you want to share the printer every time you start Windows.

Separator Pages

When sending documents to network printers for printing, it's useful to include a separator page. This is a sheet of paper that separates one print job from the next in the output tray of the printer. To use separator pages, choose the Separator Pages option on the Options menu. The following dialog box appears:

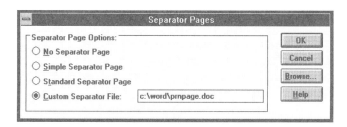

12

TIP: Print jobs from some MS-DOS applications do not properly form-feed the last page of the print job. Separator pages provide a useful way of forcing the last page of the job to output to the paper tray so the next job doesn't print over it.

The separator page you define is used to separate all print jobs on your system, even those sent by other network users. If more than one printer is attached to the system, you cannot define different separators for each printer. The following defines which separator page type you should use:

✦ *Simple Separator Page*   Use this type if your printer is a daisy-wheel printer that doesn't accept special downloadable fonts from your computer.

✦ *Standard Separator Page*   Use this type if you have a laser printer that can print downloadable and scalable fonts.

✦ *Custom Separator File*   Use this option if you want to define the text that is printed on the separator page.

Custom Separator Pages

You click the Custom Separator File option on the Separator Pages dialog box to specify the name of a text file that should be used when printing the separator page. The custom separator page accepts Windows *metafiles,* or Clipboard information. A metafile is a graphical file created with some Windows applications, such as the Draw program supplied with Microsoft Word for Windows. You can specify metafile formats when saving graphics in many Windows applications. You can also save information on the Clipboard in a metafile format and transfer the information to other documents, such as the custom separator file.

You can create a custom separator page in an application such as Word for Windows, using its built-in Draw utility. You can include graphics in the separator page, and the following strings.

    %1% The name of the document being printed

%2% The name of the person printing the document

%3% The date and time the document is printed

For example, your separator page might have the following entries:

```
D O C U M E N T   S E P A R A T O R
File Name:, %1%
Owner:, , %2%
Date:, , %3%
```

You can also include a graphics image in the file or other text information. Save the file, then open the Separator Pages dialog box and type the path and filename of the separator page in the Custom Separator File field.

How to Stop Sharing Printers on Your System

When you're done sharing your printer, click the Stop Sharing Printer button, or choose Stop Sharing Printer from the Printer menu. You'll see a list of shared printers. Choose the printer to stop sharing and click the OK button. To stop using a shared printer on another system, click the Disconnect Network Printer button or choose Disconnect Network Printer on the File menu.

Connecting and Disconnecting from Shared Printers

You can connect with a shared printer attached to another computer on the network by following the procedures outlined in the earlier section in this chapter, "Connecting to Network Printers."

To disconnect from a shared network printer, click the Disconnect Network Printer button, or choose the similar option from the Printers menu. Choose the printer you want to disconnect from in the list and click the OK button.

12

Using Printers on NetWare Servers

You can connect with shared printers on NetWare servers if your system is attached to those servers and you have been granted the appropriate rights to access the printers. The following steps describe how to connect with the printers.

1. Click the Connect Network Printer button on the Toolbar.
2. When the Connect Network Printer dialog box appears as shown in Figure 12-4, click the NetWare button. The Network-Printer Connections dialog box shown in Figure 12-9 appears.

In NetWare, you connect with a print queue instead of directly to a printer. Several queues might be connected to the same printer with each providing a different service. For example, one queue might provide higher-priority service than another, but access to the queue might be for managers only and password-protected. Another queue might hold files for printing at a later time. For example, in Figure 12-9, the LATE_NITE queue prints any documents it holds after midnight.

To connect with a NetWare printer, work through the sequence listed on the following page.

The Network-
Printer
Connections
dialog box lets
you connect
with printer
queues on a
NetWare
network
Figure 12-9.

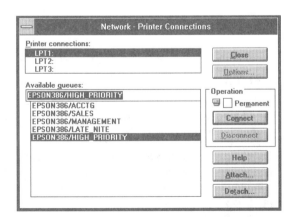

NOTE: It is assumed you are already logged onto the NetWare server before starting Windows (Novell's recommended procedure). If not, click the Attach button to log on.

1. Choose a port in the Printer connection field. Don't use a port you've already assigned to another printer.
2. In the Available queues field, choose the queue you want to attach to.
3. If you want this connection every time you start Windows, enable the Permanent check box.
4. Click the Connect button to connect with the printer.
5. You can repeat steps 2 through 4 to connect with other NetWare queues, or click the Close button to return to Print Manager.

12

CHAPTER

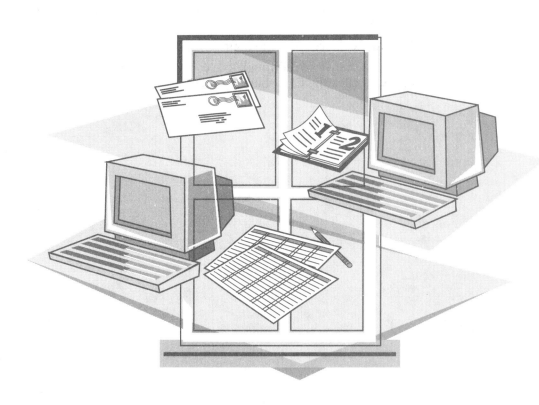

13

THE CLIPBOOK VIEWER

The ClipBook Viewer is a new accessory in Windows for Workgroups. Its icon appears in the Program Manager Main group. Double-click the icon now to open its window. ClipBook provides the functionality of the Clipboard for cutting and pasting information among applications. In addition, it provides a cataloging *feature that lets you permanently store Clipboard images and other information for later use in an area called the Local ClipBook.*

Figure 13-1 shows the ClipBook Viewer. On the left is the regular Clipboard, which displays the most recent image copied to it. On the right is the Local ClipBook, which displays images in a reduced view called a *thumbnail*. To display ClipBook images full size, or simply list them by name, you can choose a view method on the View menu. Notice that each image in the Local ClipBook has a name that you or other users refer to when sharing or connecting with the image. A ClipBook Viewer can hold as many as 127 pages of information.

NOTE: For simplicity, graphic images, text, and spreadsheet data that you copy or paste using the Clipboard are referred to collectively as *objects* in this chapter. Objects copied to the Local ClipBook are pasted into pages that you "flip" or scroll through.

Objects on the Clipboard are temporary and overwritten every time you execute another Copy or Cut command within an application. However, you can paste Clipboard objects to the Local ClipBook, which retains them for later sessions. You can close the ClipBook Viewer and even exit Windows. The next time you open the ClipBook Viewer, the pasted objects are still available.

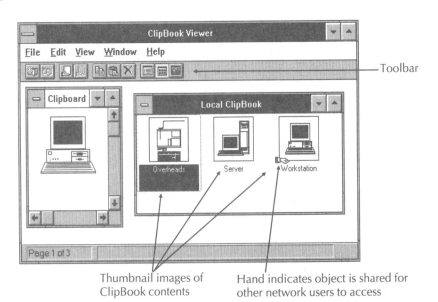

The ClipBook
Viewer
Figure 13-1.

Thumbnail images of   Hand indicates object is shared for
ClipBook contents   other network users to access

The most exciting feature of the ClipBook Viewer is that you can share Local ClipBook objects with other network users. You can share some or all of the objects, and users can copy them for pasting into their own documents. Other network users use their ClipBook to connect with your ClipBook. Figure 13-2 shows how a ClipBook window from another computer appears when you connect with it over the network. In this example, the ClipBook on the network computer called GATEWAY is available. Notice that the Clipboard and Local ClipBook are still available. You can use ClipBook images from other computers in the same way you use your Local ClipBook; however, you cannot paste images to other users' ClipBooks. Instead, users must copy objects from your ClipBook and paste them to their ClipBooks.

NOTE: You must be running Windows in 386 enhanced mode to share your ClipBook with other users.

ClipBook on \\GATEWAY is a shared ClipBook from another computer

Figure 13-2.

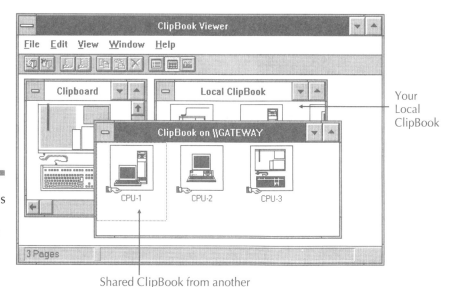

Shared ClipBook from another network computer

13

Imagine you are talking on the telephone with a co-worker about a joint project. You are discussing the art or spreadsheet information that will go in the project report. Your co-worker wants to see the art you've developed so far, so you place it on your Local ClipBook and share it over the network. Your co-worker then connects with your ClipBook and looks at the art. All this happens during your conversation. Now consider how the ClipBook can help integrate information for the report, including spreadsheet data from the accounting department, text from the marketing department, and art from the graphics department. Each department places its information on their ClipBooks and shares it. The project manager then integrates the shared information into the final compound document.

NOTE: In the next chapter, you'll see how to create even more sophisticated compound documents by combining linked information that is automatically updated when necessary.

ClipBook Features

This section describes ClipBook features and how to use them. Table 13-1 describes the buttons on the Toolbar. Each Toolbar button is also represented by a menu option on the ClipBook menu, as discussed later in the section, "Setting ClipBook Features."

TIP: When you first start ClipBook, the Clipboard is minimized. Before you read further in this chapter, you might want to restore the Clipboard and rearrange the ClipBook Viewer so you can see both the Clipboard and Local ClipBook similar to Figure 13-1.

The Clipboard

In Chapter 4, you learned how to use the Copy, Cut, and Paste commands on the Edit menu of Windows applications. You still use these same commands when working with the ClipBook. To place information on the Clipboard, you first outline or highlight the information as listed in the following, then choose Copy or Cut from the Edit menu, or press Ctrl-C or Ctrl-X respectively.

✦ To select text in a word processing program, you typically drag through the text with the mouse pointer.

Click		To
	Connect button	Connect to a ClipBook on another computer
	Disconnect button	Disconnect from a ClipBook on another computer
	Share button	Share a ClipBook page
	Stop Sharing button	Stop sharing a ClipBook page
	Copy button	Copy the selected ClipBook page onto the Clipboard
	Paste button	Paste the contents of the Clipboard onto the ClipBook
	Delete button	Delete the contents of the Clipboard or selected ClipBook page
	Table of Contents button	Display the titles of the the pages saved on the ClipBook
	Thumbnails button	Display small pictures (thumbnails) of each page on the ClipBook
	Full Page button	Display the contents of the selected ClipBook page

The ClipBook
Toolbar Icons
Table 13-1.

13

✦ In drawing applications, you usually click the graphic object you want to copy, or drag a box around it.

✦ In a spreadsheet program such as Excel, you click and drag the mouse pointer through the cells you want to copy.

Once the information is on the Clipboard, you can paste it elsewhere. Open the application where you want to paste the information, then position the mouse pointer or insertion point and choose the Paste command, or press [Ctrl]-[V].

Capturing the Screen and Windows to the Clipboard

You can capture the entire screen or the active window to the Clipboard using the following methods. The objects are captured as bitmaps that you can paste into Paintbrush or other bitmap editors. You can then change the images as necessary.

Capturing the Entire Screen   Press the [Prt Sc] key to capture the entire screen. On older keyboards, you may need to press [Alt]-[Prt Sc] or [Shift]-[Prt Sc].

Capturing the Active Window   Press [Alt]-[Prt Sc] to capture only the active window.

Saving Clipboard Objects to Files

While ClipBook provides a method for saving Clipboard objects to the Local ClipBook for later use, you can also save a Clipboard object to a separate file. For example, you might need to save a Clipboard object on disk and mail the disk to another user. Or, you might have an object that you want to save, but you just don't want it on the Local ClipBook. Follow these steps to save the object:

1. On the Clipboard, capture the graphic, text, or other information you want to save.

2. Open the ClipBook and click the Clipboard icon or document window.

3. Choose Save As from the File menu. Type a name for the file and click the OK button. Clipboard files are automatically assigned the .CLP extension.

Remember that Clipboard objects are overwritten when you capture a new object. Use the Save As option as an alternative method of saving an object you don't place on the Local ClipBook. To retrieve a previously saved object, choose the Open command on the ClipBook File menu and specify the name of the previously saved file.

Setting ClipBook Features

The View menu pictured in Figure 13-3 has options for customizing the ClipBook window and choosing the type of view you want to see in the Clipboard and Local ClipBook. These options are described in the following sections.

Toolbar   Enable this option to display the Toolbar. Disable it to remove the Toolbar so you can reduce the size of the ClipBook Viewer window. When the Toolbar is disabled, you can still access related options from menus.

Status Bar   The status bar displays messages related to your activities. You can disable the option to reduce the size of the ClipBook window if necessary.

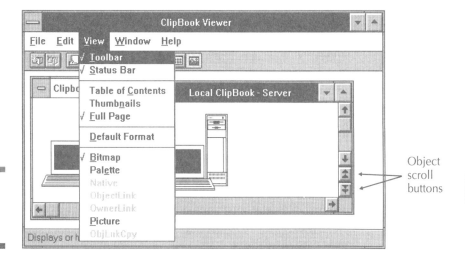

The ClipBook Viewer View menu
Figure 13-3.

13

Table of Contents   This option is only available when the Local ClipBook (or a ClipBook shared from another network computer) is active. If you enable it, the Local ClipBook (or shared ClipBook) window appears as shown here. Each object is listed by name. If the object is shared, a hand appears in the left corner under its icon.

Thumbnails   When this option is enabled, you see a reduced view of the objects on the Local ClipBook with enough detail to discern the image. The Local ClipBook in Figure 13-1 shows how thumbnails appear. Each image on the Local or shared ClipBook is called a *page*. Compare the object in the Local ClipBook called Workstation to its normal image size in the Clipboard on the left.

Full Page   Click this option to display images in the Local ClipBook (or shared ClipBook) at their full size. When you click this option, an extra set of buttons appears in the scroll bar of the window for jumping between object pages.

Format Options

The remaining options on the View menu depend on the type of image on the Clipboard or object selected in the ClipBook. The Clipboard accepts a number of text or graphics formats so you can transfer information between different applications. For example, when you copy an image in Paintbrush, the object is placed on the Clipboard in a default format, a bitmap format, and a picture format. When you paste the object into another application, the application uses the format that it understands the best. In other words, the application doesn't need to convert the image because the source application (in this case, Paintbrush) has already supplied several different possible formats.

You can view how the image or text appears in the different formats by clicking any of the available options. This step has no permanent effect on the image or text.

Text is stored in three formats:

✦ *Owner Display* is the way text looks in the document, based on the character formatting you applied to it.

✦ *Text* displays the characters as plain text.

✦ *OEM Text* is the MS-DOS-based text format.

Graphic image formats vary widely. You'll see a list of different formats, but some are usually grayed, which means they are not available for the current image.

Working with Your Local ClipBook

When you have information on the Clipboard that you want to save for later use or share with other users on the network, you can paste it to the Local ClipBook. Remember, however, that you can't paste objects to other users' ClipBooks. To paste an object, follow these steps:

1. Capture the graphics, text, or other information on the Clipboard using the Copy or Cut option on the Edit menu of the application that holds the information.

2. Open the ClipBook. You'll see the captured information in the Clipboard window.

3. Click the Local ClipBook window to make it active.

4. Choose the Paste option on the Edit menu, or press ⌨Ctrl⌨-⌨V⌨. The following dialog box appears when you paste the object to the Local ClipBook:

5. Type a name for the object in the Page Name field.

6. Enable the Share Item Now field if you want to make the item shareable. If not, disable the check box. If you're not sure whether

13

you'll need to share this object, disable the box. You can share it at any time by choosing the Share As option on the ClipBook File menu.

7. Click the OK button to paste the object.

If you are sharing the object, the Share ClipBook Page dialog box appears as shown in Figure 13-4. Go to the next section now to complete the dialog box. If not, the image is pasted to the Local ClipBook. You can leave ClipBook open, or close it without further action. The image you pasted to the Local ClipBook will be available automatically the next time you start ClipBook.

Sharing a Local ClipBook Object

This section describes how to share your ClipBook pages. When a ClipBook page is shared, other users at remote network computers can access that ClipBook page.

If you are continuing here from the last section, the Share ClipBook Page is open on your screen as shown in Figure 13-4 and you can start with Step 3. If you are sharing a page you previously pasted to the Local ClipBook without sharing, start with Step 1.

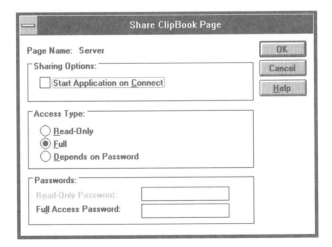

The Share
ClipBook Page
Figure 13-4.

1. Click the page you want to share in the Local ClipBook.

2. Choose Share from the ClipBook File menu. The Share ClipBook Page dialog box appears as shown in Figure 13-4.

3. Enable the option Start Application on Connect to allow remote users to establish a link to the application you used to create the shared object.

4. In the Access Type field, click one of the options depending on the type of access you want remote users to have to the shared page.

5. In the Passwords field, type a read-only and/or full-access password if you only want specific users to access the page. Give the passwords to those users, depending on their access rights.

When everything is the way you want, click the OK button. The shared object appears in your Local ClipBook with a hand next to it. Other users can now connect with your ClipBook and access the object.

Connecting with Other ClipBooks

You connect with other users' ClipBooks to use the shared items on those ClipBooks. When you make a connection, a window appears in your ClipBook with the computer name of the remote ClipBook in its title bar. Follow these steps to make the connection:

1. Open ClipBook Viewer if it is not already started.

2. Choose Connect from the File menu.

3. The Select Computer dialog box appears, similar to that in Figure 13-5. Choose a computer as follows:

   ✦ If you've recently connected with the computer that has the ClipBook you want to access, click the down-arrow button in the Computer Name field and click the name on the drop-down list box.

   ✦ If the name is not in the drop-down list, use the procedure you learned in previous chapters to select a computer in the Computers field.

13

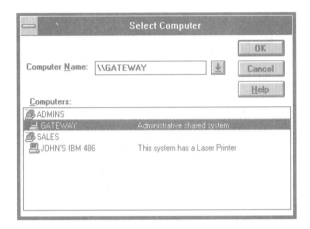

Use the Select
Computer
dialog box to
choose the
computer with
the ClipBook
you want to
access
Figure 13-5.

4. Click the OK button when the correct name appears in the
   Computer Name field.

In a moment, the ClipBook of the remote computer appears in your
ClipBook Viewer window. You can now copy the ClipBook objects to
the Clipboard and paste them in documents, as reviewed in the next
section.

Using ClipBook Objects in Your Documents

When you need to use an object on your Local ClipBook or the
ClipBook of a remote user, you simply locate the object and copy it to
the Clipboard as described in the following steps:

1. Open the ClipBook.
2. If the object you need is on a remote computer's ClipBook, follow
   the procedures in the previous section to connect with that
   ClipBook.
3. Make the Local ClipBook or remote ClipBook window active by
   clicking it with the mouse.
4. Change the view by choosing Table of Contents (name listing),
   Thumbnails (small pictures), or Full Page (full-size image) from the
   View menu.

5. Click the page you want to use.

6. Click the Copy button on the Toolbar, or press Ctrl-C to copy the object to the Clipboard.

7. Switch to the program and document where you want to paste the object and position the insertion point where you want to paste the object.

8. Choose Paste from the Edit menu or press Ctrl-V. The object appears in the document.

Object Linking and Embedding

Most Windows applications now provide support for object linking and embedding (OLE). You learn more about OLE in the next chapter, but for now, you should know that objects pasted from other applications can be much more than static items in your documents. Objects can be embedded in documents, or linked to the original file from which they were copied.

Embedded Objects   Most objects you paste are embedded. If you double-click an embedded object, the application used to create it is started with the object in its workspace so you can edit it. In this way, you don't need to be aware of the application that created an object. For example, if you create a company logo in Paintbrush, then copy and paste the logo into a Write document, you can double-click the pasted object at any time to quickly start Paintbrush and make editing changes to the object. An embedded object "remembers" the application that created it. Note, however, that the application must be available on the local system.

Linked Objects   A linked object is an embedded object with a few extra properties. A linked object reflects any changes made to the original object. For example, you could paste-link a column of numbers from an Excel spreadsheet called BUDGET.XLS into a Write document. Later, if you make changes to BUDGET.XLS from Excel, those changes are automatically made to the pasted information in the Write document. If you copied the spreadsheet information from another network user's ClipBook, and that other user makes changes to the spreadsheet on their system, the ClipBook information is changed and the information in your document also changes! Linking is an

13

extremely useful feature that lets you create "compound documents" over the network. If you paste art into your documents from the art department's shared ClipBook, any changes the artists make to the art are automatically updated in your documents the next time you open the document. This relationship is pictured in Figure 13-6.

Creating Document Links

Creating compound documents with network links enables workgroups to collaborate on projects without a lot of running around and organizational management. Information links keep information in compound documents updated as it changes. Here are the steps for linking ClipBook information into your document:

1. Start your ClipBook and click the Connect button.
2. Connect to the ClipBook of the remote computer that has the object you want to integrate into your document.
3. Select an object on the remote ClipBook and click the Copy button.
4. Switch to your application and position the insertion point where you want the object pasted.
5. Choose Paste Special from the Edit menu. A dialog box similar to the one on the next page appears:

The ClipBook serves as a link between network computers and allows pasted information to be updated automatically

Figure 13-6.

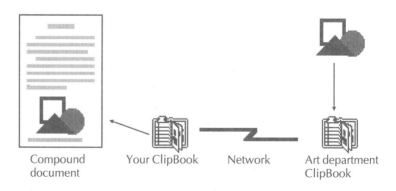

Compound document   Your ClipBook   Network   Art department ClipBook

6. In the Data Type field, click the format you want to use for the pasted data. The highlighted default format is usually sufficient.

7. Click the Paste Link button.

The information is pasted into your document and a link is established to the source document file that contains the information the remote user pasted to their ClipBook. Note that the information must exist in a file, as well as on a shared ClipBook page. Any changes made to the source file are automatically updated in your document.

For more information on object linking and embedding, continue reading in the next chapter.

13

C H A P T E R

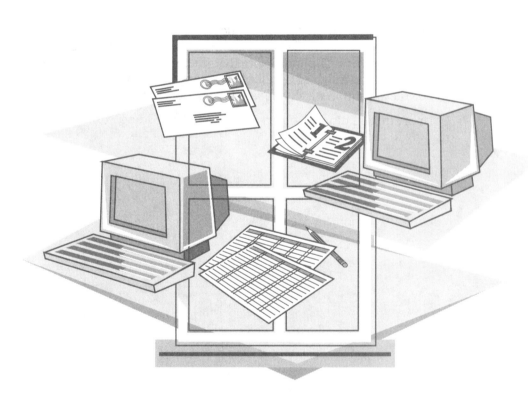

14

CREATING COMPOUND DOCUMNENTS

Don't let the title of this chapter scare you off. It's about traditional Clipboard cut-and-paste techniques. It's also about object linking and embedding (OLE), a Windows 3.1 feature that gives you additional power when you're copying pictures, text, and other information into your documents. Think about how you use the Clipboard to copy and paste between applications—you paint a picture in Paintbrush, for instance, then copy the picture to the Clipboard, and finally paste it into another document. Before the development of OLE, it was not possible to alter a picture that was already pasted in a document. You had to change the picture in Paintbrush and then copy and paste again to get the edited picture back into the document.

OLE provides *dynamic data exchange* (DDE). Dynamic is the key word here, as opposed to *static*; pictures, text, charts, and other information that you've pasted into documents can be automatically updated when you make changes to the original object in the application that created it (assuming you maintain the link).

TIP: Think of an object as a package of information (a graphic, a drawing, some text, or other data) that you paste into "containers" in other applications.

OLE frees you from having to think about the applications among which you are transferring the objects, and lets you focus on the information being manipulated. OLE lets you create *compound documents*—documents containing information that comes from many different applications. In a compound document environment, applications appear within each other. Compound documents are part of Microsoft's Information at Your Fingertips strategy.

Host applications that support OLE will appear to have features they don't normally have. For example, you can copy sound files from Sound Recorder into a Write document and then double-click the pasted sound objects to play them back. Write thus appears to have this sound capability; in reality, however, the objects call the playback functions from the application used to originally create the sounds. Both Write and Sound Recorder have built-in OLE functions, as do Cardfile and Paintbrush. Check your applications to see if they are OLE compatible.

Understanding OLE Concepts

As the name implies, OLE provides linking and embedding of objects into one or more compound documents. You double-click an embedded object to open the application that originally created it, and edit the object as necessary. A *linked object* maintains an automatic link to the creating application, so any changes made to the original object affect the linked copies even if the link is between two computers on a network. Objects may consist of

✦ Text from word processors, text editors, and electronic mail packages

✦ Spreadsheet data from Microsoft Excel, Lotus 1-2-3, or other Windows 3.1-compatible spreadsheet applications

✦ Graphs and animations from presentation packages like Microsoft PowerPoint

✦ Pictures from drawing and painting programs

✦ Video and sound from multimedia applications

In some cases, objects look like icons similar to the ones you see in Program Manager. These icons contain a package of information related to the command or application that runs when you double-click the icon. For example, a recorded sound can only be displayed as an icon that you double-click to play back, whereas a graphic image or spreadsheet appear as they are normally viewed.

Embedding

In its simplest form, OLE provides *embedding*. An embedded object knows how to call the application that created it. When you double-click the object, the application opens so you can make needed changes, as shown in Figure 14-1. When you close the application the changes to the embedded object are made to the documents that contain the object.

The most obvious place to embed an object is in text documents such as those created by Write or Word for Windows, as illustrated in Figure 14-1. The Cardfile illustration in Figure 14-2 presents another example. Each card in the stack contains a graphic image for use as a slide in a presentation. Notice that the numbered index headers indicate the order the slides should appear in the presentation. Cardfile helps organize the slides for creating and editing the presentation. Simply double-click the image on a card, and the application used to create the

14

Embedded object

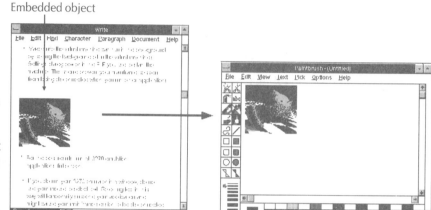

An embedded
object calls the
application that
created it when
double-clicked
Figure 14-1.

image then opens with the graphic in its workspace. In this example,
Cardfile serves as an organizer, and OLE lets you quickly access the
objects for editing.

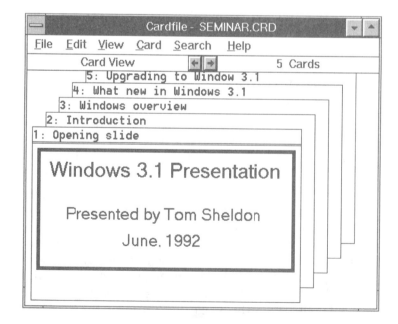

To edit this
graphic
embedded in
Cardfile, just
double-click it;
the creating
application
opens so you
can make
changes
Figure 14-2.

Linking

Linking provides a sort of communication channel between a pasted object and its original, as shown in Figure 14-3.

Changes made to the original object are automatically made to the pasted objects. This even works over a network so that objects from different departments can be combined in a compound document. Changes made to any object are made in the compound document without the need to do a lot of cutting, pasting, and organizing.

An Example of Linking and Embedding

Let's compare OLE with the cut-and-paste methods you already know. Imagine you're putting together a conference and trade show later in the year. You've created documents related to the conference using several different Windows applications—you used Windows Write to prepare press releases and other in-house documents, Microsoft Excel to create schedules, Paintbrush to draw a map of the conference rooms, and Cardfile to keep track of exhibitor and speaker information.

Linking establishes a "communication" link between an object and its pasted copies in compound documents

Figure 14-3.

14

Let's say you need to piece all this information together into several compound documents: a general press release, a brochure for attendees, an in-house document to inform the rest of your company of the conference schedule and events, and a handout for the exhibitors and speakers. Each document will, of course, be designed for its intended audience, but all will contain some of the information described earlier, such as the map and the schedule of events.

Initially, you need to create, copy, and paste various objects into your four documents, so the amount of work is the same whether you're using OLE or not. The real savings in time begins when you start to make changes to your schedules, floor plans, and the other information you've pasted into the compound documents. In non-OLE applications, you would need to copy and paste the edited information into each of the four documents. In contrast, OLE makes this part easy, because the objects in the documents contain links to the applications that created them. Changing the originals also changes the linked objects in all four documents, automatically. For example, alter the floor plan in Paintbrush, and the floor plan changes in all four linked compound documents.

Using OLE Over the Network

Now let's look at how you might use OLE over your network. If you have a multimedia sound board in your system, you can record voice messages and embed them in Microsoft Mail messages that you send to other people on the network. Of course, the recipient must have the proper equipment to play them back, but more and more Windows systems now include audio components or drivers that play sounds over the built-in computer speaker.

Assume you are a department or group manager who needs to create a business report that includes charts, tables of numbers, and text. You rely on other people in the department for this information. Start by creating an outline that describes the elements you want in the report—such as graphics, text, and spreadsheet information—and who in the department or workgroup is responsible for editing that information. Use Microsoft Mail to send this outline to each person.

There are two ways to build the compound document as each person creates the elements he or she is responsible for.

◆ *Common directory method*   In this method, all users in the workgroup connect with a common shared directory and copy the elements they create into the directory. The workgroup manager then assembles the compound document from all the objects in the directory.

◆ *ClipBook method*   In this method, workgroup users place objects they have created on their ClipBook and share them. The workgroup manager then accesses the shared ClipBook and copies objects from it to paste in the compound document.

Of course, objects are paste-linked into the compound document. That way, project workers can change the objects of the compound document they are responsible for by working directly on the object itself. The OLE link ensures that changes they make to the objects are automatically copied into the compound document. There is no need for them to ever open the compound document.

For example, assume the first page of the document has a graphic image created with an OLE-compatible drawing program. An artist in the graphics department places the image on the ClipBook and shares it. She contacts you using Chat, or sends a Mail message to let you know the image is available on her ClipBook. You connect with her ClipBook, copy the image, and paste-link it into the compound document. Later, at a project meeting, a decision is made to change the image. After the meeting, the artist simply makes the appropriate changes to the image and saves the file. There is no need to place it back on the ClipBook or into the compound document. The OLE link takes care of updating the object in every document where it is pasted.

OLE Components

To create compound documents, you use various components of Windows that provide OLE support. These components are included as options on the Edit menu of most applications, or may be integrated into the functions of a program. For example, the File Manager's OLE features are integrated. When you click a file icon and drag it to a document in an OLE-compatible application, the icon becomes embedded as an OLE object that you can double-click to open or playback (in the case of a sound or video file).

An *object* (in this instance) is a package of information that originates in a *source* document and is pasted to a *destination* document. The source and destination documents are created in server and client applications respectively, as discussed next.

Servers and Clients

A compound document is as easy to create as any other document. You use the same Clipboard cut-and-paste options that you use when copying information such as pictures and graphs into a document. If the applications support OLE, the information can be pasted as embedded or linked objects. The application the information is copied from is the *server* of OLE data, and the application the information is pasted to is the *client*. Double-clicking on embedded objects opens server applications. Note that applications are not restricted to being either servers or clients. Some applications are both. Here are some examples.

Paintbrush   Paintbrush is a server application that only provides OLE bitmap graphic objects to client applications. The object appears as an image in the client document.

Write   Write is solely a client application.

Cardfile   The Cardfile accessory is solely a client application.

Sound Recorder   Sound Recorder is a server application. Use Sound Recorder to create sounds and embed them in your documents. Embedded sounds are displayed in the client document as Sound Recorder icons, unless you use Object Packager (discussed later in this chapter) to specify a different icon.

Microsoft Excel   Excel is both a server and a client. You can paste Excel spreadsheet data into most client applications. You can also paste sound files, graphics, and other information into an Excel spreadsheet.

Microsoft Word for Windows   Word is primarily a client application (that is, you paste objects into it); however, you can paste Word document icons into other applications. The readers of those documents can double-click the icons to view the Word documents.

Microsoft PowerPoint   PowerPoint is another application that is either a server or client, but is primarily a client. PowerPoint is used to create graphics presentations.

Some objects can only be pasted as icons or packages. For example, when pasting a Sound Recorder sound into a document, a Sound Recorder icon appears, since you can't display a sound.

Verbs

A verb is the action an object takes when double-clicked; the type of action that results depends on the type of object it is. The most common verb is *play*. An object such as a sound file or an animation routine in a multimedia document plays. You could also paste a program icon into a document, such as Media Player, that more appropriately "runs" instead of plays.

The other important verb is *edit*. An edit object opens for editing in the workspace of the application that created it when double-clicked. The type of document dictates whether objects are played or edited. In the previous example, a graphic image was placed in a report document that was going through revisions. The image is an edit object, since you double-click it if you want to change it. A voice annotation, on the other hand, is a play object because it plays back when double-clicked.

Linking and Embedding

This section defines linking and embedding in more depth. There is a big difference in what happens to a pasted object in a document, depending on whether it supports OLE or not, as described here.

Normal Objects   If neither the source nor the destination support OLE, then the paste results are non-OLE. You must repaste an updated version of the information.

14

Packaged Objects   If the destination supports OLE but the source does not, the Clipboard contents are pasted as normal information into the document. However, you can use Object Packager as discussed later to create OLE-compatible packages for these non-OLE objects. They then appear as icons that, when double-clicked, play, run, or open for editing.

Embedded Objects   If both the source and the destination are OLE-compliant, a pasted object is embedded into the destination document. Double-clicking the object plays, runs, or opens it for editing. The object maintains an association with the application that creates it.

Linked Objects   A linked object maintains a two-way dynamic link between a file and the pasted portion of the file in compound documents. You choose the Paste Special or Paste Link command from the Edit menu of OLE-compatible applications to create a link.

Clipboard Methods of Linking and Embedding

The most common method of linking and embedding objects is to use the Clipboard. In the source application, you highlight or select the information or image to copy and choose the Copy command on its Edit menu, or press Ctrl-C. You then switch to the destination application and choose one of the following paste commands from the Edit menu. You can see these commands on the Edit menu of programs such as Write, Cardfile, Word for Windows, Excel, and others. Note that Paste Link is only available if the source information is saved as part of a file.

The Paste Option   Choose Paste to embed the object as it is on the Clipboard. It is embedded if the source is an OLE-compliant application.

The Paste Special Option   Use this option only if the object can't be pasted in the normal way. Paste Special is similar to Paste, except that a dialog box opens so you can choose a format for the pasted object. If you want to embed the object, you usually choose the top item in the list called "object," but if embedding is not supported, you won't see this option. The other items paste the object as a normal object. You can also click a Paste Link button in most cases to paste-link the object.

The Paste Link Option If the object on the Clipboard is from a file and linking is supported, the Paste Link option is available. Choose it to paste the object with a link back to the original file.

The Links Option Use this option to change the links of an object. You might do this when a link has been lost because the original file was moved or when one machine on a network can't find the original file located on another network machine.

The Insert Object Option Use this option to create a new object or link. It displays a dialog box so you can choose which application you want to paste from.

Changing Embedded or Linked Objects

When you double-click an object in a client document, the object appears in its source application for editing. After making changes, you choose one of the following options from the File menu.

The Update Option Choose Update to add the changes you have made to the object into the client document. You remain in the source application for further editing.

The Exit and Return To Option Choose the Exit and Return To option to return to the destination application. If you've made changes, you'll be asked if you want to update the destination with those changes.

Icons as Objects

OLE extends the use of icons beyond the Program Manager to your applications. You can insert *packages* in your documents that open other documents or start other applications. These packages use icons similar to those you see in the Program Manager. For example, look at the Cardfile illustration in Figure 14-4. This cardfile contains a stack of cards used to keep notes for writing the book you're reading now. Notice that the top card contains an icon that when double-clicked, opens another cardfile stack called FEATURES.CRD that contains notes about new Windows 3.1 features. So in this case, one cardfile tracks other cardfiles, and provides a quick and easy way to access them.

14

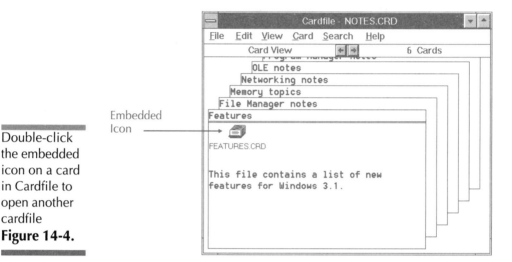

Embedded
Icon

Double-click
the embedded
icon on a card
in Cardfile to
open another
cardfile
Figure 14-4.

In Figure 14-5, notice that the Write document contains two
embedded icons. You can double-click one icon to open a set of
instructions in English and the other to open a set of instructions in
Spanish. Using Sound Recorder, you could even include audible
instructions.

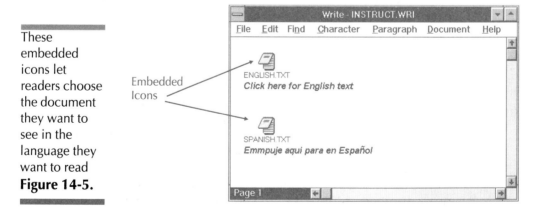

These
embedded
icons let
readers choose
the document
they want to
see in the
language they
want to read
Figure 14-5.

Embedded
Icons

The English and Spanish instruction files can also contain embedded icons providing access to other text files. In this way, a single file does not need to contain the bulk of the text. Instead, individual files can contain specific lessons or procedures that are easier to edit when necessary—and, moreover, easier to understand by the user. By double-clicking icons, readers can choose the exact topics they want to see. Figure 14-6 illustrates an instructional file for new employees.

Special documents that provide security information should not be accessible to just anyone. By using OLE, you can lock certain files and restrict access to selected readers. In the foregoing example, and also in Figure 14-6, not all employees should know the security alarm procedure. To limit access to this document, just remove the linked file from the systems of restricted employees; on a network, you can put the linked file in a directory that has restricted access so restricted empoyees can't open it.

Figure 14-7 shows how you can attach both sounds and pictures to a Write document. In this example, the ear with the musical note is a sound package created with Sound Recorder. A young reader of the document could double-click the icon to hear a prerecorded sound for the animal pictured.

This embedded icon lets authorized readers view a special security procedure
Figure 14-6.

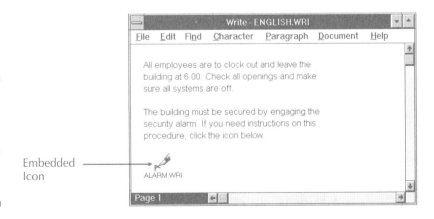

14

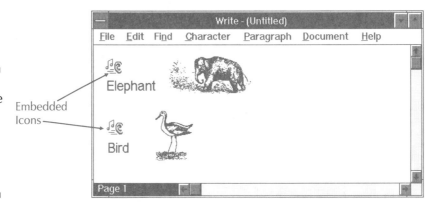

Sounds and
graphics can be
combined to
create true
"multimedia"
documents
Figure 14-7.

Embedding Objects

To embed an object from a source application to a destination document, use the copy-and-paste procedures with which you are already familiar. If both the source and destination applications support OLE, the pasted object will become embedded. If neither the source nor the destination applications support OLE, the pasted object becomes static.

Try the following exercise to see how embedding works:

1. Open Write and Paintbrush.
2. In the Paintbrush window, paint a picture to copy and paste, or open an existing picture file.
3. Use the Pick tool to surround part of the image; then choose Copy from the Edit menu to place the selection on the Clipboard.
4. Switch to the Write window, and choose the Paste command from the Edit menu.

Because both Paintbrush and Write support OLE, the selection is embedded in the Write document. Now try editing the image.

5. Double-click the image you pasted into the Write document. The Paintbrush window becomes active, with the image in its workspace.
6. Change the image in any way.

7. Open the File menu. You will see the menu shown here:

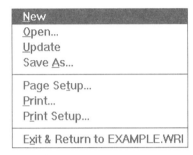

| New |
| Open... |
| Update |
| Save As... |
| |
| Page Setup... |
| Print... |
| Print Setup... |
| |
| Exit & Return to EXAMPLE.WRI |

8. Notice the third (Update) and last (Exit & Return) options on the File menu. You can choose Update to store the changes you made to the image in Write, and leave Paintbrush open. For this exercise, however, choose the Exit & Return option. This updates the image in Write, closes Paintbrush, and returns you to the Write document. When the following dialog box appears, choose Yes to update the Write document.

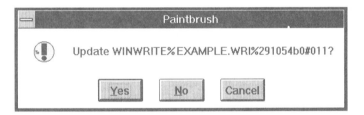

| Paintbrush |
| Update WINWRITE%EXAMPLE.WRI%291054b0#011? |
| Yes   No   Cancel |

TIP: You can follow a procedure similar to the one just discussed to embed objects on Cardfile cards, Mail messages, and most other Windows applications.

Now try embedding a sound from Sound Recorder into the Write document. The following exercise assumes that you have a sound board or speaker driver installed.

14

1. Start Sound Recorder.
2. Open any sound, or record a new sound.
3. Choose Copy from the Sound Recorder Edit menu.
4. Switch to your Write document.
5. Choose Paste from the Edit menu.

The sound is pasted into the document. Double-click the icon to hear the pasted sound.

Linking Objects

The procedure for creating a linked object is the same as the procedure for creating an embedded object, except that you choose Paste Link from the destination application's Edit menu to paste the image. The source object must be from a saved file. This maintains the dynamic link between the pasted object and its original. Try the following exercise with Paintbrush and Cardfile. Keep in mind that you can use this procedure to create a catalog of graphic images or sounds in Cardfile.

1. Open Cardfile and Paintbrush.
2. In Paintbrush, create an image. (You will paste this to a card in Cardfile.)
3. Save the image as a Paintbrush file. This is an important step, because the file of the source application contains the link information (explained in the next section) for a linked object.
4. Use the Pick tool to select part of the object to copy; then choose Copy from the Edit menu.
5. Switch to Cardfile, and choose Picture from the Cardfile Edit menu. (This is an important step.)
6. Choose the Paste Link option from the Edit menu to paste the object in the card.

Because the Cardfile object and the Paintbrush application are now linked, you can edit the Paintbrush file at any time to make changes to the Cardfile image, even when the Cardfile application is not open on the desktop. The next time you open Cardfile, it gets the latest version of the Paintbrush image, including whatever edits you've made. To see

how dynamic this link is, continue with the Paintbrush/Cardfile exercise and experiment with the sample image:

7. Double-click the linked and embedded image in Cardfile. The Paintbrush window becomes active, with the image in its workspace.

8. Arrange the Cardfile and Paintbrush windows side by side, so you can see both images at once.

9. Make some changes to the image in the Paintbrush file, such as altering the color or drawing some lines. Notice that as you edit the image in Paintbrush, the Cardfile image also changes.

If you wish, you can continue this example even further by opening Write and paste-linking the image from Paintbrush into the Write window. Then change the image in Paintbrush and watch how the linked objects in *both* Cardfile and Write change simultaneously.

Using Linked Documents Over Networks

A document with linked objects contains information about where those objects are located. Therefore, you can't just move the document or its linked objects around. If other users need to read a compound document or make changes to it, try to keep all the information for the document including linked files in one directory. Then give other users shared access to that directory. When they connect with the directory, they will be able to access its files and use the links without problems.

If the server documents must reside on other network machines, use the ClipBook. In the example discussed earlier, the artist kept a graphic file on her own machine, and pasted it to her shared ClipBook so other users could access it. Those users copied the image on the shared ClipBook and paste-linked it to their documents. Note that it may be necessary to manually update links when you open a compound document that uses server documents from other network computers. This is discussed in the next section.

To create network links using ClipBook, follow these steps:

1. At the server machine, copy the object to the Clipboard, then paste it to the Local ClipBook.

14

2. When the Share dialog box appears, type in a page name, then enable the Share Item Now option.

3. Fill out the Share dialog box as discussed in Chapter 13 and click the OK button. The object appears on the ClipBook as a shared item.

4. At the client machine, open ClipBook and choose the Connect command from the File menu, then choose the remote computer that contains the client information. Its ClipBook appears in the ClipBook Viewer window.

5. Click the item you want to paste-link and choose Copy from the Edit menu.

6. Start the client application where you will create the compound document.

7. Position the insertion point and choose Paste Link. The object is pasted with a link to the server application.

You can save and close the compound document. The next time it is opened, a dialog box appears to inform you that the document contains a linked object that may need updating, and you are given the option to update it. If you choose Yes to update the linked object, OLE is used to get the latest object from the server document over the network.

Viewing and Updating Link Information

You can view and update the *link information* for a linked object by first selecting the object, then choosing Links from the Edit menu. You'll see a dialog box similar to this one:

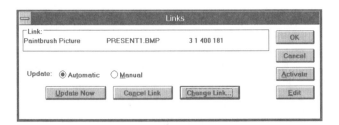

The type, name, and size information for the linked object appear in the Link display box.

NOTE: This dialog box appears when you open a document on a shared directory that contains link information. Click the Change Link button to verify the link information, then click the OK button.

The two Update options, Automatic and Manual, determine the current update method for the linked object; you can switch to Manual if you want changes to occur in the linked object only when you choose to make them. To update a link manually, choose the Update Now button after you've made your edits. Another way of editing the linked object is by clicking the Edit button and making your changes; this is the same as double-clicking the linked object.

For linked objects that play back a script or sounds, click the Activate button to play the objects.

To cancel a link, choose the Cancel Link button; or choose Change Link if you want to define a new file for the link.

Embedding Icons

As explained earlier in this chapter, embedded icons can execute commands, open other documents, or start other applications. These icons contain a set of instructions for accomplishing the icon's assigned task. To create embedded icons, you can click and drag icons from the File Manager to your documents. Or you can use the Packager accessory in the Program Manager Accessories group.

In the following example, you use the click-and-drag method to place an icon for a file on a card in Cardfile.

1. Open both Cardfile and File Manager, and arrange the windows side by side.
2. Locate a file, say a Paintbrush .BMP file, in the Windows directory.

14

3. Click the filename and drag it over the top card in Cardfile, then release the mouse. This embeds an icon for the file on the card. You can now double-click the icon in Cardfile to open the file you just pasted.

Try the same procedure with a Sound Recorder .WAV file, or even another Cardfile. Double-clicking the embedded icon will play the sound or start the application. Remember that you can use these techniques in Write or other OLE-compatible applications to create links to other documents. Try copying an icon for a text file into a Write document.

Using Packager

With Packager, you can create a *package* to embed as an icon into your documents. Packager is an alternative to the click-and-drag method just described for embedding an icon. Packager provides you with a way to specify each element of a package, such as its filename, location, and icon type. For example, you could use an envelope icon for a recording of your voice. Try the following exercise to see how this works:

1. Open Write.

2. Choose Insert Object from the Edit menu. The following dialog box appears, listing all the currently available applications that can supply OLE objects.

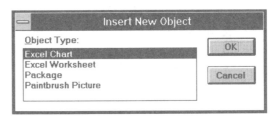

3. In the Object Type list box, choose Package, and click the OK button. You'll then see the following dialog box:

Packager contains all the tools you need to create your own embedded icons. In this case, Packager will insert the icon in the Write document when you're done. Let's create a link to another document, such as README.TXT in the Windows directory.

4. Select an icon for the new object. Click the Insert Icon button, and choose one of the suggested icons that appear. To choose from a larger selection of icons, specify one of the following filenames in the File Name field:

    \WINDOWS\PROGMAN.EXE
    \WINDOWS\MORICONS.DLL

5. Create a label for the icon you have selected, by choosing Label from the Edit menu. Type **README.TXT** in the text box of the Label dialog box and click OK.

6. Define the command that is executed whenever the package is double-clicked. Choose Command Line from the Edit menu and type **C:\WINDOWS\README.TXT** (You may need to replace C with the drive letter for your Windows directory.)

7. To create the embedded icon in the document, you may elect to choose Update from the File menu. This keeps Packager open so you can create other objects. For this exercise, however, choose Exit from the File menu. Packager asks if you want to update the object; choose Yes.

Your Write document now contains the embedded icon, and you can double-click the icon to open the README.TXT file. Use this same procedure to add other icons to your documents as you create them.

14

NOTE: The preferred method for copying sound files is to drag their file icons from the File Manager to the destination document.

Editing a Packaged Object

If you need to change the properties of a packaged object in your linked documents, follow this procedure:

1. Click once on the object to highlight it.
2. Choose Package Object from the Edit menu, and then choose the Edit option.
3. When Packager opens, make the needed changes using the menu options described earlier in this chapter.
4. Choose the Update or Exit option on the File menu to complete the change.

CHAPTER

15

MICROSOFT MAIL

Microsoft Mail provides electronic mail services to Windows for Workgroups users. You can write memos and send them to other users or groups of users in your workgroup. You can also forward messages you've received to other users. In addition, you can attach files to memos, which greatly simplifies the transfer of information between co-workers. Just about any type of information can be attached to a mail message, such as pictures, spreadsheet data, voice-annotated sound files, and even video clips.

A *postoffice* is set up and used as a clearinghouse for user mail. One system on the network serves as the postoffice and one user serves as the postoffice administrator. To send a memo with Mail, simply compose the memo, select the recipients, and click a button to distribute the memos. The steps of printing, copying, and hand delivering memos are eliminated. You can also keep a personal address book of users and groups that you send mail to on a regular basis.

Microsoft Mail is a "store and forward" application. That means messages from users are stored in a central postoffice location where they are forwarded to the recipient. The important point is that recipients can "pick up" mail at their convenience and that senders don't need to contact recipients to alert them that they have mail. Each user has a mailbox in the postoffice to hold messages and they access those messages when they log onto Mail.

The Mail postoffice is efficient in that it stores only one copy of each mail message, even if that message is addressed to multiple recipients. When messages are retrieved, they are removed from the postoffice. However, recipients can choose to store messages on their own computers.

Mail includes its own editor so users can create messages within Mail, but one of the best features is that it allows users to attach files created in other applications to Mail messages. For example, you can attach a monthly report that contains graphics, spreadsheet information, and text to a mail message and send it to one or more people. You can also embed objects such as pictures and spreadsheets directly into a message you are creating with the Mail message editor. Cut and paste is supported, so you can work on multiple messages at once and transfer information among them.

Mail uses the folder metaphor as a way to help users organize the messages they receive. While many messages can be discarded immediately, others need to be saved for future reference (or for legal reasons). You can create a folder to store business messages, another to store personal messages, and still another to store messages you need to archive (backup to a disk and remove from your hard drive). You can search for messages in folders using keywords, such as the sender's name, dates, or other descriptions.

Postoffice Components

Before you can use Mail, you'll need to create a postoffice. An *administrator* (postoffice manager) creates, manages, and maintains the postoffice. The administrator sets up a shared directory on one of the computers in the workgroup and creates a postoffice in that directory. The administrator then sets up an *account* for each person who wishes to access the postoffice.

Each Mail user is assigned a private *message file* or *mailbox* that is used to store messages. The message file is located on the user's own computer, and the postoffice is located in a shared directory on a central system set up by the administrator. Each mailbox is protected by a *password*. This restricts users other than the owner of the mailbox from accessing the mailbox. The owner is the only person who can change the password (except, of course, the postoffice manager).

When you sign in to Mail, you are presented with an *Inbox* window similar to the one shown in Figure 15-1. The Inbox window contains information about messages you have received from other postoffice users, including who sent the message, the subject of the message, and the date and time the message was placed in your mailbox.

Messages contain icons as shown here:

⊠	Unopened mail
⌂	Opened mail
!⌂	High-priority indicator
↓⊠	Low-priority indicator
⌂0	Mail with attached file

If the message is high priority, you see an exclamation point, and if it is low priority, you see a down arrow. An open envelope indicates the message has already been read, and a closed envelope indicates unread messages. An envelope with an attached paperclip indicates messages with attached files, such as text documents, spreadsheet data, graphic images, or even voice messages created with a sound utility.

To create a message, click the Compose button, type your message, address it, and finally click the Send button. You address messages by selecting names from *address lists*. The *Postoffice Address List* contains

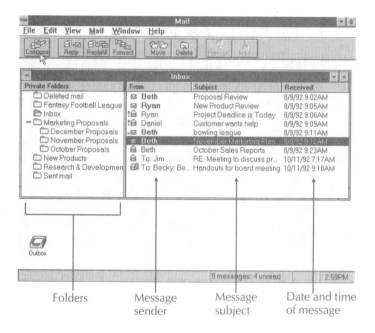

Startup screen
Figure 15-1.

Folders   Message   Message   Date and time
           sender   subject   of message

the names of users in the postoffice. You can also maintain a *Personal Address List* to track a list of users that you correspond with frequently or a *Personal group* list for groups of people you correspond with frequently. When you address a message with a group name, the message is sent to all the individuals included in the group.

The *Outbox* provides a handy place to drop your mail for delivery. You simply drag messages from your Inbox or any other folder to the Outbox, where they are automatically forwarded to the recipients. Messages that you compose and send are stored immediately in your *Sent Mail* folder.

Folders provide a way to organize your mail messages. For example, you could create a folder called "Board Presentation" and use it to store messages related to an upcoming meeting. You could also create a folder called "Archive" and use it to store messages you've already read, but want to keep on hand for future reference. A folder can be exported to a floppy disk to free space on your hard disk, then imported back to Mail in the event you want to read one of the archived messages. It's

possible to share folders to make messages in them accessible to other members of the workgroup.

15

Using Mail

Before anyone can use Mail, the Mail administrator must create the postoffice. The procedures for doing so are covered later in this chapter, in "Administrative Tasks". This section describes how nonadministrative users log on to Mail for the first time and get started. Double-click the Mail icon in the Program Manager Main group. If your account is already set up, you see the Mail Sign In dialog box shown here:

Type your mailbox name and password to gain entry to Mail. If you can't get past the logon screen, check to make sure you are using the correct mailbox name and password. If Windows is unable to find a postoffice, the following dialog box appears:

You have the option of creating a new workgroup postoffice or connecting to an existing postoffice. Read through the next section if a postoffice has already been created, or refer to "Administrative Tasks" later in this chapter if you need to create a new postoffice.

Connect to an Existing Postoffice

Click this option to connect to an existing workgroup postoffice. The Network Disk Resources dialog box comes up. You use this box to browse for the postoffice directory in the same way you use other network browse boxes to connect with shared directories as discussed in previous chapters.

Enter the network path if you know it or click the shared directory where the postoffice is located. The Network Path field is automatically filled in. Click the OK button to create the postoffice connection. If the shared directory has been password-protected, enter the password of the shared directory if you have been given rights to access it.

After you have successfully entered a password for the shared directory, the following dialog box appears. Fill it out as described in the following paragraphs. The first three fields are required, but the others are optional.

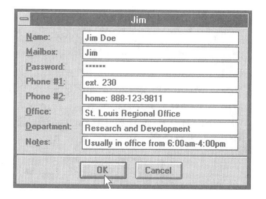

Name   Enter your first and last name. Other users will specify this name when addressing messages. The default is the name you used when installing Windows for Workgroups. The maximum length of the account name is 30 characters.

Mailbox   Enter the name of your mailbox. Typically, this is the first letter of the first name, then the last name, such as JDoe. The maximum length of the mailbox name is 10 characters. Note that the space between the first initial and the last name is usually left out, but you should check to see what your companies' policy is on this. Everyone should use the same format to avoid confusion.

Password   Enter the password you will use to gain access to Mail. Choose a password that is easy for you to remember but not easy for intruders to figure out. The maximum length of the password is 8 characters and the default is PASSWORD.

15

Phone #1   Enter your primary telephone number. The maximum length of the telephone number is 32 characters.

Phone #2   Enter an alternate telephone, fax, or modem number. The maximum length is 32 characters.

Office   Enter your office number or name. The maximum length is 32 characters.

Department   Enter your department name. The maximum length is 32 characters.

Notes   Enter notes or comments about your account in this field, such as your normal office hours or emergency information. The maximum length is 128 characters. The text will scroll as you fill up the visible area.

Click OK when the fields are filled out the way you want. You are now ready to use Mail. The next time you start Mail, you will be presented with the Mail Sign In dialog box. Simply type your mailbox name and password to gain access to Mail.

Mail Startup Trick

You can alter the Mail startup icon in Program Manager so it automatically enters your mailbox name when you start the program. You can also include your password, but that is not recommended since other users could gain access to your mail by simply double-clicking your Mail icon. To add your mailbox name, do the following:

1. Highlight the Mail icon in Program Manager and choose Properties from the Files menu.
2. Change the Command Line to include your mailbox name, similar to the following:

3. Click OK when done.

NOTE: If other people use your system and want to use this technique, they should create their own Mail startup icons. Use icon names like Mail-Jim or Mail-Ann.

Changing Your Password

Changing your password periodically is a good idea if you are concerned with security in your work environment. Follow these steps to change your password:

1. Select Change Password from the Mail menu by using a mouse or by pressing Alt-M-C.
2. Enter your old password.
3. Enter your new password.
4. Verify your new password.
5. Click OK when done.

The OK button will be grayed out until you successfully enter your current password and enter and verify a new password. On screen, you will see asterisks instead of the characters you type so that other people are unable to read your password as you enter it. Mail will notify you when the operation has been completed successfully. Be sure to make a mental note of your new password.

Exiting Mail

When you're done with Mail, you can choose from two exit options on the File menu. Choosing Exit ends your Mail session but leaves your mailbox open for other applications such as Schedule+ to use. Choosing Exit and Sign Out ends your Mail session and closes your mailbox.

Composing and Sending Messages

Once you've logged on to Mail, you're ready to compose notes and send them to other users. Here's an outline of the procedure for creating a message:

1. Click the Compose button.
2. Select the Mail users you want to send the message to as outlined in the following section.
3. Use the [Tab] key or mouse to move about within the various fields in the Send Note form, as described in the following sections.
4. Type the subject of the message and your message text.
5. Click the Send button to send the message to the recipients.

Address the Message

To address the message, you type the account names or click the Address button to access the Postoffice address list. Click the personal address book icon to display your personal address list. In this example, notes are addressed to Ryan and Daniel and a courtesy copy is sent to Becky, as shown in Figure 15-2.

1. Click the Address button.
2. Click Ryan's name.
3. Click the To button.
4. Click Daniel's name.
5. Click the To button.
6. Click Becky's name.
7. Click the Cc button.

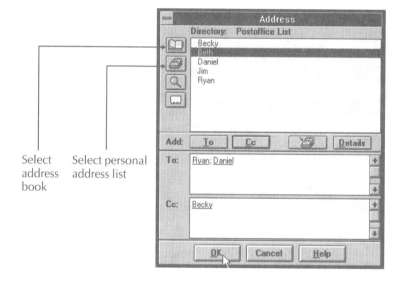

Select
address
book

Select personal
address list

Address dialog
box

Figure 15-2.

TIP: Typing a letter will allow you to zero in on names in the
address list. For example, typing *J* will position the scroll bar at the
first name beginning with J.

The names are placed in the appropriate To and Cc fields at the bottom
of the dialog box. When you click OK, the Send Note dialog box
appears, similar to Figure 15-3.

Using Groups to Address Messages

You can create groups of users that you need to send mail to on a
regular basis, such as the people in your department. It's easier to send
mail to a group than it is to address mail messages to individual users.
To create a group, follow these steps:

15

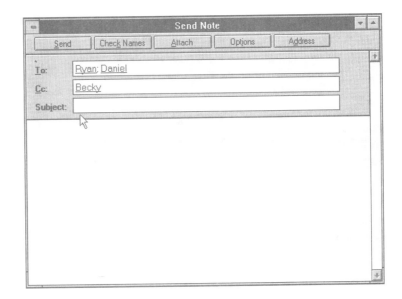

An addressed
Send Note form
Figure 15-3.

1. Choose Personal Groups from the Mail menu to create the new group in your personal address book.
2. Click the New button.
3. Type the name of the new group (for example, "Board Presentation").
4. Click a user's name in the list, then click the Add button.
5. Continue choosing new group members and clicking the Add button until you have added everyone to the group.
6. Click the OK button. The new group name appears in your Personal Address Book, similar to what you see in Figure 15-4.

To address a message to a group, click the personal address list icon. When the list appears, click the group, then click the To button. The To portion of your Send Note form is filled in with the group name as shown in Figure 15-5.

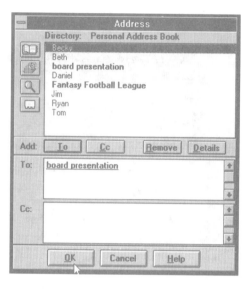

The new group name appears in your Personal address Book **Figure 15-4.**

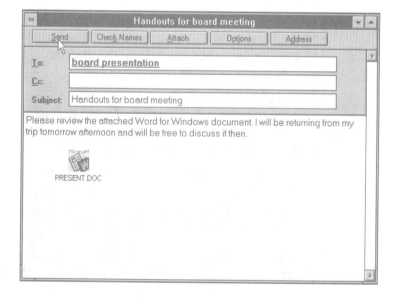

The To portion of your Send Note form is filled in with the group name **Figure 15-5.**

Type the Subject and Message

In the Subject field, type a short description of the message. This field appears as part of the message header information in the Inbox of the recipient. Make sure this field is as descriptive as possible.

In the lower part of the dialog box, type the text of your message. Many standard word processing features such as word wrap are available. The lines of text scroll as you fill up the page.

Attaching Files to Messages

One of the best features of Mail is that you can attach files of any kind to your messages. This makes it easy to send documents to other people. You could share a directory on your system using File Manager, then give other users access to the directory. After users have copied the files, you then stop sharing the directory. Mail provides a better way to do this. You simply attach the file to a mail message and send it to the recipient, who then picks up the file at their convenience.

Here are the steps for attaching a file to a message. In this example, a Microsoft Word for Windows document for an upcoming board presentation is attached to a message.

1. Click the Attach button or press [Alt]-[A].
2. Locate the file you want to attach and click it.
3. Click the Attach button.

An embedded icon is inserted into your message text. Figure 15-6 shows a message with a Word for Windows icon imbedded in the text. The recipient of the message can double-click the icon and the document is automatically loaded into Word for Windows. You can also attach voice annotations created with Sound Recorder or pictures created with programs like Paintbrush.

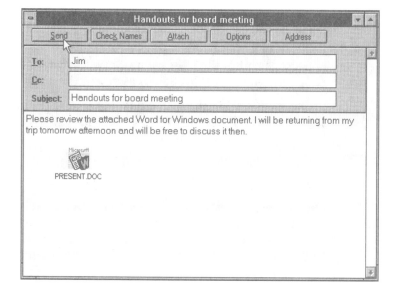

Message with
attached file
icon
Figure 15-6.

NOTE: If the File Manager window is placed next to the Mail
window, you can drag and drop file icons from File Manager to
your mail messages.

Mailing Packaged Objects

Recall from Chapter 14 that Object Packager is used to create a
packaged object with OLE links. You can add a packaged object to a
mail message that includes a pointer to a file located on another
network computer's shared directory. This is useful if you want to send
a message to another user that includes a reference to a file on your
system. Since the package points to the file on your system, you don't
need to embed it in the message itself. When the recipient reads the
message, the packaged object icon created by Object Packager should be

15

double-clicked. Then the commands in the package run and connect the user with the document on your system so it can be read without actually transferring the text to the recipient's system.

Here are the steps for creating a packaged object:

1. Start Mail and prepare a message to send to another user.
2. To create the package, choose Insert Object from the Edit menu and choose Package from its Insert Objects list.
3. When Object Packager opens, choose Command Line from the Edit menu and type the Universal Naming Convention (as mentioned in Chapter 7) in the field. For example, to include the document REPORTS.WK1 in the EXCEL directory on your computer (which is called THEBOSS for this example), you would type the following:

    \\THEBOSS\EXCEL\REPORTS.WK1

4. Click the Insert Icon button and select an appropriate icon.
5. Choose Label from the Edit menu and type the name you want to appear under the icon.
6. Choose Exit from the Edit menu, then choose Yes when asked if you want to update the package.

The packaged object now appears in the message text area. You can finish creating the message and send it to the recipient.

Send the Message

When you are done creating the message, you can click the Send button to send it to the recipients, or you can specify additional options by clicking the Options button, which brings up the Options dialog box shown here. Set options on the dialog box as described in the following paragraphs.

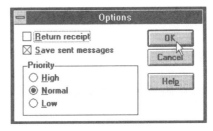

Return Receipt   Check the Return Receipt option if you want to receive notification that recipients have received and read your message.

Setting Priority   Click the appropriate button indicating the priority of the message. The default is Normal. Click the top button to change the priority to High. Click the bottom button to change the priority to Low.

Save Sent Messages   Check this option to save messages in a folder called Sent Mail. The default is to save messages.

Reading Messages You've Received

To read messages, first scan through the list of received messages that appear in your Inbox. Use the mouse or arrow keys to highlight the messages you want to read. Recall that a closed envelope icon indicates an unread message. Double-click the message you want to read, or highlight it and press (Enter). A form similar to the following appears:

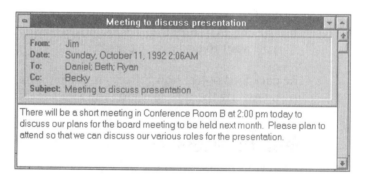

The header displays who the message is from, the date and time it was placed in your mailbox, any other people who received the same message, and the subject of the message.

Replying to Messages You've Received

Once you have opened and read a message, you can reply to it by clicking the Reply button on the main Mail window. Mail presents a reply form similar to the one shown in Figure 15-7. The message is automatically addressed to the person who sent the original message.

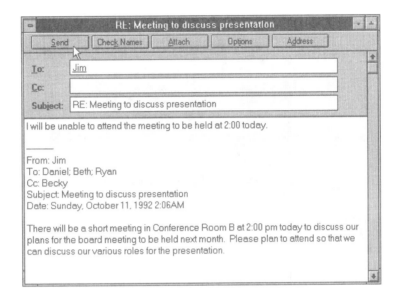

Reply note form
Figure 15-7.

Type your reply, then click the Send button on the reply dialog box.
The original message is placed in the new message area.

Forwarding Messages You've Received

You can forward messages you've received to other people who need to
review them. Choose Forward on the Mail menu, or simply drag the
envelope icon to your Outbox. Mail will present a forwarding dialog
box as shown in Figure 15-8. Address the message as you would any
other message and click the Send button. The options you consider
when you send your own messages—Return receipt, Save sent messages,
and Priority settings—are also available for messages you forward.

Folders

Mail does not force you to perform message housekeeping chores. You
could simply leave all the messages that you receive in your Inbox.
However, it won't be long before your Inbox starts looking like a
kitchen drawer with too much in it. Locating messages becomes
increasingly hard. You could use the Message Finder described later in
this chapter, but it's better to organize messages into folders.

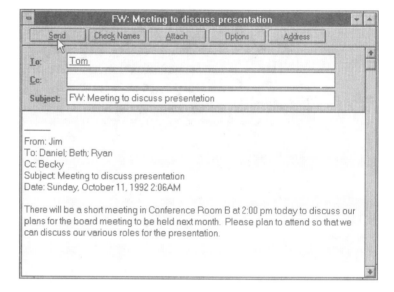

Forwarding
dialog box
Figure 15-8.

Once you've read a message, you can move it to a folder by dragging
and dropping its icon. For example, you could create a top-level folder
called Board Presentation and create a subfolder for each of the topics
to be presented at the meeting. The subfolder could be called Monthly
Sales Figures and contain documents related to monthly sales.

Creating a New Folder

To create a new folder, choose New Folder from the File menu. The
New Folder dialog box appears as shown here:

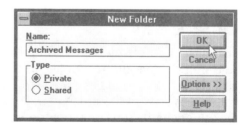

15

This dialog box contains fields for the folder's Name and Type. Clicking the Options button brings up the New Folder dialog box, shown in Figure 15-9 and described in the following sections.

Name   Enter a descriptive name for the new folder.

Type   Click either the Shared or Private button. Shared folders reside at the location of the workstation postoffice. Private folders reside on your own machine. If you select Shared, you can set whether other users will have the ability to Read, Write, or Delete the message in the folder.

TIP: Make folders shared if you have limited disk space on your own machine.

Level   In this box, choose whether the folder will be a Top Level Folder or a Subfolder of another folder. For example, you could have a top-level folder called "Meetings" and a sublevel folder for each month.

New folder
dialog box
Figure 15-9.

```
┌─────────────────────────────────────────────┐
│ ▭            New Folder                       │
│                                               │
│ Name:                          ┌──────────┐   │
│ ┌──────────────────────────┐   │    OK    │   │
│ │ Archived Messages        │   └──────────┘   │
│ └──────────────────────────┘   ┌──────────┐   │
│ ┌─Type─────────────────────┐   │  Cancel  │   │
│ │ ○ Private                │   └──────────┘   │
│ │ ◉ Shared                 │   ┌──────────┐   │
│ │                          │   │Options >>│   │
│ └──────────────────────────┘   └──────────┘   │
│                                ┌──────────┐   │
│                                │   Help   │   │
│ ┌─Level────────────────────┐   └──────────┘   │
│ │ ◉ Top Level Folder       │                  │
│ │ ○ Subfolder Of:          │                  │
│ │    📁 Board Presentation  │                  │
│ │                          │                  │
│ │                          │                  │
│ └──────────────────────────┘                  │
│                                               │
│ ┌─Other Users Can──────────┐                  │
│ │ ⊠ Read  ⊠ Write  ☐ Delete │                  │
│ └──────────────────────────┘                  │
│ Comment:                                      │
│ ┌──────────────────────────┐                  │
│ └──────────────────────────┘                  │
└─────────────────────────────────────────────┘
```

Other Users Can In this box, choose the access rights other users will have to the new folder. Click any combination of the three options, which are Read, Write, and Delete. Remove the check mark on all three to prevent other users from accessing your shared folder.

Comment In this field, type any comments about the folder such as a detailed explanation of the folder contents.

Moving Messages into Folders

After your folders have been created, you can copy messages into them by dragging and dropping the message envelopes into the new folder icons. Drag a message by following these steps:

1. Click the message you want to drag.
2. Hold the mouse button down as you move the envelope to the desired folder.
3. Release the mouse button.

Archiving and Deleting Messages

Since each message in your mailbox takes up disk space on your hard disk, you will want to go through your folders occasionally and delete messages that are no longer needed. This is done by dragging messages to your Deleted mail folder. Note that the messages aren't actually deleted until you exit Mail.

You'll often have messages you want to keep a copy of for future reference, but that you don't want cluttering up your existing Mail screen. You can copy these messages to an archive folder and export the folder to disk or another drive before deleting the messages. So, you would continue to use your Deleted mail folder for messages that you want to remove permanently and use your archive folder for those messages you wish to keep a copy of.

When the archive folder is full or you're ready to archive it, choose Export Folder from the File menu. The Export Folders dialog box appears so you can type the name of the export folder. Type a name such as A:EXPORT.MMF. When you click the OK button, you are asked to select the folders you want to export as the example in Figure 15-10 shows.

15

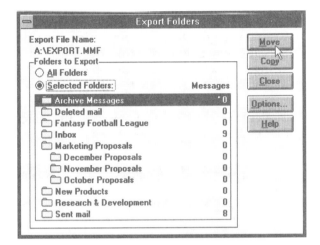

Click the folder you want to export, or to export all folders (for backup reasons), click the All Folders option. Note the Move and Copy buttons. Move places the files in the folder in the export file, then empties the folder you selected. Copy keeps the files in the folder you selected. In either case, the folder's contents are saved to the export file. You can retrieve its contents at any time by selecting Import Folder from the File menu.

Message Templates

Use message templates when you frequently send messages that follow the same general format. For example, you could compose a message to use when sending weekly bowling results to members of your company bowling league. To save a message on a template, simply write it, then close it without sending the message. It is placed in your inbox for future use.

The next time you need to send out your weekly bowling results, drag the message to your Outbox or type Alt-M-F to Forward the message as discussed earlier in this chapter. You then get a chance to add your bowling results or make any other changes to the message before clicking the Send button.

Message Finder

Even if you do a good job organizing your messages using folders, there are times when you want to search through your messages for a text string. For example, you may remember receiving a message describing a new product having to do with laser printers. You could search for messages using the keyword "laser." To start a search, choose Message Finder from the File menu and type the search criteria in the Message Finder dialog box as shown here:

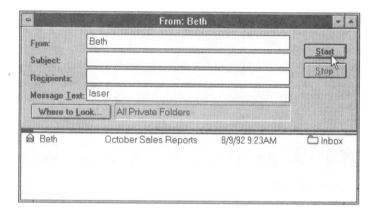

Select the Where to Look button to choose the folder you want to search through. The Where to Look dialog box shown here is displayed:

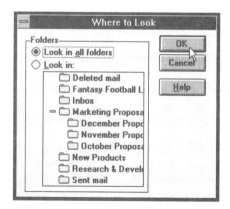

Click the Look in All Folders button to search through all the messages in all folders, or click a folder in the listing to search through just that folder. Click the Start button to begin the search. Any messages that contain the text are listed in the Message Finder dialog box. To view the contents of any message, double-click it with the mouse.

Working Offline

You can compose messages in Mail even if you are not connected to the postoffice. The messages are saved and sent the next time you connect with the postoffice. This is useful for traveling salespeople, or when the postoffice system is not up and running.

Administrative Tasks

The administrator of a workgroup creates the postoffice and is responsible for maintaining the postoffice accounts. Some of the tasks of a postoffice administrator are discussed in this section.

Creating the Postoffice

When you enter Mail for the first time, you are presented with the Welcome to Mail dialog box. On this dialog box, you can choose to connect with an existing postoffice or create a new one. If you choose to create a new postoffice, Mail displays the Create Workgroup Postoffice dialog box shown here:

In the directory listing, choose the directory for the postoffice. Mail defaults to the Windows directory, which you should use unless you have reasons not to. Click the Network button if you want to choose a directory on another computer for the postoffice. Once you click the OK button, you are prompted with the administrator account details dialog box as shown in the following:

Fill out the dialog box with the postoffice administrator's information. Recall from the Connecting to An Existing Postoffice section earlier in this chapter that the Name, Mailbox, and Password fields are required. The remaining fields are optional. Once you click the OK button, Mail reminds you that you need to share the directory in which the postoffice resides. Follow these steps to share the directory:

1. In the File Manager, click the Windows directory.
2. Click the WGPO subdirectory.
3. Click the Share button.

Mail displays the Share Directory dialog box shown on the next page:

15

```
+------------------------------------------------------+
| [-]              Share Directory                     |
+------------------------------------------------------+
| Share Name:  [WGPO                    ]   [  OK  ]   |
|                                                       |
| Path:        [C:\WINDOWS\WGPO         ]   [ Cancel ] |
|                                                       |
| Comment:     [                        ]   [  Help  ] |
|              [X] Re-share at Startup                 |
| ,-Access Type:------------------------------------,  |
| | O Read-Only                                     |  |
| | O Full                                          |  |
| | (o) Depends on Password                         |  |
| '-------------------------------------------------'  |
| ,-Passwords:--------------------------------------,  |
| | Read-Only Password:  [READPASS  ]               |  |
| | Full Access Password: [FULLPASS  ]              |  |
| '-------------------------------------------------'  |
+------------------------------------------------------+
```

Enter the following information:

Share Name   Enter the name of the shared directory. This field defaults to the subdirectory name you selected in the File Manager.

Path   Enter the path of the shared directory. This information is required and is filled in when you select the subdirectory in the File Manager.

Comment   Enter a comment about the shared directory. This information is optional.

Access Type   Check the appropriate button for Read-Only, Full, or Depends on Password access to the postoffice. Users can only browse messages in the postoffice if you select Read-Only access. Users can perform any actions in the directory if you assign Full access. If you click the Depends on Password button, the user is prompted for a password to gain access to the directory the first time he or she starts Mail.

Passwords   If you checked the Depends on Password button in the Access Type box, enter a Read-Only Password and Full Access Password.

Click the OK button in the dialog box when you are finished.

Postoffice Manager Duties

If you are the postoffice manager, you can access the Postoffice
Manager dialog box as shown in the following illustration and make
changes to postoffice mailboxes and users. Choose Postoffice Manager
from the Mail menu, then refer to the following sections for
instructions on using the dialog box features.

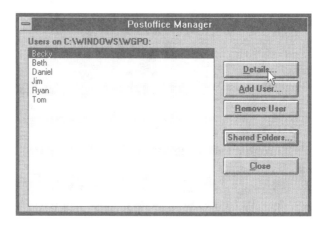

Viewing and Modifying Existing Accounts

To view or change an account, click the account name in the list and
click the Details button. A dialog box appears with information about
the account that you can change if necessary.

Adding Users

Click the Add User button to add a new account. An Add User dialog
screen appears. All of the fields are empty with the exception of the
password field. The password is defaulted to PASSWORD. You must
enter the Name and Mailbox fields. All of the other fields are
optional.

Removing Users

To delete an account, first click the account name on the Postoffice
Manager dialog box, then click the Remove User button. You are then
asked to verify the deletion.

Checking and Compressing Folders

As the administrator, you will need to monitor and manage the disk space on the computer where the postoffice resides. To check the status of a folder, select Postoffice Manager from the Mail menu, then click the Shared Folders button to display the Shared Folders dialog box shown here:

```
┌─────────────────────────────────────────────────┐
│ ─           Shared Folders                       │
│ ┌─Current Status of Shared Folders──────┐  ┌─────────┐ │
│ │        Number of folders:  2          │  │Compress │ │
│ │   Total messages in folders:  0       │  └─────────┘ │
│ │   Bytes used by messages:  2,364      │  ┌─────────┐ │
│ │ Recoverable bytes in folders:  1,786  │  │  Close  │ │
│ └───────────────────────────────────────┘  └─────────┘ │
└─────────────────────────────────────────────────┘
```

Be sure to note the number of recoverable bytes in folders. The bytes are unused because messages in the folders have been deleted. Click the Compress button to free up the recoverable space.

Reinstating First-Time Startup

In the event that a user enters the wrong information the first time Mail is started, you can make the following changes so that Mail repeats its initial startup procedures. Once you have completed these steps, the correct information can be entered.

1. Go to the user's system and edit the MSMAIL.INI file using an editor such as Notepad.
2. Disable the ServerPath= and Logon= lines by placing a semicolon in front of them, as shown below:

    ;ServerPath= *a path*

    ;Logon= *a name*
3. Add or edit the CustomInitHandler= line so that it reads as follows:

    CustomInitHandler=WGPOMGR.DLL, 10
4. Save and close the file.

Now the user can restart Mail and enter the correct information for the first-time startup.

Enhancing Microsoft Mail

The version of Microsoft Mail that comes with Windows for Workgroups is limited to a single workgroup. If you want to expand the connections to other workgroups and provide advanced administrative features, you'll need to add the *Mail and Schedule+ Extensions for Windows for Workgroups*. With this product, you can connect multiple workgroups, connect with other mail and scheduling systems, and provide remote dial-in support for Mail. The full set of features is described below:

✦ Provides an upgrade to the full-featured version of Microsoft Mail which includes spell-checking, a training module, and advanced online help.

✦ Includes MS-DOS, Macintosh, and OS/2 client software.

✦ Includes advanced features such as routing of messages between workgroups, directory synchronization, network group names, user access privileges, and mail log files.

✦ Provides a Message Transfer Agent (MTA) that connects postoffices and remote users.

✦ Provides a Schedule Distribution component that sends Schedule+ schedules to other postoffices.

The main purpose of the extensions is to allow connections among many postoffices. The Message Transfer Agent is like a postal carrier that transports messages between postoffices. Since the extensions support remote connections, you can even connect over the telephone lines with workgroups at other sites.

An administrative program gives managers the tools they need to monitor and control communications across the whole network. For example, the administrator can add or delete user accounts in any workgroup from a central location, or monitor disk storage space and the use of long distance lines.

Global address lists and directory synchronization are used to ensure that postoffices exchange information about changes made to their directories. Any changes made at a workgroup or departmental level are reflected in the address list viewed in another part of the organization, even if it is at a remote site.

To ensure that addressing of messages remains relatively simple across large remotely-connected networks, Microsoft provides gateway products that connect Mail users to most host-based, public, and LAN-based electronic mail systems and services. Typically, users of non-Microsoft Mail systems (including Macintosh and OS/2 users) will be listed in the Mail global address list so users can simply click the name of mail recipients.

CHAPTER

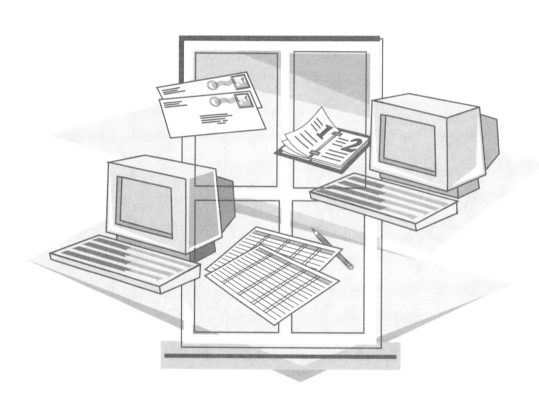

16

MICROSOFT SCHEDULE+

The Schedule+ accessory helps keep you and your workgroup on track. This personal and group scheduling tool registers upcoming meetings and appointments. It also notifies you of upcoming important events, such as birthdays and anniversaries. When you use Schedule+ in a workgroup, you can view other users' schedules and coordinate meetings with them. Schedule+ automatically scans the appointments of members in your workgroup and helps you schedule meetings during times that everyone is available.

Before using Schedule+ for the first time, you or someone else in your workgroup must create a Mail postoffice, as discussed in the previous chapter. Anyone who has a postoffice mailbox will show up in your scheduling system. Schedule+ contains an Appointment Book, Task List, and a Planner. It also has a message window that contains a list of meetings you've requested and the responses from other workgroup members as to whether they can attend the meeting or not.

Appointment Book

The basic Schedule+ window is shown in Figure 16-1. You use the Appointment Book to create all kinds of appointments—definite, tentative, recurring, and private—as described in the following list.

+ *Normal appointment*   A normal appointment is definite, not tentative. Normal appointments appear as white blocks of text in the Schedule+ window.

+ *Tentative appointment*   A tentative appointment may be cancelled or changed. You create tentative appointments to set aside a block

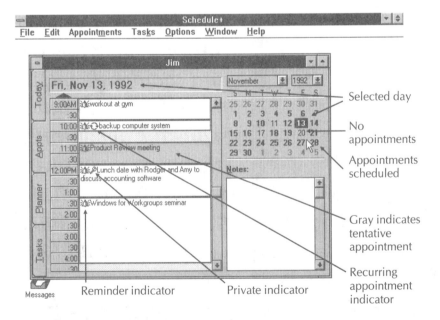

Basic Schedule+ window
Figure 16-1.

16

of time when you think you might be busy or when you are trying to arrange meetings with other users. Tentative appointments appear as gray blocks of text in the Schedule+ window.

✦ *Recurring appointment*   You set recurring appointments for meetings that occur every week or every month, or for regular activities that are important to remember, like paying the mortgage.

✦ *Private appointment*   Normally, other Schedule+ users can view your appointments so they can schedule an appointment with you when you are not busy. You can designate some appointments as private so other users can not see those activities, but can see that you are busy.

Schedule+ also provides a Daily Note section located in the lower right of its window. Use this section to enter general notes about the day.

Viewing Your Appointments

To change the dates you can view other appointments, click day, month, or year buttons. When you first start Schedule+, the calendar is positioned at the current day, month, and year as shown here:

Days that have scheduled appointments are displayed in boldface text. To change to a different day, click the numeral of the day you want to view. The new day is displayed, but note that the current day appears indented.

To change the month, click the down arrow button in the month field and choose a different month from the drop-down list box. To change the year, click the down arrow button in the year field and choose a different year from the list.

TIP: Click the Today button located in the upper left portion of the schedule window to return to the current day.

Go To Date

Instead of selecting a new date from the drop-down menus, you can use the Go To Date dialog box by pressing ⌈Ctrl⌉-⌈G⌉ or by selecting Go To Date from the Edit menu. You can manually type in the date you want or click the up and down arrow buttons to change the date. Use this option to jump to dates that don't appear on the calendar.

Adding a One-Time Appointment

After you've selected a day, you're ready to enter appointments. The left portion of the schedule window is divided into time slots in half hour increments, as you can see in Figure 16-1. Click the time slot where you want to make an appointment you want to make with the mouse or press the ⌈↑⌉ and ⌈↓⌉ keys to change time slots. You can also click and drag through several time slots if an appointment lasts longer than a half hour.

You can use either of the following methods to create an appointment:

✦ Simply type the text for the appointment in the time slot. It scrolls to the left as you type. If you drag through several time slots, they all convert to text fields when you start typing.

✦ Double-click the time slot (or press ⌈Ctrl⌉-⌈N⌉), then fill out the Appointment dialog box as shown in Figure 16-2.

The second method lets you specify additional information for the appointment, such as whether it is tentative or private. The fields of the Appointment dialog box are described in the following sections. Once you've filled out the fields, click the OK button.

16

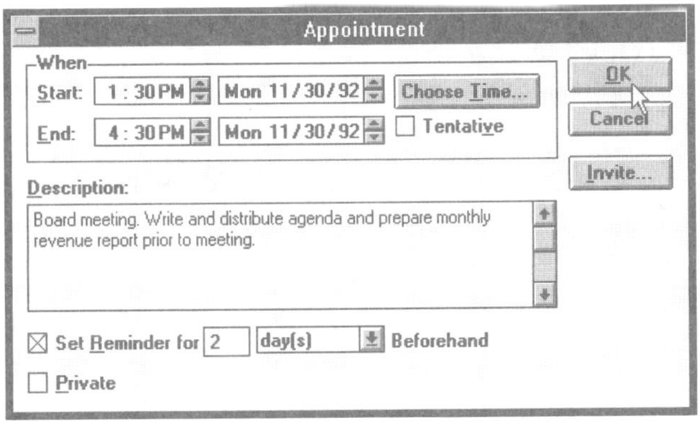

Appointment window
Figure 16-2.

Entering Times and Dates   Type the starting and ending time and
date for the appointment or change the time or date by clicking the up
and down arrow buttons in the Start and End fields. If you dragged
through several time slots before opening the Appointment dialog box,
the time field reflects the time slots you selected.

Making the Appointment Tentative   Check the Tentative box to make
the appointment tentative. As mentioned previously, use this option to
reserve a block of time when arranging meetings with other users. A
tentative appointment appears gray instead of white in the main
schedule window and in the Planner reviewed later in this chapter.

Entering Appointment Description   Type information about the
appointment in the Description field, but keep in mind that not all of
this text will appear in the time slot for the appointment on the
Schedule+ window. Be sure to type information that uniquely identifies
the appointment. For example, instead of typing just "lunch," you
could type "lunch date with Rodger and Amy to discuss accounting
software." Adding more information helps you easily search for and
identify the appointment. In some cases, you might need to locate a
previous appointment. It's much easier to search for keywords like
"Rodger," "Amy," or "accounting," rather than scan through all the
appointments described as "lunch."

Set Reminder   Enable the Set Reminder box to set a reminder for an
appointment. Click the down arrow button in the Beforehand field,
then choose either minute(s), hour(s), day(s), week(s), or month(s). In
the field preceding it, type in the quantity, such as 2 minutes, 2 hours,

and so on. A bell icon appears next to appointments that have reminders. When the reminder is activated, Schedule+ displays a reminder message similar to the one shown here:

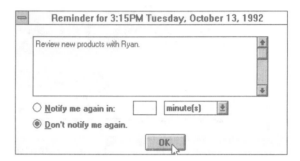

You then read the text of the appointment or click the Notify me again in button if you want another reminder. You can make reminders appear when you first start Windows by copying the file MSREMIND.EXE into the Program Manager Startup Group.

NOTE: You can disable all reminders by selecting Turn Off Reminders from the File menu. To reenable reminders, choose Turn On Reminders from the File menu.

Making Appointments Private   Click the Private box to make an appointment private. A key icon appears next to private appointments on the main Schedule+ window. The text of private appointments can't be read by other Schedule+ users who connect with your schedule over the network.

Inviting Meeting Attendees
Click the Invite button on the Appointment dialog box to display a list of other possible meeting attendees from your workgroup, as shown in Figure 16-3. The list displays all users with Mail mailboxes in your workgroup. Click the icon labeled "other lists" in Figure 16-3 to display

16

Other lists ———

Personal address ———
book

Search for name ———

Create new address ———
book

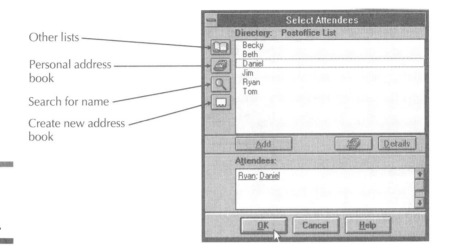

Select
Attendees
dialog box
Figure 16-3.

a list of other address books you can search through, or click the personal address book icon to display your personal address list. To select attendees, click their names in the top list, then click the Add button. Their name then appears in the lower list. Alternately, you could choose a *group* of preselected names. For example, you might select a group called "board presentation" that you had previously set up in Mail.

After selecting attendees for a meeting, click the OK button on the Select Attendees dialog box. If you are then finished filling out the Appointment dialog box, click its OK button. The Send Request window then appears as shown in Figure 16-4. Fill out this dialog box with information you want to send to other users about the meeting. The information will appear in their Mail Inbox and in their Schedule+ Message window. You can make changes to the Subject box and type additional information about the meeting in the lower text box. Enable the Ask for Responses box to request a reply.

When everything is filled out, click the Send button. Schedule+ sends the messages and displays a handshake icon in the appointment slot.

NOTE: If attendees haven't responded to your meeting request, you can pester them by choosing the Re-Send Mail option from the Appointments menu.

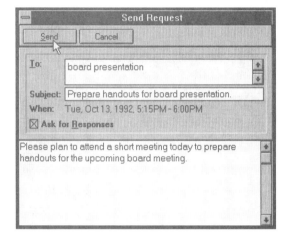

Send Request
dialog box
Figure 16-4.

Replying to Appointment Requests

If someone requests your presence at a meeting, the request appears in
the Schedule+ Message window. Double-click the message to pull up a
Meeting Request dialog box as shown in Figure 16-5. To respond, check
the Send Response box, then click one of the following buttons:

✦ Click View Schedule to see if the meeting can be arranged within
your schedule.

✦ Click Accept to notify the sender that you will attend the meeting.

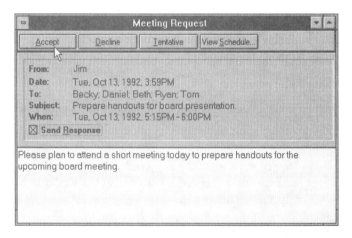

Meeting
Request dialog
box
Figure 16-5.

16

◆ Click Decline to notify the sender that you will not attend the meeting.

◆ Click Tentative to notify the sender that you are unsure of your attendance.

If you click Accept, Decline, or Tentative, the Send Response dialog box as shown in Figure 16-6 appears. Fill in the message area if you wish and click the send button.

Request Receipts

Once attendees have responded to a meeting request, their responses appear in the meeting organizer's Message window. Figure 16-7 shows the various message headers and icons that indicate responses to meeting requests. Double-click any message header to view the request receipts.

You can also double-click the appointment in the Schedule+ window to view similar information on the Appointment dialog box as shown in Figure 16-8. Note that a closed envelope next to the addressee indicates a person has not responded or that there is an incomplete response from a group.

Recurring Appointments

You can set recurring appointments for events or meetings that occur on a regular basis. Schedule+ automatically adds the appointments to your schedule at the appropriate time and dates.

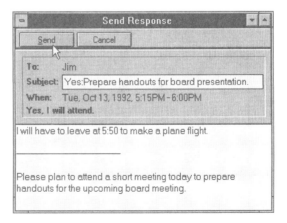

Send Response
form
Figure 16-6.

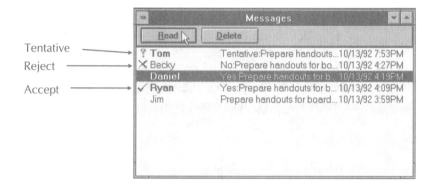

Tentative
Reject

Accept

The first step to creating a recurring appointment is to select the time and date of the first appointment. Next select New Recurring Appointment from the Appointments menu. Schedule+ presents the Recurring Appointment window shown in Figure 16-9. Each section of the dialog box is described in the following sections. Once you have created a recurring appointment, a circular-arrow icon indicating recurring appointments appears next to the appointment description on the main schedule window.

Recurring Details

Click the Change button to open the Change Recurrence dialog box shown in Figure 16-10. Fill out the box as discussed in the following.

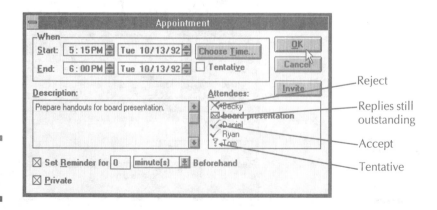

Reject
Replies still
outstanding

Accept
Tentative

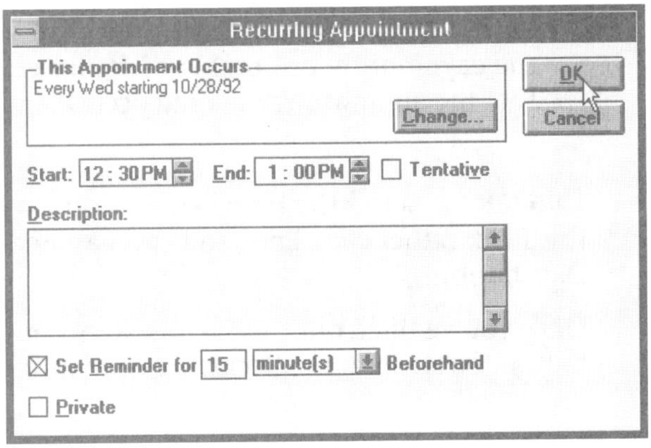

16

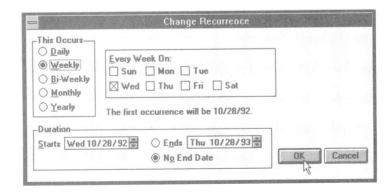

Recurring
Appointment
dialog box
Figure 16-9.

Time Increment Enable Daily, Weekly, Bi-Weekly, Monthly, or
Yearly in the This Occurs field. The box on the right changes depending
on the option you selected.

✦ *Daily* When you click Daily, you can choose Every day or Every
Weekday on the right.

✦ *Weekly* When you click Weekly, you can choose the day of the
week on the right.

✦ *Bi-Weekly* When you click Bi-Weekly, you can choose the day of
the week on the right.

✦ *Monthly* When you click Monthly, you can select either the
number of days into the month or the actual day of the month.

Change
Recurrence
dialog box
Figure 16-10.

♦ *Yearly* When you click Yearly, you can set a specific date or select the day, month, or number of days, weekdays, or weekend days that the appointment should occur.

Duration   Select the time period for the recurring appointments in this field. Either click Ends and enter an End date or click the No End Date button.

Once you've filled out the Change Recurrence dialog box, click the OK button to return to the Recurring Appointment dialog box.

Starting and Ending Times

In the Start and End fields, enter the starting and ending time. Click the up and down arrow buttons to adjust the Start and End time in 15-minute intervals.

Making the Appointment Tentative

Enable the Tentative box to make the appointment tentative. Tentative appointments appear in gray rather than white in the main schedule window and Planner.

Entering Appointment Description

Enter a brief description of the recurring appointment such as "sales meeting—monthly" or "bowling night" or "Windows for Workgroups class." Try to put the most descriptive word first. Here is an example that shows what happens when more than one appointment is scheduled for the same time slot:

Here is the same schedule entry with the keyword entered first:

12:00PM	🔔👤Mortgage!		🔔👤Lunch!
:30			
1:00	👤Weekly sales meeting		
:30			
2:00			
:30			

You can see that placing keywords first helps you quickly identify an appointment. Also notice that an entry doesn't necessarily need to be an appointment. You can also type reminders, so there will be instances when you have multiple entries at the same time slot.

Reminder

Check the reminder box and set the time interval for the reminder message. For example, you could set Schedule+ to remind you two days before an anniversary or birthday.

Making Appointments Private

As with regular appointments, you can make an appointment private by checking the Private box. A key icon next to the appointment description on the main schedule window indicates a private appointment. Other users cannot see details of your private appointments.

Editing Recurring Appointments

Select Edit Recurring Appointments from the Appointments menu to edit recurring appointments. A window containing your existing recurring appointments appears similar to this:

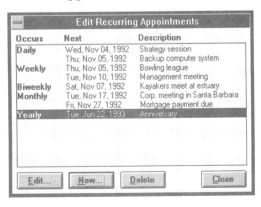

Use a mouse or the ⬆ or ⬇ keys to select an existing recurring appointment. Edit the recurring appointment details just as you would when adding a new one.

Changing Appointments to Recurring Appointments

You can change a one-time appointment to a recurring appointment. For example, assume you have an appointment with a research and development group, and the group decides to meet at the same time and date each month. Follow these steps to change a one-time appointment to a recurring appointment:

1. Click the appointment.
2. Select New Recurring Appointment from the Appointments menu or press Alt-M-R.
3. Enter the recurring appointment information.

The boxes in the recurring information window default to the information for a one-time appointment.

Finding Appointments

You can have Schedule+ search for appointments by choosing Find from the Edit menu. For example, let's assume you know you have a lunch date with Sally sometime this week, but you can't remember when. You would type **Sally** in the Search For field of the Find dialog box as shown in the following. Then choose one of three buttons: Forward from today, Backward from today, or Whole schedule. Click OK when you are ready to search.

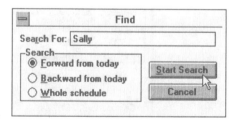

16

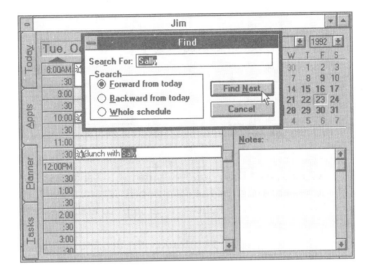

The Find dialog
box
Figure 16-11.

Schedule+ displays the first appointment where it finds the text. The
keyword is highlighted in the appointment as shown in Figure 16-11. The
Find dialog box remains on the screen so you can continue searching for
other appointments. The Start Search button becomes a Find Next button.
Click the Cancel button to stop searching or the Find Next button to
continue searching. You can also type other text to search for.

If the Initial search or the Find Next search is unsuccessful, you'll see a
message box. Click OK and check your spelling of the keyword. Correct
your spelling or look for a different keyword. You may have misspelled
Sally's name in the appointment itself. Search for a different keyword
such as "Sal" or "lunch" in further attempts to find the appointment.
Change your search criteria to search the entire schedule just in case
you already missed your appointment. If you did miss your
appointment, make sure you enable the reminder feature of the
appointment next time.

Setting Access Privileges

You can set the access privileges that other users have to your schedule.
Choose Set Access Privileges from the Options menu to display the Set
Access Privileges dialog box as shown here:

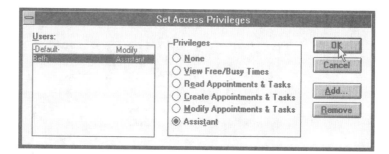

Click one of the Privileges buttons to set access levels for other users. All
users are assigned the default privileges unless you add their name to
the list of Users. Follow these steps to assign access privileges:

1. Click the Add button on the Set Access Privileges window. A list of
   names appears.
2. Click a name.
3. Click the Add button on the user list screen.
4. Click the OK button.
5. Click a privilege button.

NOTE: If you have a secretary or other assistant who helps you
manage your schedule, give that person the Assistant privilege.

Opening Other Users' Appointment Books

You can open other users' appointment books to schedule joint
appointments. Note that you can only open another user's
Appointment Book if you have appropriate access privileges. Select
Open Other's Appt. Book from the File menu to open someone else's
schedule. A list of names or groups appears to choose from, similar to
that in Figure 16-12. Click the name and Add button for each name (or
group name) you want to include. Click the OK button when you are
done. If you selected multiple users, the windows are displayed in
cascade formation.

Open Other's
Appt. Book
dialog box
Figure 16-12.

Exporting and Importing Appointments

You can export your Schedule+ data to disk or another computer and later recall its contents back to your own computer. This is useful for backing up or moving a specific range of appointments.

NOTE: If you need to take a copy of your schedule with you on a trip, you can move the schedule to a floppy disk by choosing the Move Local File command from the File Menu. To archive appointments, refer to the following section.

Click Export Appointments from the File menu to bring up the Export Appointments dialog box shown here:

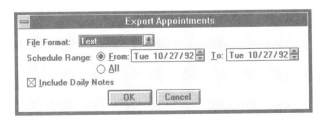

In the File Format field, choose the schedule format to export the entire schedule. If you choose text format, you can enter a date range of appointments in the Schedule Range field. You can also choose Include Daily Notes to copy daily notes to the exported schedule.

The Export Appointments file section dialog box appears when you click the OK button. Enter a file name or choose an existing file from the directory. The file name defaults to the name of your mailbox and a "SCH" extension. Click the OK button to export the schedule.

Select Import Appointments from the File menu to import schedules that were previously exported. Schedule+ also provides the ability to import schedules from other programs, such as Windows Calendar or WordPerfect Office. Type the name of the file and click the OK button. The Import Format dialog box shown here appears:

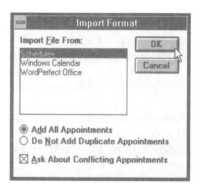

Choose a format and select one of the following options from the Import Format dialog box, then click the OK button.

✦ *Add All Appointments* Click this button to add all appointments regardless of whether they already exist in your current schedule.

✦ *Do Not Add Duplicate Appointments* Click this button to merge the imported appointments with those already in your schedule.

✦ *Ask About Conflicting Appointments* Click this button if you want Schedule+ to get your OK prior to adding any conflicting appointments.

Archiving Appointments

You can remove appointments from your schedule, but save them for later by using the archiving option. Select Create Archive from the File menu to create an archive file. You can later open the archive file and view or modify its schedule entries. Select Open Archive from the File menu to open an existing archive file. Follow these steps to restore archived schedule entries back into your primary schedule:

1. Open an Existing Archive.
2. Export the schedule entries in the archive.
3. Select your primary schedule.
4. Import the schedule entries from the exported file.

Task List

Tasks, unlike appointments, are activities to which you assign priorities and desired completion dates. You can use the Schedule+ *Task List* to create tasks, then you can assign priorities and completion dates to each task and group them into *projects* if necessary. You can optionally tell Schedule+ to create appointment entries from your tasks.

Adding A One-Time Task

Select the Task tab button from the schedule window or press (Ctrl)-(T) to add a new task. The following Task dialog box appears:

To create a task, fill out the fields on the Task dialog box as described in the following:

+ *Description* Type the description of the task.

+ *Project* Type a project name or select from existing projects if there are any.

+ *Due Date* Select the date the project is due.

+ *Start Work* Enter the number of days, weeks, or months prior to the due date that you should begin work.

+ *Set Reminder* Enable this to be reminded of a start work time.

+ *Priority* Set the priority level. The tasks are ordered by priority. In addition, you can print reports based on the priority of your tasks.

+ *Private* Enable this box if you do not want others to see the task details.

Recurring Tasks

You can set tasks to recur on a repeating basis. Select New Recurring Task from the Tasks menu and fill in the boxes as you would for a one-time task. In addition, click the Change button to change the recurrence of the task. The Change Recurrence dialog box appears and you can fill it out as discussed previously in this chapter under "Recurring Appointments."

Viewing Tasks

To view your current tasks, click the Tasks tab button. Schedule+ displays a list of tasks similar to that shown in Figure 16-13. To edit or view the details of task, simply double-click it, or use the arrow keys to first highlight a task, then click the Edit button. You can also create a new task from this dialog box by typing a name for it in the New Task field and clicking the Add button.

There are several options for viewing that make it easy to find the item you are looking for or to determine which task you should work on next:

16

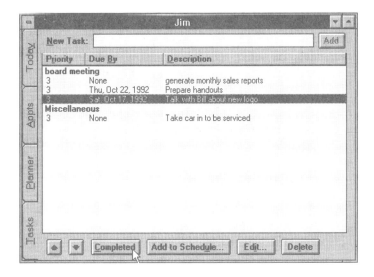

Task list
Figure 16-13.

View by Project   Select View by Project from the Tasks menu to sort tasks by projects and project names. Use this in combination with the sort options described next to manipulate the view of your tasks.

Sort by Priority   Select Sort by Priority from the Tasks menu to sort tasks by priority. If you enabled View by Project, then your tasks are sorted by priority within each project. Otherwise, you will see a combined task list sorted by priority.

Sort by Due Date   Select Sort by Due Date from the Tasks menu to sort your task view by due date. If you have enabled View by Project, then your tasks are sorted by due date within each project. Otherwise, you will see a combined task list sorted by due date.

Sort by Descriptions   Select Sort by Descriptions from the Tasks menu to sort tasks by description. Your tasks are sorted by due date within each project if you have enabled View by Project. Otherwise, you will see a combined task list sorted by due date.

Show Active Tasks   Select Show Active Tasks from the Tasks menu to view only tasks that are currently active. Any tasks with a due date prior to the current date are excluded from the display.

Planner

The *Planner* is used to scan your own and other users' appointments in order to set up group meetings. Browse through the days in Planner to view others' and your own availability. The *Auto-Pick* feature automatically selects times in which all parties are available.

The planner window shown in Figure 16-14 appears when you click the Planner tab button or press (Alt)-(P). The blocks are shaded to indicate attendees availability:

✦ *Dark block* You are busy.

✦ *Gray block* At least one other attendee is busy.

✦ *Striped block* You and at least one other attendee are busy.

Schedule+ displays a checkmark or an X next to the attendees' names to indicate their availability. Look next to the attendees when you click on a time slot. A checkmark indicates the person is available and an X indicates they already have an appointment scheduled.

Select Auto-pick from the Appointments menu to automatically search for the next time slot in which all attendees are available.

Click Request Meeting once you have selected a time for an appointment to pull up a Send Request form as shown in Figure 16-15.

Planner
window
Figure 16-14.

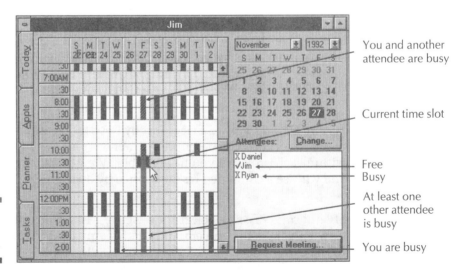

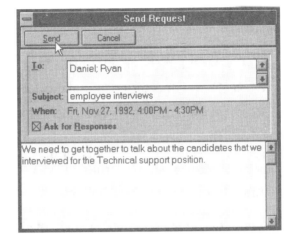

Send Request
dialog box
Figure 16-15.

The To box is filled in with the attendees you had selected in the
planner window. Enter a subject, check the Ask for Responses box, fill
in a short memo, and click the Send button. You are notified that the
meeting is booked successfully.

Printing Appointments and Tasks

Select Print from the File menu or press [Ctrl]-[P] to print a copy of your
appointments and tasks. Select the criteria for the report from the
dialog box shown here:

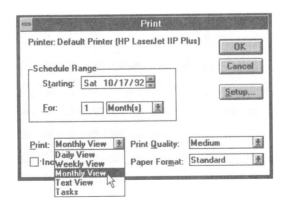

You have the option of printing your schedule or tasks in the following formats:

✦ *Daily View* Prints the appointments for a single day.

✦ *Weekly View* Prints the appointments for a single week.

✦ *Monthly View* Prints the appointments for a month in calendar format.

✦ *Text View* Prints appointments for the day in text format. It does not include time slots like the daily view does.

✦ *Tasks* Prints a complete listing of active tasks.

Click Print Quality to select either High, Medium, Low, or draft quality. Click Paper Format to choose either Standard (8.5"x11.5"), Junior (5.5"x8.5"), or Pocket (3.75"x6.75") size for the printout. These sizes match most appointment books.

Setting Display Defaults

Click Display from the Options menu to change default colors and font sizes used by Schedule+. You can change the following items in the Display dialog screen as shown here:

✦ *Appointment Book Background* Color used for time slots that have not been filled.

✦ *Planner Background* Color used for time slots that are available for all attendees.

✦ *Planner User* Color used in Planner to indicate that you are busy.

✦ *Planner Others* Color used in Planner to indicate that others are not available.

✦ *Page Background* Background color used on Appointment Book, Planner, and Task List.

✦ *Font Size* The size of the characters on the screen. Choose either the 8-point or 10-point size.

General Options

Click General Options from the Options menu to change many of the default settings in Schedule+ as shown in Figure 16-16.

Enable the Startup Offline option if you want Schedule+ to start in the offline mode rather than attempting to connect with the network. Select one or more of the options in the Reminders box to set how you want reminders to operate. Set the remaining fields according to how you want Schedule+ to display your schedule.

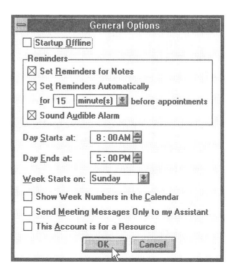

General
Options dialog
box
Figure 16-16.

More About Schedule+

Schedule+ is an application that uses Microsoft Mail for many of its functions such as logging on, and sending and receiving messages. It also uses the address books created in Mail. User account information is automatically translated from Mail to Schedule+.

While Schedule+ has its own initialization file called SCHDPLUS.INI, it also uses Mail's MSMAIL.INI initialization file. User preferences such as colors and option settings, as well as the location of calendar files and archives are stored in SCHDPLUS.INI. Logon information, server location, and custom message types are read from the MSMAIL.INI file.

TIP: If you need to change the time and date display format, choose the International icon in the control panel. If you want to change the reminder sounds (assuming you have a sound board), choose the Sound option in the Control Panel.

The following sections present additional information about Schedule+.

Offline and Online Modes

You can use Schedule+ in offline or online modes. When working in the offline mode, Schedule+ operates as a stand-alone application and maintains a local calendar file on your hard disk. When working with Schedule+ in the online mode, a calendar file in the WGPO\CAL directory of the workgroup postoffice is used. You can use the offline file when the Schedule+ server is unavailable. Both online and offline files are kept synchronized as follows:

✦ The offline file is updated to match the online file every time you start and quit Schedule+ or connect and disconnect from the server.

✦ Appointments in the offline file are added to the online file.

✦ Deleted appointments in the offline file are removed from the online file.

✦ Changes made to the offline file take precedence over changes made to the online file.

Viewing Reminders at Windows Startup

Normally, you won't see any appointment reminders until you actually start Schedule+ and log on. If you want to see appointment reminders as soon as Windows itself starts, you'll need to create a startup icon for the file MSREMIND.EXE (located in the Windows directory) in the Program Manager Startup group. The following steps explain how to do this.

1. Highlight the Startup Group in the Program Manager by clicking it once.
2. Choose New from the Program Manager File menu.
3. Choose Program Item when the New Program Object dialog box appears.
4. On the Program Item Properties dialog box, click the Browse button, then select the file MSREMIND.EXE in the Windows directory and click OK.
5. When you return to the Program Item Properties dialog box, click OK to create the icon in the group.

The next time you start Windows, the Mail logon dialog box appears. Enter your logon name as usual. If there are any appointment reminders to display, a reminder dialog box appears for each.

Creating Resource Accounts

Although Schedule+ helps people organize their time, it can also be used to schedule the use of high-resolution printers, conference rooms, and other company resources that many people need to share. The network provides an excellent way for many users to view the schedule of the resource and book it for future use. To create a resource, follow these steps:

1. Create an account for the resource using Mail in the same way you would to create an account for a regular user. You must assign your password to each new resource account so you can log onto them from your workstation and perform step 2.

2. Start Schedule+, and logon using the new resource account name. Since you used your existing password for each resource, Schedule+ lets you sign into a different account during the same session.

3. Choose General Options from the Options menu, then enable the This Account is for a Resource check box.

Enabling this option changes the access privilege for the resource account to the "create appointments and tasks" option so that other people can access and reserve the resource. For example, if the resource is a conference room, a user organizing a meeting can select the conference room at the same time they choose attendees for the meeting. If the resource is a printer or other equipment, they can reserve it for future use by choosing the Open Other's Appt Book option on the File menu. They can then specify a time to use the resource in the same way they would create an appointment.

The Schedule+ Extensions

Microsoft provides the Microsoft Mail and Schedule+ Extension for Windows for Workgroups as an add-on package that enhances the features and capabilities of Schedule+. The main advantage is that Schedule+ users can exchange schedule information with other workgroups and communicate with users of other mail systems. An administrator program provides central control of Schedule+ data on the Mail server. Network administrators can delete old calendar files and set up communications options.

CHAPTER

17

NETWORK GAMES: HEARTS

Hearts is a game of luck and skill that you can play over the network with other users. Good strategy will often overcome a bad draw of the cards. Hearts is always played with four players. However, you can play Hearts against any combination of computer and workgroup users. Unlike most other computer games, in Hearts each player sits at a different computer.

One player must be a dealer. If you play by yourself you become the dealer. The computer takes over hands of any users that drop out of the game except for the dealer and the game ends if the dealer drops out.

The object of Hearts is to score as few points as possible. You want to avoid getting hearts and the queen of spades in your hand since you are penalized points for those cards (13 points for the queen of spades!). The game is over when one player reaches 100 points and the winner is the player with the fewest points.

Hearts Basics

The cards are ranked with the 2 as the low card and the ace as the high card. The card's ranking determines who wins tricks. A *trick* is comprised of four cards—each player plays a single card in a clockwise rotation. The person who lays down the highest ranked card of the lead suit "wins" the trick. The *lead* is the first card played in a trick.

The holder of the 2 of clubs starts the game by laying that card on the table. Each person must *follow the suit* of the lead card. In the first hand, everybody lays down a club, but if you don't have a club, you *play off* by laying down a card of any other suit. You play off cards in other hands as well if you can't follow the suit of the lead card.

NOTE: You cannot play a heart or the queen of spades during the first trick.

"Hearts are broken" the first time someone plays a heart because he or she can't follow the suit of the lead card that was played. From that point on, any player can lead hearts.

At the end of the game, you are penalized one point for each heart suit card and 13 points if you hold the queen of spades. One exception is when you attempt to *shoot the moon*. To successfully shoot the moon, you must collect all the hearts and the queen of spades during a hand. If you are successful, then every other player is penalized 26 points while you collect zero points. The game is over when one player reaches 100 points. The winner is the player with the fewest points.

Begin Play

When you first start Hearts, the dialog box in Figure 17-1 appears. Type in your name, then click one of the button options.

If you want to start a new game, or just play by yourself, click the I want to be dealer option. If you become the dealer, you have a choice:

✦ Press F2 immediately to play by yourself.

✦ Wait for other users to connect to the game you started (use Chat to alert other users that you've started a game). Once other users have attached, press F2 to start the game. Any missing players are filled in by the computer.

17

TIP: To improve game performance when other users are playing over the network, the user with the fastest computer should be the dealer.

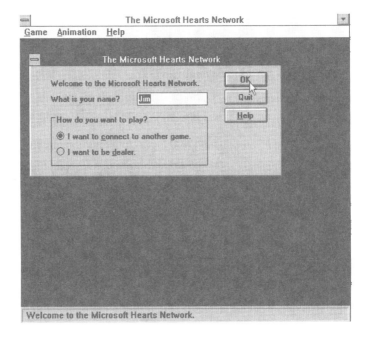

Startup dialog box
Figure 17-1.

Click the I want to connect to another game button to attach to another dealer's computer. Enter the dealer's computer name in the Locate Dealer dialog box shown here:

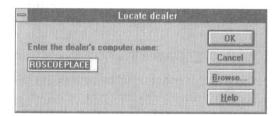

If you don't know the other user's name, click the Browse button to browse through a list of dealers on the network, then select a dealer and click the OK button.

The dealer starts the actual game by pressing F2. Your hand is shown face up at the bottom of the table and sorted by suit (as shown in Figure 17-2). Each person sees only his or her own hand.

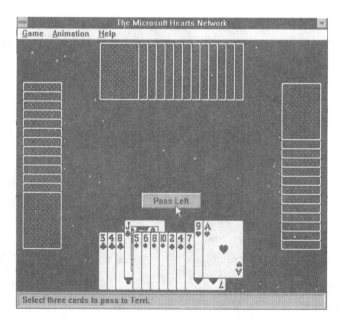

Sample game layout

Figure 17-2.

Passing Cards

A version of Hearts called Greek Hearts requires each player to pass three cards prior to each hand. Hearts for Windows uses a variation of Greek Hearts. Cards are passed in this order:

◆ *First Hand* Pass three cards to opponent on your left.

◆ *Second Hand* Pass three cards to opponent on your right.

◆ *Third Hand* Pass three cards to opponent across from you.

◆ *Fourth Hand* Do not pass cards.

17

The cycle begins over again starting with the fifth trick.

Click three cards that you want to pass to your opponent. This will raise the selected card slightly from your hand as shown in Figure 17-2. If you decide you don't want to pass a card you picked, click the card again to lower the card back into your hand. Click the Pass (Pass Left, Pass Right, or Pass Across) button once you have selected three cards. You will receive three cards from one of your opponents.

Passing Strategy

Pass any cards in your hand that you think are likely to win tricks. Here's a general strategy for passing or holding cards:

1. Pass the queen of spades.
2. Pass high hearts.
3. Pass high cards of any suit.
4. Keep spades lower than the queen, but if you have a lot of spades, get rid of the highest cards first.

You keep other spades lower than the queen of spades to protect yourself from being forced to play the queen of spades when someone else leads out spades. For example, if someone leads spades, and the queen is all you have, you must play it, and subsequently win the trick.

Game Strategy

Never lead out the king or ace of spades unless the queen of spades has already been played in a previous trick. Lead out with low cards and play off with the queen of spades, hearts, or high cards. An exception is if you are trying to shoot the moon. In that case, you want to lead out with high cards in order to collect all of the tricks. Be watchful of other players attempting to shoot the moon. You may need to sacrifice a trick to stop them.

The last person to play a trick has a distinct advantage. He or she can play a high card to take a trick without the risk of getting stuck with a heart or the queen of Spades. Don't get stuck with high cards that you might be forced to play later. For example, if the first two players played a jack and queen, it would be better to play a 10 rather than a 3. Otherwise, you might need to play your 10 later in the game where it would take the trick and possibly win hearts or the queen of spades along with it.

Take calculated risks in order to get rid of high cards. For example, you could safely lead the ace of clubs if it is your only club and clubs has not been played yet. You know that the remaining 12 clubs are spread out among the three other players. The odds are good that each player has at least one club. By leading the ace, you could safely get rid of it early while saving your low cards for later.

Avoid leading out suits if you are holding many cards of a single suit. For example, don't lead an ace of clubs if you are holding seven other clubs. The remaining five clubs are divided among the three other players, and there's a good chance one of them will be able to play off a heart or the queen of spades.

CHAPTER

18

NETWORK ADMINISTRATOR INFORMATION

Now that you've explored features and benefits of the Windows for Workgroups environment, you may be ready to expand your technical knowledge. This chapter goes into details for those who need background information on Windows for Workgroups. It also contains information for people who are administering a Windows for Workgroups network.

There are two other helpful sources for network administrator information.

For the first source, start the Windows Write application and open the file NETWORKS.WRI in the Windows directory. You can also order the Microsoft Windows for Workgroups Resource Kit, which contains more technical information about networks and a disk with useful utilities for monitoring the network. Contact Microsoft at (800) 642-7676 to order the kit and refer to Appendix D for more information.

Installing Windows for Workgroups

Before installing Windows for Workgroups, install the network cards in the computer and resolve any conflicts if possible. Some conflicts don't appear until after you've installed Windows. For more information on installing network cards and resolving these conflicts, refer to the next section.

The procedure for installing Windows for Workgroups is similar to the installation of Windows 3.1. You place the number 1 disk in the floppy drive of your system, switch to the drive, and type **SETUP**.

After the opening screens appear, you can choose Express Setup or Custom Setup. As with Windows 3.1 installation, Express Setup identifies your equipment and performs the installation with little response needed from you. If you have a previous installation of Windows 3.1, its settings and printer setup are preserved. Custom Setup gives you more control over the devices, accessories, and software utilities to install.

You need to know the following information to complete either Express or Custom setup:

✦ A name for your computer, up to 15 characters long.

  This name appears to other users when you share your system or access other shared systems.

✦ A workgroup name of up to 15 characters long.

  Your manager may assign your workgroup name. If you're part of administration, it may be ADMIN, or if you work in marketing, it may be MARKTG. Workgroups provide a way to easily send messages or files to groups of people, and to quickly locate a system you're trying to share.

◆ Your printer type, if any, and the port it is attached to.

◆ The type of network card, its interrupt (IRQ), base I/O port address, and base memory address (if any).

◆ If you are already connected to a network such as Novell NetWare or Microsoft LAN Manager, you will be asked to identify it during the setup.

Network Hardware

18

A computer network consists of two or more computers tied together into a communications system that lets users share files and resources among systems. Connections are made by installing network interface cards (NICs) in each machine and linking them with network cable. Windows for Workgroups will operate on the four most popular networks as described in the following sections. The network cards you buy for every computer in the network must support the network type you choose.

Network Types

The following sections provide a brief introduction to each network type. Your local computer dealer or network installer can help you determine which system is best for your needs. In some cases, you might be able to use cable that is already installed in your building, and that will determine which network type is best for your company.

Thin Ethernet

Thin Ethernet, often referred to as *10Base2*, uses a thin coaxial cable (similar to television cable) that links one computer to the next in a daisy-chain fashion, as shown in Figure 18-1. The coaxial cable is shielded and thus protected from outside noise interference. The entire length of the network cable cannot exceed 606 feet unless a special repeater device is used . The number of workstations attached cannot exceed 30. Ethernet has a data transfer rate of 10 megabits/sec. The transfer rate is meaningful when comparing network types.

Ethernet is relatively easy to configure and install. Its *topology*—its layout—is similar to a snake of wire. You start at one end of an office

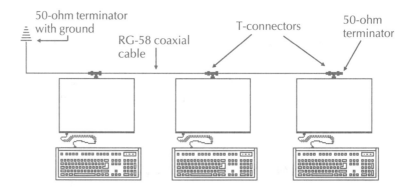

Thin Ethernet
network
Figure 18-1.

and connect machines in line until you reach the last machine. Both ends of the cable get terminated with a special cap, and one end (only one end!) gets grounded.

Ethernet is also relatively inexpensive. You can purchase an Ethernet NIC for as low as $80, and cable costs about 20 cents to 30 cents a foot in rolls of 1,000 feet. A T-connector is required to attach the cable segments at the back of each NIC (network interface card) and the terminators attach to the T-connectors at each end of the network.

Twisted Pair Ethernet

Twisted Pair Ethernet (often referred to as 10BaseT) has the same data transfer rate as Thin Ethernet, but uses simple telephone wire (also called twisted pair) that costs approximately 15 cents per foot. The topology of 10BaseT is slightly different than Thin Ethernet. The cable to each workstation branches from a central concentrator box in a star configuration, which makes wiring the network somewhat easier. In some cases, you can even use existing (unused) telephone wire that terminates in the telephone wiring closet of your building, as shown in Figure 18-2. The concentrator simply serves as a central connection point for all the computers in the network.

While twisted pair wire is less expensive and easier to handle than the coaxial cable used in Thin Ethernet, you must buy an additional concentrator box, which starts at about $500. The maximum length of the network cannot exceed 328 feet, about half that of 10Base2. Most 10BaseT network cabling systems use RJ-45 cable connectors. You can buy cable in set lengths, or make the cables yourself.

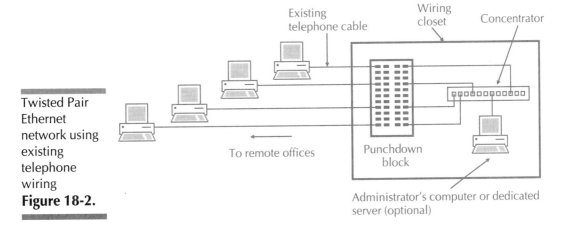

Twisted Pair
Ethernet
network using
existing
telephone
wiring
Figure 18-2.

18

Token Ring

Token Ring is an IBM networking scheme that uses a special twisted
pair wire and star topology like that shown in Figure 18-3. Each station
branches from a central concentrator box known as the Multi-Station
Access Unit (MAU). Token Ring provides data transfer rates of 4
megabits/sec or 16 megabits/sec, depending on the type of cards you

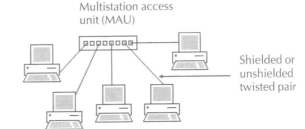

Token Ring
network
Figure 18-3.

purchase. The faster cards are more expensive. In fact, Token Ring tends to be more expensive than other network types, but unlike other networks, it does offer some protection from cable breaks and other problems. The MAU is actually a switching device that keeps the network up and running if one of the cable segments breaks or is disconnected.

The cable used to connect Token Ring is either shielded twisted pair (STP) or unshielded twisted pair (UTP). The type you choose depends on your budget, number of workstations, and distances you want to connect. Each computer can be up to 328 feet from the MAU device with STP cable, or 148 feet using UTP cable. You can connect multiple MAUs together to support up to 260 workstations with STP cable and up to 72 workstations with UTP cable. Token Ring MAUs can be placed in a phone closet and wired to workstations in the same way as Twisted Pair Ethernet (see Figure 18-2).

ArcNet

ArcNet is a wiring topology that consists of a series of stars. As shown in Figure 18-4, ArcNet is useful when you need to connect groups of workstations at distant locations. Note that each group is wired to a hub device in a star configuration, then connected to other groups using long linear cable segments of up to 2,000 feet. This is useful if some workstations are at distant locations, such as a warehouse or manufacturing floor. The data transfer of ArcNet is only 2.5 megabits/sec, but this speed should not be a problem on small networks. ArcNet is also the least expensive network to configure.

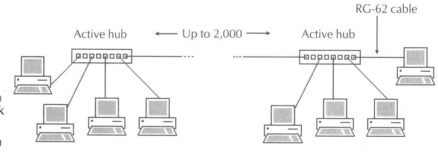

ArcNet network
Figure 18-4.

18

Network interface cards are available in the $50 range and cable is about 20 to 30 cents per foot.

You can directly connect two computers together without further hardware, but you'll need passive and active hubs to connect three or more computers together. Passive hubs (under $50) connect groups of three computers and active hubs (starting at $300) connect larger groups of computers.

Installing Network Interface Cards

Installing network interface cards is not often a simple matter. You usually need to ensure that settings on the cards don't conflict with the settings of other devices in the computer. These settings are the interrupt (IRQ), base I/O port address, and base memory address, as reviewed in the following sections.

Interrupts   An interrupt, or IRQ, is like a telephone call that the devices connected to your computer make to your computer when they need service. The computer must "answer" the interrupt and service the request. No two devices in the computer can use the same interrupt at the same time. The most commonly used settings are listed in Table 18-1.

	IRQ	Base I/O
EGA/VGA video adapters	2	3C0 to 3CF
EGA/VGA video in color mode	2	3D0 to 3DF
COM1, COM3	4	3F0 to 3FF
COM2, COM4 (if used)	3	2F0 to 2FF
Floppy disk controller	6	3F0 to 3FF
Parallel port LPT1	7	3B0 to 3BF
Parallel port LPT2 (if used)	5	370 to 37F
System clock	8	
Math coprocessor	13	
Hard disk controller	14	320 to 32F
Game port		200 to 20F
Bus mouse		230 to 23F

Common interrupts and I/O ports
Table 18-1.

You'll want to install your network card with an interrupt that is not already in use. Use the Microsoft MSD utility in the Windows directory to determine the current interrupt usage for your system. Type **MSD** to start the utility, then type Q to select IRQ Status from the main menu. Use an IRQ number that lists No in the Detected column, or that is not marked (Reserved) in the Description column.

I/O Port Addresses   An I/O port address is a memory location that the network card and other devices installed in your computer use to transfer information to the CPU. No two devices can use the same I/O port address at the same time.

Base Memory Address   This is the location in memory that a network card uses to transfer information between itself and the CPU. No two devices can use the same block of memory. The base memory address is the start of a block of memory used by the network card to move information on and off the network. Not all network cards need a memory address but if your card does, make sure the starting address does not conflict with the address used by another device, as described in a moment. Also make sure the block of the memory used does not overlap the block used by another device. Typical starting addresses are in upper memory blocks (see Appendix A for a description of memory) at C000, C800, D000, and D800. Cards usually require 16K or 32K of memory starting at one of these addresses.

It's usually best to install the network cards and resolve conflicts before installing Windows for Workgroups on the computer, but problems often occur after the installation. If you can't get a computer to operate after installing a network card, or if you can't get Windows for Workgroups to recognize other computers on the network, you'll need to do a little investigative work. Restart the computer and make sure that the commands in the CONFIG.SYS and AUTOEXEC.BAT file install properly without errors. These commands are reviewed in the next section. If the commands don't load properly, you'll probably need to change the settings on the cards and the settings that Windows uses, as noted in the following sections.

The following points and steps can help you resolve network card problems or connection problems.

♦ Run the Microsoft MSD utility in the Windows directory to determine current system settings.

♦ Typically, if your system fails to boot from the start, try a different IRQ setting on the card. If a device such as a mouse fails to work after your system is started, the network card is probably using the same IRQ as the mouse. Try setting a different IRQ for the mouse or the network card.

18

NOTE: If you change a network card setting, you'll also need to alter the PROTOCOL.INI file to match the new settings as discussed in the next section.

♦ If your system locks up after running a utility that uses one of the upper memory areas (C000, C800, D000, and D800), your network card is probably using part of the same memory. Try a different memory setting.

♦ If Windows starts, but locks up when you perform a network activity such as connecting with a shared drive, try changing the IRQ and I/O settings. Refer to the next section for instructions on how to do this.

♦ Make sure all the cables are installed properly and that each has a good connection. If the network failed only when you added the new station, the new cable segment may be bad. If possible, use an ohm meter to check continuity between the center pins at each end. If they test OK, then check continuity between the ground (the connector casing itself) at each end.

TIP: Keep in mind that on large networks, Windows may take a while before it recognizes new computers on the network. You might, at first, think you have a connection problem. Just wait a few moments and try the connection again. In some cases, you might need to restart the new computer, or all the computers.

Trying Different IRQ and I/O Settings

In many cases, you need to try numerous different settings and restart your system and Windows each time before everything works as it should. When you change the settings of the board, you'll need to change the settings in the PROTOCOL.INI file to match the new board settings. You don't need to do this from Windows using the Control Panel Networks icon. Instead, use Notepad to directly edit the file. In some cases, you might not even be able to start Windows, in which case you can make the changes using a DOS editor such as DOS EDIT.

Here are the lines you'll need to change in the PROTOCOL.INI file to match the new settings made on a network interface card:

```
IOADDRESS=
IRQ=
```

For example, the file may list the following settings for the network card:

```
IOADDRESS=0x300
IRQ=3
```

To change the I/O address to 260 and the interrupt to 5, you would change the lines as follows:

```
IOADDRESS-0x260
IRQ=5
```

Save the file, then turn off your computer and change the settings on the network interface card. Restart your computer and be sure to watch the messages displayed during the boot process to make sure the network commands in the CONFIG.SYS and AUTOEXEC.BAT file load properly. These commands are discussed in the "Windows for Workgroups Startup Files" section.

Windows for Workgroups Network Communications

Windows for Workgroups uses the Network Device Interface Specification (NDIS) to provide communications and data exchange between computers on the network. NDIS is a software interface

18

between a network card and the protocols within a computer that define how network communications are handled. The communications software (often called a *protocol stack*) in Windows for Workgroups, is called NetBEUI and NetBIOS. Other types of networks use different communications standards. For example, Novell NetWare uses the SPX/IPX communications protocol.

As mentioned earlier, each type of network (Ethernet, ArcNet, and Token Ring) has its own method for handling the actual transfer of data over the network cable. NDIS simply provides a standard method of connecting the network protocol stack (NetBEUI and NetBIOS) with the particular type of network card installed in a computer.

Windows for Workgroups adds commands to the CONFIG.SYS and AUTOEXEC.BAT files to install network drivers when a system boots. A software driver called the Protocol Manager *binds* the protocols used by Windows for Workgroups with the particular network card installed in the computer. The interesting thing about NDIS is that it allows you to install up to four different network interface cards in the computer and each of those network cards can support up to four network protocols. For example, Windows for Workgroups supports both the NetBEUI/NetBIOS and SPX/IPX (Novell NetWare) protocols on a single network card. In that way, the computer can access both Windows for Workgroup computers and NetWare servers. Alternatively, you might install two network cards to access two completely different networks.

Windows for Workgroups automatically installs all the proper drivers and inserts the proper initialization commands in the startup files during installation, depending on the choice of network cards you make. You can also install new cards or change protocols by using the Network utility in the Control Panel at any time. After changing the configuration, Windows reboots to initialize the new settings in the startup files.

Once Windows for Workgroups is up and running, the Protocol Manager handles requests to and from each of the networks that the computer is attached to. If a user makes a request to a NetWare server, that request is directed over the appropriate communications protocol and network cable to the NetWare server.

NetBEUI and NetBIOS

NetBIOS and NetBEUI are the standard protocols that Windows for Workgroups uses to communicate with other network computers. NetBEUI provides the basic functions for communications, much like the telephone company provides the basic equipment and procedures for establishing telephone calls. NetBIOS is an application-level communications protocol. Once a communications session is established between two machines using NetBEUI, two programs (such as Chat or File Manager's Share and Connect commands) use NetBIOS to communicate with one another.

NetBEUI This protocol provides communication flow control and error detection between computers that communicate on the network. It conforms to IBM's NetBEUI, so it can provide links to IBM networking products. It is also small and efficient, so it doesn't take up much room in a computer's memory.

NetBIOS The NetBIOS interface is used by applications to communicate with other NetBIOS-compatible applications using the NetBEUI communications protocol. It performs high-level tasks, including establishing network names, sessions between two computers, and the start and completion of data transfers. NetBIOS uses the computer name entered for each computer during Windows for Workgroups setup. A session is a connection between two computers that is maintained until disconnected. Many tasks may occur during that session, such as messages exchanges or file transfers.

NetWare SPX/IPX Support

The NDIS driver provides support for multiple protocol stacks on one network interface card. That means you can load the NetBEUI protocol required by Windows for Workgroups, and load the IPX protocol required to communicate with a NetWare server.

You can specify both protocols during Windows for Workgroups setup, or you can open the Network utility in the Control Panel after installation and choose the Networks button to install the support. Choose the Novell NetWare option and click OK. Windows asks you to insert one of the Windows disks, then it installs the necessary drivers and makes changes to the startup files. You then reboot the computer to load the NetWare protocol support. NetWare support is discussed later in this chapter.

Windows for Workgroups Startup Files

In this section, let's examine the startup commands that Windows for Workgroups places in the CONFIG.SYS file and AUTOEXEC.BAT file during installation.

Commands similar to the following are placed in CONFIG.SYS:

```
DEVICE=C:\WINDOWS\PROTMAN.DOC /i:C:WINDOWS
DEVICE=C:\WINDOWS\NE2000.DOS
DEVICE=C:\WINDOWS\WORKGRP.SYS
```

18

The first command loads the Protocol Manager and binds the network transport protocols into an NDIS-compliant network interface card driver. This command must be specified before the other commands. The Protocol Manager looks at the information in the PROTOCOL.INI file that resides in the WINDOWS directory. Normally, changes to the Windows for Workgroups configuration are made by accessing the Networks icon in the Control Panel, but you can view and edit this file to make changes from the DOS command line. This is often convenient and necessary. For example, an incorrect network card setting might not let you start Windows to specify new settings. In this case, you would edit PROTOCOL.INI using an editor such as DOS EDIT, as discussed in "Trying Different IRQ and I/O Settings."

The second line loads the network interface card driver. The driver name depends on the network card installed in your system. In the example, an NE2000 network card is specified.

The last line loads the Workgroups driver. This driver provides support for accessing network functionality.

One command is added to the AUTOEXEC.BAT file, as shown next. This command starts the network software and binds the network drivers specified in the CONFIG.SYS file:

```
NET START
```

Standard Mode

When Windows for Workgroups runs in standard mode, it can only act as a client for network services. It cannot share its resources with other users. The reason for this is that sharing is a background process that requires a special form of multitasking only available when Windows runs in 386 enhanced mode.

Before starting Windows in standard mode, you must type the **NET LOGON** command. This command loads the transport protocols identified in the PROTOCOL.INI file, loads the NetBIOS interface routines (in NET.EXE), and starts the network redirector.

Once the user logs on, the Windows for Workgroups driver WFWNET.DRV loads and provides user access to the network. It allows users to connect with other computers and access resources on those computers.

386 Enhanced Mode

When Windows for Workgroups runs in 386 enhanced mode, the computer can share its resources with other network users, and thus is a server on the network. The computer can, of course, also be a client of shared resources on other computers. An 80386 processor or later with 3MB of memory (4MB is recommended) is required to run Windows for Workgroups in 386 enhanced mode.

Several components provide network support in 386 enhanced mode. These are briefly described in the following sections. You don't normally need to be concerned with these components, because they load in the background to handle networking tasks. You will see these files listed in the \WINDOWS\SYSTEM directory. Understanding what they are and what they do helps you understand how Windows for Workgroups handles network support.

VNB.386   This component is a device driver that provides NetBEUI support.

VNETBIOS.386   This component allows multiple network-aware Windows and MS-DOS applications to use the NetBIOS interface at the same time.

VREDIR.386   This component is the network redirector that multiple programs can use simultaneously. A redirector determines whether commands are for the local system or for a remote network server.

VSERVER.386   This component implements file and printer server functions. It allows workstation clients to access the computer as a server.

VBROWSE.386   This component provides the browsing features that let a user view a list of shared network computers and resources.

VNETSUP.386   This component provides network support functions to the modules described above.

18

VSHARE.386   This component provides an MS-DOS-compatible SHARE.EXE command for the networking environment of Windows for Workgroups. It dynamically allocates memory for file-sharing functions more efficiently than the DOS-based SHARE.EXE. When Windows for Workgroups is running, the version of SHARE loaded at the DOS prompt is ignored.

VWC.386   This component maps devices that a user connects to or disconnects from while working in an MS-DOS window.

Windows for Workgroups Initialization Files

The following initialization files hold startup parameters for Windows for Workgroups, or some of the applications you run with Windows for Workgroups. The files are located in the WINDOWS directory and can be edited from the DOS command line, or by using Notepad or Write. If you use Write, don't convert the .INI files to Write format when opening the files. You can use the System Editor (SYSEDIT.EXE in the \WINDOWS\SYSTEM directory) to change the SYSTEM.INI and WIN.INI files, but not the remaining files listed here.

WIN.INI   This file holds preference settings for the Windows environment, such as the window colors, desktop patterns, keyboard and mouse settings, font settings, printer settings, and others. You have little need to edit this file manually, since most changes are made from the Control Panel. For a complete description of WIN.INI entries, view the file WININI.WRI in the Windows directory using Windows Write.

TIP: You'll also find important information on the initialization files in the NETWORKS.WRI file.

SYSTEM.INI This file contains parameters that specify the type of hardware your system has and how Windows for Workgroups is to use that hardware. For example, the file lists the type of video display driver you have and the mode Windows should use with that driver. Many of the settings in this file are made during setup, or by using the Setup utility in the Program Manager Main menu. For a complete description of its entries, view the file SYSINI.WRI using Windows Write.

PROTOCOL.INI This file contains entries that define the network interface card and the protocols that use it.

PROGMAN.INI This file contains startup information and settings for Program Manager.

CONTROL.INI This file contains some of the entries set by the Control Panel utilities.

WINFILE.INI This file contains startup information and settings for File Manager.

MSMAIL.INI This file contains startup information and settings for Microsoft Mail.

SHARED.INI This file contains entries that you can use to share Mail custom commands and custom messages with other workgroup members.

SCHDPLUS.INI This file contains startup information and settings for Schedule+.

You should view the first few pages of the SYSINI.WRI or WININI.WRI files for instructions on how to make changes to any .INI file.

The PROTOCOL.INI File

This section describes the PROTOCOL.INI file, which is of interest to network administrators. Normally, you use the Networks utility in the Control Panel to make changes to this file, but as mentioned earlier, you might need to make changes from the DOS command line if Windows won't start because its settings are incorrect.

NOTE: The PROTOCOL.INI and other .INI files are discussed in the Microsoft Windows for Workgroups Resource Kit (see Appendix D).

18

The [network.setup] Section

The [network.setup] section has entries that define the network setup. An example and definitions are shown here:

```
[network.setup]
version= 0x3100
netcard= ms$ee16, 1, MS$EE16
transport= ms$netbeui, MS$NETBEUI
lana0= ms$ee16, 1, ms$netbeui
```

Entry	Definition
version=	The current network software version. The default version 0x3100 is assigned by Setup.
netcard=	The network adapter driver name for each card that is used in the network as defined in NETWORK.INF.
transport=	The name of the network transport driver protocol for Windows for Workgroups.
lana#=	Identifies the binding between the network adapter and the network protocol, as configured by Setup.

The [protman] Section

The [protman] section defines the settings for the Protocol Manager. An example and definitions are shown on the next page:

```
[protman]
drivername= PROTMAN$
priority= MS$NETBEUI
```

Entry	Definition
drivername=	The PROTMAN$ entry defines the driver name for the Protocol Manager.
priority=	The priority entry determines the order in which incoming frames are processed. If used, the highest priority is given to the first protocol stack, MS$NETBEUI.

The [netcard] Section

The [netcard] section defines the parameters for NDIS network adapters. If more than one network adapter is installed in the computer, a [netcard] section appears for each card. An example entry is shown in the following. The setting in this section will vary, depending on the network card you use.

```
[ms$ee16]
drivername= EXP16$
IOADDRESS=0x300
IRQ=5
IOCHRDY=Late
TRANSCEIVER=Thin Net (BNC/COAX)
```

The [protocol] Section

The [protocol] section defines the parameters used by network protocols. If multiple protocols are used, a [protocol] section is present for each protocol with different parameter settings for each. An example that defines the Microsoft NetBEUI protocol is shown and explained here:

```
[MS$NETBEUI]
drivername= NETBEUI$
sessions= 10
NCBS= 32
bindings= MS$EE16
lanabase= 0
```

Entry	Definition
drivername=	The name of the driver
sessions=	The number of allowable connections to remote computers. Automatically adjusted as necessary when running in 386 enhanced mode.
NCBS	Identifies the maximum number of NetBIOS commands that can be used. The value is dynamically adjusted when running in 386 enhanced mode.
bindings=	The entry indicates to which network adapter card drivers each transport binds. The netcard name for the network driver and protocol must appear in the bindings= entry for at least one of the transport drivers. The bindings= entry may specify one or more [netcard] sections (separated by commas).
lanabase=	The entry to define the first LANA number the protocol is to accept. Refer to lana#= in the [network.setup] section.

18

Network Settings in WIN.INI

The following information is extracted from the WININI.WRI file for your convenience. It provides a description of settings in the WIN.INI file of interest to network administrators.

The [network] Section

The [network] section describes network settings used by secondary Windows network drivers and are not used by the Windows for Workgroups WFWNET.DRV driver. The section can contain a list of network directory and printer connections that are restored when Windows is restarted.

The [MRU_Files] Section

This section maintains the 12 most recently used file share connections for this workstation. The values for these entries are displayed in the Path field of the Connect Network Drive dialog box in File Manager.

The [MRU_Printers] Section

This section maintains the 12 most recently used printer share connections for this workstation. The values for these entries are displayed in the Path field of the Connect Network Drive dialog box in Print Manager.

Network Settings in SYSTEM.INI

The following information is extracted from the SYSINI.WRI file for your convenience. It provides a description of settings in the SYSTEM.INI file of interest to network administrators.

The [ClipShares] Section

The [ClipShares] section is used by the ClipBook Viewer to identify the names of ClipBook pages that have been shared for use by other Windows for Workgroups workstations. The ClipBook Viewer should be used to change the information present in this section; this information should not be edited manually.

NOTE: The format and location of information present in the [ClipShares] section is subject to change in a future version of Windows. Modifying or creating ClipBook shares should be done only through the ClipBook Viewer.

The [network] Section

This section contains settings that affect how your computer interacts with the network. Use the Network option in Control Panel to change these settings, except where specified. The list of possible entries in this section is extensive. For more detailed information, refer to the [network] section in SYSINI.WRI.

The [PasswordLists] Section

This section contains settings that specify the location of the password-list files for each user who logs on to your computer. Each password-list file contains a list of the passwords you can use to connect to password protected resources. Each entry in the [PasswordLists] section has this format:

username= drive:directory\PasswordListFilename

Each parameter is defined as follows:

username	The logon name of the user.
drive	The drive that contains the password-list file.
directory	The name of the directory where the password-list file is located.
PasswordListFilename	The name of the password-list file.

18

Restricting Share Options

As a network administrator, you can control whether users on Windows for Workgroups network can access server functions. For example, you could disable the Share As and Stop Sharing functions from the File Manager to prevent users from changing the network configuration that other users depend on.

Completely Disabling Sharing

You can completely disable the user interface for sharing resources by adding the following command to the [network] section in the SYSTEM.INI file.

```
NoSharingControl=1
```

When set to 1, Windows for Workgroups will not allow users to change the Enable Sharing section on the Network Settings dialog box that appears when they open the Network icon on the Control Panel.

Disabling File Manager Share Options

You can disable the Share As and Stop Sharing options on the File menu in the File Manager by adding the following line to the [restrictions] section of the WINFILE.INI file:

```
NoShareCommands=1
```

When set to 1, File Manager will not display the commands and the user of the system won't be able to share a drive on the system, or more importantly, stop sharing a drive that other users might be accessing. This option also disables the related buttons on the Toolbar.

Disabling Print Sharing

You can disable the printer sharing interface in Print Manager by adding the following line to the [spooler] section of the WIN.INI file:

```
NoShareCommands=1
```

It prevents Print Manager from displaying the Share Printer As and the Stop Sharing Printer options on the Printer menu. It also disables the related buttons on the Toolbar. When set to 1, the user of the system won't be able to share a printer attached to the system, or more importantly, stop sharing a printer that should remain available for others to use.

Server Priority Values

This section describes how to adjust the allocation of processing time on a computer that runs as a Windows for Workgroups server. The performance of programs that run on the server system are affected when other users access its resources. You can adjust the Performance Priority slider on the Network Settings dialog box as shown in Figure 18-5 to allocate more or less processing time to the programs running on the computer, as opposed to its server processes. You open the Network Settings dialog box by choosing the Network icon in the Control Panel.

As you probably know, Windows will multitask applications. That means the computer's processing time is allocated to each program to make the programs appear as if they are running at the same time. Think of the processor dealing a round of cards at a table. Each card is analogous to a slice of the processor's time and the players are Windows applications and DOS applications.

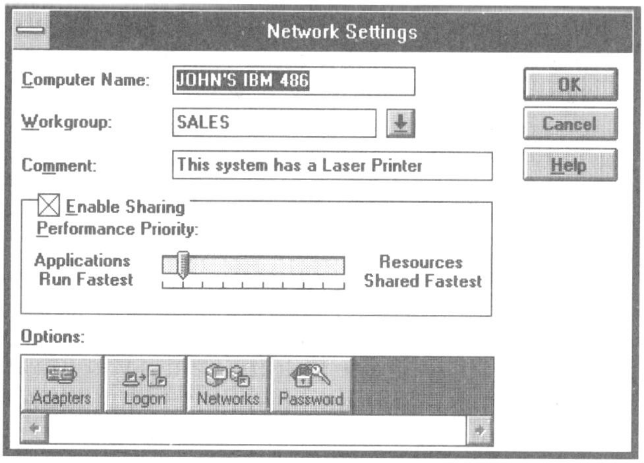

The Network
Settings dialog
box
Figure 18-5.

When 80386 or later systems multitask, they use the special virtual
8086 mode of the processor that simulates one or more self-contained
computers. Each virtual machine has its own memory and CPU, so
applications running in the virtual machines think they are running by
themselves on their own machine. In Windows for Workgroups, there
are three possible types of virtual machines: System VM, Server VM,
and DOS VM.

System VM   There is always one System VM that runs the Windows
program itself. All Windows-based applications run in the System VM
as well.

Server VM   The Windows for Workgroups file and printer server
functions are implemented in this virtual machine. It provides other
network users with access to resources on the computer. As more
network users access the shared resources, the processor must allocate
time to the Server VM and deallocate it from the other virtual machines.

DOS VM   When you start a non-Windows, DOS-based application,
Windows creates a DOS VM. If you start more than one DOS-based
application, Windows creates a DOS VM for each.

From the above descriptions, you can probably ascertain that there can
be three or more players at the Windows card table. The System VM is

always present. If the computer is used as a server, the Server VM is also present. The following discussion assumes your system is used as a server and that the Server VM is always present. Finally, there can be one or more DOS VMs. Every time you start a DOS application, another DOS VM is allocated. Figure 18-6 illustrates the relationship of each VM to the total processor time.

Setting Values for Each VM

You can set how much processor time each virtual machine gets, as reviewed here. Note that the values you use are arbitrary in themselves. However, it is useful to ascertain the percentage of processing time allocated to each VM, as you'll see in the example following this list:

+ To set a value for the Windows System VM, open the 386 Enhanced icon in the Control Panel and sets its foreground and background values. The default values are 100 when Windows applications run in the foreground, and 50 when Windows applications run in the background. Leave these values as they are for the examples.

+ The Server VM values are set by adjusting the Performance Priority slider on the Network Settings dialog box (Figure 18-5). The notches on the slider from left to right are 40, 80, 110, 175, 200, 250, 300,

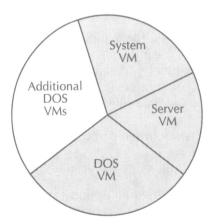

Windows for
Workgroups
virtual machines
Figure 18-6.

500, 5,000, and 9,000 as shown in the illustration. When the Enable Sharing box is checked, the server process runs in the background. It is never a foreground process.

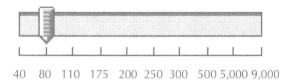

40   80   110   175   200 250 300   500 5,000 9,000

18

✦ DOS VM values are set by creating a PIF file for the application, which is read when you start the application. PIF files are discussed in Appendix B. You can also adjust the foreground or background priority settings on the fly by pressing [Alt]-[Enter] in the DOS application, then choosing Settings from its Control menu. The default settings are 100 when the application is used in the foreground and 50 when used in the background.

NOTE: If you don't run DOS applications from Windows, you don't need to be concerned with DOS VM values when calculating server priorities.

Now lets look at these values to see how adjustments to the Performance Priority slider affects the performance of the Windows programs or DOS programs you run on the server system. First, we'll calculate the percentage of processor time allocated to each VM with the default settings, assuming that one DOS VM is running and the Performance Priority slider in the Network Settings (Figure 18-5) dialog box is set to the second notch (80).

> Value of System VM running in the foreground = 100
> Value of Server VM running in the background = 80
> Value of DOS VM running in the background = 50

To calculate the percentage values, sum the values to get 230 (100+80+50), then calculate the ratio of each VM by dividing its value by the sum. For example, the percentage allocation to the System VM is calculated as follows:

$$\frac{100}{230} = 43\%$$

The Server VM is calculated as follows:

$$\frac{80}{230} = 35\%$$

Finally, the DOS VM application running in the background is calculated as follows:

$$\frac{50}{230} = 22\%$$

The above percentages would change if you brought the DOS VM application to the foreground. Because the System VM moves to the background with a value of 50, the sum stays the same, but the percentage for the DOS VM is recalculated to 43% (100/230).

Now suppose you start another DOS application. Windows creates another DOS VM and gives it a foreground value of 100 and a background value of 50. Assume the above values for the rest of the VMs. The System VM runs in the foreground with a value of 100 and the two DOS VMs run in the background with a value of 50 each. But also suppose you adjust the Priority Slider in the Network Settings dialog box to the 5000 position (second from the right). You do this because you want the system used mainly as a server and the two DOS applications are rarely used (so you don't care that they get so little allocation).

Here are the calculations with the new sum of 5200 (100+5000+50+50).

$$\frac{100}{5200} = 2\% \text{ for the System VM}$$

$$\frac{5000}{5200} = 96\% \text{ for the Server VM}$$

$$\frac{50}{5200} = 1\% \text{ for the first DOS VM}$$

18

$$\frac{50}{5200} = 1\% \text{ for the second DOS VM}$$

Note that processor allocation values are only meaningful when each VM is processing a task. For example, a word processor doesn't do anything in the background (typically) because it waits for you to type or issue commands. However, a database application could be sorting a mailing list in the background. The Server VM sits idle unless another user accesses your system.

When all is said and done, the best policy is to change the values as necessary while running your programs. For example, if your system bogs down because several users suddenly access its server functions, and you have a need for immediate performance, open the Network Settings dialog box and move the Performance Priority slider all the way to the left. If you need more performance from a DOS application running in the foreground, open its Settings dialog box and increase its foreground value.

Connecting with Novell NetWare Networks

You can choose to install support for Novell NetWare networks during the installation of Windows for Workgroups or anytime afterwards. To install NetWare support after installation, double-click the Network icon on the Control Panel, then click the Networks button on the Network Settings dialog box that appears. This opens the Compatible Networks dialog box. Click Novell NetWare in the list on the left and click the Add button.

You'll be asked to insert one of the Windows for Workgroups disks to complete the installation. Several new drivers are added to your system and its startup files are altered as described in the next section.

Novell NetWare Drivers

When Novell NetWare support is added to a Windows for Workgroups workstation, the drivers listed in the following sections are copied to the Windows directory and appropriate load commands are placed in the CONFIG.SYS, AUTOEXEC.BAT, and Windows initialization (.INI) files. Note that these drivers assume the workstation is an 80386 or later system that can share its resources as a server. The primary component is the MSIPX driver, which provides IPX-compatible transport protocol support. It is different from standard Novell IPX in that it can be loaded alongside an NDIS driver on a single network card, thus allowing the workstation to communicate with both NetWare servers and NetBEUI/NetBIOS-compatible networks.

MSIPX.SYS　　This driver file binds the MSIPX transport protocol to the NDIS drivers. It is loaded at boot time with the command DEVICE=C:\WINDOWS\MSIPX.SYS in the CONFIG.SYS file.

MSIPX.COM　　This command file loads the NDIS-compliant implementation of the IPX protocols. It is typically loaded from the AUTOEXEC.BAT file.

NETX.COM　　This command file loads the NetWare redirector shell, which diverts commands to the NetWare server when appropriate. It is typically loaded from the AUTOEXEC.BAT file.

VIPX.386　　This file virtualizes the IPX protocol in 386 enhanced mode to provide one or more MS-DOS virtual machines with IPX support. The command to load this driver is found in the SYSTEM.INI file.

VNETWARE.386　　This file virtualizes the NETX shell in 386 enhanced mode to provide one or more MS-DOS virtual machines with IPX support. The command to load this driver is found in the SYSTEM.INI file.

NETWARE.DRV　　This driver file provides NetWare support in the Windows environment.

NWPOPUP.COM This command provides a messaging system for the NetWare environment.

Native Novell IPX is not compatible with NDIS. You must use the Microsoft MSIPX drivers with Windows for Workgroups. Additionally, Novell ODI network drivers are not compatible with Windows for Workgroups. When Windows for Workgroups is installed, the existing IPX.COM file is replaced by the MSIPX drivers. However, the current IPX settings are used to configure the MSIPX driver. For example, the interrupt and I/O settings are retained. Because of this, you can't move MSIPX from one machine to another unless the network card settings are exactly the same.

18

NOTE: If you use ArcNet Cards, be aware that Windows for Workgroups and NetWare client software cannot share the same ArcNet adapter. This is discussed further in the Windows Resource Kit mentioned at the beginning of this chapter.

Other NetWare Information

Be aware of the following information when connecting with NetWare servers in the Windows for Workgroup environment.

+ The LASTDRIVE= command This command sets the drive letter for the NetWare server and reserves drive letters for shared directories in Windows for Workgroups. Generally, set the lastdrive equal to P, which makes the first NetWare drive Q.

+ It's best to log on to the NetWare server before starting Windows for Workgroups. You can include commands to do this in the AUTOEXEC.BAT file.

+ If you create a SHELL.CFG or NET.CFG file, place it in the same directory as the NETX.COM file.

+ Add the following line to the SHELL.CFG or NET.CFG file. Refer to the Novell manuals for further explanations.

```
show dots = on
```

Connecting with LAN Manager Networks

Windows for Workgroups was designed with Microsoft LAN Manager integration in mind. LAN Manager is a much more extensive networking system that provides more security than Windows for Workgroups. For example, LAN Manager provides share-level security similar to Windows for Workgroups, in which a user who knows the password of a resource can access that resource. LAN Manager also provides user-level security. In this scheme, the password is associated with the user rather than the shared resource. A system administrator typically sets the type of access a user has to each resource.

Connecting to LAN Manager Servers

There are two scenarios for LAN Manager integration with Windows for Workgroups. In the first, Windows for Workgroups users are allowed to see and use the LAN Manager server. In the second, users on the LAN Manager network can work with Windows for Workgroups workstations.

LAN Manager Server Availability

To make LAN Manager servers available to Windows for Workgroups users, at least one Windows for Workgroups workstation on the network must be a part of a LAN Manager domain. Double-click the Network icon in the Control Panel at the workstation you want to connect with the LAN Manager domain, then type the name of the domain in the Workgroup field.

Once the workstation becomes part of the LAN Manager domain, it makes the names of LAN Manager servers within the domain available to other workstations on the Windows for Workgroups network. If there are other domains, you'll need to duplicate the above strategy for each one.

LAN Manager User Access

A Windows for Workgroups workstation that is connected to a LAN Manager network does not usually broadcast its presence. This helps reduce traffic on the network. However, users at LAN Manager workstations won't see Windows for Workgroups workstations that are operating as servers. To fix this problem, add the following entry underneath the [network] heading in the SYSTEM.INI file. You can use Notepad to make this change.

```
LMAnnounce=yes
```

You may need to disable this option if you notice an appreciable slowdown in the network's performance due to extensive broadcasting.

Using LAN Manager Security

18

A Windows for Workgroups user can be given a guest account or higher-level privilege on LAN Manager servers. A guest account is typically used by a number of users who have limited access to the same resources. For example, the guest account might allow Windows for Workgroups users to access a printer and a public directory where they can read but not write files. The account itself provides adequate security since it is limited by the network administrator.

The network administrator can also create a separate group account for Windows for Workgroups users if they need access rights different from the guest account. Additionally, separate accounts can be created for individual users if those users have specific needs beyond a groups needs. However, it's easier to create special security rights for a group of people than for individual users, assuming that all the users in the group get the same access rights.

Groups have other advantages that make management of security much easier for the network administrator. Since the access rights to the LAN Manager servers are assigned to the group, rather than to each individual user, new users added to the group automatically get the same access rights as everyone else in the group. Of course, there can be many different groups sharing access to a server. Some groups may have more rights than others.

Password Management

The LAN Manager network administrator can set various password controls to enhance security; however, these controls are not always compatible with Windows for Workgroups users. For example, a password can expire after a certain amount of time, forcing the user to enter a new password. But, a Windows for Workgroups user won't see the message that his or her account is about to expire because messaging is not supported in the Windows for Workgroups environment. If the password expires, the user may not be able to log on to his or her Windows for Workgroups workstation. To log on to the Windows for Workgroups workstation if a LAN Manager password expires, it is necessary to disable the Log On to LAN Manager Domain check box in the LAN Manager Settings dialog box, which is accessible from the Network icon in the Control Panel.

APPENDIX

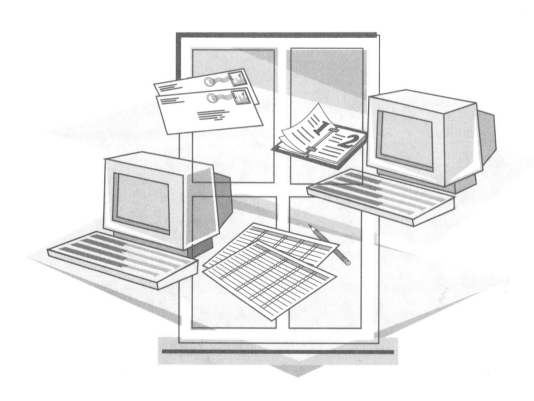

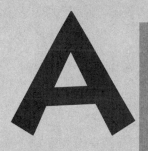

A

WINDOWS MODES AND MEMORY

This appendix provides a basic discussion of memory and how it is used in the Windows standard and 386 enhanced modes. Its purpose is to help you determine which mode to use, and to show you how to overcome memory-related problems when running non-Windows applications in Windows. Non-Windows applications are DOS applications not specifically designed to work with Windows.

Products like Microsoft's

MS-DOS 5.0, Digital Research's DR DOS 6.0, Quarterdeck's Expanded Memory Manager, and Qualitas's 386Max all help you use the memory in your system efficiently. Having the additional memory provided by these applications often makes the difference between successfully running an application and viewing an out-of-memory message. You will, however, need an 80386 or 80486 system to take advantage of some of these products.

When you run short of memory on an 80286 system, you can add more memory to your system and/or upgrade to an operating system that makes more memory available. Memory problems on 80386 systems are less severe, because you can use a Windows feature called *virtual memory* that makes hard disk space look like system memory. This gives applications all the memory they need.

Types of Memory

The random access memory (RAM) in your system holds program code and document data while you work. Programs are loaded from disk files into RAM, and are then executed by your computer.

NOTE: RAM is volatile; data in it can be lost if your system loses power, so it is essential that you save your work to disk often.

Memory is measured in bits and bytes. A bit is either 1 or 0 (on or off) in the binary number system, and is the smallest unit of information in RAM. A byte is a group of eight bits (in various on and off states) that is used to represent letters of the alphabet and numbers. Certain abbreviations are generally used in discussions about computer memory: K is used to represent kilobytes; 1024 bytes equals a kilobyte, so a file with 1024 characters is 1K in size. A million bytes of memory is referred to as one megabyte (abbreviated 1MB).

Systems that run DOS and Windows have three types of memory: *conventional memory*, *upper memory*, and *extended memory*. All systems come with some amount of conventional memory, usually 640K, but upper memory and extended memory must be made available by using some of the techniques described in this appendix. Each memory type is illustrated in Figure A-1, and discussed in the paragraphs that follow.

Conventional Memory   Conventional memory is the lowest part of memory, starting at 0K and going to 640K. DOS uses this memory to load itself and to run DOS applications. Because there is often insufficient conventional memory for these applications, newer versions of DOS—such as Microsoft's MS-DOS 5.0 and Digital Research's DR DOS 6.0—can load part of their operating code into other parts of memory, thus making more conventional memory available for applications.

Upper Memory   Upper memory blocks (UMB) make up the area of memory between 640K and 1MB. This is the area sometimes called the adapter area. DOS uses this area to store program code (called *drivers*) for your video display, disk drives, and other hardware. Because the UMB often contain blocks of unused memory addresses, various strategies have been devised to move program code from conventional

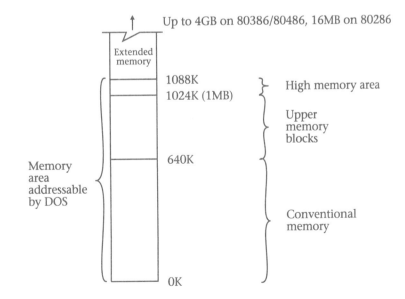

A typical
memory map
for a
DOS-based
system
Figure A-1.

memory to the UMB, thus freeing conventional memory, as discussed in the foregoing paragraph.

Extended Memory   Memory that extends beyond 1024K (or 1MB) is called extended memory. An 80286 system can access up to 16MB of extended memory; 80386 processors can access up to 4GB (gigabytes) or 4000MB of extended memory. Windows and Windows applications use extended memory extensively, so the more you have, the better. However, to maintain compatibility with 80286 systems and software, Windows addresses only 16MB of extended memory.

NOTE: Another type of memory is called expanded memory. It provides up to 8MB of additional memory to DOS applications that are written to take advantage of it. Expanded memory requires a special memory board and/or software. With the advent of Windows, expanded memory is falling into disuse, and many expanded memory applications have been converted to Windows applications.

CAUTION: The line DEVICE=HIMEM.SYS in your CONFIG.SYS file is the command that lets Windows access the high memory area (HMA) and extended memory. Do not remove this command unless you have an 80386 system and intend to use Quarterdeck QEMM, Qualitas 386Max, or another similar memory manager instead. The HMA is an extra 64K of memory (located in extended memory) that DOS can address.

Windows Operating Modes

Windows starts in either *standard mode* or *386 enhanced mode*, depending on your processor type and the amount of memory in your system. During setup, Windows determines which mode your system can start in, but may be able to start in the other mode under certain circumstances.

Standard Mode   If you have an 80286-based system, or a 386 or 486 system with only 2MB of memory, Windows starts in standard mode automatically. But you can "force" Windows to start in standard mode and gain some performance benefits, even if you have an 80386 (or more advanced system) with 3MB or more of memory. Doing so, however, precludes the use of features provided by the 386 enhanced mode. Standard mode is typically 10 to 20 percent faster than 386 enhanced mode, but it does not provide the ability to let you share resources on your system. You can, however, access resources shared on other systems.

✦ To start Windows in standard mode, type **NET LOGON**, then **WIN /S** at the DOS prompt.

386 Enhanced Mode   The 386 enhanced mode is the normal operating mode for 386 and 486 systems with 3MB or more of memory, although Microsoft recommends 4MB. This mode provides virtual memory and the ability to share resources with other network users.

✦ To start Windows in 386 enhanced mode, type **WIN /3** at the DOS prompt.

Standard Mode and Memory

Standard mode uses extended memory to provide an optimal environment for running multiple Windows applications. You should add as much memory to your system as possible and configure it as extended memory.

Some of you may have systems with an expanded memory board for running DOS expanded memory applications. Windows does not use expanded memory, so if you no longer need the expanded memory application, reconfigure the memory on the board as extended memory, if possible. Your manual should provide details on how this is done. If you must run the expanded memory application, you can do the following:

✦ On a 386 or 486 system with 3MB or more of memory, start Windows in 386 enhanced mode when you need to run the expanded memory application. In this way you can configure all memory as extended memory, and Windows will emulate the expanded memory needed by the applications. The memory used in the emulation is taken from extended memory.

✦ On a 286 system, you need to configure some of the memory on an add-in memory board as expanded memory. The board must have built-in expanded memory support. Determine exactly how much expanded memory the application needs, and then configure only that much on the board. Configure the remaining memory as extended memory for use by Windows. You also need to load the expanded memory manager supplied with the board. Place its command in your CONFIG.SYS or AUTOEXEC.BAT file.

386 Enhanced Mode and Memory

Systems with 386 or 486 processors can run in the 386 enhanced mode. This mode provides several important features that standard mode does not, as described in the paragraphs that follow. Evaluate your need for these features; if you don't need them, run Windows in standard mode to improve performance.

✦ *Resource Sharing*   This means your system can act as a server, sharing its resources (directories and printers) in the background while you work on programs in the foreground.

✦ *Virtual Memory*   This allows Windows to run more applications than will fit in RAM memory, by using part of your hard disk as if it were memory.

✦ *Multitasking*   This means DOS applications can be run in a separate window, simultaneously with Windows applications or other DOS applications.

✦ *Expanded Memory*   This can be emulated for DOS applications that need it, allowing you to configure all your system memory as more efficient extended memory.

Virtual Memory

Virtual memory techniques move information in RAM to a temporary or permanent *swap file* on your hard disk. Swap files can be used only on 80386 and 80486 systems. The type of swap file depends on the amount of free space on your disk.

✦ A temporary swap file is installed when Windows starts and is removed when you exit Windows. It only uses available disk space.

✦ A permanent swap file is set up on a hard drive and used every time you start Windows. Because the swap file occupies a contiguous area on the drive, it provides better performance.

If, during installation, Setup finds adequate contiguous disk space available, it sets up a permanent swap file that theoretically provides better performance. As a beginning Windows user, you need not be too concerned with the type of swap file—just know that it is there to provide you with more memory should you need it.

To check your system's virtual memory capabilities,

1. Start Windows in 386 enhanced mode by typing **WIN /3** at the DOS prompt.

2. Choose the About Program Manager option from the Program Manager Help menu. You'll see a dialog box similar to that in Figure A-2.

If a swap file is in use, the memory setting at the bottom of the dialog box will indicate more memory than your system has. Figure A-2 is from a system with 4MB of memory that thinks it has 10MB!

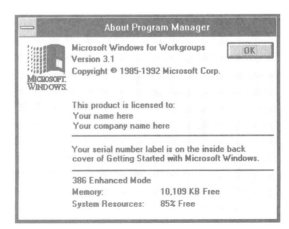

About Program Manager dialog box
Figure A-2.

Virtual memory depends on the existence of a swap file. You can add, remove, or change the settings of a swap file by following these steps:

1. Double-click the 386 Enhanced Mode icon on the Control Panel.

2. Click the Virtual Memory button on the 386 Enhanced dialog box. You'll then see a dialog box that lists the current setting. Click the Change button to display the dialog box in Figure A-3.

3. The current swap file settings are listed at the top of the dialog box. Note whether the Type field says Permanent or Temporary, and the drive location of the swap file.

4. In the Settings box, you can add a swap file, change a swap file's settings, or remove a swap file. Look at the number in the Space Available field, and

   ✦ If you have large amounts of available disk space, use the dialog box to set up a permanent swap file if it doesn't already exist.

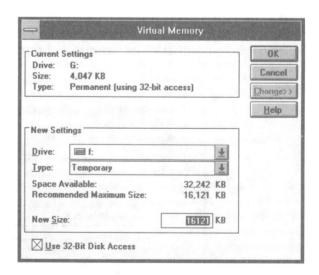

Virtual Memory dialog box
Figure A-3.

TIP: You might want to reduce the recommended swap file size. It is usually much larger than you will actually need, unless you are working with sound, video, or graphics editors, or programs like Ventura Publisher or Aldus PageMaker that use graphic images.

◆ If you're running low on disk space, use the dialog box to set up a temporary swap file, reduce the swap file's size, or disable the swap file completely by choosing None in the Type field.

5. In the Drive field, choose the drive for the swap file.

6. In the Type field, choose Permanent, Temporary, or None. (Choosing None disables virtual memory and removes existing swap files.)

7. In the Approximate Size field, Windows recommends a size for the swap file that is usually larger than you need. Change this setting to reduce the size of a swap file. It's not recommended that you increase the size of the swap file beyond Windows's suggestions. If you're running low on disk space, reduce the value.

8. Enable the Use 32-Bit Disk Access option in most cases to improve performance. Do not enable this option on laptop computers that use power-saving features that shut down the hard drive during periods of non-use.

9. When you are finished, choose OK to activate the new settings.

10. Follow the instructions on the screen to restart Windows.

CAUTION: Do not use Ctrl - Alt - Del to restart your system after changing swap file settings. Simply click the Restart Windows button.

A P P E N D I X

B

RUNNING NON-WINDOWS APPLICATIONS

This appendix examines how non-Windows applications are used with Windows. Non-Windows applications are DOS programs that aren't specifically designed to work with Windows. They do not use the windows graphical interface, nor do they share memory in the same way as Windows applications. Certainly you should upgrade all your applications to newer Windows versions whenever possible, but many applications will never be designed to work under Windows.

When you do need to run a non-Windows application, there are good reasons to run it under Windows: you can quickly switch to a non-Windows application while other Windows applications stay loaded, and you can cut and paste information between Windows and non-Windows applications.

A primary topic in this appendix is the *Program Information File*, or *PIF*. Normally, Windows uses a standard set of parameters to start non-Windows applications. If you can't get the application to run properly in this way, however, or you need to specify other startup parameters, you can create a special Program Information File to supply Windows with specific information about the application. You can then double-click a PIF to start the program. Program Information Files are created and edited with the PIF Editor, found in the Program Manager Main group.

Even though non-Windows applications don't always need a PIF to run properly, some settings in the PIF can help the program run more efficiently; or you can designate startup parameters and data file locations.

Types of Applications

Here are the various types of applications that can run with Windows; they are discussed in the sections that follow.

✦ *Windows 3.0 Applications* are designed to run with Windows 3.0 and will probably run fine with Windows 3.1.

✦ *Windows 3.1 Applications* are designed to take advantage of new features in Windows 3.1, such as object linking and embedding (OLE), and Drag and Drop features.

✦ *Pre-Windows 3 Applications* are written for versions of Windows earlier than version 3.0. You need to upgrade these applications for use with Windows 3.1, or run them in Windows 3.0 real mode.

✦ *Non-Windows Applications* are normally run under DOS and were not designed for use with Windows. You can run them from Windows by switching into a full-screen or windowed DOS environment.

♦ *Memory-Resident Software Utilities (TSRs)* are small programs that load and stay resident in memory. Examples are pop-up programs such as Borland's Sidekick, or software drivers that provide the operating system with information to run special hardware or network support.

Non-Windows Applications

Non-Windows applications were written by programmers who did not have Windows in mind. These programs do not take advantage of the Windows graphical interface or memory access method. Think of Windows applications as being very generous with memory. They will give up a portion of their memory, if necessary, when another application needs it. Non-Windows applications, on the other hand, are selfish with memory. They do not share it with other applications and, in the process, limit the total number of applications you can run at the same time.

There are some other things to keep in mind regarding non-Windows applications. For instance, they normally run full screen in all Windows modes. In 386 enhanced mode it is possible to run them in a separate, resizable window.

NOTE: You must load MOUSE.COM to use a mouse in non-Windows applications when running in standard mode or 386 enhanced full-screen mode.

Processing in all other applications temporarily halts when you switch to a non-Windows application in standard mode. In 386 enhanced mode, non-Windows applications can be multitasked, which means they can continue processing in the background when you switch to other applications.

In standard mode, a full screen of information can be copied to the Clipboard. In 386 enhanced mode, specific sections of the screen can be copied to the Clipboard.

Non-Windows Applications Requiring Expanded Memory

Some non-Windows applications use expanded memory. If you have an 80286-based system, you need to add expanded memory on a memory expansion board, and then load the expanded memory manager that comes with the board into your system startup files. Instructions for doing this will be in the board's manual.

If you have an 80386 or 80486 system, run expanded-memory applications in the 386 enhanced mode to take advantage of its ability to emulate expanded memory. To run expanded-memory applications in DOS when your system does not have an expanded memory board, be sure to load the EMM386.SYS expanded-memory emulator by including the following command in your CONFIG.SYS file:

    DEVICE=C:\WINDOWS\EMM386.SYS

If necessary, replace the C in this command with the letter of the drive that holds your Windows directory.

Up to 256K of memory will be set aside as expanded memory. You can specify a larger amount of expanded memory by including a parameter for it at the end of the DEVICE command. For example, the following command sets aside 512K of memory:

    DEVICE=C:\WINDOWS\EMM386.SYS 512

N OTE: If you use DOS 5, include the DOS=HIGH,UMB option in your CONFIG.SYS file. Also, refer to your DOS manual for a discussion of the LOADHIGH and DEVICEHIGH commands.

Memory-Resident Software

Memory-resident utilities are programs that start and stay loaded in memory while other applications run. Commands in the CONFIG.SYS and AUTOEXEC.BAT files usually load this software when your system first starts. There are two types of memory-resident utilities:

✦ *Noninteractive memory-resident software* typically provides instructions to the operating system for handling peripheral equipment such as tape drives and optical disk drives. These programs may also provide support for connections to networks or electronic mail systems.

✦ *Interactive memory-resident software* is sometimes referred to as pop-up software because it appears on the screen when certain keys are pressed.

When you want a memory-resident utility to be available to applications when Windows is not running, start the utility in the CONFIG.SYS or AUTOEXEC.BAT file. If the utility takes up too much memory and prevents other non-Windows applications from running, try loading it after Windows starts since Windows allocates its use of memory more efficiently. (Note that some of these utilities can only be started with commands in the CONFIG.SYS file and never from within Windows.) If you still run out of memory when running non-Windows applications, exit Windows and run the utility and applications that use it from DOS.

Start pop-up programs after starting Windows. In this way, Windows can allocate memory for its own use first, and then provide the utility with the memory it needs. You may have to create a Program Information File to get the pop-up utility to run from Windows. In some cases, keys used by the pop-up program may be the same as those used by Windows. If so, reconfigure the keys in the pop-up utility as described in the utility's manual.

B

Working with Non-Windows Applications

To start a non-Windows application, do one of the following:

✦ Double-click the icon of the application in the Program Manager (you may have to create a startup icon first).

✦ If the application has special memory or startup requirements, you may have to create a PIF. You then double-click the PIF to start the application, or create a startup icon for the PIF in the Program Manager.

♦ Start the application from the File Manager by double-clicking its executable filename or its PIF.

♦ Double-click the DOS Prompt icon in the Program Manager Main group, and then run the application from the DOS command line.

NOTE: If an application locks up or you lose mouse control in 386 enhanced mode, Windows will let you terminate the faulty application without rebooting your entire system, by pressing Ctrl-Alt-Del.

Running Non-Windows Applications in a Window

When a non-Windows application runs full screen, it has no window borders or menu options. A Control Menu exists, but can only be accessed by pressing Alt-Esc to switch from the full-screen display back to Windows. You then click the application's icon on the desktop to display its Control Menu. The options on the Control Menu are limited—unless you're running in 386 enhanced mode, in which case the application can be run in a resizable window, as shown in Figure B-1.

If you're in 386 enhanced mode, there are two ways to get a non-Windows application to run in a window:

♦ Start the application as usual, and then press Alt-Enter. If this doesn't work, press Alt-Esc to return to Windows, and click the icon of the application. On its Control Menu, click Window in the Display Options box, and click the OK button.

♦ Create a PIF to specify that the application always start in a window as discussed in "Using Program Information Files" in this appendix.

Once your non-Windows application is in a resizable window, click its Control Menu button and choose a new font and screen size to match your needs.

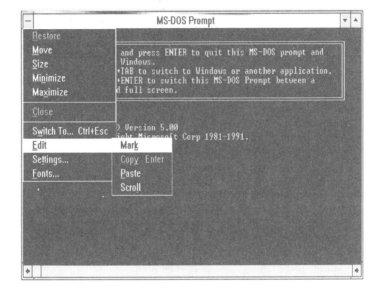

A non-Windows
application
running in a
window
Figure B-1.

TIP: Choose the Fonts option to display the Fonts dialog box. Select any of the listed fonts and then click OK.

Copying and Pasting in Standard Mode

Copying and pasting to and from non-Windows applications in standard mode is somewhat limited, but workable. Only text can be copied and pasted; and when copying from a non-Windows application, you must copy a full screen of information.

Here are the steps for copying from a non-Windows application to a Windows application:

1. Switch to the non-Windows application. It appears full screen.
2. Press the (Prt Sc) key to copy the entire screen to the Clipboard.
3. Press (Alt)-(Esc) to switch back to Windows.

B

4. Position the insertion point where you want to paste the information; then choose the Paste command from the Edit menu.

5. Delete any lines or characters that you did not wish to copy.

Here are the steps for copying from a Windows application to a non-Windows application:

1. In the Windows application, highlight the text to copy.

2. Choose Copy from the Edit menu.

3. Switch to the non-Windows application, and position the insertion point where you want the text pasted.

4. Switch back to Windows by pressing Alt - Esc .

5. On the Windows desktop, click the non-Windows application icon to open its Control Menu.

6. Choose Paste on the Control Menu to paste the text into the document.

7. Switch back to the non-Windows application to continue working with the document.

Copying and Pasting in 386 Enhanced Mode

When running a non-Windows application in 386 enhanced mode, you can copy specific portions of the screen to the Clipboard using commands on the Control Menu. If the window is running full screen, run it in a window, as discussed earlier in this appendix. You can then open its Control Menu to access the Copy and Paste options, as illustrated in Figure B-1.

To copy information from a non-Windows application to the Clipboard,

1. Make sure the application is running in a window.

2. Highlight the area you want to copy by clicking and dragging with the mouse.

3. Choose Edit from the Control Menu, and then choose the Copy option; or choose the Mark option, highlight the text to copy by pressing the arrow keys, and then choose Copy.

4. Switch to another application, and choose the Paste option from its Edit menu.

To paste information to a non-Windows application running in a window,

1. In the Windows application, highlight the text to copy.
2. Choose the Copy command on the Edit menu to copy the text to the Clipboard.
3. Switch to the non-Windows application, and position the insertion point where you want the text to be pasted.
4. Choose the Edit option on the Control Menu, highlight Paste, and release the mouse.

Setting Options for 386 Enhanced Mode

B

To control how a non-Windows application runs in 386 enhanced mode, you can choose the Settings options on the Control menu of a running application, or you can set system-wide defaults in the Control Panel. You can also create or edit a PIF to designate permanent startup settings for the application. Each method is described in the paragraphs that follow.

NOTE: The following discussion assumes non-Windows applications are running in a resizable window.

Using the Settings Dialog Box

In the non-Windows application window, choose Settings from the Control menu to display the dialog box pictured in Figure B-2. The options in this dialog box are used to switch from full-screen display to window display, to change the way the application works with other Windows applications, and to change the way processing time is allocated to the non-Windows application. There is also a button you can use to "informally terminate" applications that have locked up. All these options are explained in the following paragraphs.

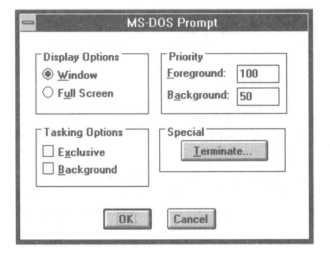

The Settings
dialog box for a
non-Windows
application
running in 386
enhanced mode
Figure B-2.

NOTE: Changes made to the Settings dialog box affect only the current settings of the program. Use Control Panel options or a PIF to make permanent changes.

Display Options   Click Full-Screen for best performance, but click Window if you want to switch easily between Windows and other DOS programs running under Windows.

Tasking Options   Click Background to run the application in the background (inactive) window when working in other windows. Click Exclusive to give the application exclusive use of your system processor when the application is in the foreground (active) window.

Priority Options   Use the Priority options to specify how much processor time the application should receive in relation to other applications. Refer to Chapter 18 for information on setting these options.

Terminate Button   Click the Terminate button to quit a non-Windows application when it has locked up. Use this option only as a last resort, because data may be lost. After terminating an application in this way, always save your other work and restart the computer, because the operating system could become unstable.

Setting Control Panel Options

Double-click the 386 Enhanced icon in the Windows Control Panel to display the dialog box pictured in Figure B-3. The options in this dialog box are used to set *default* multitasking options, which are used by any non- Windows application you may start. Note that the Scheduling options are used to set options for Windows, not DOS applications.

N**OTE:** To change startup options for individual DOS applications, create PIF files for those applications.

B

Device Contention Settings   Some non-Windows applications may try to use a COM or LPT port while it is in use by another application.

The Control Panel 386 Enhanced dialog box
Figure B-3.

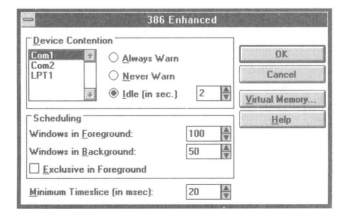

To change the warning method for this situation, click a device name, and then click one of the option buttons. In most cases, choose Always Warn. If you select Never Warn, the non-Windows application can use the device at any time; select this option only when you're sure no other devices will be using the port. Select Idle when two devices may use the port, one after the other. Designate an idle time interval for the time that must elapse before the next application uses the port.

Scheduling Options   The Scheduling options let you divide the processor time between foreground and background operations for Windows applications, as discussed next and in Chapter 18.

Multitasking Options

The microprocessor in your system can multitask by giving processing time to each running application, one after the other. If you have an 80386 (or more advanced system), you can multitask non-Windows applications, as well.

The *foreground application* is the currently active application, whether it is running in a window or full screen. *Background applications* may be running in a window, or full screen "behind" the active foreground window. *Exclusive processing* is when an application is given the full processing power of your system, and no other applications are processed.

In multitasking, the amount of processing time an application receives can be adjusted based on whether its window is currently active in the foreground or running in the background. Alternatively, processing can be stopped altogether when the application is in the background, or the application can be given exclusive processing when it is in the foreground.

In most cases, the default settings of the multitasking options are sufficient, but you can control them in special cases by increasing or decreasing the values of the scheduling options. For more information, refer to Chapter 18.

Using Program Information Files

Program Information Files (PIFs) are used to supply Windows with startup information for non-Windows applications. The files will normally have the same name as the program file, with the extension .PIF. PIFs are normally stored in the Windows directory. You create or edit existing PIFs using the PIF Editor, in the Windows Main group.

There is a difference between PIFs created for applications that run in standard mode and PIFs created for applications that run in 386 enhanced mode. A PIF for 386 enhanced mode contains multitasking options used to control how the application behaves when running with other applications.

Remember that you are not required to create a PIF for every non-Windows application. Windows will attempt to run the application using its own default values, but if the application doesn't run properly, you can try creating a PIF to specify custom parameters.

NOTE: You should always run the Setup utility after installing a non-Windows application to automatically create a PIF for the new application. Choose Setup Applications from the Options menu. You then tell Windows to find the application and attempt to create a PIF for it. Windows is aware of the required PIF settings of hundreds of non-Windows applications, so Setup is your best bet to get the application running properly under Windows.

B

Keep the following features and functions of Program Information Files in mind. If a PIF already exists for an application, you can use the PIF editor to make some of the listed changes:

✦ PIFs are usually given the filename of their corresponding application, with the extension .PIF. For example, a PIF to start Microsoft Word would be named WORD.PIF.

✦ Information in PIFs is used to specify the path to the directory where the program is located, and the path to be used for retrieving and storing documents.

✦ Startup parameters for non-Windows applications can be specified in PIFs.

✦ You can start a non-Windows application by double-clicking its associated PIF.

♦ An application can have several PIFs, each with different settings. One PIF could be created to use files from a business directory, and another to use files from a personal data directory. You might also want to change the memory settings of one PIF if you need to load documents or run programs that require full system memory.

♦ You can create PIFs for batch files. Commands in batch files are executed sequentially and can be used to run other commands before or after running a non-Windows application. For example, you might load a memory-resident package before starting an application.

Using the PIF Editor

To start the PIF Editor, double-click its icon in the Program Manager. In a moment the PIF Editor dialog box appears. The first four items in the PIF Editor dialog box are common for all Windows modes. Complete these four text boxes first, as described in the following paragraphs. Then refer to the Help option for information on setting the other options. To edit an existing PIF, choose Open from the File menu.

Program Filename

In the Program Filename text box, type the path and filename of the program you want to run. Files can be executable files with the extension .EXE or .COM, or batch files with the extension .BAT.

TIP: To avoid startup problems when Windows can't find a non-Windows program, specify the path to program directories in the AUTOEXEC.BAT file.

Window Title

The Window Title text box is optional. You can type a descriptive name for the PIF in this box. The name you type will appear under the application's icon on the desktop. Try to keep the name short so it doesn't overlap other names.

Optional Parameters

In the Optional Parameters box, type any additional startup parameters the application may require. For example, some versions of Microsoft Word for DOS can be started in graphics mode by typing **WORD** /**G**. To start Word in this way from a PIF, you would type /**G** in the Optional Parameters box. If you are creating a PIF to start a program and then load an existing file in its workspace, you can include the filename in the Optional Parameters box. Be sure to include the drive and path, if necessary.

If you want Windows to prompt you for a parameter whenever you start the application, type a question mark in the Optional Parameters box. This allows you to start applications in a different way every time they are run.

Start-Up Directory

In the Start-up Directory field, type the name of the directory where files are to be opened and saved for this application. Typically, the directory where data files are stored is specified in this field. You can create several PIFs for a single application, each pointing to a different data directory. In this way, you can start applications with one PIF to access business files, and with another PIF to access personal files.

Other Settings

A complete explanation of the remaining settings in the PIF Editor dialog box is available on the PIF Editor help system.

Some applications don't need all the memory allocated to them in a PIF. You can reduce these allocations and provide more memory for your Windows applications. To do this, reduce the value in the KB Desired field in small increments until the application refuses to run; then return the setting to the last workable value.

If your application requires expanded memory, specify the amount of expanded memory it needs in the EMS Memory KB Required field of the 386 Enhanced version of this dialog box. If your application requires extended memory, specify the amount in the XMS Memory KB Required field.

B

If you're running low on memory, try setting the Video Memory to the Text option first; then switch to Low Graphics, and finally to High Graphics until you get the application to work.

In the 386 enhanced mode, applications will run faster if you choose the Full Screen option for the Display Usage setting, rather than the Windowed option. Then when you run the application, you can switch to a window when you need to by pressing Alt-Enter. Also, don't select the Background option for the Execution setting unless you really need to run the application while working in other windows. Background operation slows performance.

Be sure the Detect Idle Time option is marked in the Advanced Options dialog box. Windows will then borrow unused time allocated to your non-Windows application and give it to other applications.

A P P E N D I

OPTIMIZING WINDOWS' PERFORMANCE

The best system configuration for Windows is an 80386 (or later model system) with 4 megabytes or more of memory. If you have an 80286 system, you'll be satisfied with Windows' performance—until you see it run on a 386 or 486. When you do, you'll probably want to upgrade your hardware, and the best way to do that is to add more memory. In fact, the majority of Windows performance problems are caused by insufficient memory. Once you've installed enough memory to keep your system running smoothly, you can achieve additional gains in performance by "tweaking" various system parameters, or changing the way you use Windows. This appendix offers some suggestions in these areas.

Choosing a Windows Mode

If you have a 386 or 486 system with more than 3MB of memory, Windows automatically starts in 386 enhanced mode. This mode lets you multitask non-Windows applications and use virtual memory. However, your system may operate faster if you start Windows in standard mode (by entering the command **WIN /S** at the DOS prompt). This is because in 386 enhanced mode your processor spends extra time maintaining the virtual environment used to multitask non-Windows applications and prevent them from conflicting with the memory and system resources of other applications. If your system is a server on the network, access by other users will also reduce its performance. You might want to stop sharing temporarily to run an application at full performance.

Although there are definite advantages to using the 386 enhanced mode, speed is not usually one of them, unless you have the fastest system on the market. As mentioned before, the primary advantage of 386 enhanced mode is its ability to multitask non-Windows applications and share resources on your system with network users. But is multitasking essential for your needs? Is the slowdown in performance really worth it?

One of the first things you should do, if possible, is upgrade your DOS-based applications to Windows-compatible versions. Windows 3.0 was announced in early 1990, and by now most major applications are available in Windows versions at a typically small upgrade price. By upgrading all of your applications, you can work in the Windows environment most of the time and benefit from its graphical interface.

If you must run a non-Windows application, decide whether to run it in the multitasking environment of 386 enhanced mode. Remember that multitasking lets applications continue to process in the background while you work with other applications in the foreground. A non-Windows application can run in a resizable window in 386 enhanced mode, as well as full screen. Do you really need these features when running non-Windows applications? If not, start Windows in standard mode for better performance. However, applications running in standard mode can only be displayed full screen.

Another aspect of this discussion is memory. If your system is low on memory, you may need the virtual memory capabilities of 386 enhanced mode. Because Windows applications share memory cooperatively, out-of-memory errors are more likely to occur when running non-Windows applications. Non-Windows applications run in conventional memory, so you need to take steps at the DOS level to increase conventional memory. You can do this by upgrading to Microsoft's MS-DOS 5.0 or Digital Research's DR DOS 6.0.

TIP: If you get out-of-memory problems when working with large graphic files and scanned images in a Windows application, start Windows in 386 enhanced mode. The swap file will make up for memory deficiencies. If you still have out-of-memory problems, try increasing the size of the swap file.

Improving the Performance of Non-Windows Applications

When running non-Windows applications in 386 enhanced mode, there are a few things you can do to improve performance. The options described in the following paragraphs are available from the Settings dialog box while an application is running in 386 enhanced mode, or you can specify them in a Program Information File, or PIF (see Appendix B) for the application. To open the Settings dialog box, as shown in Figure C-1, press (Alt)-(Esc), click the application's icon, and then choose Settings from its Control Menu.

NOTE: When the startup settings for 386 enhanced mode are established using a PIF, you can still change the settings when the application is running, using the options described here.

510

The dialog box
to edit the
settings of a
non-Windows
application,
available from
its Control
Menu in 386
enhanced mode
Figure C-1.

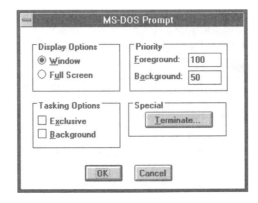

Window Versus Full-Screen Display Options   The best performance is
realized when non-Windows applications run full screen, instead of in
a window. So select Full Screen from the dialog box for the fastest
mode, but select Window when you need to compare the contents of
the non-Windows applications with other windows.

Exclusive Processing   Mark the Exclusive Processing check box under
Tasking Options to give the non-Windows application exclusive use of
the system processor.

NOTE: If you don't want the non-Windows application to process
in the background or exclusively, leave both the Exclusive and
Background check boxes unmarked. In this way, processing in the
non-Windows application is suspended when you switch to Windows
applications.

Optimizing System Startup

When your system does not have enough memory, no matter what
type of system it is or what type of applications you run, it will operate
inefficiently, or it will prevent you from running more than one or two
applications at a time. You can gain extra memory by running
Windows in 386 enhanced mode and using virtual memory, or by
attempting to gain memory used by utilities and applications at system
startup. This second method is covered here.

Using Windows SYSEDIT

The SYSEDIT utility is a convenient tool for changing the contents of your startup files. When you start SYSEDIT, the startup files are automatically loaded into its workspace in separate document windows, as shown in Figure C-2. You can thus quickly make changes to any file, save it, and exit SYSEDIT.

To start SYSEDIT, select Run from the Program Manager or File Manager File menu, and type **SYSEDIT** in the Command Line box. (Chapter 8 tells you how to create a startup icon for SYSEDIT.)

TIP: The following sections recommend disabling some commands in the startup files. Rather than deleting the command altogether, insert a REM statement before the command to disable. In this way, you can easily reinstate the command later. When your system boots, you'll see error messages for commands that start with REM statements in the CONFIG.SYS file, but you can ignore them.

Once you've made changes to the startup files after reading the following section, close the SYSEDIT window. SYSEDIT will ask if you want to save the changes you've made. Answer Yes to save changes in all four of the files that appear in the SYSEDIT window. Then reboot your system.

Use SYSEDIT to edit DOS and Windows startup files

Figure C-2.

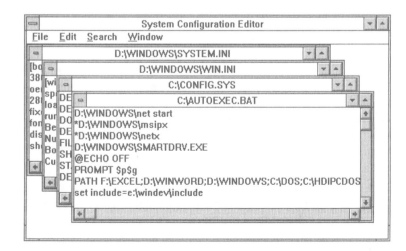

NOTE: Changes made to startup parameters do not take effect until you reboot your system.

Changing the CONFIG.SYS File

The CONFIG.SYS file is used to load device drivers for peripherals attached to your system, such as a mouse or special video equipment. The file may also hold DOS commands that configure the DOS operating parameters. For more information on these commands, refer to your DOS manual. To make the following changes, click the CONFIG.SYS document window in SYSEDIT.

✦   Remove any unnecessary device drivers for equipment that is no longer installed on your system. For example, if you use your mouse only with Windows applications, and not DOS applications, you can remove the command DEVICE=MOUSE.SYS, because mouse support is handled internally by Windows.

✦   The FILES command is used to specify the maximum number of files that can be open at once. Set its value at 40, using the following command:

FILES = 40

 NOTE: Set the FILES value higher only if you receive the error message "Insufficient file handles" when running an application.

✦   The BUFFERS command lets you specify the number of buffers used to improve disk access. If CONFIG.SYS contains a DEVICE= command that loads SMARTDrive, set BUFFERS to 10 with the following command:

BUFFERS = 10

✦ The LASTDRIVE command is used to specify how many hard drives, RAM drives, and optical drives your system supports. This value is important if you are attached to network drives. Windows typically sets this value to P, but you may need to increase it if you don't have enough drive letters to accommodate the directories you are sharing on other systems.

LASTDRIVE = P

✦ The SHELL command uses the parameter /E to specify a larger amount of environment space. You may want to remove this value from the SHELL command to free up memory. If you receive an "Out of environment space" message, reinstate the command or increase its value.

✦ If you are using DOS 3.3 or higher, make sure this command is in CONFIG.SYS:

STACKS=9,256

✦ If your system has an EGA monitor, and you want to run non-Windows applications in standard mode, include this command in CONFIG.SYS:

DEVICE=C:\WINDOWS\EGA.SYS

✦ *Do not remove* any lines that load the HIMEM.SYS extended memory manager or SMARTDRV.SYS cache program.

RAM Drives

Because the Windows SMARTDrive utility is very efficient at speeding up a system, RAM drives are usually not necessary under Windows. You may, however, gain some performance improvement by using a RAM drive for the storage of temporary files. Applications often create temporary files on disk to store information as you work with the application. These files are removed when you exit the application or Windows. Because these files are temporary, it makes sense to place them in a RAM drive. Moreover, access to a RAM drive is faster than to a disk drive. In addition, Print Manager queues its print files to a temporary directory; thus, its performance improves if the temporary directory is a RAM drive.

To install a RAM drive, include a command similar to the following in the CONFIG.SYS file. (Be sure to specify the correct drive and directory for your Windows directory.)

    DEVICE=C:\WINDOWS\RAMDRIVE.SYS 512 /E

The number at the end of the command specifies the size of the RAM drive. Here 512K is specified, but you can change this value based on the amount of RAM memory you are willing to give up for use as a RAM drive. The /E parameter installs the RAM drive in extended memory; to install a RAM drive in expanded memory, use the /A parameter instead.

Once the RAM drive is installed, you direct temporary files to it by including a SET command in the AUTOEXEC.BAT file. For example, let's say the RAM drive will be drive E when your system reboots. You will need to include the following command in AUTOEXEC.BAT to direct temporary files to drive E:

    SET TEMP=E:\

Some applications recognize the command TMP instead of TEMP. Therefore, include this command as well:

    SET TMP=E:\

NOTE: If your system has many hard drives, network drives, and optical drives, you may need to increase the LASTDRIVE setting to specify an additional drive letter for the RAM drive.

The AUTOEXEC.BAT File

The AUTOEXEC.BAT file automatically starts programs and utilities when your system is started. For example, commands you'll find in AUTOEXEC.BAT are those that load terminate-and-stay-resident programs (TSRs). On a Windows system, TSRs should be loaded from within Windows, so you need to disable these commands in AUTOEXEC.BAT (using REM statements) and start them from within

Windows. You can create startup icons for the TSRs, or start them using the Run command on the Program Manager File menu. TSRs started from within Windows are loaded into extended memory, leaving conventional memory free for non-Windows applications that need it.

If you installed a RAM drive, as discussed in the previous section, be sure to include in AUTOEXEC.BAT the SET command that directs temporary files to the RAM drive.

Improving Disk Performance

Performance diminishes if your system runs low on disk space. This section tells you how to periodically remove old files and optimize the way files are stored.

File fragmentation occurs when files are stored in several noncontiguous sectors on a disk. Reading fragmented files takes more time and causes the disk to work harder, since the read/write heads must jump to several different places to access the complete file. File fragmentation begins the first time you erase a file and save a new one in its place, because the old and new files are usually different in size. Each erased file leaves a blank area where a new file can be stored; however, if this area is not large enough to accommodate the new file, part of the new file is stored elsewhere. As more old files are erased and more new files are stored, fragmentation increases. Eventually, you must unfragment the disk.

CAUTION: Never run a disk fragmenting utility when a disk cache utility like SMARTDrive or DOS FASTOPEN is active. Temporarily disable the disk cache command in AUTOEXEC.BAT and restart your system first.

Hard Disk Cleanup

To keep a hard drive running efficiently, you need to remove unnecessary files and *optimize* the drive to remove file fragmentation. Files you want to keep but that are not currently needed can be archived to disks or tape for future use.

NOTE: You can use File Manager to archive and remove files, but you must close all other applications when doing so. To remove files in the Windows directories and subdirectories, use only the Setup utility, as described in "Removing Unnecessary Windows Files with Setup," later in this appendix.

Deleting .BAK Files   Major candidates for deletion are .BAK files, which are the previous versions of files you've edited. These backup files are created so you can quickly restore a file to the way it was before editing. When you're sure you don't need them, you can delete these .BAK files.

One of the best ways to delete .BAK files is to use the File Manager Search command. The Search dialog box is shown here:

Type ***.BAK** in the Search For field, and in the Start From field specify the drive to search. For this task, the Search All Subdirectories box should always be marked. (The preceding example tells Windows to search all directories on drive C for .BAK files.) When Windows displays the list of .BAK files, highlight the files you want to remove and press the ⬚Del key.

Removing Unnecessary Windows Files with Setup

When you really run short on disk space, it may be necessary to delete some of the Windows files. You can do so by starting the Setup utility in the Control Panel and choosing the Add/Remove Windows Components option. You'll then see the dialog box shown in Figure C-3 on the next page.

To remove an entire set of files, unmark one or more of the boxes in the Windows Components column. To remove individual files, click the button in the Customize column for the files you want to delete.

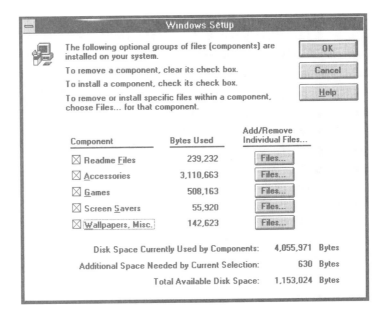

The Windows
Setup dialog
box that lets
you add or
remove
Windows
components
Figure C-3.

Disk Optimizing Techniques

After you've scanned your disk and removed unnecessary files, it's a
good idea to unfragment (optimize) the disk. You can use any of
various third-party utilities designed for this task, or the methods
described here. In fact, it's wise to put your disk on a regular optimizing
schedule, say once every month, or whenever you begin to see a
slowdown in disk performance.

TIP: Disk optimization can be conveniently scheduled to coincide
with regularly scheduled disk backups.

Disk optimizing utilities automatically unfragment files by moving
them around on the disk until they are all in a contiguous form. This
shuffling method ensures that files are not lost should the system crash
during the unfragmenting session. Popular disk optimizing programs
are Speed Disk by Peter Norton Computing (now Symantec), and PC
Tools by Central Point Software.

Backup-and-Restore Method

The backup-and-restore method of optimizing a disk can be done with the DOS BACKUP and RESTORE commands, or with a tape backup utility. The process involves first backing up your entire hard drive to disks or tape, then formatting the hard disk, and finally restoring the data. When the files are restored, they are restored contiguously.

When you use the backup-and-restore method, it is important to do a file-by-file backup, not an image backup. An image backup-and-restore would copy the files exactly as they are on the hard drive, in fragmented form. On the other hand, the file-by-file method gathers together the fragmented portions of each file on the backup medium and restores them in that state (assuming the disk has been formatted).

Formatting the hard drive is an important step because it clears the table DOS uses to keep track of files and their location on the disk. This information includes the locations of the fragmented portions of the files. If you restore without removing this table, DOS could replace the files in their old locations, based on the table.

Another important step in the backup-and-restore process is to remove old files before you perform the backup. In this way, only the files you really want get restored to the drive, thus reducing clutter and increasing available disk space.

If you plan to unfragment the boot drive using this method, keep in mind that DOS won't let you format the drive from which you booted. You'll need to create a boot disk so you can restart your system from its floppy drive. Then you can format the hard disk. Be sure the FORMAT.COM command is on the disk.

APPENDIX

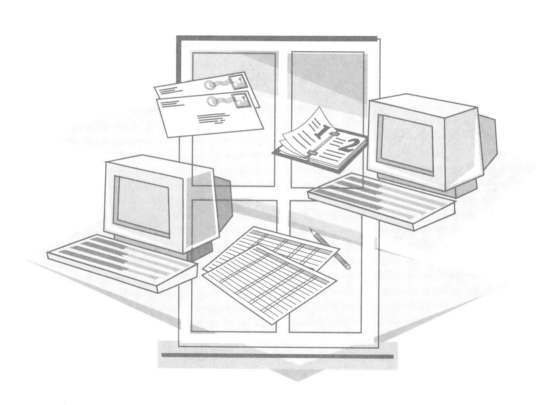

WINDOWS FOR WORKGROUPS RESOURCE KIT

The Microsoft Windows for Workgroups Resource Kit is an indispensable guide for people who need to know more about Windows for Workgroups. This technical supplement to the Windows for Workgroups documentation is designed for system administrators or users who are responsible for installing and managing Windows for Workgroups networks and for integrating the program with other network environments. The kit consists of a reference manual and a disk. The manual contains a wealth of information about networks and Windows for Workgroups program and utilities. The disk contains a set of additional utilities for monitoring and managing the network.

To obtain the kit, which sells for $29.95, call Microsoft at (800) 642-7676.

The manual provides the following information:

✦ Technical discussion of networking

✦ Overview of the Windows for Workgroups architecture

✦ Technical discussion of the installation process and how you can create custom installation routines for automated setup.

✦ A technical discussion of the Windows for Workgroups initialization files, including WIN.INI, SYSTEM.INI, PROTOCOL.INI, MSMAIL,INI, and SCHDPLUS.INI

✦ Tips for using and optimizing Windows for Workgroups

✦ Information about integrating Windows for Workgroups with other networks such as Novell NetWare and Microsoft LAN Manager

✦ Technical discussion of network dynamic data exchange (DDE), the underlying component of object linking and embedding.

✦ Information about Microsoft Mail, such as its architecture and how to customize Mail and integrate it with other Windows-based applications

✦ Information about Microsoft Schedule+

✦ A complete troubleshooting section

The Resource Kit Utility Disk

The disk accompanying the Windows for Workgroups Resource Kit contains utilities for monitoring and managing the network. A brief description of each utility follows.

NetMeter

Unlike the WinMeter utility for monitoring the utilization statistics of a local workstation, the NetMeter utility is used to view the CPU utilization statistics of a remote Windows for Workgroups workstation that is also running a copy of NetMeter.

System administrators can use NetMeter to monitor other workstations on the network. For example, you could monitor the performance level of a remote workstation such as an unattended print server or file server. Several remote workstations can be monitored at once from your local workstation. NetMeter and WinMeter should not be run on the same machine. NetMeter supersedes WinMeter.

Network Adapter Status (NetStat) Utility

The NetStat utility is executed from the MS-DOS command line and used to obtain statistics about a network adapter card. You use the utility to identify problems with a network adapter card configured in a workstation on the network or identify a network cabling problem. Most important, the utility can be used to test a computer's presence on the network and isolate hardware problems from other problems you might encounter after starting Windows for Workgroups. Error counts displayed as part of the NetStat status display can help to identify errors resulting from problems with network cabling, a network that is overloaded, or a network adapter card that is generating or receiving bad *packets*, or blocks of information.

A typical NetStat display provides the following information:

✦ The address assigned to the network adapter card, usually defined in ROM residing on the adapter card.

✦ The amount of time the network adapter card has been active on the network since it was last reset.

✦ NetBIOS information useful in debugging network problems.

✦ The number of packets that have originated from the network adapter and the number of packets that have been received by the network adapter on the specified workstation.

D

✦ Information about errors that have been logged by the network adapter card on the specified workstation. A significant number of errors identified for a network adapter card may indicate either a problem with the network card, or a possible problem with the network cabling. The error types that the network adapter card keeps track of have the following descriptions:

Retries Exhausted   The number of times that the number of retry time-out attempts have been exceeded.

CDC Errors   The number of times that corrupted data was caught by error-correction code on the network adapter card.

Alignment Errors   Indicates corrupted packets were received by the network adapter card.

Collisions   Indicates the number of times that the network adapter card encountered a collision with another packet when attempting to send information out over the network. A large number of collisions may indicate a heavily loaded network.

Aborted Transmissions   Indicates the number of times the network adapter card gave up trying to send data over the network.

Retransmissions   Indicates the number of times the network adapter card needed to retransmit data across the network due to an error encountered during an earlier transmission.

Network DDE Share Manager

The Network DDE Share Manager lets you work with the DDE Shares database so you can define Network DDE communications between DDE-aware applications. For example, you could create a DDE share that allows an application on another network workstation to establish a Network DDE conversation with an application running on your workstation. Both applications must be DDE-aware.

Dr. Turing

The Dr. Turing utility gathers local configuration and status information when an application error occurs, such as a general protection fault when an application violates its memory space. It stores the information in a local log file. The information can then be sent to a designated Mail user, such as the system administrator over the network.

Dr. Turing is useful to system administrators as a tool for tracking application errors that occur on network workstations. When an application error occurs, Dr. Turing automatically sends a message to the administrator.

Phone Message Application

Phone Message is a sample Visual Basic application that you can use to send logged phone messages as a mail message to people in your workgroup. Phone Message uses edit fields and check boxes to present a friendly interface to the user to facilitate taking phone messages. The Windows for Workgroups Setup program adds a custom command to the Mail menu in the Mail application to serve as an example of defining a custom command.

Mail 3.x Folder Conversion Program

The Mail 3.x Folder Conversion Program makes it easy to convert Mail folder files created by Microsoft Mail version 2.1 or the MS-DOS-based Mail application provided with the Microsoft Workgroup Connection product for use with Windows for Workgroups Mail. Use this utility to move the folder structure and all the messages within the folders into your Windows for Workgroup folder list.

Additional Files

The disk also contains the following files that add functionality to various Windows for Workgroups applications and accessories.

File Manager Utilities

FMUTILS.DLL automatically adds a Utility menu to the File Manager menu bar and two icons to the File Manager Toolbar to provide the following functionality:

Show File Size Information   Shows the number of files, directories, and total disk space used by the specified selection in File Manager.

This option is useful to determine the amount of disk space occupied by a given directory and any directories within the selected directory.

Find File   Enhances the File Search function supported by File Manager by also allowing the user to search for files that contain a given search string.

Sample Custom Print Separator Page File

PRINTSEP.CLP is a sample ClipBook Viewer clipboard file that Print Manager can use as a custom separator page file to separate print jobs. The information can be modified by pasting it into an appropriate editor.

Online Help Information

The Network Adapter Card Setup Help file contains information compiled by Microsoft Product Support Services (PSS) to aid in configuring network adapter cards for use with Windows for Workgroups. This help file is useful in identifying the jumper or switch settings to configure your network adapter card when you can't locate the documentation that was originally supplied with the card.

Mail Utilities

The following utilities are available for adding custom command and message types to the Microsoft Mail interface. Custom commands are commands you add to Mail menus. Once installed, custom commands appear as regular built-in features. Custom message types let you define forms for sending mail messages.

APPEXEC.DLL   A dynamic-link library you can use to create custom commands that can invoke other applications from within Mail.

Empty Wastebasket Custom Command   Adds the menu command, Empty Wastebasket, to Mail.

Help Request Custom Message   Provides forms users can complete to send help requests to the system administrator.

INDEX

$ at end of name of directory to be
   hidden, 284-285
386 Control Panel option to control 386
   enhanced mode, 20
386 Enhanced dialog box, 486, 499-500
386 enhanced mode, 15, 20, 157-158,
   482
   automatic startup of Windows in, 508
   copying and pasting non-Windows
      data using, 496-497
   features of, 28-29, 458
   forcing Windows to start in, 30
   non-Windows applications running
      in, 497-500, 508
   required for shared ClipBooks, 339
   required for shared printers, 330
   required for systems that are both
      client and server, 272
   running non-Windows applications
      in, 35
   startup files for, 458-459
386Max (Qualitas), 480, 482

A

About Program Manager dialog box,
   27-28
   available RAM and system resources
      listed in, 28, 30, 485
Accessories group
   arrangement on screen of, 73-75
   purpose of, 72
Accessories group window, 17-19
Add dialog box, 150
Advanced Options dialog box, 504
[Alt] key plus underlined letter or number
   to access a menu, 5-6, 48
   to jump to a dialog box field, 63
   to select a Task List button, 55
[Alt]-[-] to access Control menu of a group
   window, 48-49
[Alt]-[<] to browse backward in Help
   history file, 108
[Alt]-[>] to browse forward in Help history
   file, 108
[Alt]-[A] to attach a file in Microsoft Mail,
   389

527

Alt-B to display Browse dialog box, 194

Alt-D to delete a bookmark, 115

Alt-Enter
  to collapse full-screen DOS prompt to window, 35-36
  to run non-Windows application in a window, 494, 504

Alt-Esc
  to switch among application windows, 53, 81, 494, 509

Alt-F4
  to close a window, 61
  to exit Windows, 38

Alt-F-A to save a file and specify its name, 182

Alt-F-C to copy a program item, 189

Alt-F-R to open Run dialog box, 31, 50, 68

Alt-F-S to save a file, 34

Alt-G to go to specific help text, 109

Alt-H to display help drop-down menu, 103

Alt-H-A to open About Program Manager dialog box, 27

Alt-I to change an icon, 195

Alt-M to minimize the File Manager when it runs, 69

Alt-M-C to change a password in Microsoft Mail, 384

Alt-M-F to forward mail messages, 397

Alt-S to show Help topics, 109

Alt-Backspace to open Control menu, 38, 48-49, 69

Alt-T to view history file of help topics, 107

Alt-Tab
  to activate Program Manager, 27, 57
  to open minimized window, 69
  to preview windows when they are hidden, 52-54, 81
  switching, fast, 138-139

Alt-V-B to sort files by extension type, 94

Alt-W to open Window menu, 34, 50

Alt-W-N to open a new window, 97

American Standard Code for Information Interchange (ASCII), 163

Annotate dialog box, 113

Application
  background versus foreground, 500
  help display for an entire, 102-103
  in memory, removing, 51
  reduced to an icon when program starts, 192, 207
  selecting an icon to use for, 193

Application, starting
  by adding its startup icon to the Program Manager StartUp group, 32-33, 206-207
  by double-clicking its icon, 30-31, 47-48, 237-238
  by entering its name on the command line, 31
  by highlighting its application icon and pressing Enter, 51-52
  by specifying it in the AUTOEXEC.BAT file, 31-32

Applications
  moving among multiple, 52-56, 81
  organizing, 185-207

Applications File menu, 173

Applications group, 201

Appointment dialog box, 410-413, 415

Archive flag (A), 254

Arrange Icons button, 83

Associate dialog box, 258

Attribute flags, file, 254-256

AUTOEXEC.BAT file
  applications listed in PATH command of, 32
  conflicting commands in, 34

disabling other programs' startup
  commands in, 35
expanded memory manager
  command in, 484
Novell NetWare's changes to,
  297-298, 472
RAM drive's changes to, 514
TSR commands in, 492-493, 514-515
Windows startup command in, 33-34,
  457

B

Background application, 15
Background Printing dialog box, 328-330
Banyan VINES, vii
Bitmap image format for graphics, 163
Bookmark Define dialog box, 114
Bookmark menu, 113-114
Bookmarks. *See* Help system
Browse button, 192, 203
Browse Connections dialog box, 298, 300
Browse dialog box, 62-63, 68, 194-195
By File Type dialog box, 97, 226-228

C

Calendar Windows appointment utility,
  18
Cardfile Windows minidatabase utility,
  18
  as client application, 360
  embedded cardfiles in, 363-364
  embedded icons on cards in, 367,
    371-372
Cascade button, 82
CD-ROM drives
  playing audio CDs in, 149
  sharing, vii, 283
Change Icon button, 195, 203

Change Icon dialog box, 195, 203-204
Change Recurrence dialog box, 416,
  418, 426
Character Map Windows special
  character utility, 18
Chat Edit menu, 290
Chat Windows information-sharing
  utility, viii, 18-19, 282, 291
Check boxes, 65
  marking and unmarking, 63, 69
  multiple enabled, 66-67
Clicking and holding the mouse
  defined, 5
Clicking the mouse defined, 5
Client
  OLE application, 360-361
  system, v, 271-272
Clipboard, 340-342
  capturing screens and windows to,
    342, 491, 495
  copying help topic text to, 113
  for cutting and pasting, 2, 83-86,
    353-374, 496-497
  linking and embedding using, 362-363
  minimized, 340
  saving contents of, 86-88, 342-343
  temporary storage with, 15-16, 88
ClipBook accessory. *See also* Local
  ClipBook
  compound documents built using, 359
  examining and saving contents of, 17,
    86-88
  features, 340-345
  icons and their meanings, 341
  to move text or graphics between
    applications, 15-17
  network links created using, 369-370
  objects used in documents, 348-351
ClipBook viewer, 84, 337-351, 526
ClipBooks, connecting with other users',
  347-348

Clock
changing the time display on, 61
displayed when Windows starts,
206-207
Clock Settings menu, 61
Clock Windows time utility, 18
Color Control Panel option for
customizing Windows color, 20,
90-91, 120-125
Color dialog box, 90-91, 120-123, 136
Color Palette button, 91
Color schemes, creating custom, 121-122
Colors, creating custom, 123-125
Command buttons
mouse and keyboard techniques for,
64
purpose of, 63
Compatible Networks dialog box, 471
Computer name for each computer on
network, 153, 273, 446
CONFIG.SYS file
conflicting commands in, 34
devices described in, 492, 514
disabling other programs' startup
commands in, 35
for DOS 5.0, additional commands in,
492
EGA monitor specified in, 513
expanded memory manager
command in, 484, 492
minimizing memory used by, 512-513
Novell NetWare's changes to, 297, 472
stacks listed in, 513
TSR commands in, 492-493
Windows' changes to, 297, 457
Confirm Directory Delete dialog box,
264-265
Confirm File Delete dialog box, 213-214,
252, 264
Confirmation dialog box, 263
Connect dialog box, 313

Connect Network Drive dialog box,
179-181, 281, 284, 287
Connect Network Printer dialog box,
314-315, 334
Connect Network Printer Toolbar
button, 322, 334
Connect to Shared Directory Toolbar
button, 286
Connect Toolbar button, 341
Connection menu, NetWatcher
Close File option, 293
Disconnect option, 293
Properties option, 292
Contents list. *See* Files list
Control menu
Close option, 61
closing, 49
opening, 11, 38, 48-49, 69
Control Panel, 119-158
categories of options on, 120
opening, 37, 119-120
options, customizing Windows with,
19-20, 88-91
printer settings, 319-320
Control Panel icon, 37
CONTROL.INI file, 460
Ctrl-Alt-Del to reboot system, 487, 494
Ctrl-C to copy Clipboard data, 362
Ctrl-Esc to open Task List, 47, 53-55
Ctrl-F8 to expand an entire directory
tree, 222
Ctrl-G to select a new date, 410
Ctrl-N to use a Schedule+ appointment
time slot, 410
Ctrl-P to print appointments and tasks,
429
Ctrl-Tab
exclusive to the Program Manager
window, 52
to highlight title bar of group, 50-51
Conversation menu, 290

Copy command, 16-17, 84-86
  difference between Cut command
    and, 83
Copy dialog box, 250
Copy Disk dialog box, 265-266
Copy Toolbar button, 341, 349
Create Directory dialog box, 260-261
Cross-hair pointer for graphics, 42
Cursor blink rate, 146
Customize Toolbar dialog box, 233-235
Cut command, 16-17, 84-85
  difference between Copy command
    and, 83
Cut-and-paste feature of Windows,
  83-88. *See also* Clipboard

D

Database
  record access, 280
  sorting process, processor time
    required for, 329
Date & Time dialog box, 89
Date/Time Control Panel option to set
  the date and time, 20, 89-90, 120,
  148
Del key to delete an icon, 206
Delete Document Toolbar button, 322,
  326
Delete Toolbar button, 341
Desktop
  closing applications open on, 88
  defined, 3
  metaphor for Windows, 2-4
  moving among applications on, 52-53
  organizing, 80-83
  pattern colors, changing, 137
  pattern, editing, 138
  pattern installation, 136-137
  wallpapering, 143-144

Desktop Control Panel option to
  customize desktop, 20, 135-146
Desktop dialog box, 136-139, 141,
  143-146
Desktop-Edit Pattern dialog box, 136-138
Dialog boxes, 14, 62-69
  accepting changes in, 62
  canceling, 62
  displaying, 62, 68
  Tab key to move between fields in, 24,
    62
  using, 68-69
Directory, 260-265. *See also* Shared
  directory
  concepts, 169-171
  copying, 261-262
  copying files to another, 246
  creating, 260-261
  defined, 91
  deleting, 263-265
  information displayed in the File
    Manager status bar, 215
  moving, 261-262
  moving files to another, 246
  opening, 248
  parent, 94
  purpose of, 162
  root, 170, 175, 268
  selecting another, 174-176
  space used by, determining, 526
  working, 192, 204-205
Directory sharing. *See* Shared directory
Directory tree, 92-93, 169
  defined, 210
  expanding and collapsing, 220-222
  indicating expandable branches in,
    222
  navigating, 220-222
  in a "normal" directory window, 239
  plus signs in, 222
Directory windows, 91-93

arranging, 219
creating, 239
document files, 242
for executable files, 239-240
features of, 210-211
minimizing, 219
normal or working, 239
opening multiple, 97, 217
sorting filenames in, 239
split bar in, 217-219
updating list of files in, 220
working with, 216-220
Disconnect Directory Toolbar button, 289
Disconnect Network Printer Toolbar button, 322, 333
Disconnect Toolbar button, 341
Disk cache utility, conflict of disk optimizing utility and, 515
Disk drive
CD-ROM, icon on drive icon bar for, 211
copying files to another, 246
moving files to another, 247
network, 179-181, 513
opening a File Manager window for another, 97
selecting another, 173-174
Disk menu, File manager
Connect Network Drive option, 286
Copy Disk option, 265-266
Disconnect Network Drive option, 281, 289
Format Disk option, 267-268
Label Disk option, 266
Make System Disk option, 268
Share As option, 278
Share Directory option, 283
Stop Sharing option, 288
Disk performance, optimizing, 515-518

Disk space, obtaining information about available, 215
Dithering, 312
DR DOS 6.0
efficient memory usage by, 480-481
memory freed by upgrading to, 36
Document. *See also* Documents
associations, 257-259. *See also* File type, associated
collated during printing, 318
links, creating, 350-351
warning about an unsaved, 62
Document icons
creating, 196-201, 236-237
startup, 186
Document menu, 325
Delete Document option, 326
Resume Printing Document option, 325
Documents. *See also* Document
compound, viii, 350, 353-374
displaying multiple open, 4
linked, uses over the network for, 369-370
DOS
accessed from within Windows, 35-36
command line, 209
file system, Windows for Workgroups and, 161
upgrade, 5.0, 36, 479-481
DOS VM, 467-471
Double-clicking the mouse
to close a window, 61
to collapse a directory in the directory tree, 222
defined, 5
to launch an application, 30-31
to maximize and restore original size of windows, 14, 46
to open a group of icons, 10, 30

to open an associated file within its application, 96-97
to open server applications, 360
to open the Task List, 53
to play a sound using an embedded icon, 372
to return to help topic in history file, 108
to run a non-Windows application, 501
to run the File Manager, 68
to switch to an application, 55
Dragging the mouse defined, 5
Draw utility to create custom print job separator pages, 332
Drive icon bar, 210
turning off, 215
Drive icons, 92
Drivers
adding, 150-151
Novell NetWare, 472-473
settings for, 151
stored in upper memory, 481
Drivers Control Panel option for device drivers, 20, 149-151
Dynamic data exchange (DDE), vi, 354

E

Edit menu, ClipBook
Copy option, 340-341, 345
Cut option, 340-341, 345
Paste option, 340, 349, 355
Paste Special option, 350
Edit menu, Object Packager
Command Line option, 373, 391
Exit option, 391
Insert Object option, 372
Label, 373, 391
Edit menu options, cutting and pasting with, 84-87, 362-363

Electronic label for disk, 266
Electronic mail, Windows for Workgroups support of, v, vii, 273. *See also* Microsoft Mail
Embedding graphic objects in text files, 251
Enter key equivalent to clicking OK button, 64, 69
Environment space, changing, 513
Error information about application problems, 524-525
Esc key
to close Control menu, 49
to deselect menu option, 45
Expanded Memory Manager (Quarterdeck), 480
Export Folders dialog box, 396
Extension Order Toolbar button, 93-94

F

F1 for help system, 102, 104
F2 in Hearts
to play alone, 439
to start the game, 440
F7 for File Move option, 6
Fields in dialog boxes, 62
File
attributes (properties), 224, 254-256, 279
backup and storage, centralizing, vii, 272
closing another user's, 294-295
copying, 246-248
defined, 91, 162
deleting, 252-253
finding, 526
fragmentation, 515, 517
locking, 280
moving, 246-248
opening, 248

overwriting, 294-295
printing to, 318
renaming, 252-254
revision time and date for, 224
security, 277-280
size, 224, 525-526
statistics, listing, 95
types of. *See* File types
File allocation table (FAT), 268, 518
File icons, 93-94
File Manager, ix, 91-98, 209-243,
    245-268
  accessing, 68
  clearing more room to work in, 215
  closing, 97-98
  confirmation messages, 212-213
  customizing, 212-216
  disabling share options in, 465-466
  documents window in, 240
  drag-and-drop procedures to open
      document in, 242-243
  file deletions with, controlling,
      213-214
  font selection in, 214-215
  launch windows in, 238-241
  minimizing on use, 215-216
  OLE features in, 359-360
  printing from, 256-257
  restoring default settings of, 211-212
  saving settings changed in, 216
  starting, 69
  starting applications from, 237-243
  status bar of, toggling, 215
  using, 94-96
  utilities for, 525-526
File Manager window, 91-92, 210-212
File menu, File Manager, 98, 248-260
  Associate option, 257-258
  ClipBook option, 346
  Connect option, 347
  Copy option, 249-251, 262

Create Directory option, 247, 260
Delete option, 251, 263
Move option, 249-250, 262
Open option, 248, 283
Properties option, 254-255, 279, 296
Rename option, 252-254
Run option, 241-242
Save As option, 283
Save option, 256
Search option, 259-260
Select Files option, 231-232
Share As option, 465
Stop Sharing option, 465
File menu, Microsoft Mail
  New Folder option, 394
  Properties option, 383
File menu, Notepad
  New option, 172
  Open option, 172-181
  Save As option, 182-183, 197
  Save option, 181
File menu, Paintbrush, 85
File menu, PIF Editor, 502
File menu, Program Manager
  Copy option, 188-189
  Delete option, 206
  Exit option, 190
  Exit Windows option, 75, 79
  New option, 187, 190-193
  Properties option, 205, 207
  Rename option, 212
  Run option to start an application, 31
File menu, Schedule+
  Create Archive option, 425
  Import Appointments option, 416
  Open Archive option, 425
  Print option, 429
  Program option, 423
  Turn Off Reminders option, 412
File menu, Windows for Workgroups,
    11-12, 49-50

Alt-F to access, 6
 clicking File on menu bar to access, 44
File transfers, vii, 272
File types, 161-183
 associated, 93, 96-97, 167, 238,
  242-243, 257-259
 backup (.BAK), 166, 516
 batch (.BAT), 166, 227
 Calendar (.CAL), 96, 166
 Cardfile (.CRD), 166
 Clipboard (.CLP), 166
 data (.DAT or .DTA), 163, 166, 171
 database, 279
 DIF, 163
 document (.DOC), 163, 166, 227,
  237-238
 driver (.DRV), 163
 dynamic link library (.DLL), 163
 executable (.EXE), 93, 95-96, 162, 227
 formatted text, 163
 graphics, 163
 Help (.HLP), 110, 166
 hidden, 228, 255
 Initialization (.INI), 166, 279,
  459-460, 472
 Media Player (.MID), 166
 menu (.MNU), 166
 message (.MSG), 166
 Notepad (.TXT), 4.26, 166, 176
 other, 94
 overlay (.OVL), 163
 Paintbrush (.BMP, .MSP, and .PCX),
  166
 PIF Editor (.PIF), 166, 227, 469, 490,
  493-494, 498-503
 print, 310
 program (.COM or .EXE), 162-163,
  171, 227
 Program Manager (.GRP), 166
 read only, 254, 256, 284
 Recorder (.REC), 166

Sound Recorder (.WAV), 166, 374
 startup, 457, 511-512
 support, 162-163
 swap, 484-487, 509
 SYLK, 163
 system (.SYS), 163, 228, 255, 267-268
 template, 181, 256, 279
 temporary (.TMP), 166, 513-514
 Terminal (.TRM), 166
 text (ASCII), 163
 Write (.WRI), 165-166, 176
Filename extensions. *See also* File
 common, table of, 166
 programs and documents associated
  by means of, 257-259
 rules for using, 164
 sorting files by their, 94-95
 strategies for, 165-167
 used by Windows accessories, table of,
  166
Filenames
 browsing for, 193-195
 conventions for, 162, 164-167
 displayed with detailed information,
  224-225
Files list
 changing the order of (sorting) files
  in, 94-95, 223, 225-226
 deselecting files from, 231
 icons for the types of files listed in,
  93-94
 launching applications from, 238
 listing selected files in, 226-228
 purpose of, 210
 selecting files from, 229-232
 working with, 223-228
Find dialog box, 420-421
Floppy disk
 bootable, 267
 changing labels on, 266
 formatting, 267-268

system, 268
Font dialog box, 126, 214-215, 306-308
Fonts, 125-131
    assigning a document's, 307-308
    defined, 125
    types of, 305-307
Fonts Control Panel option for
        customizing screen and printer
        fonts, 20, 120
Fonts dialog box, 128-131
Form feeds for print jobs, 332
Format Disk dialog box, 267-268
Full Page Toolbar button, 341

G

Games group window, 17-19, 72
Gates, Bill, vi
Go To Date dialog box, 410
Graphics
    embedding, 366-368
    overlapping text with, 312
    printing portions of, 318
    resolution of printed, 317, 319
    scaling, 318-319
Grid, adjusting the sizing, 145-146
Group windows, 8
    accessing Control menu of, 48-49
    changing the properties of, 201-202
    copy program items to new, 188-189
    creating, 185-188
    defined, 7
    deleting, 205-206
    document startup icons in. *See*
        Document icons
    maximized, 46
    minimizing, 51
    resizing and arranging new, 189-190
    selecting other, 50-51
    tiling, 76-77
    unhiding hidden, 46-47

H

Hard disk drive
    backing up and restoring files to, 518
    changing labels of, 266
    formatting, 518
    optimizing performance of, 515-518
Hardware
    network, setting up, 447-454
    settings customized with Control
        Panel, 120
Hearts card game, v, 19, 437-442
    basics of, 438
    dealer for, 437-439
    dealer's computer name in, 440
    game strategy in, 442
    lead in, 438
    object of, 438
    passing three cards in, 441
    queen of spades in, 438, 441-442
    shooting the moon in, 438
    starting, 439
Help button
    Back, 107-108
    backward browse (<<), 107-108
    Contents, 107-108
    forward browse (>>), 107-108
    Glossary, 107
    History, 107-108
    in the Run dialog box, 104
    Search, 107-109
Help menu, 109-113
    Contents option, 103
    Edit Annotate option, 112-113
    Edit Copy option, 111
    File Open option, 110
    File Print Topic option, 111
    Search for Help option, 108
Help system, 101-116
    accessing, 102-103
    annotating topics in, 112-113
    for an application, 102-103

bookmarks in, 102, 113-15
collapsible, 115
context-specific help from, 103-104
copying a help topic to a file from, 111-112
drop-down menus, 103
glossary items, green or underlined, 106
history file, 107-108
online, 526
printing topics from, 111
scrolling text of, 105-106
table of contents, 108
Help windows, 101-102
minimizing, 102-103, 105
opening, 103
resizing, 105
using, 104-115
Hourglass display during wait times, 43

I

Icons
changing the properties of, 201-202, 204-205
copied between windows, 188-189, 206
custom startup, creating, 185, 236-237
default spacing between, changing, 144-145
deleting, 206
desktop, arranging, 83
document. *See* Document icons
embedding, 371-373, 389
hiding, 185
in Microsoft Mail messages, 379
as objects in OLE, 363-365
in Program Manager, 10-11
rearranging Main group, 78-79
windows as, 9-11
Import Format dialog box, 424

Insertion point (I beam) for text editing, 42, 84
Install Driver dialog box, 150
Intensity Control slider bar, 312
International Control Panel option to customize country settings, 20, 89, 120, 146-147
International dialog box, 147
IPX protocol, 456, 472

K

Keyboard
accessing menu and menu options with, 49-50
group windows selected with, 50-51
navigating dialog boxes with, 62-63
opening and closing the Control menu with. *See* Control menu
starting applications with, 51-52
techniques, 48-52
usage and terminology, 5-6
Keyboard Control Panel option to customize keyboard, 20, 120, 148

L

Label dialog box, 373
LAN Manager for OS/2 servers, 272
LAN Manager for UNIX servers, 272
LAN Manager network (Microsoft)
connecting with, 474-475
guest accounts, 475
security, using, 475
setup process in Windows, 447
Windows support of connections to, vi, 300
LAN Manager Settings dialog box, 476
Link information, viewing and updating, 370-371

List All Toolbar button, 93, 95
List boxes
    displaying text in, 64-65, 68-69
    drop-down, 65-66, 68
    purpose of, 64
    scrolling the lists in, 64
Local ClipBook, 16
    object, sharing, 346-347
    saving contents of Clipboard to, 17,
        86-88, 338
    thumbnail images in, 338
    working with, 345-346
Locate Dealer dialog box, 440
Logon name, 24-26, 152-153
Logon Settings dialog box, 37

M

Mail and Schedule+ Extensions for
    Windows for Workgroups, 404, 434
Mail dialog box, 399
Mail menu
    Change Password option, 384
    Personal Groups option, 387
    Postoffice Manager option, 403
    Select Change Password option, 384
Mail menu, Postoffice Manager, 403
Mail Sign In dialog box, 381, 383
Main group, 72-75
    rearranging icons for, 78-79
Marquee Setup dialog box, 142
Maximize button, 12, 45
Media Player Windows multimedia
    utility, 18
Meeting Request dialog box, 414
Memory. *See also* Random access
    memory (RAM) *and* Virtual memory
    386 enhanced mode of Windows and,
        484, 508
    conventional, 480-481, 509
    expanded, 482, 484, 492, 503

    extended, 480-483
    map, typical, 481
    PIF requirements for, 503
    standard mode of Windows and,
        483-484
    upper, 480-482
Memory-resident
    (terminate-and-stay-resident, TSR)
    programs, 34, 491-493, 514-515
Menu bar, 3
    accessing, 49
    File Manager, 92, 210
    opening a menu from, 6, 11-12, 43, 50
Menu options. *See* Options, menu
Menus. *See also* individual menus
    accessing, 5-6, 43
    drop-down, 11, 43-44
    scanning, 44-45
Message boxes. *See* Microsoft Mail
Message Finder dialog box, 398-399
Metafiles for custom print job separator
    pages, 332
Microsoft CD-ROM Extensions, 283
Microsoft Customer Support, telephone
    number for, 150
Microsoft Driver Library (MDL), 150
Microsoft Excel
    networking features of, vi
    as server and client application, 360
Microsoft Knowledge Base information
    service, xi
Microsoft Mail, 67, 289, 377-405. *See*
    also Electronic mail
    address lists, 379-380, 385-386
    administrative tasks for, 399-404
    administrator, 379
    archiving and deleting messages in,
        396-397
    attaching shared files to messages in,
        389
    composing messages in, 385

converting files from earlier versions
for, 525
custom command and message types
for, 526
editor, 378
embedded objects sent in, 367
enhancing, 404-405
exiting, 385
folders, 378, 380, 393-397, 403, 525
forwarding received messages in, 393
groups to address messages in,
386-388
help system, 115-116
mailbox (message file), 379
mailbox name, automatically
entering, 383-384
message templates, 397
outbox, 380, 397
packaged objects mailed in, 390-391
postoffice, 378-383, 399-401, 404, 408
postoffice manager duties for, 402
purpose of, viii
reading received messages in, 392
reinstating first-time startup for,
403-404
replying to received messages in,
392-393
Schedule+ use of, 408, 432
sending messages in, 391-392
as "store and forward" application, 378
users, adding and removing, 402
using, 381-385
Microsoft MSD utility, 453
Microsoft Network (MS-NET) servers, 272
Microsoft PowerPoint as primarily a
client application, 361
Microsoft Schedule+, 273, 407-434
access privileges, 421-422
adding appointments using, 410-412,
415-420
Appointment Book, 408-423

appointment reminders, viewing, 433
archiving appointments using, 425
display defaults, setting, 430-431
exporting appointments using,
423-424
extensions and enhancements, 434
help system, 115
importing appointments using, 424
issuing meeting requests using,
412-414
Microsoft Mail required for, 408, 432
online and offline file
synchronization for, 432
Planner, 428-430
purpose of, viii, 407
replying to meeting requests using,
414-415
resource scheduling accounts
managed using, 433-434
Task List, 425-427
types of appointments in, 408-409
Microsoft Technical Support, xi
Microsoft Windows NT servers, 272
Microsoft Word for Windows
application and document windows
for, 7-9
as client application primarily, 361
multiple open documents possible in, 4
networking features of, vi
window view settings in, selecting,
66-67
MIDI Mapper Control Panel option to
control MIDI devices, 20, 120
Minesweeper game, 19
Minimize button, 12, 45
Mouse
buttons, swapping functions of, 135
double click speed, setting, 135
tracking speed, setting, 134
trails of pointers during dragging, 135

used in non-Windows applications,
491
Mouse Control Panel option to
customize mouse settings, 20
Mouse dialog box, 134-135
Mouse usage
for activating a window, 46-47
for clicking buttons, 45-46
for copying and moving files, 246-248
to open menus and choose options.
See Options, menu
in Program Manager, 42-48
for resizing windows, 56-58
for scanning menus, 44-45
for starting an application, 30-31,
47-48
and terminology, 4-5
Move dialog box, 249-250
Move Document Down Toolbar button,
322, 325
Move Document Up Toolbar button,
322, 325
MS-DOS Prompt icon, 35
MSIPX
command to load internetwork
packet exchange software, 298
driver, 472-473
MSMAIL.INI file, 460
Multitasking
386 enhanced mode for, 484, 508-509
DOS applications, 29
processing time allocations for,
466-467, 500
with Windows, 14-15
Mystify Setup dialog box, 141

N

Net Watcher Windows network monitor
utility, 18-19, 282, 289, 292-293

NetBEUI communications protocol,
455-456
NetBIOS communications protocol,
455-456
NetWare-Drive Connections dialog box,
299
Network adapter, status of, 523-524
Network administrator, x-xi, 445-476
connections with other networks
managed by, 471-476
hardware setup by, 447-454
help requests to, forms for, 526
initialization files managed by,
459-465
installation process for Windows used
by, 446-447
network communications managed
by, 454-456
password management by, 27, 281
processing time priorities adjusted by,
466-471
share options restricted by, 465-466
sources of information for, 445-446
startup files managed by, 457-459
workgroups assigned by, 273-274
Network button, 173, 179, 195
Network cabling
coaxial, 447-448
RG-62, 450
shielded (STP) or unshielded (UTP)
twisted pair, 449-450
twisted pair (telephone wire), 448-449
Network communications, 454-456
Network Control Panel option, 152-157
Network DDE, viii
Network Device Interface Specification
(NDIS), 454-455
Network dialog box, 152, 155-157
Network files, sharing and accessing,
271-300
Network icon, 37

Network interface cards (NICs), v, x, 447
  base memory address for, 452
  binding protocols Windows uses
    with, 455
  for different network topologies,
    449-451
  I/O port addresses for, 452, 454
  installing, 451-454
  interrupt (IRQ) settings for, 451, 454
  problems with, 452-453
Network links, 369-370
Network performance monitors, 276
Network-Printer Connection dialog box,
  334
Network printers, v
  connecting printer drivers to, 313-315
  connecting to, 312-316, 333
  disabling print sharing on, 466
  disconnecting from, 333
  installing drivers for, 313
  on NetWare servers, 334-335
  printing directly to, 330
  separator pages between print jobs
    on, 331-333, 526
  stopping the sharing of, 333
  on your system, 330-333
Network Settings dialog box, 465-471
Network types
  ArcNet, 450-451, 473
  thin Ethernet (10Base2), 447-448
  Token Ring, 449-450
  twisted pair Ethernet (10BaseT),
    448-449
Networks Control Panel utility
  to customize network connections, 20
  disabling network sharing
    temporarily using, 276-277
NETWORKS.WRI file, 446, 460
NETX command to provide DOS
  support for accessing Novell
  NetWare, 298

New Folder dialog box, 395
New Program Object dialog box, 187,
  191
Non-Windows applications, 489-504
  associating filename extensions with,
    257-259
  DOS VMs for, 467
  memory problems in running, 479
  performance of, improving, 509-510
  PIFs for, 490, 493-494, 498-503
  quitting, 56
  running, 34-36, 493-495, 508
  speed of, enhancing, 504
  terminating locked up, 499
  types of, 490-493
Non-Windows Applications group, 72,
  201
Notepad Windows note-writing utility,
  18
  copying and pasting text using, 84
  copying help topic text to, 113
  to edit AUTOEXEC.BAT file, 34
  printing a Notepad file without
    loading, 256-257
  timelog, 196-197
Novell NetWare, vi
  drivers, 472-473
  servers, 272, 276, 334-335
  setup process in Windows, 447,
    471-473
  SPX/IPX support, 456
  support for shared resources with
    users of, 296-300

Object linking and embedding (OLE),
  349-350, 353
  changing objects in, 363
  components, 359-365
  concepts, 354-359

embedding in, 355-356
example, 357-358
linking in, 357
network support of, vii, 272-273,
   358-359
Object Packager Windows group data
   transfer utility, 18
   to add file to mail message, 390-391
   creating embedded icons using, 371
   using, 372-373
Objects
   applications that can supply, 372
   changing embedded or linked, 363
   creating packaged, 391
   editing packaged, 374
   embedding, 366-368
   icons as, 363-366
   linking, 368-370
   mailing packaged, 390-391
   types of, 361-362
Open dialog box, 34, 172-181, 193
Open Files dialog box, 296-297
Option buttons, 65-66
Options dialog box, 311, 391
Options, menu
   accessing, 5-6, 43-44
   check mark to left of enabled, 43-44
   deselecting, 45
   grayed out, 6
   speed keys for, 6
   turning off enabled, 44
Options menu, Chat, 290
Options menu, File Manager
   Confirmation option, 213, 263
   Customize Toolbar, 233
   Font option, 214
   Open New Window on Connect
      option, 288, 299
Options menu, NetWatcher, 293
Options menu, Print Manager, 326
   Background Printing option, 328-330

Font option, 328
Separator Pages option, 331
Set Column Width option, 328
Status Bar option, 328
Toolbar option, 327
Options menu, Program Manager
   Auto Arrange option, 75, 189
   changing, 75
   Save Settings on Exit option, 43-44,
      75, 79, 97-98
Options menu, Schedule+
   Display option, 430
   General Options option, 431
   Set Access Privileges option, 421
Options menu, Setup, 501
Out-of-memory problems, 507-509. *See
   also* Random access memory (RAM)

P

Packager accessory. *See* Object Packager
   Windows group data transfer utility
Packages
   creating, 362, 373
   inserting, 363
   sound, 365
Pg Up and Pg Dn keys to scroll lists in list
   boxes, 64
Paintbrush Windows painting utility, 18
   embedding graphics using, 366-368
   files created by, 165-166, 178-179
   as server application, 360
Paper sizes and tray sources, specifying,
   304, 311
Password
   changing, 27
   entering, 24-25, 287-288
   for full-access right, 278, 284
   LAN Manager, 474-476
   list, 280-281
   logon, 26, 281, 288

mailbox, 379, 381, 383-384, 401
  for read-only access right, 278, 284
  resource access, ix, 26, 277
  for screen saver, 140-142
  settings, changing, 157
  for shared printer, 331
  two-level access with, 285
Password-list file, 26
Paste command, 16-17, 83-86
Paste dialog box, 87, 141
Paste Toolbar button, 341
Path, search, 162, 164-165, 284
Pause Printer Toolbar button, 322
Pause Printing Document Toolbar
    button, 322, 326
PC Tools (Central Point Software), 517
Peer-to-peer network system, Windows
    for Workgroups as, 276-277
Performance Priority Slider, 155, 466-471
PIF Editor, 502-504
PIF Editor dialog box, 502-503
Pointer
  moving, 4-5
  shapes and their functions, 42, 56-57
Pointing the mouse defined, 5
Port
  adding, 315-316
  contention settings for non-Windows
      application using, 499-500
  fictitious shared printer, 315
  file connection, 310
  I/O network, 451-452
  printer, 313
  setup by network administrator, 447
Ports Control Panel option to customize
    serial ports, 20, 131-134
Postoffice Manager dialog box, 402
PostScript fonts, 307
PostScript printer, 307
Print dialog box, 305-306
  Paintbrush, 318-319

print quality and resolution specified
    in, 317-318
  print range specified in, 317
  setting print options in, 316-319
  Write, 306
Print Manager, ix, 320-330
  accessing, 304, 323
  connecting with network printer
      using, 312
  disabling, 320
  flashing icon for, 330
  purpose and functions of, 320-321
  sending a print job to, 323-324
  status bar, 328
  Toolbar, 327
Print menu Share Printer As option, 330
Print Queue jobs
  changing order of jobs in, 304,
      323-325
  displayed in window with date and
      time, 327
  displayed in window with file size, 327
  list of, refreshing outdated, 327
  pausing the printing of, 325
  priority of, setting, 328-329
  resuming the printing of, 325
  separator pages between multiple,
      331-333
  viewing, 304, 323-324
Print Setup dialog box
  choosing paper size in, 311
  choosing your printer in, 309-310,
      312, 319
  setting options in, 14, 304-305,
      311-312
  setting print orientation in, 311
Printer driver, 304
  connecting, to a network printer,
      313-315
  installing a network printer's, 313
  for multiple-printer system, 309-310

Printer menu, Print Manager 327
   Disconnect Network Printer option, 333
   Pause Printer option, 326
   Resume Printer option, 326
   Share Printer As option, 466
   Stop Sharing Printer option, 466
Printers
   choosing from among, 309-310
   default, setting, 319-320
   network. *See* Network printers
   password for, 331
   pausing and resuming, 326
   switching between, 304
Printers Control Panel option for printer configurations, 20, 304, 310
Printers dialog box, 319-320
Printing, 303-335
   assigning fonts before, 307-308
   to a file, 318
   multiple copies, 318
   orientation, 304, 311
   process, 304-305
   processor time allocated to, 328-27
   speed, 310, 320
   starting, 304
Processing time
   adjusting, 466-471, 500
   divided between your applications and other users, 155
   exclusive use of, 500, 510
   monitored by WinMeter utility, 291
Processor time for print jobs, allocating, 328-329
PROGMAN.INI file, 460
Program Group Properties dialog box, 187
Program Item
   deleting, 205-206
   icons, creating, 190-198

Program Item Properties dialog box, 191-193, 195-196, 204, 207
Program Manager, 72-79
   groups, 72
   keyboard navigation techniques, 48-52
   mouse navigation techniques, 42-48
   reorganizing, 72-75
   returning from Control Panel to, 52
   saving customized window layout for, 79
Program Manager icons, starting applications by double-clicking, 10
Program Manager window, 2, 27
   Accessories group window of, 7-8
   activating, 27
   Ctrl-Tab effective only in, 52
   Main group window of, 7-8
   moving and resizing, 76
Properties dialog box, 279-280, 296
Protocol Manager, 455
Protocol stack, 455
PROTOCOL.INI file, 457-458, 460
   [netcard] section, 462
   [network.setup] section, 461
   [protman] section, 461
   [protocol] section, 462-463

Q

QEMM (Quarterdeck), 482

R

RAM drive, 513-514
Random access memory (RAM)
   checking available, 28, 30
   closing application windows to restore, 88
   conventional, 480

freed by upgrading to DOS 5.0 or DR DOS 6.0, 36
improving Windows' performance by adding, 507-508
minimizing usage of, 34-35, 479-480, 503-504, 510-515
Record locking, 280
Recorder Windows mouse movement- and keystroke-saving utility, 18
Recurring Appointment dialog box, 418
Rename dialog box, 212, 252-254
Restore button, 12, 45, 46
Resume Printer Toolbar button, 322, 326
Resume Printing Document Toolbar button, 322, 325
Run dialog box, 31, 62-64, 68, 241-242

S

Save As dialog box, 179, 181-183, 279
SCHDPLUS.INI file, 460
Scissors cutout tool, 85
Screen resolution, adjusting, 311-312
Screen saver
    customizing, 140, 142-143
    password-protected, 27, 37, 140-142
    using, 139
Scroll bars, 13
    removing, 59-60
    using, 58-59
Search dialog box, 108-109, 259
Search Results dialog box, 259-260
Security features
    LAN Manager, 474-475
    network, ix, 25, 277
Select Attendees dialog box, 413
Select Computer dialog box, 347
Select Files dialog box, 231-232
Send Note dialog box, 386
Send Response dialog box, 415
Separator Pages dialog box, 331-333

Server, v
    connecting an MS-DOS based PC to a Windows, v
    dedicated, 275-276
    LAN Manager, 272, 474-475
    name for each network computer, 164
    Novell NetWare, 472-473
    of OLE data, 360-361
    priority data, 466-471
    usage, monitoring, 296
Server system, 271
Server VM, 467-471
Set Access Privileges dialog box, 421
Set Default Printer Toolbar button, 322
Set Selection dialog box, 232, 249
Settings dialog box, 497-499, 510-511
Settings menu, WinMeter, 292
Setup Applications dialog box, 199-200
Setup dialog box, 65, 140
Setup utility
    to create startup icons, 198-201, 237
    to remove files in Windows directories, 516-517
    run after installing a non-Windows application, 501
    swap file created by, 485
Share Clipbook Page dialog box, 346-347
Share dialog box, 370
Share Directory dialog box, 278, 283-285, 400
Share Directory Toolbar button, 283
Share name for each shared directory, 164, 284-285
Share Printer As Toolbar button, 322, 330
Share Printer dialog box, 330-331
Share Toolbar button, 341
Shared computer
    listing, 286
    performance, monitoring, 276, 282
    temporarily stopping sharing for, 155, 276-277, 508

Shared directory, 25-26, 282-289
  accessing, 280-281
  accessing network files in, ix,
      179-181, 273, 284-288, 292-293,
      296
  availability of, 277
  choosing a different drive for, 180-181
  closing another user's files on, 294-295
  comments for, 284
  compound documents built using, 359
  copying and moving files for, 249-250
  disabling a connection to, 288
  disconnecting from another system's,
      289
  disconnection problems with, 281,
      294
  driver letter for, reserving, 473
  hiding, 284-285
  listing most recent, 282
  passwords to access. *See* Password
  program, 278-279
  reshared whenever Windows starts,
      281, 284
  rights, read-only and full-access,
      277-280, 295
  servername and sharename of, 180
  share name for, 164, 284-285
  temporary, 287
  on your system, 283-285, 288-289
Shared disk, 266
Shared folders, 395, 403
Shared Folders dialog box, 403
Shared peripherals, vii-viii, 272. *See also*
    Network printers
Shared resources, v, 271-300
  386 enhanced mode for using, 29, 484
  disabling, 465
  responsibilities to network users for,
      277
  restricting, 465-466
SHARED.INI file, 460

Shift-Alt-Esc to reverse order of
    switching between windows, 53, 81
Shift-Alt-Tab to reverse scroll a list of
    open windows, 81
Shift-F1 and clicking to access
    context-specific help, 103
Shift-Tab to move backwards through
    dialog box fields, 62
Shortcut key
  changing, 201-202
  creating, 202
  to start an application, 192, 196
Slider buttons and slider bars, 58-59
SMARTDrive utility, 512-513, 515
Software settings, Control Panel options
    for customizing, 120
Solitaire card game, 19
Sort by Name Toolbar button, 223, 240
Sort by Type Toolbar button, 223, 229,
    240
Sound Control Panel option to assign
    sounds, 20, 151-152
Sound Recorder Windows sound utility,
    18
  embedded sounds created using,
      367-368
  as server application, 360
  sound packages created using, 365
Spacebar to mark and unmark check
    boxes, 63
Speed Disk (Symantec), 517
Speed keys, 6, 38, 48
Split bar, 211, 217-219
Standard mode
  copying and pasting non-Windows
      data using, 495-496
  forcing Windows to start in, 29-30,
      482-483
  memory and, 483-484
  tradeoffs of using, 28, 457-458, 483,
      508

Starter kits for Windows for
    Workgroups, ix
StartUp group of Windows, 32-33, 72,
    206-207
   creating new icons for, 185, 236-237
Status bar
   File Manager, 211-212
   Print Manager, 328
Stop Sharing Printer Toolbar button, 322
Stop Sharing Toolbar button, 341
Subdirectories, 94, 170
   copying, 261-262
   deleting, 263
   directory tree displaying branching,
    221
   full access to shared directory's, 278
   included in sorted files list, 227
SYSEDIT utility to change startup files,
    511-512
System administrator. *See* Network
   administrator
System resources, checking available, 28,
   30
System VM, 467-470
SYSTEM.INI file, 459-460
   [ClipShares] section, 464
   driver commands in, 472
   [network] section, 464-465
   [PasswordLists] section, 464-465

T

Tab key
   to move among command buttons, 64
   to move between dialog box fields,
    24, 62
Table of Contents Toolbar button, 341
Task dialog box, 425
Task List
   buttons, 55
   opening, 47, 52-53

to organize the desktop, 81-83
Task menu Select View option, 427
Template file, 181
   access rights for, 279
   defined, 256
   for mail messages, 397
Terminal Windows communications
   utility, 18
Text boxes, purpose of, 64
Thumbnail images, 17
Thumbnails Toolbar button, 341
Time log for file revisions, creating,
   196-197
Time, setting, 20, 89-90, 148
Title bar
   clicked and dragged to move a
    window, 14
   highlighted in active window, 3-4
Toolbar, ix, 92
   ClipBook, 341
   File Manager buttons on, 93, 232-235
   Print Manager, 327
   purpose of, 210
   rearranging, 235
   reverting to original, 235
   turning off, 215
Tree menu
   Expand All option, 222
   Indicate Expandable Branches option,
    222
TrueType dialog box, 130-131
TrueType fonts, 305-307

U

User kits for Windows for Workgroups,
   ix
Users
   disconnecting, 294
   locking out unauthorized, ix

monitoring directories and files
      accessed by other, 292-293
properties of, 292
refreshing obsolete display of, 293
sending documents to be printed to
      other, 306
sharing processing time with other,
      155
Utility menu, File Manager, 525

V

Verb as an object's action, 361
View All File Details Toolbar button, 224
View menu, ClipBook Viewer
    Full Page option, 344, 348
    Status Bar option, 343
    Table of Contents option, 344, 348
    Thumbnails option, 344, 348
    Toolbar option, 343
View menu, File Manager
    All File Details option, 95, 213-225
    By File Type option, 95-96, 226-229
    Directory Only, 218, 240
    Name option, 223-224
    options available on the Toolbar, 223
    Partial Details option, 223-225
    Sort By Date option, 226
    Sort By Name option, 225, 230
    Sort By Size option, 226
    Sort By Type option, 94, 226
    Split option, 218
    Tree Only, 218
View menu, Print Manager, 327, 343
    Other Network Printer option, 327
    Print File Size option, 327
    Refresh option, 327
    Status Text option, 327
    Time/Date Sent option, 327
Virtual 8086 mode, 467
Virtual machines, 467-471

Virtual memory
    386 enhanced mode for using, 29,
        484, 508-509
    checking your system's capabilities
        for, 485
    purpose of, 484, 510
    swap file used for, 484-487
Virtual Memory dialog box, 486-487

W

Warning boxes, 67
Welcome to Windows for Workgroups
    dialog box, 24-25
Where to Look dialog box, 398
Wildcards, ? and *, 168-169, 178
    selecting files using, 231-232
    sorting file list using, 229
Window
    activating, 46-47
    active, 3-4
    borders, 13, 42-43, 56-58
    closing, 61-62
    customized, 45
    elements, 11-14
    maximizing, 12, 14, 45
    minimizing, 9-10, 12, 45
    moving, 60-61
    resizing, 56-59, 74-75, 77-78
    running a non-Windows application
        in, 494-495
    sizing, 12-13
Window menu, 51
    Accessories option, selecting, 50
    Cascade option to overlap windows,
        47, 77-78, 97, 219
    New Window option, 97, 220
    Refresh option, 220
    Tile option to rearrange windows side
        by side, 47, 76-77, 219
Windows

application, 7-9, 47, 88
background, 15
cascading, 46-47, 77-78, 82
displaying multiple open, 2-3
document, 7-9
group. *See* Group windows *and*
    individual groups
as icons, 9-11
moving among multiple open, 52-53,
    81
previewing, 52
tiled, 46-47, 76-77, 82
types of, 7-9
Windows 3.0 applications run under
    Windows for Workgroups, 490
Windows 3.1
    applications run under Windows for
        Workgroups, 490
    OLE feature of, 353, 490
    upgrading to Windows for
        Workgroups from, ix-x
Windows Applications group, 72
Windows for Workgroups
    accessories and games for, 17-19
    advantages of connecting systems
        with, 272-273
    automatically starting, 33-34
    benefits of, vi
    closing, 38
    compatibility of servers with, 272
    configuration, changing, 457
    customizing, options for, 19-20, 88-91
    DOS file system and, 161
    environment, navigating, 71-98
    exit methods for, 37-38, 69
    features, vii-ix
    graceful exit to, 36
    installation of, 23, 446-447
    interface, using, 41-69
    logging on to, 24-27, 41-42
    logging out of, 37

logon settings, changing, 156-157
multitasking with, 14-15
operating modes, 27-29, 32, 482-487,
    508-509. *See also* individual modes
optimizing performance of, 507-518
overview of, 1-20
packaging (configurations), ix-x
as peer-to-to file-sharing system, 276
processors for running, 29
restarting, 487
starting, 24-30, 272, 457-458
starting to use, 23-38
startup mode for, 23-24
support by other products and
    vendors of, v
system requirements for using, x, 458
update notes for, xi
upgrading to, ix
Windows for Workgroups Resource Kit,
    296, 446, 521-526
    Dr. Turing utility of, 524
    Mail 3.x Folder Conversion Program
        of, 525
    NetMeter utility of, 523
    NetStat utility of, 523-524
    Network DDE Share Manager of, 524
    Phone Message application of, 525
    obtaining, 522
    utility disk, 522-526
Windows Setup dialog box, 516-517
WINFILE.INI file, 211-212, 460
    [restrictions] section, 465
WIN.INI file, 177, 459
    [MRU_Files] section, 463
    [MRU_Printers] section, 464
    [network] section, 463
    [spooler] section, 466
WinMeter Windows system usage
    utility, 18-19, 276, 282, 291-292
Workgroup Connection for MS-DOS, v
Workgroups, 273-276

assigning computers to, 155, 273-274
benefits of, 274-276
listing shared computers in, 286
names for, 154, 446
postoffices for, 381-383
purpose of, 273
shared printers assigned to, 314-315
Workspace of window, 3-4
Write Windows word processor utility, 18

as client application, 360
embedding graphics in text using,
    366-368
embedding sounds in text using,
    367-368
pasting graphic from Paintbrush into,
    85-86
pasting text from the Notepad into, 85

Windows for Workgroups Update Notes

Send a $12 check or money order to the following address to receive the Windows for Workgroups Update Notes:

Tom Sheldon
P.O. Box 947
Cambria, CA 93428

California residents, add 86 cents sales tax.

Add $2 shipping if you live outside the United States.

Name: _____

Company/Phone: _____

Address: _____

City/State/Zip: _____

Comments about the book: _____

_____

_____

_____

_____